TWELVE AMERICAN WARS
NINE OF THEM AVOIDABLE

TWELVE AMERICAN WARS

NINE OF THEM AVOIDABLE

Great is the guilt of an unnecessary war
——John Adams (1735-1826)

EUGENE G. WINDCHY

TWELVE AMERICAN WARS
Nine of Them Avoidable

iUniverse books may be ordered through booksellers or by contacting:

iUniverse LLC
1663 Liberty Drive
Bloomington, IN 47403
www.iuniverse.com
1-800-Authors (1-800-288-4677)

ISBN: 978-1-4917-3053-9 (sc)
ISBN: 978-1-4917-3055-3 (hc)
ISBN: 978-1-4917-3054-6 (e)

Library of Congress Control Number: 2014906009

Printed in the United States of America.

iUniverse rev. date: 07/18/2014

For Erik, Mio,
and the Queen of the Forest

CONTENTS

ACKNOWLEDGMENTS

(For Two Books)

Tonkin Gulf veteran Dale Evans provided important assistance for this book and, previously, for my book *Tonkin Gulf*. Also very helpful with the latter volume were a great many other Navy men. I regret that the circumstances of the time did not permit me to acknowledge their assistance. Standing out in my mind are the late Captain John J. Herrick, Commander George Edmondson, Lieutenant Commander William Buehler, Ensign C. Ward Bond, and Chief Petty Officer Murray T. McRae. Flag officers were less communicative but interesting. In response to my first question, the late Admiral Robert B. ("Whitey") Moore said, "I'm not sure how far you're cut in on this." Asked about a false statement in the official reporting, he responded, "That was just short hand."

With respect to *Twelve American Wars*, helpful criticisms and advice came from my friend Lee Baseman, a Defense Department retiree, and my dynamic daughter, Elizabeth Windchy. Especially helpful at the Library of Congress were librarians Judy Robinson and Abby Yochelson. At the circulation desk I received friendly assistance from Christopher Baer and Regina Thielke. Fairfax County's Martha Washington library was another major source of books. Very helpful there were Ingrid Bowers, Jill Burgard, and Joshua Cruciotti. "Josh" performed an important internet search which had defied my efforts. Interlibrary Loan, a magnificent service, supplied many hard-to-get books.

PREFACE

Can we prevent wars in the future by investigating wars in the past and how they could have been prevented? That is the object of this book. We shall examine twelve American wars to see what lessons can be learned. Some of these wars you might have forgotten about or never even heard about. American participation in China's Second Opium War still is unknown to our textbooks, although not to the people of China. This arcane event might not have attracted my attention if I had not spent a dozen years in the Far East, serving in the U. S. Army and the U. S. Information Agency.

We shall begin with the Vietnam War, which remains vivid in the memory of many Americans. How we got into that long bloodbath, why we failed to achieve our objective, and ways in which South Vietnam could have been saved will be discussed. Next, we shall turn back to the nation's very first foreign war. Did you know that we had a war with France? It was a naval conflict that lasted from 1798 to 1800. From there we shall proceed chronologically up to World War I.

A profoundly transformational event, World War I erupted, mysteriously, from a period of relative tranquility known as *La Belle Epoque*. It shook Western civilization to its foundations, and produced enough disputes and grievances to fuel World War II. How did all that happen? Making use of neglected scholarship and high level memoirs, we shall discover what took place behind the scenes, both in Europe and in the United States.

Only three of those twelve wars were unavoidable. In the nuclear age, we need to do better.

CHAPTER ONE

Vietnam War (1965-1975)

Those who do not remember the past are condemned to repeat it—George Santayana (1863-1952)

During the Vietnam War, the U. S. Information Agency transferred me from Japan to its Office of Policy in Washington and having some background in science, I was designated assistant science adviser. In 1967, I left that position to research and write a book, *Tonkin Gulf*, which explained how our leaders, making a mockery of the Constitution, had blundered, lied, and schemed their way into a seemingly endless conflict. They had not learned much from our predecessors in Vietnam, the French colonialists and their German mercenaries.

Although it did not appear that way at the time, critical events had taken place in 1964, the last year of peace. It was a presidential election year, and a major issue was South Vietnam's Communist-led insurgency. For fourteen years we Americans had supported anti-Communist efforts in Vietnam, first the French campaign, which failed, and following that, desultory efforts by a series of corrupt South Vietnamese governments. Result: the Communists were growing stronger. In 1964, we asked ourselves, should we continue providing aid short of war? Or should we jump directly into the conflict and "get it over with"? Quitting was hardly an option. Neither political party wished to be responsible for losing another country to Communism, as the Democrats had "lost China." Besides, it was feared, if South Vietnam went Communist, all of southern Asia might do so in a domino effect.

Running for president were the Democratic incumbent, Lyndon B. Johnson, and Republican Senator Barry M. Goldwater. Johnson favored aid short of war. Goldwater blamed the insurgency in South Vietnam on Communist North Vietnam, and he wanted to bomb that country. That seemed a far-fetched idea. Goldwater also recommended fewer restrictions on the use of nuclear weapons. In a survey, 1,189 psychiatrists said the Republican candidate was unfit to be president.

Surprise Attack

In the midst of these controversies, torpedo boats from North Vietnam surprised the world by reportedly attacking a ship of the U. S. Navy, and soon after that two ships of the U. S. Navy. The American ships were destroyers cruising off the North Vietnamese coast in the Tonkin Gulf. President Johnson ordered a retaliatory air raid, and at his request the Congress voted its approval in what informally was called the "Tonkin Gulf Resolution."

President Johnson, the peace candidate, won the election in a landslide.

In the following year, 1965, Johnson showed his true colors. He began bombing North Vietnam, as Senator Goldwater had recommended. Next, Johnson sent marines to protect an American air base in South Vietnam. That overturned a long settled policy of not putting American combat troops on the Continent of Asia (in addition to those stationed in South Korea).

The Army chief of staff, General Harold K. Johnson, made a trip to South Vietnam, and he came back recommending the deployment of five hundred thousand troops, a number that stunned President Johnson and Defense Secretary Robert S. McNamara. Prior to the request for marines, Johnson and McNamara thought bombing would win the war and *no combat troops at all* would be required. That is what McNamara said in his postwar book *In Retrospect: The Tragedy and Lessons of Vietnam.*[1] McNamara's critics said he feigned ignorance of the troop need in order to cover for the President, who during the election campaign promised not to send any ground forces. As evidence for McNamara's possible duplicity, in the summer of 1964 the State Department warned President Johnson that bombing North Vietnam almost inevitably would result in retaliation and a need for American combat personnel.[2] How did the State Department know that in 1964 and not the Defense Department in 1965?

Joint Chiefs Stick Together

At the Pentagon, it was the Marine Corps and the Air Force that had recommended bombing North Vietnam. The Army doubted the value of bombing, and the Navy "wasn't too sure about it," according to McNamara's book. Despite dissension among them, the Joint Chiefs of Staff unanimously recommended bombing so that they would not have to present a "split paper" to the secretary of defense. (Remember that the next time you hear the Joint Chiefs are recommending something unanimously.) President Johnson knew the decision was split, and he knew that Secretary of State Dean Rusk opposed bombing. But South Vietnam was near collapse, and Johnson decided to go with the Air Force's recommendation in addition to sending troops. The bombing drew the North Vietnamese army full-scale into South Vietnam. Perhaps the Communist army would have come anyway, but in the eyes of the world we Americans took on the role of aggressor. Perhaps also the Air Force had been too eager to find a job for itself.

Secretary of War Robert McNamara and Secretary of State
Dean Rusk (Photo courtesy of the LBJ Museum)

President Claims War Power

The use of both air and ground forces had been authorized by Congress in the Tonkin Gulf Resolution, said President Johnson, and that forgotten document now was seen to have taken on new meaning. It authorized the President to "repel any armed attack against the forces of the United States *and to prevent further aggression*" [emphasis added]. Not only the torpedo boat attacks but the insurgency in South Vietnam was North Vietnamese aggression, said the Administration. The President also asserted that he had the right to make war on his own authority as Commander-in-Chief, without any authorization from Congress.

The Vietnam War dragged on for years, lawmakers complained that the Tonkin Gulf Resolution was not meant to authorize a war, and the news media cast doubt on whether anything actually had happened in the Tonkin Gulf. Information on that subject was scarce and for years no pictures were released. Actually, significant events had taken place in that far off body of water, but they were lied about and shrouded in official secrecy. The controversial summer of 1964 could be written up as a course in Deceptive War Making.

In the sea off North Vietnam, the fateful events began with a strange encounter.

De Soto Patrol

In July of 1964, the destroyer USS *Maddox* proceeded to the Tonkin Gulf in order to carry out a previously established routine called the "De Soto patrol." The ship reached the gulf early in the morning of Friday, July 31 (the same day that the State Department warned President Johnson about bombing North Vietnam.) The American destroyer began refueling from an oil tanker, which the Navy calls an "oiler." While the *Maddox* was in that vulnerable position, hooked up to the oiler, the ship's radar detected four fast boats rapidly bearing down from the north. The destroyer's Combat Information Center (CIC) identified their radar "fingerprint" as friendly and sent a messenger to inform the captain and one other officer, Commodore John J. Herrick.

Destroyer USS *Maddox* (U. S. Navy photo)

In visual distance, the approaching craft were seen to be flying no flags and still traveling at a very high speed, 50 knots. On *Maddox's* bridge, Lieutenant William Buehler grabbed an intelligence book and tried to identify the speedsters, but with no success. He felt relieved when Commodore Herrick hurried up to the bridge, taking a fall on the way, and told him, "Those are friendly. They're Nasty-class patrol boats." The Nasties were 80-foot Norwegian torpedo boats converted to gunboats. The ones approaching had been up north during the night shelling North Vietnamese military facilities.

A Friendly Greeting

Two of the four boats veered toward the *Maddox*. Emerging from CIC to get a look, Lieutenant Dale Evans examined the nearer of the two. A Caucasian man with reddish brown hair was standing up, and he waved at the destroyer. Apparently the skipper, he wore a khaki uniform like Evans's but no headgear, which would have blown off at high speed. Later, Evans wondered whether the auburn-haired adventurer was Norwegian. For the gunboat operations, which were initiated by the Central Intelligence Agency (CIA), Norwegians and Germans were hired to command boats with South Vietnamese crews. This was supposed to establish plausible deniability for the U. S. Government's involvement. Reportedly the Norwegians left South Vietnam in May. At some point the Navy fired the Germans for drinking beer on duty, although the Germans objected that they had contracts with the CIA.[3] Since it would make no sense to hire Germans for plausible deniability and give them American uniforms, perhaps the man Evans saw was American.

During their advance briefings, the *Maddox's* officers had envisioned a scenic coastal cruise. After encountering the gunboats, they wondered what they were getting into. For one thing, they were going to collect information useful to the gunboats, as the North Vietnamese surely would assume. The American warship also would constitute a threat. To Communist eyes, the gunboats already represented a threat, and the *Maddox,* with its 5-inch guns, would represent a bigger threat.

Skipper of the *Maddox* was Captain Herbert L. Ogier. He and Commodore Herrick, who had higher responsibilities, were old friends and Naval Academy graduates. Commodore is an honorary rank usually given to an officer commanding more than one ship. We will get to that.

Near the entrance of the gulf cruised the carrier USS *Ticonderoga,* whose aircraft carried out reconnaissance operations in South Vietnam and southern Laos. Communist forces, the Pathet Lao, were active in Laos. The CIA operated aircraft in northern Laos, and they attacked Communist soldiers on sight. Thinking to rescue a downed Navy pilot, a CIA man set down his helicopter and was shot between the eyes.

Maddox Heads North

After refueling, the *Maddox* headed north, toward where the Nasty bombardments had taken place. The day was peaceful, the scenery beautiful. Stony cliffs rose abruptly from the sea, festooned with green foliage. The crew took hydrographic soundings, which the French had done already, and they looked for North Vietnamese soldiers who might be headed for South Vietnam. None was observed. It all seemed like busywork. But some people, not regular crew members, apparently had plenty to do. They were an intelligence team monitoring North Vietnamese communications. The strangers, both sailors and marines, used a van installed on the ship especially for this patrol. They called their facility the "comvan." *Maddox* sailors called it the "mad box." The monitors were picking up "good stuff," as one later informed me. There ought to have been plenty of radio traffic, since the Nasty boats were blasting military facilities.

In charge of the comvan was Lieutenant Gerrell Moore, a quiet and soft-spoken Texan. Some of *Maddox*'s crew members called him the "hair ball man." They had seen a moving picture about a witch doctor who worked magic with a ball of hair, and they noticed that every time Moore went to the bridge with a piece of paper in his hand, something happened.

Air Attacks on North Vietnam

Probably the monitors caught word of combat operations over near Laos. On Saturday, August 1, CIA propeller aircraft strafed and bombed two North Vietnamese military posts. The CIA's aircraft were marked as Laotian Air Force, but the North Vietnamese viewed them as American. The aircraft were two-seat T-28 trainers armed for counter-insurgency operations.

The *Maddox* encountered many fishing craft. Whole families lived aboard them. The destroyer was patrolling peacefully, but the fisher folk had a sullen look.

On Saturday night Lieutenant Moore gave Commodore Herrick three messages which, taken together, indicated that the North Vietnamese intended to attack the ship. Herrick interpreted the messages to mean that some small craft with explosives aboard was ordered to pull alongside. With a kamikaze threat in mind, the commodore ordered the ship away from the coast when radar showed a large number of fishing junks massing in the darkness up ahead. At 4 a. m., Herrick sent a message to higher command. The message said he had received intelligence indicating possible hostile intent on the part of the North Vietnamese.

As a result of the evasive move, Captain Ogier learned that the ship had steam in only one of its four boilers. He ordered another to be fired up in case there was a requirement for more speed. Besides suicide junks, the Americans had to be wary of torpedo boats. Naval Intelligence said the North Vietnamese had twelve of them. They were Russian boats with aluminum hulls and Chinese boats with wooden hulls. The North Vietnamese also had approximately forty gunboats. Somebody remarked that *Maddox* could not take on the whole North Vietnamese navy, and Ogier snapped, "What's the matter? Are you afraid to die?" Ogier had a reputation for being sarcastic. But it was his duty to quell such talk.

Come daylight, the *Maddox* was still in one piece, and it moved back toward the coast. About an hour after sunrise, Herrick sent another message. This time he confirmed that the earlier report was accurate, and he recommended that the patrol be canceled. Herrick's exact words:

Consider continuance of patrol presents unacceptable risk.[4]

Admiral Roy L. Johnson, commander of the Seventh Fleet, ordered that Herrick continue the patrol but deviate from the planned route as might be needed.[5] The planned route consisted of moving from one point of military interest to the next.

The "Laotian Air Force" raided another North Vietnamese position.

Torpedo Attack

On Sunday afternoon, Herrick again had threatening intelligence from the comvan, and *Maddox's* radar showed three motorized craft heading toward the ship. Moving fast, they had to be either gunboats or torpedo boats. The torpedo is a powerful short range weapon, and if three torpedo boats came too close to the destroyer, they could blow it to smithereens. *Maddox* turned away from the coast, testing the North Vietnamese intentions. The boats followed. They and the destroyer speeded up. Radar operators could see that the pursuing craft were too fast for North Vietnamese gunboats. They had to be torpedo boats. As such, they were much faster than the destroyer. *Maddox* turned southeast. So did the boats. The torpedo craft started a three-boat weave to confuse the Americans' fire control radar. Then they formed a column and began zigzagging. Their bow waves shone white in the sun and at the stern each boat featured a "rooster tail" thrown up by its powerful engine. The North Vietnamese were doing 50 knots; they were faster than what Naval Intelligence had reported. *Maddox* was doing 27 knots.

"General Quarters, General Quarters," rasped the loudspeaker. "This is not a drill. This is not a drill." The crew rushed to combat stations, and CIC called *Ticonderoga* for air support.

Commodore John J. Herrick and Captain Herbert L. Ogier ready for battle (U.S. Navy photo)

As a warning to the North Vietnamese, *Maddox* fired a salvo of four shells. (Three shells were intended, but a gunner misunderstood.) The boats were commanded by three brothers, and they kept coming. *Maddox* began rapid fire. Braving all that shellfire, the North Vietnamese made a surprisingly determined attack. At least three torpedoes were launched. One of them could punch a hole in the ship thirty feet wide. *Maddox* evaded the bubbly wakes. The North Vietnamese fired machine guns. Their aim was poor. One bullet put a half-inch hole in *Maddox's* after fire director. Shellfire prevented the third boat from getting close enough to launch. All three boats turned back toward the coast. Four jet planes arrived and briefly chased the Communist craft. The boats were damaged but did not sink. On the radar, two boats appeared to be towing the third. Their original V-shaped formation now was inverted. Four North Vietnamese had been killed and six wounded.

North Vietnamese torpedo boats under fire (U. S. Navy photo)

Commodore Herrick decided to leave well enough alone. As he told me, Herrick did not know "how far they would want us to push this thing." The decision was taken from his hands when higher command ordered the ship to retire from the gulf.

The *Maddox's* Luck

Early warnings helped the ship to survive, and so did poor tactics by the North Vietnamese. The high-speed, daylight charge was a warning in itself and, with advance information, it was easy to fend off. If the North Vietnamese had not broadcast their intentions and if the boats had approached slowly after dark, among fishing craft, the destroyer might have been sunk with all hands. "Remember the *Maddox*!" would have been the war slogan. The Pentagon would have flooded the media with pictures of the victims, and President Johnson would have made a dramatic speech.

Back home the skirmish was big news and the Navy was praised for defending itself successfully from a surprise attack. The Pentagon said the *Maddox* was on a "routine patrol" and the attack was "unprovoked."[6] Few took notice of the fact that, although the Johnson Administration as a rule preferred to release important news in Washington, the sensational Tonkin Gulf report came from an Air Force colonel in Hawaii, as if nobody in the Navy or in Washington wanted to be responsible for it.

Privately, President Johnson was not all pleased with the naval action. He fumed that the U.S. Navy could not sink "three little old torpedo boats." The admirals said that by peace time rules their ships were to fire back if fired upon, but not to pursue and destroy. Press and public could not understand why the North Vietnamese would want to challenge the U.S. Navy. It seemed to be a "mad dog" kind of attack. More than a half dozen theories were published. One held that Communist China had ordered its puppet, North Vietnam, to sink the destroyer in order to draw attention away from an imminent invasion of Taiwan. Was this the beginning of a new war with China?

The public at this time did not hear about air raids or gunboat raids on North Vietnam.

To show the flag and maintain freedom of the seas, *Maddox* on Monday, August 3, was sent back into the gulf accompanied by another destroyer, the *Turner Joy*, named for Admiral C. Turner Joy, who had helped to negotiate peace in Korea. "TJ," as the men called it, was a newer and bigger destroyer with fast firing automatic guns. The *Maddox*, one might say, was a more expendable ship. Commodore Herrick took command of both destroyers. He remained on the *Maddox*. In case of attack, Herrick was ordered to pursue and destroy.

On Monday, during the daytime there was no shooting. At night the two ships moved toward the middle of the gulf, far from land. At about 11 p. m., a radar picture shattered the calm. The picadors were coming. Four fast boats were moving north. They shelled a radar site and a security post, according to Radio Hanoi. Nobody bothered the destroyers, but at least some of the *Maddox* men wondered whether their mission was to cruise in the gulf until sunk.

Admiral's Decoy Plan

The two ships had another peaceful cruise during the daylight hours of Tuesday, August 4. But the gunboat men still planned to harass the North Vietnamese, and the De Soto ships were to have a role in that. Admiral Thomas L. Moorer, commander-in-chief of the Pacific Fleet, decided to use the destroyers as decoys in order to draw North Vietnamese attention away from the Nasty operations planned for the night. Following is the relevant portion of a message sent by the admiral:

> The above patrol [the night steaming plan] will
>
> (a) clearly demonstrate our determination to continue these operations.
> (b) possibly draw NVN [North Vietnamese] PGMS [patrol gunboats, motor] northward away from the area of 34A OPS [Nasty boat operations].
> (c) eliminate De Soto patrol interference with 34A OPS.[7]

That contradicted what Defense Secretary McNamara told the Senate Foreign Relations Committee and the Senate Armed Services Committee four years later in a secret hearing. McNamara said the Navy was not aware of the gunboat operations. He called the gunboats "South Vietnamese" and talked as if they were engaged in anti-infiltration operations.[8]

Tuesday night was heavily overcast and extremely dark. The destroyers found some radar contacts and opened fire. *Turner Joy* shot first, followed a few minutes later by the *Maddox*. The latter's sonar men repeatedly detected torpedoes and the ship dodged them. Air support arrived. The aircraft found no attackers, and in the morning no wreckage was seen. There was nothing physical to prove a battle had taken place.

Commodore Herrick expressed his doubts to higher command. Had the ships merely been firing at false contacts? A message from Herrick concluded,

> Entire action leaves many doubts except apparent attempt to ambush at beginning.[9]

Pigeon Trick

In an attempt to settle the matter, some destroyer men were called to the *Ticonderoga* and questioned. They were officers except for a few *Turner Joy* enlisted men who claimed visual sightings. First the group met with a balding staff officer, Captain James Daniels, a veteran of the Pearl Harbor attack of 1941. He was rancorous from having lost sleep during the long night of dispatching aircraft and receiving battle reports. Growled the captain, in front of *Turner Joy's* enlisted men:

> I suppose you people think you were pigeons up there. Well, [raising his voice] *that's exactly what you were.*[10]

My informant, the impeccably conscientious Lieutenant Evans, on second thought wasn't sure whether the captain said "pigeons" or "sitting ducks." Either way, the meaning is about the same, and Admiral Moorer's decoy plan we have from the 1968 hearing. Following publication of *Tonkin Gulf*, Captain Herrick (giving here his permanent rank), sent me a friendly letter in which he made no objection to the book's contents.

Playing pigeon was not new to the *Maddox*. During the Korean War the ship teased the Communist coast in order to draw fire and divert attention from landings. The destroyer claimed a record for getting shot at: 720 rounds of major caliber fire. Some did not miss. Deploying a unit to draw fire is a common tactic used by military forces. Used to initiate a war, the pigeon assignment can be extremely valuable. Politically, it is important to put the blame on the other side. We will see more of that.

The destroyer men were interviewed individually aboard *Ticonderoga* by Admiral Robert B. Moore. Next, *Maddox* officers wrote up a report of the night action. The Navy was satisfied that a battle had taken place. There would be no court of inquiry. At least one of the pilots who took part in the search for torpedo boats decided that there had not been a battle. This was James Stockdale, who became a highly decorated officer and, as a retired admiral, ran for vice president on the Ross Perot ticket of 1992. Informed of the *Ticonderoga's* retaliation mission, Stockdale asked, "Retaliation for what"?

In Washington, evidence for an August 4 attack included a few North Vietnamese messages concerning the August 2 battle that were mixed into the August 4 file. This false evidence was reported by Anthony Austin in his book *The President's War*, and Austin attributed the misplacement to "bureaucratic muddle" and "clerical error." Austin said the mix-up took place within the Pentagon.[11]

As for the Nasties' planned August 4 sortie, Radio Hanoi said nothing about it. Apparently that was canceled. Hanoi denied that its forces had made any attack that night. In America, Hanoi's charge that the night battle was a "fabrication" sounded ridiculous.

President Takes Action

Two reported naval attacks were enough for President Johnson. He ordered retaliatory air raids and briefed congressional leaders at the White House. Johnson asked the leadership to pass a resolution of support for his actions. He did not mention that the second attack might have been illusory.

President Lyndon B. Johnson addresses the nation after the second
Tonkin Gulf incident. (Photo courtesy of the LBJ Museum)

On the floor of the Senate, Wayne Morse, Democrat from Oregon,
offered an explanation of the North Vietnamese attacks. He claimed that
South Vietnamese gunboats had been attacking North Vietnam, and he
said that the *Maddox's* patrol ought not to have been scheduled at such
a time. Morse was contradicted by Senator Frank Lausche, Democrat
from Ohio, who had attended the same briefings. Heated words were
exchanged. Secretary McNamara told newsmen he did not know of any
"South Vietnamese" raids. Little credence was given to Morse, who had
the reputation of being a maverick.

Senator Morse denounced the proposed resolution as an
"unconstitutional, pre-dated declaration of war." He predicted it would
pass and that the senators voting for it would regret having done so.
The press condemned Morse's "reckless and querulous dissent," but he
was able to put into the *Congressional Record* hundreds of telegrams
in support of his position. In both houses of Congress, the vote took
place amid overwhelming support from press and public. Only two

lawmakers, one of them Morse, voted against what was called the "Tonkin Gulf Resolution."

Provocation Intended

Unknown to the public, the resolution had been prepared months before the naval incidents, and President Johnson had been waiting for an opportunity to get it passed. Undersecretary of state during the Tonkin Gulf crisis was George Ball, one of the top Vietnam planners. After the war Ball was interviewed by a British journalist, and he admitted that among his colleagues there had been some thought of provoking an incident. He said of the De Soto patrol that it had an intelligence objective, but Vietnam planners were looking for an excuse to start bombing North Vietnam and "the sending of a destroyer up the Tonkin Gulf was primarily for provocation."[12]

The Washington *Evening Star* reported passage of the Tonkin Gulf Resolution and also an explanation for the August 2 attack, which was similar to Senator Morse's explanation. According to an anonymous source in the Pentagon, South Vietnamese craft had raided a naval base on the North Vietnamese coast, and when the *Maddox* approached the raided territory, the Communist torpedo boat men assumed the ship was hostile and went after it. President Johnson refused to confirm that "speculation." However, the Pentagon's explanation seemed to make sense, and it helped to cool tempers in the United States. People forgot about the naval incidents and the possible invasion of Taiwan. The crisis was over. The true nature of the gunboat raids remained unknown.

A "Different Kind of War"

Having won the presidential election as the peace candidate, President Johnson in 1965 entered the war in a gradual manner with bombings and flag-flying troop arrivals. Gradualness was not recommended by our military men. They wanted a "knockout blow." On July 28, Johnson, in a low-key noontime telecast, explained "why we are in Vietnam." He said this was a "different kind of war," but "really war." The Congress had not declared war, and the speech was not taking place in prime time. Editorial writers puzzled over what Johnson meant. They decided we must be at war. For support, some editorial writers quoted other editorial writers. In short, the nation was at war, but lulled into a confused complacency. Johnson knew how to manage the news.

Not such a big deal, it seemed. Military men experienced in Vietnam advised me, "It can't get as big as Korea." The enemy, although on paper not too numerous, could recruit more soldiers as needed. Innocuous-looking women played their parts. Our civilian and military facilities were riddled with spies. In the autumn of 1965, American troops began clashing with units of the North Vietnamese army, which was infiltrating southward on the Ho Chi Minh Trail. The Americans won victories, and the enemy vanished into the jungle. More North Vietnamese kept coming. In time the Viet Cong forces were greatly weakened, especially by their failed Tet offensive of 1968. However, the size of the Tet offensive surprised and discouraged the American public, and the U.S. Army began to scale back its efforts. The North Vietnamese army remained strong and able to recruit as many men as required. The Communist strategy was not to win battles, but to keep inflicting casualties until the growing anti-war movement in the United States was strong enough to bring the troops home.

As noted above, President Johnson justified legally the war by his authority as Commander-in-Chief and by the Tonkin Gulf Resolution. True, going to war was not the intent of Congress, but there was the authorization in black and white, and although ambiguous it had been approved almost unanimously by two legislative bodies, both of which were composed chiefly of lawyers.

Behind the Scenes

As we have seen, the North Vietnamese attack on the *Maddox* was not "unprovoked," as the Defense Department claimed. The destroyer had not committed any provocations, but the gunboats and CIA aircraft had. Were these coordinated operations? They were. They were coordinated by a secret committee which met at the Executive Office Building next to the White House. The group was called the "303 Committee," taking its name from the room in which its meetings initially were held. Chairman of the committee was McGeorge Bundy, the president's national security adviser. The committee directed various special operations in North Vietnam.[13] Operations became more frequent when *Maddox* entered the Tonkin Gulf.

It was President John F. Kennedy who first recommended special operations in North Vietnam. He wanted to counter that country's assistance to Communist guerrillas in South Vietnam. Agreeing with him was Secretary of State Dean Rusk who thought that aggressive special operations would demonstrate to North Vietnam that the United States had "no intention of quitting" in South Vietnam. Defense Secretary McNamara enthusiastically endorsed the special operations, which, he believed, needed more people and support. McNamara was famous for thinking in numbers and quantifying everything. Crisp, decisive, and showing an interest in the poetry of T. S. Eliot, Robert McNamara was the darling of the Washington press corps.

The CIA found that inserting agents into North Vietnam was counter-productive. Even if the agents were North Vietnamese refugees who knew the place well, they were caught and used to generate anti-American sentiment. Bombarding the North Vietnamese coast had little value, and that also stirred up anti-American sentiment. The CIA preferred to operate in South Vietnam, which Secretary of State Rusk agreed was "98 percent of the problem." [14]

President Johnson decided to have the Defense Department take over special operations from the disenchanted CIA, and that these operations would be supervised in Washington by the 303 Committee. No doubt having the decisions made in Washington appealed to Johnson, who liked to micromanage military operations. Each special operation had to be approved, and this was a four step process. It involved the Joint Chiefs of Staff, Secretary McNamara, Secretary Rusk, and the national security adviser. There was a fifth step when President Johnson's approval was required.[15] If anything required a fifth step, it ought to have been coordinating the De Soto patrol and the special operations.

A Naval Advisory Detachment was established at the South Vietnamese port of Da Nang to drop agents in North Vietnam and raid the coast. Put in charge was a Navy commander with no experience in special operations. He was assisted by a Marine Corps lieutenant colonel who had had some kind of experience with the CIA (and maybe was CIA?). The intelligence agency was ordered to assist the Navy, but disapproving of the plan, the agency kept its involvement to the minimum

The Navy was not really keen, either. For a naval officer getting involved with special operations was not a good career move, and the Navy culture was not geared to cloak and dagger work. The latter deficiency became apparent right away. When the first Nasty boats were acquired, the Navy showed them off at a press conference in Washington, and again at a press conference in Honolulu as the boats proceeded toward Vietnam. For the Navy it was routine to publicize new equipment, and the Nasties were a proud acquisition. They were super-fast and built of mahogany. Wood is less radar reflective than metal.

Not Secret to Hanoi

The gunboat operation, although highly classified, never was going to be secret from the North Vietnamese. They knew all about it because they were bombarded by the boats, and because their spies worked at port of Da Nang, where the gunboats were based. Radio Hanoi complained about "ships of the Americans and their henchmen." Few Americans listened to Radio Hanoi.

We need to correct something. What the Congress voted for in 1964 was not the Tonkin Gulf Resolution, the popular term for that legislation, but correctly—and prophetically—the Southeast Asia Resolution, a term which applied to a much larger geographical area. Few suspected the Southeast Asia Resolution would live up to its name, authorizing military operations outside of Vietnam, but even before the resolution passed, we had a secret war going on in Laos. Of course, the Laotian war was secret only in the sense that the American people did not know about it. We can be sure the Laotians knew about it—not to mention our enemies in Moscow and Beijing. The war later spread to Cambodia as the North Vietnamese army moved into that area and established a base.

Communist Holocausts

Republican President Richard M. Nixon in 1970 attacked the North Vietnamese base in Cambodia, and this led to a civil war that the Cambodian Communists eventually won with the help of the North Vietnamese. The Communist regime subsequently murdered approximately two million of its own people, an event dramatized in a moving picture, *The Killing Fields*. Totalitarian regimes are inclined to wipe out whole classes of people. The Nazis killed six million people. Far bigger holocausts, in the tens of millions, occurred in the Soviet Union and Communist China.

As students of war-making, we must note that President Nixon's invasion of Cambodia was preceded by another mysterious ship incident. Reportedly, the *Columbia Eagle*, an American ship headed for Vietnam with munitions, was hijacked by two young anti-war Americans and taken to Cambodia, where a few days later the Cambodian army overthrew the neutralist government of Prince Sihanouk. The hijackers told the press the *Columbia Eagle* was carrying napalm meant for Vietnam. Communist sources said the ship delivered arms to the Cambodian army. When *Columbia Eagle* departed the port of Sihanoukville, a photograph showed the ship riding high in the water. Something heavy had been unloaded. Apparently, President Nixon had made a deal with the Cambodian generals.

Lost Opportunity to Win

The American campaign in Cambodia might better have been directed at Laos. When in 1975 South Vietnam fell to the Communists, North Vietnam sent one of its most distinguished soldiers to accept the surrender. He was Colonel Bui (family name) Tin, who had been fighting with the Communist forces for thirty years. In 1990, Bui defected from North Vietnam, disgusted by its tyranny and corruption. Later, an American human rights activist asked him whether there was anything the United States could have done to win the war. Bui's answer was, "Yes, cut the Ho Chi Minh trail in Laos." He added, "If President Johnson had granted General Westmoreland's request to enter Laos and block the Ho Chi Minh Trail, Hanoi could not have won the war." Bui meant that if we had blocked the trail with ground forces, instead of just bombing it, North Vietnam could not have moved its regular army into South Vietnam.[16] The former colonel discussed this subject more fully in his book *From Enemy to Friend*. Later we shall discuss another way in which South Vietnam could have been saved.

A Way to Prevent War

In *Tonkin Gulf* I recommended that the Congress establish an office of its own for the "swift and expert inquiry into international incidents and sudden crises."[17] The book's reviewers thought this an excellent idea, considering how President Johnson and his "Tonkin Gulf Resolution" had duped the nation into a ten-year war in the jungles of Southeast Asia. A quick trip to the *Maddox* might have prevented all that. Indeed, the mere *probability* of such an investigation might have kept everybody on the straight and narrow. If the *Columbia Eagle* had not been "hijacked," that alone could have saved millions lives.

In 2003, a congressional investigative office might have prevented the Iraq War. President George W. Bush's allegation that Iraq possessed weapons of mass destruction was based on little evidence, our invading forces failed to substantiate the charge, and it generally was decided that the President had erred (or lied as some said).

In 2006, however, we heard that Iraq did in fact possess large quantities of toxins and other contraband, but not nuclear weapons, which were the chief concern. This we were told by the man who had been the dictator's air vice marshal, General Georges Sada, an Armenian Christian. According to him, Saddam shipped hundreds of tons of contraband, disguised as disaster relief, to neighboring Syria, where a dam had collapsed. To disguise the shipments, they were carried by commercial airliners which had their seats removed.[18] Commercial trucks were used as well. This could explain how Syrian dictator Bashar al-Assad came into possession of poison gas, which he reportedly has used on rebels trying to overthrow him.

In 2012, an experienced investigative office might have found answers to important questions about why an American ambassador and three other Americans met their deaths at the hands of terrorists in Benghazi, Libya.

Investigation on the Cheap

Something else the investigators could do would not cost much. They could recommend timely and significant reading material. This might sound like a boring suggestion, but of the two lawmakers who withstood tremendous public pressure and voted against the Tonkin Gulf Resolution, one did so because he had read a book. He was Democratic Senator Ernest Gruening, a medical doctor from Alaska. Gruening explained to me his vote by saying he had read *The Two Viet-Nams* by Bernard B. Fall. Fall was a Vienna-born writer who acquired French citizenship by fighting with the French Resistance in World War II and later in the French army. On trips to Vietnam as a civilian, he witnessed first-hand the French military campaign there and, subsequently, the American effort. *The Two Viet-Nams,* first published in 1963, tells the history of French rule and its Vietnamese opposition. The book makes it clear that the Vietnamese insurgents were patriots unalterably opposed to foreign rule and not the puppets of a worldwide Communist conspiracy.

The erroneous "puppet" notion badly skewed American policy. As one example, our policy-makers wasted time trying to end the war in Vietnam by making a deal in Moscow. (In those days we had no diplomatic relations with Communist China.)

The Other Naysayer

The other heroic naysayer, Senator Morse, came to politics from academia, and perhaps he also read *The Two Viet-Nams.* However, Morse told me that he voted against the resolution because he had received a tip from the Pentagon that events in the gulf were not what they appeared to be. "I know their lingo," he said in reference to the Pentagon informant. My proposed investigative office would have to learn the Pentagon's "lingo" and other lingoes as well, in order to be prepared in times of crisis.

After we went to war in Vietnam, Senator J. William Fulbright, chairman of the Senate Foreign Relations Committee, read *The Two Viet-Nams* and discovered that the author lived in Washington, D. C., where he taught at the predominantly African-American Howard University. Fulbright began conferring with Fall, and the powerful chairman became a prominent figure in the anti-war movement. He bitterly regretted having aided passage of Johnson's resolution.

Senator Fulbright and President Johnson in characteristic poses

In 1995, a late-coming disciple of Bernard Fall turned up. He was General Colin Powell, former chairman of the Joint Chiefs of Staff. As a captain in Vietnam, Powell was wounded and much decorated. He read a different book by Fall, *Street Without Joy: the French Debacle in Indochina,* which was first published in 1961. Powell says in his autobiography, *My American Journey,* that if President Kennedy or President Johnson had read that book, he would have found a way "to extricate ourselves from the quicksand of Vietnam":

> Fall makes it painfully clear that we had almost no understanding of what we had gotten ourselves into. I cannot help thinking that if President Kennedy or President Johnson had spent a quiet weekend at Camp David reading that perceptive book, they would have returned to the White House Monday morning and immediately started to figure out a way to extricate ourselves from the quicksand of Vietnam.[19]

In the same year that General Powell published his autobiography, 1995, former Defense Secretary McNamara published *In Retrospect: The Tragedy and Lessons of Vietnam,* and in it he complained that the Johnson Administration lacked Vietnam experts who could have helped to prevent mistakes. Did McNamara ever look for a Vietnam expert? While the U.S. Government commissioned studies and frantically tried to figure out what to do about its misbegotten adventure, Bernard Fall was residing in the nation's capital, where he was surveilled as a trouble-maker by the FBI. His widow, Dorothy Fall, says the bureau tapped their telephone and intercepted their mail, as early as the Administration of President John F. Kennedy.[20]

Flirting with Fascism

Our national security establishment did not want any pessimistic advice, and critics were viewed as unpatriotic. Retired Admiral Arnold S. True wrote to Senator Fulbright questioning the official account of the Tonkin Gulf incidents, and the Navy reminded him that regulations prohibited his commenting adversely on a military service. True thought he was being threatened with a court martial. I heard that retired military officers could not speak out against the war because that would jeopardize their pensions. Correct or not, that was the atmosphere of the time. Some pro-war retired officers, worried about losing the war, observed darkly that a government run by the military would be "more efficient." If you were a civilian in the national security establishment, you had to support the war, and if your support was muted, some gung-ho individual was liable to be promoted over you.

Large, often violent anti-war demonstrations filled our television screens. At Kent State University in Ohio, anti-war students threw rocks at National Guardsmen, who opened fire killing four students and wounding nine, one of whom was paralyzed. Marxist "Weathermen" set off bombs at the Capitol, Pentagon, and other government buildings.

In such circumstances I began writing *Tonkin Gulf* and applied for a study desk at the Library of Congress. Seeing in the hall men wearing security badges, I cautiously gave as the subject of my research "naval history." That worked, but in this era of "hawks" and "doves," both sides were militant. A dovish library administrator repeatedly warned me there was a shortage of study desks and advised me to write about the Montessori schools. (Notice how easily bureaucratic power can be switched to thought control.) In a small way, I felt some identity with my European ancestors, who were blown this way and that by the winds of war.

Despite a serious illness, in 1966 Bernard Fall made another trip to Vietnam. This was the sixth of his forays, and his life came to a tragic end. Early in 1967, the intrepid writer was killed by a land mine while accompanying U.S. Marines. They were patrolling an intricately defended coastal area that the French called "the street without joy." Bernard Fall, soldier-scholar, died with his boots on.

Reformers on Capitol Hill

One of *Tonkin Gulf's* reviewers was Carl Marcy, chief of staff of the Foreign Relations Committee. An easy-going, somewhat portly gentleman with eyebrows bushy enough to comb, Carl at middle age had taken on the folksy characteristics endemic to Capitol Hill. He and I began meeting at his Capitol office to talk about war prevention and other problems of national security. Achieving popularity on the Hill at that time was a proposed "War Powers Resolution" intended to prevent unnecessary wars. Thoroughly disgusted with the Vietnam experience, many legislators identified the *presidency itself* as a cause of war, and they planned to limit by law the Chief Executive's ability to plunge the nation into deadly conflict. The reformers wanted the President to explain any new war plans to the Congress, and to follow the proper constitutional procedure by asking permission before committing military forces. The reformers recognized that emergencies could require the President to act quickly. In that case, they wanted him to seek congressional authorization within a definite period of time.

During one of our chats, Carl brought up the proposed War Powers Resolution and said, "Fulbright wants to know whether you think that will work."

"No, I don't think so," said I.

"Fulbright doesn't think so, either," said Carl.

25

Carl's response might surprise some people who remember Senator Fulbright, his courageous opposition to the Vietnam War, and his support for the War Powers Resolution. But it was Senator Jacob J. Javits (Republican of New York) who took the lead on that legislation, and as Carl later told the Senate historian, Donald Ritchie, "Senator Fulbright never became very deeply involved."

Presidency a Hazard

Sponsors of the War Powers Resolution were right about the presidency as a source of warfare. James Grafton Rogers, a former assistant secretary of state, in his 1945 book *World Policing and the Constitution* reviewed the history of American military actions and concluded,

> War has habitually followed a series of executive acts or steps taken by the President, or both the President and the Congress, which rendered it inescapable.[21]

Getting trapped by series of steps is precisely what happened to us in Southeast Asia. Familiarity with Rogers's work might have enabled observers to appreciate better the portents that heralded the Vietnam War. A series of presidents took forward steps, each expedient at the time, until turning back became politically almost impossible.

What were the major steps? In 1954, the French, following military reverses, decided to give up their rule of Vietnam, and a multilateral conference in Geneva provided temporarily for a Communist North Vietnam and a non-Communist South Vietnam. In 1955, anti-Communist Ngo Dinh Diem was elected President of South Vietnam in a rigged election. The Geneva Accords called for unifying the two Vietnams in 1956 with nationwide elections, but Diem refused to cooperate. As President Eisenhower admitted, "possibly 80 percent of the population would have voted for the Communist Ho Chi Minh."[22] Guerrilla warfare began in the South. Eisenhower promulgated the domino theory. The next American President, John F. Kennedy, sent thousands of "military advisers," and although supposed to avoid combat, these men because of their numbers inescapably became involved. In other words, they got shot at. President Johnson, brandishing his Southeast Asia Resolution, went whole hog.

Approximately 58,000 Americans died in the ten-year war. The *Encyclopedia Americana* lists Vietnamese military fatalities as 220,357 South Vietnamese and 444,000 North Vietnamese. According to *Collier's Encyclopedia*, total Vietnamese fatalities, counting both military and civilian, came to 1.7 million.

The Communists won in South Vietnam, but the effects are not so bad as had been expected. The formerly two Vietnams are unified under a Communist government, and like North Korea, this impoverished part of the globe is dark at night as seen by satellite. However, the Vietnamese regime permits thousands of private companies, and except for the small neighboring states of Laos and Cambodia, there has been no domino effect of Asian nations collapsing into Communism. The U.S.—Vietnam Trade Council is helping Vietnam to fit into the world economy, and American investors are buying Vietnamese stocks. McDonalds and several other American fast food companies have invaded formerly enemy territory and are doing business there. Unlike North Korea, Vietnam is not building nuclear weapons and threatening its neighbors with annihilation.

A Test in Libya

Since the War Powers Resolution was passed in 1973, it has not prevented any wars. In 2011, a bipartisan group of lawmakers, led by Speaker of the House John Boehner (Republican from Ohio), questioned Democrat President Barack Obama's war in Libya and insisted that the President obey fully the requirements of the War Powers Resolution. Obama's compliance was sketchy and inadequate. Had the war critics tried to cut off funds, the Democrat-controlled Senate would not have agreed, and the President had his veto power. Impeachment by the Republican-controlled Lower House would not have been followed by conviction in the Senate, although it would have put some pressure on the President. The constitutionalists planned to go to court, but in the past the courts had refused to adjudicate this sort of dispute between the President and the Congress. The issue became moot when the brief war in Libya ended.

At that point it looked nearly impossible for the Congress to wrest back the war power from the President. In the summer of 2013, however,

President Barack Obama suddenly needed help from the Congress and the latter's position strengthened a bit. Obama had threatened military action against Syria if its dictator, Bashar al-Assad, used poison gas against the rebels in Syria's civil war, and with Assad apparently having done that, Obama prepared to take action. The American president, however, found himself with little support, foreign or domestic. Among our foreign allies, not even the British would lend a hand. The President then sought a resolution of support from Congress, while claiming that, legally, he as Commander-in-Chief did not really need congressional approval. The Lower House appeared likely to vote against the President, and a constitutional crisis loomed. What would happen if the Congress disapproved action against Syria and the President ordered it anyway? That was a troublesome question indeed. Fortunately, like the deus ex machina in an ancient Greek play, Russia's President Vladimir Putin stepped forward and offered to mediate the removal of chemical weapons from Syria, and that ended the crisis. In Washington, there must have been many sighs of relief. Putin's initiative also kept in power his client Bashar al-Assad and enabled the Russian leader to write a smug *New York Times* op-ed criticizing President Obama.

During the debate on Syria, Washington pundits and former government officials said that the War Powers Resolution enabled the President to carry out a military action anywhere for a period of ninety days before seeking congressional approval. That is not true. The War Powers Resolution gives the President a free hand *only in the case of emergency*—when there is insufficient time to consult the Congress. Syria was no emergency; it had been debated for weeks. I fired off a corrective e-mail to the *Washington Times,* and it was printed on September 9. A few days later another pundit on television made the same War Powers mistake.

The ninety day period, to be precise, provides sixty days for military action and thirty more days, if need be, for withdrawal.

Intent of the Founding Fathers

The Founding Fathers wanted Congress to have the power to initiate war, not the President, and we can see that in James Madison's notes concerning the Constitutional Convention of 1787. Americans were keenly aware of how monarchs would drag their people into a war for sometimes obscure reasons, and then demand everybody's support as a patriotic duty. Madison, a delegate from Virginia, helped to prepare before the convention the Virginia Plan of government, which proposed a bicameral legislature with population-weighted representation. This gave the delegates a place to start on their design for governance. For that and other reasons, historians have called Madison the "Father of the Constitution."

At the convention, Madison recorded that John Rutledge of South Carolina "was for investing the executive power in one person, though he was not for giving him the power of war and peace." George Mason of Virginia said the President was not "safely to be trusted" with the war power. Neither was the Senate, according to Mason. Agreeing with him was Elbridge Gerry of Massachusetts. The whole legislature, it was decided, would be less corruptible than just the President or the Senate. Notice that our Founding Fathers were both idealistic and cynical. They knew that people were corruptible. They planned a government of laws, not of men, and they designed checks and balances.

The convention voted to give only Congress the power to "make war." Later the delegates changed that wording to "declare war" so that the President would have the "power to repel sudden attacks." In agreement with that, the War Powers Resolution of 1973 preserves the emergency option and requires the President to obtain a war authorization within a limited period of time.

Mason was for "clogging" the process of going to war, and for "facilitating" the process of making peace, and that is what the convention ended up doing. The Congress, unwieldy and contentious, is suited to discussing and thereby slowing the initiation of war, a perceived need which in time might go away. The President, nimble and secretive, is better able to conduct diplomatic negotiations and make peace. The Founders put together a sensible plan. To the nation's regret, the plan has not always been followed. Nimble and secretive Presidents have been known to hornswoggle both the Congress and the public, creating emergencies and usurping Congress's right to initiate war. Turning the tables, the Congress in 1898 bullied President William McKinley into asking for a declaration of war against Spain. Overall, the

Congress has tended to lose power by not always insisting meticulously on its war-making prerogative.

Truman's "Police Action"

In the latter half of the twentieth century, there took flight the notion that the President has a right to initiate war without consulting Congress. Levitating this idea was a combination of bureaucrats and college professors who were trying to justify President Harry S. Truman's unauthorized war in Korea. Truman had acted in quick response to North Korea's invasion of South Korea, the American people strongly approved, and the President, instead of seeking congressional authorization, cited a favorable vote in the United Nations Security Council. Truman called the war a "police action." As the war grew bigger and less popular, supporters called it the "Korean Conflict." Critics insisted on calling it the "Korean War." When the North Koreans were defeated, the Communist Chinese flooded into the conflict, which ended with a truce line approximating the prewar boundary. South Korea gained some territory.

Truman suffered so much criticism about the lack of congressional authorization that President Johnson in 1964 felt that, for political reasons, he needed some kind of congressional approval for fighting in Vietnam.

During the lengthy and unpopular Vietnam War, a few professors changed their minds about the presidential war power, and among them was Henry Steele Commager, Columbia University authority on American history. Commager had supported President Truman's action, but he now felt that this extension of Executive power subverted political institutions at home and threatened the peace abroad.

"We find ourselves turning into a military society," Commager warned the Senate Foreign Relations Committee.

In defense of President Johnson's war in Vietnam, the State Department cited the Southeast Asia Resolution and added these arguments: (1) The right to make war was implied by the President's constitutional designation as Commander-in-Chief, and (2) Presidents have been making war on their own authority since the founding of the Republic. Those contentions were advanced by Leonard C. Meeker, legal adviser to the State Department. On March 4, 1966, Meeker signed a memorandum to that effect, and it was sent to the Foreign Relations Committee. The memorandum afterward appeared in the *Department of State Bulletin* of March 28, 1966. Meeker said of the Commander-in-Chief's duties:

> These duties carry very broad powers, including the power to deploy American forces abroad and commit them to military operations when the President deems such action necessary to maintain the security and defense of the United States.

As evidence of that claim, the State Department's attorney said,

> Since the Constitution was adopted there have been at least 125 instances in which the President has ordered the armed forces to take action or maintain positions abroad without obtaining prior Congressional authorization, starting with the "undeclared war" with France

False and Disappearing Evidence

Meeker either lied about the undeclared war with France or made an unconscionable error. Our second President, John Adams, obtained congressional authorizations to attack French warships and privateers (privately sponsored, government authorized raiders) that were preying on American commerce.[23] On May 28, 1798, Congress authorized our navy to subdue, seize, and bring into port armed French vessels encountered off the Atlantic coast. Less than two months later, on July 9, Congress authorized seizing such vessels found anywhere on the high seas. In sum, the Quasi-War, as it was called, was authorized but not declared.

The unpopular Vietnam War and its controversial authorization brought about a "constitutional crisis," according to the constitutional authority Professor Alpheus T. Mason of Princeton University. In that circumstance, the State Department's legal adviser misinformed the Foreign Relations Committee in a way that upheld the President's claim to the war power.

Now, what about Leonard Meeker's other 124 instances in which the President has "ordered the armed forces to take action or maintain positions abroad without obtaining prior congressional authorization"?

The list has disappeared.

At this writing, the State Department's legal adviser is Harold Koh, a former dean of the Yale Law School. I twice asked Koh about Meeker's list, once by e-mail and once by the U.S. Postal Service, as well as attempting to reach him by telephone. Koh never responded to my queries. In addition, I contacted the State Department's Office of the Historian, which told me that a 1966 document would have been sent to the National Archives. The National Archives says that it does not have such a document.

A Surprising Fate

Is that not a surprising fate for a document of such great consequence, on which is based the President's alleged right to make war on his own authority?

Perhaps, indirectly, I was the cause of the disappearance. In January of 1972, *New Republic* carried my article debunking the claim that the Founders intended to give the President the war power.[24] It discussed Madison's notes, and it examined military incidents early in the nation's history, finding them irrelevant, erroneous, or trivial. Senator Fulbright subsequently disparaged the Johnson Administration's historical claims concerning the war power.

Meeker must have had in mind incidents that James Grafton Rogers listed in his book *World Policing and the Constitution*. Rogers reviewed 149 military operations of various kinds. Almost all were minor actions, such as evicting pirates from Caribbean strongholds. Our Navy fired on tropical villages where American castaways or surveyors had been murdered. We landed marines in Latin America to protect American residents in times of revolt. In 1870, the USS *Jamestown* landed marines in Honolulu to force the U.S. Consulate (yes, *the U.S. Consulate*) to put its flag at half-staff in order to commemorate the death of Hawaii's Queen, a controversial figure.

The Rogers book chronicles a gradual increase of power exercised by the Commander-in-Chief, and a concurrent diminishment of congressional oversight. Small interventions became so frequent that the Congress lost interest. It is clear, however, that Presidents did not claim the war power during the early part of the Republic's existence as alleged by Leonard Meeker. Those Presidents knew what was the intent of the Founding Fathers. Four of them were Founding Fathers.

New Century, Bad Precedent

A damaging precedent was set in 1900. With the Congress not in session, President William McKinley sent five thousand troops to China during an uprising called the "Boxer Rebellion." The American people saw McKinley's action as justified by the circumstances. The Boxers were killing hundreds of foreigners and thousands of Chinese Christians. The Americans joined an eight-country force of twenty thousand that fought for about two months. Early on, it appeared that the enemy was just an anti-foreign peasant uprising, but it turned out that the Boxers were supported by the Empress of China, who ordered the killing of all foreigners, and backed up by the Imperial Army. The U.S. Congress upon reconvening in December, if not sooner, ought to have fulfilled its constitutional duty by approving or disapproving the President's action. That never was done, and this failure set a precedent for the President's undertaking military action against a foreign state on his own authority as Commander-in-Chief. The Congress did appropriate the necessary funds.

The Boxer campaign was a small and temporary aberration. Later, President Woodrow Wilson sought congressional authorization when he invaded Mexico and when he took the United States into World War I. President Franklin D. Roosevelt obtained a declaration of war when entering World War II, but had not been so punctilious in his earlier secret operations against German submarines.

Analysis

In 1964, Britain's Manchester *Guardian* saw right away what was happening in Vietnam:

> Many people—not only Communists—will be tempted to suspect that the U.S. air attacks, and the great movement now proceeding of military power into Southeast Asia, had long been planned and required only a suitable occasion— easily manufactured—to set them off.

And so the USS *Maddox* was given a pigeon assignment.

In the 1968 hearing, McNamara angrily rejected the notion that the United States Government meant to provoke a conflict in the Tonkin Gulf. Contemptuously, he said, "I can only characterize such insinuations as monstrous." The Pentagon Papers tell us, however, that in of September of 1964 the military situation was deteriorating in South Vietnam, and our strategists at that time were discussing how to provoke an incident in order to get a bombing campaign started. A written "Plan of Action for South Vietnam" listed possible provocations, such as shelling the North Vietnamese coast and attacking by air the Ho Chi Minh trail in Laos. The memorandum said that if one of our De Soto ships were sunk, this would make possible a "full fledged squeeze" on North Vietnam. The document also said that the De Soto patrols should be "fully protected" and "far out in international waters."[25]

Both political parties feared to lose Vietnam to Communism. President Johnson used the Tonkin Gulf incidents to shoehorn the nation into getting formally involved. Johnson diluted American military effectiveness by applying power in small increments to which the enemy was able to adapt. In a business-like cost-benefit analysis, McNamara and economist Walt Rostow decided that the gradual increase of American military action would persuade the North Vietnamese that the game was not worth the candle. Perhaps they also thought that the "graduated response" strategy would not unduly provoke the Chinese, who in 1950 entered the Korean War as our forces approached their border. Yet for several years, beginning in 1966, the Chinese Communists were engrossed by their "Cultural Revolution," a series of mass purges that followed the failure of dictator Mao Zedong's economic initiative called the "Great Leap Forward." For whatever reason, anyway, our Commanders-in-Chief would not invade Laos to cut the Ho Chi Minh trail, and bombing the dense jungle had little effect.

Some American flag officer, I forget which, said after the war, "No military man in his right mind would have fought that war the way we did." The military had recommended a knockout blow. Graduated response having been approved instead, our military men staunchly and quietly continued their deference to civilian rule, letting Washington's bean counters and micromanagers have their way.

An Avoidable War?

The Vietnam War was a war of choice. Keeping out of it certainly would have been preferable.

As an alternative to war—or to win the war, we might have saved South Vietnam from Communism by recruiting more South Vietnamese to the side of democracy, and that might have done by insisting on land reform. Where in South Vietnam the poor sharecroppers were the most numerous, so were the Viet Cong guerrillas. In South Korea, we had supported land reform, and American troops would not have been needed if North Korea had not invaded the South. We also supported land reform in Japan and Taiwan, two more success stories. In South Vietnam our land reform effort was stymied by the ruling elite, which included many landowners.

Economist Robert L. Sansom observed that the Viet Cong offered the peasant land while we offered him a constitution.[26] Sansom and also Bernard Fall commented that the American officials in South Vietnam were slow to give land reform a high priority or grasp its importance. In 1970, we undertook a serious "land to the tiller" program, but it was "too little, too late,"[27] and the recipients of land knew that their ownership would last only so long as did the ineffectual regime in Saigon[28] From the beginning, land reform ought to have been a necessary condition of American support.

Land reform might have gone better in South Vietnam if in 1955 Wolf Ladejinsky, our leading expert on that subject, had not been fired from the U. S. Government. Senator Joseph McCarthy (Wisconsin Democrat turned Republican) had accused him of being pro-Communist, even though Ladejinsky's work in Japan and Taiwan had proved effective as a deterrent to Communism. It was Ladejinsky's bad luck to have been born in the Ukraine, which became part of the Soviet Union. Furthermore, land reform acquired a bad name because of events in China. The Chinese Communists achieved power as "agrarian reformers" promising "land to the landless." Collectivization was their real aim and, as happened earlier in the Soviet Union, many millions of farmers died by execution or starvation. The very words *land reform* became toxic. Whatever remains of the legions of McCarthy haters, they arguably could add the loss of South Vietnam to their list of complaints.

After the Communists took over South Vietnam, they collectivized the land, and famine resulted. In 1988, Vietnam switched to a market oriented system with individual households responsible for production. People then began growing enough rice for their own needs and even enough to export. Had the North Korean regime taken that course, it would have no need to cover its failures with bluster about nuclear weapons.

Useful Principles

In a crisis situation, be skeptical. First reports usually are wrong. Check the facts as much as possible.

Be prepared to check the facts. The Congress needs is own rapid reaction investigative facility.

Somebody has to know key people and their "lingoes."

The Joint Chiefs of Staff like to present a united front. When they make a unanimous recommendation, they might be obscuring dissension.

This is important to know. When the Joint Chiefs recommend something unanimously, they ought to be polled like a jury, which McNamara did do, and unanimity ought not to be trumpeted if it does not exist. McNamara probably had learned something from the 1961 Bay of Pigs operation in Cuba. After that failed, there was some question about whether the Joint Chiefs actually had been in favor of it or whether, viewing it as a CIA project, they had dissembled.

> *Do not let inter-service rivalries determine policy or strategy.*

> *Watch out for pigeon assignments and other provocations.*

> *Do not automatically reject what the other side has to say.*

The North Vietnamese broadcast reports of gunboat and aircraft attacks on them. Considering their reports would have put the Tonkin Gulf incidents in a different light.

> *An alert investigative facility could discourage some deceptions before they began.*

> *Consult the best available experts on the area in question.*

No President, secretary of state, or secretary of defense met with Bernard Fall. Neither was he recruited by an Ivy League university. At the policy-making, "best and brightest" level, not enough attention was paid to Vietnam's need for land reform or the Vietnamese peoples' profound desire for unalloyed independence. We Americans did not plan to replace the French as colonial overlords, but since we had supported the French, the Communists were able to make their recruits think otherwise.

Despite criticism, Special Forces at Fort Bragg, North Carolina, invited Bernard Fall to lecture there. He had patrolled with them.

References

[1] Robert S. McNamara, *In Retrospect: The Tragedy and Lessons of Vietnam*, pages 174-175

[2] Edwin E. Moise, *Tonkin Gulf and the Escalation of the Vietnam War*, page 42

[3] Edwin E. Moise, *Tonkin Gulf and the Escalation of the Vietnam War*, page 14

[4] Senator Wayne Morse, *Congressional Record—Senate February 29, 1968, page 4693*

[5] *U. S. Congress, Hearings Before the Committee on Foreign Relations*, February 20, 1968, page 31

[6] Eugene G. Windchy, *Tonkin Gulf*, Appendix I

[7] Senator Wayne Morse, *Congressional Record—Senate*, February 29, 1968, page 4695

[8] U. S. *Congress, Hearings Before the Committee on Foreign Relations*, February 29, 1968, page 37

[9] Senator Wayne Morse, *Congressional Record—Senate*, February 29, 1968, page 4695

[10] Eugene G. Windchy, *Tonkin Gulf*, page 248

[11] Anthony Austin, *The President's War*, pages 333-345

[12] Edwin E. Moise, *Tonkin Gulf and the Escalation of the Vietnam War*, pages 99-100

[13] Richard H. Shultz, *The Secret War Against Hanoi*, pages 187-188

[14] Richard H. Shultz, *The Secret War Against Hanoi*, page 39

[15] Richard H. Shultz, *The Secret War Against Hanoi*, page 188

[16] Stephen Young, "How North Vietnam Won the War," *Wall Street Journal;* August 3, 1995

[17] Eugene G. Windchy, *Tonkin Gulf*, page 339-340

[18] Georges Sada, *Saddam's Secrets*, pages 258-261

[19] Colin Powell, *My American Journey*, pages 147-148

[20] Dorothy Fall, *Bernard Fall, Memories of a Soldier-Scholar*, page 207

[21] James G. Rogers, *World Policing and the Constitution*, page 54

[22] Dwight D. Eisenhower, *The White House Years*, volume 1, *1953-56*, page 372

[23] Alexander DeConde, *A History of American Foreign Policy*, volume 1, first edition, page 69

[24] Eugene G. Windchy, "The Right to Make War," *New Republic*, January 29, 1972

25 John McNaughton, "Plan of Action for South Vietnam," second draft, September 3, 1964, *Pentagon Papers,* Gravel edition. volume 3, pages 556-559

26 Robert L. Sansom, *The Economics of Insurgency,* page 234

27 Mark A. Lawrence, *The Vietnam War,* page 149

28 David W. Elliott, *The Vietnamese War,* page 83

CHAPTER TWO

Quasi-War (1798 to 1800)

Here lies John Adams, who took upon himself the responsibility of Peace with France in the year 1800—Epitaph favored by our second President (but not used)

During the American Revolution, Benjamin Franklin arranged an alliance with France's King Louis XVI, and this proved crucial to the American cause. In 1781, at the decisive Battle of Yorktown, French and American troops outnumbered by more than two to one the British and their hired Germans. French warships blockaded the British encampment and delivered heavy siege guns to assist the American field artillery. After three weeks of bombardment and infantry encroachment, Lord Cornwallis, the British commander, and his men surrendered. Cornwallis did not surrender personally. Pleading illness, he sent Brigadier General Charles O'Hara to deliver the ceremonial sword. According to legend, a British band played "The World Turned Upside Down." The lyrics:

> If buttercups buzz'd after the bee
> If boats were on land, churches on sea
> If ponies rode men and if grass ate the cows
> And cats should be chased into holes by the mouse
> If the mamas sold their babies
> To the Gypsies for half a crown
> If summer were spring
> And the other way 'round
> Then all the world would be upside down!

First American Disarmament

Following the Revolution, there took place the first of America's optimistic disarmaments. The Founding Fathers thought it imperative to pay off the national debt and balance the budget, and many Americans believed that possessing a navy would entangle us in foreign conflicts. We sold off almost all of the Revolutionary War's Continental Navy. Not sold was the new warship *America*, which was given to France as a present. Otherwise, the spanking new vessel would have been commanded by our great Revolutionary War naval hero Commodore John Paul Jones. Jones urged the importance of having a navy and warned, "Without a Respectable Navy, Alas America!" The illustrious but unemployed sailor went to Russia, where Empress Catherine the Great made him an admiral. Although insufficiently appreciated in the United States, Jones retained his American citizenship, and he now is interred at the U.S. Naval Academy in Annapolis, Maryland.

The lack of a navy did not prevent war. Soon the need for warships became apparent as the "Barbary pirates," a thousand-year-old scourge, captured American merchant ships on the European side of the Atlantic. (Before the Revolution our ships were protected by the British navy.) Some of these predators were pirates and others privateers sponsored by Arab states on the North African coast, which was called the "Barbary coast." (*Barbary* was a corruption of the term *Berber,* which referred to the inhabitants of North Africa west of the Nile.) In those days, pirates when captured were hung. Privateers were held as prisoners of war.

Americans Enslaved

The Barbary predators seized not only money and goods but men, women, and children, whom they sold as slaves or kept until ransomed. Most captives were too poor to be ransomed. Certain Roman Catholic orders purchased freedom for captives by using money from special collection boxes in the churches.

In 1789, the world was turned upside down again with the French Revolution. Louis XVI was executed, and the new French government went to war with Great Britain, Holland, and Spain. Louis XVI being dead, President George Washington discussed with his advisers whether to honor the Treaty of Alliance. It was decided to steer a middle course. The President recognized the revolutionary government but proclaimed American neutrality in the war. We Americans wanted freedom from the endless cycle of European wars. Congress abrogated the French alliance.

To deal with the Barbary predators, the Congress in 1794 authorized the construction of a small navy, including several medium-sized, fast warships called "frigates." Construction stopped in the next year as we, imitating some European states, began making treaties with the North African rulers. The treaties ransomed American captives and provided for the paying of annual tribute ("protection money" in today's parlance). It was thought that paying tribute would be cheaper than maintaining a navy. Warships then, as now, were extremely expensive. Many Americans also feared that to build a navy would give the President too much power in terms of patronage (read naval-industrial complex).

Freedom from European conflicts would not be easy to attain. Despite the demise of Louis XVI, the French felt entitled to American help in their new wars, and they objected to our trading with their enemy Great Britain. In 1795, just after we stopped building warships, the French set privateers upon American commerce. Unlike the Barbary corsairs, the French stationed themselves on this side of the Atlantic, and by 1797 they had seized more than six hundred American merchant vessels.

French Demand Bribes

President John Adams sent three prominent Americans to negotiate peace with France, but informal representatives of the French government demanded bribes to get the negotiations started. They wanted 50,000 pounds sterling, a $12 million loan, and a $250,000 personal bribe for the foreign minister, Charles Maurice de Talleyrand.

Talleyrand's agents tried various tricks. They threatened a bigger war, hinted at personal violence, and, according to some authorities, deployed an attractive widow, Madame de Villette, to charm the Americans. Two of our envoys decided to rent lodgings in the lady's house. They were Elbridge Gerry, later to become vice president of the United States, and John Marshall, later to become chief justice. Gerry and Marshall spent a long weekend at Madame de Villette's country chateau, accompanying her and another French lady.[1]

President John Adams (Picture Courtesy of U.S. Navy)

When President Adams made the bribery demands public, he termed the French negotiators "W, X, Y and Z." What became known in the press as the "XYZ" affair sparked outrage, and in 1798 we Americans decided to fight. No war was declared, but the Congress authorized attacking armed French vessels.[2]

Naval Success

In the resulting Quasi-War with France, the new U.S. Navy performed very well. It seized ninety-three French warships and privateers. Our side lost one warship but grabbed it back. Paintings have celebrated the new U.S. Navy's first victory over a foreign warship: the frigate USS *Constellation*'s defeat of the French frigate *L'Insurgente*. Another frigate, the USS *Enterprise,* subdued eight French ships and freed eleven American merchant vessels.

The American frigates were designed by Joshua Humphreys, a Philadelphia shipbuilder. Humphreys was new to building warships, but he was good at it and made technological improvements. Compared to foreign frigates, Humphreys' ships were more strongly built and carried heavier guns, yet they were fast enough to escape combat with the larger vessels called "ships of the line," which might carry twice as many guns.[3] The 44-gun USS *Constitution* (nicknamed "Old Ironsides"), survives to this day, berthed at Boston, Massachusetts. In 2012, it sailed across Boston harbor to commemorate the 200th anniversary of its victory over the British frigate HMS *Guerriere* in the War of 1812. The building of Humphreys' frigates involved cost overruns, as much as 260 percent, but they proved their worth in four wars, and *Constitution*, the most famous of them, now boosts the tourist industry.

"Old Ironsides" fires starboard guns on its 200th anniversary.

The President Risks His Job

In 1799, President Adams, over the opposition of most of his cabinet, sent a new delegation to make peace with France. Adams did that even though, because of war fever, the peace initiative endangered his prospect of reelection. After lengthy negotiations, France's new dictator, Napoleon Bonaparte, instructed his government to make peace with the Americans. French privateers were losing their effectiveness, anyway. American warships were patrolling, and they cooperated with the British navy in convoying each other's merchant vessels. Besides, with its farmers at war, France badly needed American grain, and French commerce was being raided by hundreds of American-commissioned privateers. They hurt France more than did the U.S. Navy.

A peace treaty was signed in the fall of 1800 at a big celebration, the most splendid since the French Revolution, and Napoleon described the recent maritime unpleasantness as a "family quarrel."[4] The three American envoys refused Napoleon's presentation of costly gold medals.[5] News of the war's end did not arrive in the United States soon enough to help President Adams win reelection.

After a lifetime of service to his country, Adams said he desired nothing more on his tombstone than "Here lies John Adams, who took upon himself the responsibility of peace with France in the year 1800." His crypt at Quincy, Massachusetts, lists other great achievements: the presidency, the Constitution of Massachusetts, and Adams's contribution to the Declaration of Independence. Neglected is the Founder's noble precedent in peace making.

Analysis

There was no way to prevent war. To satisfy the French, we would have had to go to war with Great Britain. Not having done that, we found our ocean-going commerce set upon by French privateers. We had to build a navy and commission privateers. We tried to negotiate, and we continued trying despite the XYZ affair. Peace became possible when the French wanted it. We had a president more concerned about making peace than retaining political office.

An Avoidable War?

Given the circumstances of the time, this was not a war of choice. If there had been a way in which President Adams could have prevented war, he would have done so.

Useful Principles

Weakness invites aggression. In a violent and covetous world, a well planned and robust defense is needed.

Try to elect Presidents more devoted to the public good than to personal advancement and retaining office.

References

[1] William Stinchcombe, "The Diplomacy of the XYZ Affair, "*William and Mary Quarterly*, volume 34, pages 609-610

[2] Alexander DeConde, *A History of American Foreign Policy*, page 65

[3] Michael A. Palmer, *Stoddert's War*, page 27

[4] Ian W. Toll, *Six Frigates*, page 142

[5] Alexander DeConde, *The Quasi-War*, page 257

CHAPTER THREE

First Barbary War (1801 to 1806)

It was written in their Koran, that all nations which had not acknowledged the Prophet were sinners, whom it was the right and duty of the faithful to plunder and enslave; and that every mussulman who was slain in this warfare was sure to go to paradise—Tripolitan ambassador, 1785, as quoted by Thomas Jefferson

Following the Quasi-War, we fought the Barbary Pirates. One reads that the Barbary wars were "undeclared," implying that they were not authorized by Congress. They were authorized, although the word "declare" was not used. The authorizations voted by Congress referred to a "state of war." Isn't that equivalent to declaring a war? President Woodrow Wilson thought so. When the former president of Princeton University was preparing his war message in 1917, Wilson asked his friend Colonel Edward M. House whether he should ask the Congress to declare war on Germany or merely to say that a state of war existed and ask for the means to carry it on? House said the word *declare* might cause an "acrimonious debate." Wilson used the word *declare* anyway.

As noted earlier, the Barbary pirates were both pirates and privateers. They operated from North African states that demanded tribute. A major source of their income was capturing people, ransoming them, and selling them as slaves.

Villages Kidnapped

Predation by the Barbary corsairs escalated sharply after the Spanish in 1492 expelled their Muslim ruling class. Needing employment, many of these Arabs took to piracy and slave trading. In 1509, the Spanish invaded the North African city of Oran and freed 15,000 Christian slaves. The Barbary pirates acquired captives not only by seizing ships but by kidnapping the residents of coastal towns and villages, and this or the threat of it depopulated much of the northern Mediterranean coast. Some raiders went as far away as Iceland. In Ireland the village of Baltimore was kidnapped, and in Sardinia the village of Palma. The Spanish author of *Don Quixote*, Miguel de Cervantes, was captured on a ship and kept in slavery for five years until his family could raise the demanded ransom. To ease the cruelty of their captivity, many slaves converted to Islam. That was called "going Turk." Some enslaved women did that in order to keep their Muslim children with them. It has been estimated that the Barbary pirates captured 1.25 million Europeans over a period of three hundred years.

American Prisoner's Report

One American prisoner was David Pierce, captain of the merchant schooner *Jay*, which when seized was bound for Boston with a cargo of raisins, figs, grapes, and wine. Hoping to be ransomed, Pierce wrote home:

> On our landing we were all put into chains without the least distinction and put to hard labor from daylight until night with only the allowance of two small black loaves and water & close confined at night . . . When they boarded us they even took the clothes from our backs & and brought us on board almost naked, not even a blanket to Cover us where we remained until our arrival here without even a shirt . . . Death would be a great relief and more welcome than a continuation of our present situation . . . We think ourselves happy if we escape through the day being beat by our driver, who carries a stick big enough to Knock man down, and the innocent often suffer with the guilty as they say we are all Christians.

Most of the American captives did not survive.

Some of the most notorious pirate captains were Europeans who volunteered to fight for the Muslim states. A Dutch pirate and former shipbuilder, Zymen Danseker, taught the Arabs how to build large sailing vessels, instead of rowed galleys, so that they could range beyond Gibraltar into the Atlantic.

Since American ships were being taken and their crews enslaved, Thomas Jefferson in 1785 went from Paris to London to meet with an ambassador from Tripoli and asked why his government made war on a country which "had done them no injury." The ambassador explained,

> It was written in their Koran, that all nations which had not acknowledged the Prophet were sinners, whom it was the right and duty of the faithful to plunder and enslave; and that every mussulman who was slain in this warfare was sure to go to paradise. He said, also, that the man who was first to board a vessel had one slave over and above his share, and that when they sprang to the deck of an enemy's ship, every sailor held a dagger in each hand and a third in his mouth; which usually struck such terror into the foe that they cried out for quarter at once.[1]

For one year's peace with Tripoli, the ambassador requested 12,500 guineas for his government and 1,250 guineas for himself. Algiers and Morocco, he said, would require additional payments.

President Thomas Jefferson

Jefferson decided that building a navy was a better way to protect our ships. Instead, the United States Congress, still burdened with debt from the Revolutionary War, decided to pay tribute. In 1800, however, one of the corsairs seized an American ship, and the Bey of Tripoli demanded an increase of payment. We already were paying in tribute 20 percent of the federal budget. On top of that, when Captain William Bainbridge in the USS *George Washington* delivered the annual tribute to Algiers, the Bey insisted that Bainbridge use his ship to deliver Algiers' annual tribute to the Sultan in Constantinople. Since Bainbridge was under orders to keep peaceful relations, he ended up carrying a large number of animals, a hundred African slaves, and various goods. Also on board was an Algierian diplomat with his entourage. The Algierian flag flew at the mainmast. Bainbridge later explained to the secretary of the navy that once you pay tribute to the Bey, he thinks of you as a slave.

In 1801, Thomas Jefferson became President, the war with France was over, and Tripoli declared war on the United States. Traditionally, the Arabs declared war by cutting down the flag at a consulate. Jefferson had had enough of the Barbary pirates. He began sending our battle-hardened naval squadrons to enforce agreements and defend American commerce.

Commodore Stephen Decatur

We fought Tripoli from 1801 to 1806 (most accounts say 1805, but President Jefferson did not call our ships home until 1806).[2] Initially, the U. S. Navy blockaded Tripoli with the help of a Swedish flotilla. During the war there were successes and mishaps. The frigate *Philadelphia* ran onto a reef and was captured, its guns then used for defending the harbor. Stephen Decatur, as a lieutenant, led a party that sneaked into the harbor at night and burned the ship. Admiral Horatio Nelson called that "the most bold and daring act of the age."

Attempt at Regime Change

In 1805, we made an attempt at regime change. In charge of that was a "Lawrence of Arabia" of his time, William Eaton, a former consul and soldier from Connecticut. Armed with $20,000 and some naval support, Eaton organized a force of eight U.S. Marines, seventy Greek mercenaries, and three hundred Arabs and Bedouins. This colorful battalion, the marines discouraging mutiny, marched five hundred miles from Alexandria, Egypt, to capture the port city of Derna. As commemorated in the Marine Corps hymn, Derna was located "on the shores of Tripoli" in what is now eastern Libya. The marines ran up an American flag for the first time on foreign soil. Eaton planned next to capture Tripoli and put the Bey's older brother in charge, but in Tripoli Consul General Tobias Lear forestalled that by signing a peace treaty. Lear regarded the older brother as no more reliable than the younger one. The treaty required payment of $60,000 in ransom for prisoners.[3] Eaton went home in disgust and complained for the rest of his life.

Analysis

A blackmailer is inclined to increase his demands, and we decided to fight. We learned that it was difficult to make a North African stick to an agreement on other things as well. For example, when a Tripolitan ship struck its colors in surrender, this was liable to be a trick. The Arab would use the pause to catch his opponent off guard and start fighting again. One Arab captain, after striking his colors twice, showed he was serious by throwing his flag into the water. At this writing, Americans fighting in Afghanistan have a saying: "You can't buy an Afghan, but you can rent one."

Could we have deterred the Barbary corsairs by building a larger navy? The cupidity of the corsairs was such that they probably would not have let us off without a fight

An Avoidable War?

In the circumstances of the time, this was an inevitable war and not one of choice.

Useful Principles

Plan ahead

Be prepared.

Know your enemy

Thomas Jefferson made a good start on that.

References

[1]   James Parton, "Jefferson American Minister in France," *Atlantic*, volume 30, 1872, page 413

[2]   Robert W. Love, *History of the U. S. Navy*, volume 1, page 85

[3]   Ian W. Toll, *Six Frigates*, pages 260 to 262

CHAPTER FOUR

War of 1812 (1812 to 1815)

You will find wars are supported by a class of argument which, after the war is over, the people find were arguments they should never have listened to—British Quaker John Bright (1811 to 1889)

After the war with Tripoli came the misnamed "War of 1812," which lasted until 1815. President James Madison, the Father of the Constitution, maneuvered us into an unnecessary war with Great Britain, the only nation having the potential to destroy our new republic. (Bear in mind, General Washington's victory at Yorktown was made possible by our ally France, which provided important ground and naval support.)

We all have heard about Great Britain's impressment of American seamen as the cause of the war. To be more precise about that particular casus belli, the British policy was to stop American merchant ships to look for deserters from the Royal Navy, and the British did not recognize our naturalization process. For the British the impressments were needed because they had tripled their fleet to fight Napoleon, and the British sailors much preferred to sail on American merchant ships. There they were relatively safe, better paid, and flogged less. Depending on the individual and the number of lashes, flogging could be not only painful but fatal.

In 1812, we perhaps could have eliminated the impressment issue by stopping the employment of British deserters. President Madison offered to do that in secret negotiations of 1813, when Czar Alexander of Russia tried to act as an intermediary to make peace. The Czar wanted to get his American trade going again, and he wanted his British ally to focus entirely upon Napoleon. The British, however, did not want the Russians to get involved with their American war.

Other issues: The British were believed to be giving arms to hostile Native Americans in the Northwest Territory, and the British navy would not permit neutral ships to trade with France. We could have coped with the Native Americans without attacking Great Britain. The British indeed were blockading France. However, the French were seizing more American ships going to Britain (558 by the summer of 1812) than the British were seizing going to France (389 by the summer of 1812). American companies engaged in international trade viewed the European blockades as a manageable cost of doing business.

To get better treatment from France and Great Britain, President Madison tried punishing both of them with a complete trade embargo. This did not help. In order to keep trade going, Napoleon appeared to agree to our terms. Loopholes nullified the agreement, but Madison allowed trade with France, anyway, and we continued on a collision course with the British.

Some Americans found another motive for war: honor. In those days of man to man dueling, one's honor was very important, and the Virginia House of Delegates resolved that, under the circumstances, peace was "disgraceful" and war "honorable."

Lack of Enthusiasm

Yet the votes in Congress were close, and there was no great groundswell of public opinion demanding war. Congressional "war hawks" represented, for the most part, some hotheads in the South and the West. War hawks were few in New England, which had the most concern with trade and impressment issues. Historian Henry Adams, great grandson of President John Adams, commented later on the lack of public enthusiasm:

> Many nations have gone to war in pure gayety of heart; but perhaps the United States were the first to force themselves into a war they dreaded, in the hope that the war itself might create the spirit they lacked.

The British ambassador was amazed by the declaration of war on June 18, and he believed it "unexpected by nearly the whole Nation." Following the declaration, Madison learned that a new British Prime Minister had decided to allow our trade with France. Madison sought an armistice, but the British insisted upon their right of impressment and the war continued.

Who could be enthusiastic about fighting the Royal Navy? The British, having more than six hundred warships, assigned ninety-seven of them to blockade American ports. We had only seven frigates, ten smaller ocean going warships, and a lot of little gunboats of some use within harbors. We had no big ships of the line, which were needed to break the blockade. The frigates, it will be recalled, were designed to fight pirates. Two of our frigates were trapped in port, and one of those, the *Chesapeake*, was captured trying to escape.

The frigates that made it to sea won some famous victories against other medium-sized warships. The USS *Constitution's* defeat of the HMS *Guerriere* dumfounded the British public and reelected Madison, an otherwise lackluster Commander-in-Chief. In 1812, Americans won five out of nine single-ship engagements. The enemy, with his huge navy, could afford the losses, but they were a great psychological blow to a naval power that previously enjoyed a conviction of invincibility. The British began imitating Joshua Humphreys' ship designs. Prior to engaging in battle with the *Chesapeake*, the captain of the British frigate *Shannon* said to his men:

> Shannons, you know that from various causes the Americans have lately triumphed on several occasions over the British flag in our frigates . . . they have said, and they have published in their papers, that the English have forgotten the way to fight. You will let them know today that there are Englishmen in the *Shannon* who still know how to fight.

Shannon won, but the British blockade of the long American coastline often was evaded, and the Royal Navy's Western Atlantic commanding officer was fired. In London, the Admiralty could not understand why there still existed an U.S. Navy considering how outnumbered it was. Partly to make up for this frustration, the British burned much of Washington.

American privateers did well, capturing 1,300 British merchant ships. The Americans exhibited both daring and ingenuity. The privateer *Paul Jones* left port with 120 men, 3 guns, and 14 black-painted logs ("Quaker guns"). Encountering a British merchant vessel with 14 guns but only 20 men, *Paul Jones's* skipper ordered his numerous crew into the rigging ready to board, and the merchant vessel, suitably impressed, surrendered. The privateer seized the ship, its cargo, and 14 much needed guns.

The USS *Essex,* the first American warship to cross the Equator and visit the Pacific, caught a large number of British whaling ships, and London reportedly went dark for a year for the lack of whale oil. Partially disabled by a storm, the *Essex* was captured near Chile. The ship, not one of the heavier frigates of Humphreys' design, might have survived but for its lack of long range guns. Two British vessels stood out of range and lobbed cannon balls.

The Object of the War

The U.S. Navy demonstrated courage and skill, but its exploits could not lift the blockade or end the impressments. So what was the object of the war?

The object was to acquire Canada or, according to some historians, to invade Canada and use it as a bargaining chip. Probably the Canadian issue explains why the Senate engaged in two weeks of secret debate before voting on the war. An American army marching north, it was thought, would be greeted by Canadians yearning to be free from British rule. The retired but influential Thomas Jefferson subscribed to that idea. To take Quebec, he said, was a "mere matter of marching."[1] William Eustis, secretary of war, asserted, "We can take Canada without soldiers, we have only to send officers into the province and the people . . . will rally round our standard." (Why, after invading Canada, would we just use it as a bargaining chip if the Canadians were yearning to be part of the United States?) As a general strategy, Jefferson advised,

> I hope we shall confine ourselves to the conquest of their possessions, and defence of our harbors, leaving the war on the ocean to our privateers. These will immediately swarm in

every sea and do more injury to British commerce than the regular fleets of all Europe would do.[2]

The Canadian government, too, had a plan for aggrandizement. It hoped to lure our New England states voluntarily into its fold, and evidence of that fact helped to stir in Americans some martial spirit.

Battle of Lake Erie

As a preparation for invading Canada, Master Commandant Oliver Hazard Perry built and gathered together a flotilla on Lake Erie, and with it he defeated in a close battle the British warships previously dominating the lake. This was one of the few times in history that an entire British squadron surrendered.

The American land forces were badly organized and poorly led. Right away, we lost a fort in Michigan which had not been informed of the war's outbreak. Our troops marched north, as Jefferson recommended, and some Canadians, immigrants from the United States, welcomed us. General William Hull explained to Canadians with leaflets how they would be more free and more prosperous as United States citizens (the American economy was growing faster). But Hull proved ineffective militarily. Having been deceived concerning the numbers of the enemy, Hull surrendered Detroit to British regular troops allied with Canadian militia and Native Americans.

Hull ordered the small garrison at Fort Dearborn (now downtown Chicago) to take refuge at Fort Wayne in Indiana, and they were ambushed by Potawatomi Native American allies of the British. Most of the men and children were killed. Captain William Wells fought so valiantly that upon his death the Native Americans immediately ate his heart in order to absorb his courage.[3] The rest of the party was captured and held for ransom. More than half of the captives died. The British in the Northwest routinely added to their surrender demands a warning of what their Native American allies would do if the Americans lost the battle.

On both sides the politics of the war were complicated. In Quebec, the French Canadians had no great love for the British, but they disliked more America's aggressive Protestantism. Many in the American state militias refused to cross the Canadian line. Perhaps they could see no connection between that and the war slogan: "Free Trade and Sailors' Rights!" The Canadian militia lacked enthusiasm, too. British authorities had to conjure up a "militia myth" as part of their propaganda (according to R. Arthur Bowler's "Propaganda in Upper Canada in the War of 1812" published by the *American Review of Canadian Studies*.) The New England states, the ones most concerned about trade and sailors' rights, hampered the invasion by not allowing their soldiers to enter Canada. The New Englanders wanted to trade with the enemy, and the British, for their own benefit, allowed that until 1814. Perceiving our Southerners as supporting the war, the Royal Navy blockaded their coast first.

Secession Debated

New England opposition to "Mr. Madison's War" was intense. Alexander De-Conde tells us in his *A History of American Foreign Policy*:

> During the war New Englanders supplied British troops with food and other provisions, and some did not hesitate to take an oath of allegiance to King George. So strong was Federalist and antiwar opposition that in his bid for re-election in 1812, Madison lost all but two of the states north of the Potomac River. The South and West re-elected him.[4]

Disgruntled New Englanders got together in Hartford, Connecticut, to discuss their grievances, the need for states rights, and the possibility of nullifying some federal laws. The meetings were held in secret, and the possibility of secession was discussed. All this foreshadowed what the Southerners would be saying later in the century as they railed against import tariffs and struggled to preserve their "peculiar institution" of slavery.

In 1813, we Americans burned and looted the Canadian capital of York (now Toronto).

With Napoleon's defeat at Leipzig in 1813, British forces were freed up for fighting the United States. The British offered peace talks, President Madison accepted, and the talks began in Ghent, Flanders.

The people of Great Britain were angry about the American war. They saw themselves as having been in a life or death struggle with an evil dictator (Jefferson compared Napoleon to Attila), and in their view the Americans ought not to have been taking advantage. The British negotiators demanded large territorial concessions for Canada and the Native Americans. The purpose of the latter demand was to create a buffer zone that would prevent the Americans' westward expansion. The London *Times* even wanted the Louisiana Purchase territory given to Spain, which had held that area prior to Napoleon's taking it back from Spain in a treaty of 1800.

As the talks in Ghent continued, the British burned government buildings in Washington, looted the port city of Alexandria, although it had surrendered, and destroyed many villages on Chesapeake Bay. The British would have burned Baltimore, but naval officers and army engineers (trained at the new military academy at West Point) prepared artillery defenses that kept the enemy ships at bay. A major factor was Fort McHenry of "Star Spangled Banner" fame.

A Separate Peace

Lacking food and fuel, the island of Nantucket made a separate peace with Great Britain. That enabled the islanders to fish and to obtain supplies from the mainland. Some Nantucket men were prisoners of war at Dartmoor, England. They were released, and that was lucky for them considering that of the 6,500 American prisoners there 1,500 died. After the war an Anglo-American commission awarded compensation to the families. An American naval prisoner at Dartmoor wrote in his journal, "An American in England pines to get home; while an Englishman and an Irishman longs to become an American citizen."

The atmosphere in Ghent was altered dramatically by a young American naval officer who achieved a stunning victory. Master Commandant Thomas Macdonough won control of Lake Champlain on the Canadian border. Theodore Roosevelt, in his book *The Naval War of 1812*, judged the Lake Champlain contest "the greatest battle of the war" and Macdonough "the greatest figure in our naval history" up to the Civil War. Both the Lake Erie and the Lake Champlain battles were won by last ditch maneuvers when the Americans appeared to be defeated. Perry lost his flagship and escaped to another. Macdonough saved his flagship with resourceful seamanship.

Commodore Thomas Macdonough

Robert W. Love, in his *History of the U. S. Navy* tells us of Macdonough's indomitable spirit:

> Blown across his deck twice by splinters, knocked out for a few moments by a large timber, and hurled across the deck by the head of a decapitated gun captain, Macdonough emerged from the battle amazingly unscathed. He had saved the Republic.[5]

Yet the plaudits of Perry have eclipsed those of Macdonough. Like Julius Caesar and Douglas MacArthur, Perry was good at sound bites. He reported, "We have met the enemy and they are ours." Perry's legend has benefited from the power of the brush as well. Dramatic paintings show how he was rowed, standing up amid shot and shell, to another flagship after the loss of his first

Wellington Advises Peace

The British cabinet wanted the Duke of Wellington, victor over Napoleon, to take command of its military forces in North America. The duke, however, was impressed by the American naval victories on the border lakes, and he decided that American control of the waterways would make it extremely difficult to mount an invasion from Canada. Wellington advised that continuing the campaign in North America would require more effort than could be expected from the British people, who were tired from decades of fighting the French.

Instead of acquiring Canada, we Americans were satisfied to accept fishing rights in the Gulf of St. Lawrence, and, otherwise, a return to the status quo ante bellum. Impressment remained an issue, but Napoleon was gone (except for his Hundred Days return) and there was no need for impressment. The British kept three thousand African-Americans to whom they had offered freedom during the war; the blacks settled as freedmen in Nova Scotia and New Brunswick. Keeping the blacks violated the Treaty of Ghent, and so by terms of arbitration the British paid $1,204,960 for reimbursement to the slaves' owners. The British negotiators returned home to complaints about the lack of territorial gains.

Biggest Land Battle

News of peace did not arrive in time to stop the biggest land battle of the war. The British had sent an expeditionary force to capture the port of New Orleans. Commanding there was a resourceful and ruthless militia officer, Major General Andrew Jackson, who added to the city's defenders pirates (experienced artillerymen), Kentucky sharpshooters, freed blacks, Native Americans, Creoles, and businessmen. Jackson solved the reluctant militia problem by shooting a militiaman. His motley army of approximately four thousand repulsed a force of eleven thousand British veterans. The latter, hemmed in between a swamp and the Mississippi river, took very heavy casualties attempting to advance across an open field to American breastworks supported by artillery. The British had planned to advance in the morning darkness and fog, but they experienced delays in starting.

A popular legend tells us that the Americans used cotton bales as an instant and effective breastwork. According to an eye witness (*New York Times*, April 21, 1869), the barrier was mostly earthen, and musket balls easily penetrated the cotton.

President Madison reviewed the war in a letter to Thomas Jefferson. He commented that the victory at New Orleans ought to help discourage future British invasions. Madison was pleased that the final report of the Hartford Convention did not call for secession. He must have felt insulted, however, that the convention recommended the following text for a constitutional amendment, which implied that the war with Great Britain was neither defensive nor necessary:

> Congress shall not make or declare war, or authorize acts of
> hostility against any foreign nation, without the concurrence
> of two thirds of both houses, except such acts of hostility
> be in defence of the territories of the United States when
> actually invaded.

In the end, the War of 1812 lifted America spirits. We had fought honorably against the humiliations of impressment, and we felt as if we had won a "second war of independence." But the expense and bloodshed could not be described as necessary, the end might have been catastrophic, and the specter of secession was born, along with sectional antagonism.

After the War of 1812, Americans began speaking of the United States in the singular rather than in the plural. (Some people, like Henry Adams, continued using the plural.)

Invention of Peace Societies

Anti-war Americans hoped that in the future private citizens would take a hand in preventing war, and they founded peace societies. The first one, the New York Peace Society, originated in 1812, at the home of David Low Dodge, a Presbyterian merchant distressed by the devastation of the Napoleonic wars. In the wake of the War of 1812, American peace societies grew to fifty in number, and in 1828 Dodge combined the New York Peace Society with some others to form the American Peace Society. The American Peace Society still exists. It publishes the bimonthly *World Affairs Journal,* the descendant of a nineteenth century peace society publication.

Analysis

In 1812 our leaders had a choice. There was no need to go to war. In the Congress more clogging by means of debate would have helped. The British decided to allow our trade with France, but the news arrived too late, and President Madison insisted that the British also give up impressment. He could have promised that no more British deserters would be hired. But at that time our leaders wanted to invade Canada while the British were busy fighting Napoleon. In the peace treaty, nothing was said about impressment.

An Avoidable War?

The war was avoidable. Irate New Englanders called it "Mr. Madison's War."

Useful Principles

Do not choose to go to war when a large proportion of the population is against it.

Find reliable sources of information in order to check out the premises on which the proposed war is based. For example, if

*cooperation is needed from a populace to be invaded, find out
how they would feel about getting invaded.*

Considering our experiences with Cuba and Iraq, we've had a hard time learning the latter lesson. President Eisenhower and his successors were well informed about the attitude of the Vietnamese. Rosy visions were purveyed to the public anyway. In 1812, the State Department, having no legation or consular establishments in Canada, could offer no special expertise on the political opinions of the diverse Canadian population. Overconfident about Canada, Secretary of State James Monroe tried to quit his job and obtain a military command. Failing that, he eventually became secretary of war in addition to secretary of state.

Already in 1812 the Congress needed its own investigative office.

*Delay the initiation of war so long as possible or practicable
since the causes for war might diminish or disappear.*

In 1812, the Senate did not clog the process long enough. After the war was declared, we learned that the British had decided to let us trade with France. In response to that, Madison could have offered to stop hiring British deserters.

Compromise sometimes is necessary and advisable.

References

[1] Thomas Jefferson, *The Works of Thomas Jefferson*, volume 4, page 265,

[2] Thomas Jefferson, *The Works of Thomas Jefferson*, volume 4, pages 259-260

[3] John D. Barnhart, *Indiana to 1816*, pages 400-401

[4] Alexander DeConde, *A History of American Foreign Policy*, page 106

[5] Robert W. Love, *History of the U. S. Navy*, volume 1, page 128

CHAPTER FIVE

Second Barbary War (1815)

We make war that we may live in peace—Aristotle (384-322 B.C.)

During the War of 1812, the Barbary states violated their treaties by seizing American ships and helping the British. President Madison, after making peace with Great Britain, was in a strong position for dealing with the treacherous regimes in North Africa. We had been building more warships, and in March of 1815 Congress authorized an expedition to the Mediterranean. Two naval squadrons were assigned. The first one, commanded by Commodore Stephen Decatur, made short work of the enemy ships it encountered, and largely pacified the North African coast before the second squadron arrived.[1] Decatur commanded three frigates and five smaller ships which were needed for operations in shallow waters. We planned to lose no more frigates on reefs. Even though commanding a large force, Decatur had to fight and show his prowess.

Commodore Decatur's squadron freed many Christian slaves, both American and European. The commodore and the Bey of Algiers signed a peace treaty which demanded $10,000 from the Algierians in compensation for damages. After the American ships left, the Bey repudiated the treaty. The Second Barbary War, however, ended our paying of tribute. Disappointed Algerians assassinated the Bey. For many years the U.S. Navy kept a squadron in the Mediterranean in order to protect our commerce.

CAPT CROKER HORROR STRICKEN AT ALGIERS,
on witnessing the Miseries of the Christian Slaves chain'd & in Irons driven home after labour by Infidels with large Whips. Page ibid

British officers view Christian slaves in Algiers. 1815.

In 1816, the British and the Dutch bombarded Algiers. This resulted in the freeing of 1,083 Christian slaves and a British consul. Thenceforth, technologically improving European navies gradually safeguarded the area, and European colonization subdued the troublesome North African coast.

Analysis

For good reason we Americans chose to fight, we were well prepared, and we won in a short time.

An Avoidable War?

This war might have been avoided if we had fought the First Barbary War to a more successful conclusion. That not having been done, the second war was not avoidable, and was inflicted upon us during the War of 1812 when we could not respond.

Useful Principle

When a nation goes to war, some other nation is liable to perceive this as an opportunity to attack.

In 1812 that is what we did to the British and what the Barbary pirates did to us. In 1968, North Korea seized the unarmed USS *Pueblo,* an electronic intelligence ship, as American forces were tied down in Vietnam. In that circumstance, President Johnson did not want to risk Korean War II.

References

---

[1]   Robert W. Love, *History of the U.S. Navy,* page 131

CHAPTER SIX

First Mexican-American War (1846 to 1848)

Part One

*These Americans are so contriving that some day they will build
ladders to touch the sky—General Jose Castro, 1845*

As a long-term effect of the First Mexican-American war, we have in
the United States an extraordinary number of Mexican consulates, and
their number keeps growing. At this writing there are fifty-one of them.
Our other next door neighbor, Canada, has only twelve consulates. The
Canadian officials take care of routine consular business. The Mexican
officials are engaged in a stealthy campaign to infiltrate Mexicans into
this country, especially into California and the American Southwest,
which they view as territory stolen from Mexico. California has ten
Mexican consulates and Texas eleven. This campaign the Mexicans call
the "reconquista." To that end, the consulates encourage and facilitate
illegal immigration. They assist illegal immigrants with identification
cards and legal advice, teach methods of illegal entry, complain about
American immigration laws (extremely lenient compared to Mexico's),
and tell Hispanic children that they owe allegiance to Mexico. The
following appeared in the *Washington Times* of October 20, 2011:

> The Mexican consulate in Los Angeles has distributed
> hundreds of thousands of . . . textbooks to more than 1,000
> schools in the Los Angeles area alone. Those textbooks teach
> that the Southwest, California and Texas belong to Mexico;
> that they were stolen in the 1848 Mexican-American War; and
> that Hispanic children owe allegiance to the Mexican flag and
> the Mexican state.

Did the United States steal California and Texas from Mexico? We will get to Texas later. Here is another way of looking at what happened with California. In 1848, the U.S. Government agreed to pay today's equivalent of hundreds of millions dollars for California (plus the New Mexico territory) *even though Mexico had governed California for only a short time and had lost control of it before the war began.* Had we purchased California from the Californians, who were called "Californios," perhaps we would not have today fifty-one Mexican consulates engaged in reconquista.

Some historical background is needed here. Hernan Cortes's conquest of Mexico began in 1519. Hundreds of years went by without the Spanish showing much interest in California, but in the late seventeenth century they began to worry about British designs on North America. Hence in 1697, a half-dozen Spanish soldiers helped a friar from Italy, Juan Salvatierra, establish a mission on California's Baja peninsula. In 1796, the Spanish began to build missions up north in Alta California (what we now call "California"). The Alta California settlers, including Native American converts, came from Baja in two ships, and also by land bringing livestock. As they had done down south, they established presidios (forts) and missions.

The Californias, New Mexico, Mexico, the Philippine islands, and several other territories were part of New Spain. They were ruled by a Spanish viceroy in Mexico City and locally by Spanish governors.

In 1810, Mexico rebelled against Spain and gained its independence in 1821. The fighting took place in Mexico. Having defeated the Spanish, the Mexicans claimed as their territory not only Mexico but, in addition, the sparsely populated provinces of Baja California, Alta California and New Mexico. The faraway Philippines were left undisturbed.

Spanish Governor Ousted

When in January of 1822 Alta California's Spanish governor, Pablo Vicente de Sola, heard of the new "Mexican Empire" including the Californias, he declared it "absurd." A few months later, however, no help had come from Spain (a single frigate would have been enough), and Sola on April 11 took an oath of loyalty to Mexico. He also cooperated in the formation of a new government.[1] There was no fighting. The Spanish flag was lowered in Monterey, the capital of Alta California, and the Mexican flag raised up. The Native Americans were pleased that the new flag featured an eagle instead of a lion.

During Spanish rule, *Las Californias* were administered largely by the missions. They owned spacious territories and employed Native American converts or potential converts as agricultural laborers. Could Mexico with its ever-changing, coup-prone government manage this vast and distant territory? The Mexicans complicated the task by secularization. They seized mission lands and distributed them to people favored by the authorities. This was disastrous for the Native Americans who had been working on the mission lands, where they learned to grow European crops and tend European livestock. The missions never were completely self supporting. They needed contributions from Christians abroad. With secularization, fewer hands were needed to do the same work, and suddenly ousted were Native Americans who had spent all their lives on mission farms. Alta California's Native American population declined drastically.

Governor Sola was in office for seven years. After the Mexican takeover, Alta California governors came and went rapidly. In fourteen years there were ten of them. When in 1836 another Mexican governor was ousted by the Californios, a Californio assumed the governorship, and Californio military commanders were installed permanently. From 1836 the Californios effectively enjoyed self-rule, although as we shall see, they voluntarily installed one Mexican governor, hoping (vainly) for benefits.

California for Sale

With its most remote "department" being so ungovernable and the nation hopelessly in debt, Mexico made an attempt to sell Alta California (and possibly Baja). It was after six straight years of Californio governance that Mexico in 1842 offered the territory to the Kingdom of Prussia.[2] Accepting the offer was recommended to King Frederick William IV by Baron Christian von Bunsen, a distinguished scholar who at the time was Prussia's ambassador to London. Applauding the proposal was the Prussian ambassador to Washington, Baron von Ronne, who since 1837 had been hoping to obtain part of California for

German emigrants. The King was dissuaded from the purchase by the Baron Alexander von Humboldt, the explorer and scientist for whom the Pacific Ocean's Humboldt current is named. The proposed purchase price is said to have been six million dollars, but I have not been able to confirm that. In the 1840s, seven thousand German settlers went to Texas instead of to the Californias.

From here I shall refer to Alta California simply as "California."

California had plenty of empty space, but there was not much Hispanic immigration. In 1817, Hispanics totaled only 3,000. In the mid-1840s, their number had increased to 7,000, probably almost all born in California, and most of them resided around Los Angeles. An easy going people, the Californios enjoyed ranching, horse racing, and fandangoes. Non-Hispanic foreigners, chiefly Americans up north, numbered perhaps 1,000. Most of the population, 30,000 or more, was Native American. (United States population in 1840 was seventeen million.) Allied with the Californios, the Suisun tribe enforced treaties with the Native Americans. The Suisun people have been described as very tall, very well built (suitable for a sculptor's model), and possessing small feet. Their chief towered 6 feet 7 inches. The Suisun diet consisted mostly of fish, leached acorn flour, and miner's lettuce (*Claytonia perfoliata*).

Traveling from Mexico to California was not easy. Since 1781 the hostile Yuma and Apache tribes of Native Americans had rendered hazardous the Anza trail. Getting to California by ship was slow. If one caught a ride on a commercial vessel, it went by way of Hawaii, so that even from Mexico's Pacific coast the trip took thirty to fifty days. Some years no ships at all went from Mexico to California. Foreign whalers stopped there to trade manufactured goods for vegetables and water. Some trading ships, largely from Boston, came to load up with cow hides and tallow (for candles). Having noted the travel difficulties, it still was much easier to get from Mexico to neighboring California than, say, from Illinois to California. Americans migrating westward had to cross rivers, mountain ranges, and deserts. Many thousands did not survive. Cholera, smallpox, and accidents were the chief killers. Few died fighting with Native Americans.

Gold Discovered

The lack of Mexican immigration is the more surprising when we consider that gold was discovered in March of 1842.[3] This gold was found in southern California on a ranch formerly belonging to a mission. It was gold discovered in northern California that in 1848 inspired the great California gold rush.

A new era arrived in the early 1840s when the Americans, by trial and error, established a California trail branching off from the Oregon trail. From that time there was a continual flow of settlers. They were motivated by glowing reports of the area's advantages. One early writer was Richard Henry Dana, author of a popular autobiographical book, *Two Years Before the Mast*. Between 1834 and 1836 Dana was a crew member on the brig *Pilgrim*, out of Boston, which traded for cow hides. California, Dana said, embraces

> four or five hundred miles of sea-coast, with several good harbors; with fine forests in the north; the waters filled with fish, and the plains covered with thousands of head of cattle; blessed with a climate, than which there can be no better in the world; free from all manner of diseases, whether epidemic or endemic; and with a soil in which corn yields from seventy to eighty fold. In the hands of an enterprising people, what a country this might be!

Californio General Jose Castro admired how enterprising were the American settlers. He made a startling prophecy:

> These Americans are so contriving that someday they will build ladders to touch the sky, and once in the heavens they will change the whole face of the universe and even the color of the stars.[4]

An almost empty paradise, California seemed likely to be acquired by a foreign power. Eugene Duflot Mofras, a French visitor of 1840, said,

> It is . . . evident to us that California will belong to whatever nation chooses to send there a man-of-war and two hundred men.[5]

Having talked to officers of the British Hudson's Bay company, which was active in California, Mofras was confident that the British would be able to acquire California in payment of Mexican debts.

False Alarm

The U. S. Navy had standing orders to occupy the California ports if there were war with Mexico or if a European power was about to seize the ports. In 1842, the unknown whereabouts of France's Pacific Squadron worried the commander of the U. S. Navy's Pacific Squadron, Commodore Thomas Jones. Then, while visiting Peru, Jones received from the American consul in Mazatlan, Mexico, a report that war between the United States and Mexico was about to begin because of the proposed annexation of Texas. The consul also sent a piece from the Boston *Advertiser* that said California had been sold to Great Britain for seven million dollars. In those tense circumstances, Thomas saw the flagship of Britain's Pacific squadron head north from Peru, and so the commodore, taking two of his ships, raced to Monterey. There Jones found no British or French warships. Nevertheless, he landed 150 men and occupied the port, doing so with no bloodshed. Most officials fled to the hills.

Jones saw himself as upholding the Monroe Doctrine. Official papers in Monterey mentioned no cession to Britain, and they cited the Monroe Doctrine as an obstacle to that. A local American merchant, Thomas O. Larkin, showed the commodore newspapers from Mexico and persuaded him there was no war going on. Jones apologized, retired, and fired a gun salute. The incident underlined how defenseless was this vast and valuable territory. Complaints from the Mexican government resulted in the appointment of a new commodore for the Pacific Squadron. More important, Jones's little invasion incurred such umbrage in Mexico City that the American envoy, Waddy Thompson, had to give up his attempt to buy California for the United States.[6] The collapse of Thompson's plan occurred in the same year as Mexico's offer to Prussia.

In 1843, Thomas Larkin became California's first (and only) American consul. He had been writing for Eastern newspapers articles that extolled the advantages of settling in California, and he continued doing that.

San Francisco Needs Wharf

When Commodore Jones visited Monterey, a new Mexico-appointed governor was just arriving in California and had not yet reached the capital. A new governor had been requested by the area's military commandant, a Californio who reported that the current governor, also a Californio (and his brother), had become dissipated and useless. The commandant, General Mariano Guadalupe Vallejo, also requested from Mexico some basic services. He wanted a postal service and schools. For the splendid harbor at San Francisco, he wanted a rebuilt fort, a customs house, and a wharf. The general asked for two hundred soldiers, and he recommended sending a large number of Mexican artisans and farmers in order to counterbalance the influx of foreigners. Evidently Vallejo realized that if Hispanics were going to populate California, the Mexican government would have to take them there, as the British shipped their people to Australia. Not many Mexicans would trek to the Pacific paradise on their own, not in the nineteenth century.

General Mariano Guadelupe Vallejo

Even if the Californio governor was a drunk, why after six years of self-rule, would Vallejo want to replace him with a Mexican governor?

Presumably he hoped that a Mexican governor would have some influence in Mexico City and be able to bring about the improvements and increased Hispanic population that Vallejo wanted. If so, that did not work out. To the officials in Mexico City, California was just an ungovernable nuisance.

Among his duties, General Vallejo had to keep under control a mysterious and enterprising immigrant, Johann Augustus Sutter. He was a German who had acquired Swiss citizenship but locally was reputed to be French since he spoke French and claimed to have been a captain in the French army. Sutter also spoke English and Spanish. He arrived in California with eight to ten Hawaiian servants, both male and female, whom he had purchased in Honolulu. (Polynesia's custom of slavery continued in Hawaii until 1900, two years after the territory was annexed by the United States.) Sutter paid his "Kanakas" $10 each per month. The feudal lord and his Hawaiian concubines scandalized the Californios.

German Fort Constructed

When in 1842 the Russians gave up on settling California, the Mexican government refused to buy their fort, and Sutter was able to purchase on credit the whole property including cattle, ten iron cannon, two mobile field pieces made of brass, and various other items. At present day Sacramento, Sutter then built a fort with high adobe walls, and he established a prosperous community boasting fields of grain and considerable livestock. Native American women made hats and wove blankets. A security force of Native American men marched to the accompaniment of fife and drum. The first house built in what would become Sacramento, was not adobe but made of wood and grass, thanks to skilled Hawaiian labor. The polyglot pioneer called his multicultural community "New Helvetia," *Helvetia* being the Roman name for Switzerland. If the governor of California had given Sutter a piece of San Francisco bay, he surely would have built a wharf and made money on it. Indeed, he very likely would have added a warehouse and other profitable structures.

Johann Augustus Sutter

When displeased with the California government, Sutter threatened to establish a French protectorate with the help of a French frigate.

Sutter's fort became the destination for American settlers coming overland. The "overlanders" often arrived in poor health and in desperate need of supplies. All visitors ate for free. The standard fare: beef, beans, and boiled wheat. Five or six oxen were slaughtered per day (the animals from Baja had run wild). Sutter sent men into the mountains to guide the overlanders. Many worked for Sutter until they could find their own way to make a living. To some he sold land. In effect, this German-Swiss-French lord of the manor was building an American colony in northern California. Sutter was destined to become famous for the discovery of gold near where he was building a sawmill. However, the chaotic gold rush destroyed his domain.

Sutter's Fort in 1851

Another Rebellion

Ironically, the Mexican soldiers requested by General Vallejo had the effect of bringing down what was left of Mexican rule. They were not real soldiers in colorful Mexican uniforms. They were pardoned convicts in dirty, ragged blankets. The ex-cons arrived unpaid, and Mexico did not send the funds promised for their keep. Soon they took to sneak thievery and armed robbery, and after two years of these depredations, the Californios rebelled. The final crunch came in February of 1845. Armed Californios confronted soldiers supporting the Mexico-appointed governor. Both sides recruited American settlers, but the Americans refused to fire at each other. Following a bloodless artillery duel at long range, the government side surrendered. The laid back Californios had a way of settling disputes with little or no bloodshed, while in Mexico a battle might end with a massacre of the losers. The Mexican governor and the ex-convicts were shipped home.

If the Mexican government wanted to keep California, it could have bought the Russian fort, on credit if need be, and filled it with real soldiers.

For their new governor, the rebels selected an Afro-Hispanic Californio by the name of Pio de Jesus Pico. Pico customarily is referred to as the "last Mexican governor of Califonia." Actually, he was a Californio born during the period of Spanish rule. Pico moved the capital from Monterey to Los Angeles, where he owned a tavern and a leather tannery. He governed from there until Los Angeles was captured by American forces in August of 1846. Today, Pico's eighteen-month governance is memorialized by the Pio Pico state park in Whittier, California.

The Californio rebellion was one of many during the Latin American independence movement of the nineteenth century, which was inspired by the American and French revolutions of the eighteenth century. First came Haiti, in 1804, where Toussaint Louverture, another rebel of African descent, became the national leader, with help from the U. S. Navy.[7] Chronologically, in the middle of the Latin American independence parade, came Mexico, which overthrew Spanish rule in 1821. In Mexico so much internal conflict continued that it took many years for Spain to give up the hope of regaining this province. In a separate development, the Mexican department of Texas, which was populated chiefly by American settlers, rebelled in 1835.

Californios Debate Their Future

The Californios did not declare their independence, but they talked about it, and the merchants, fearing for their property rights, wanted separation from Mexico. In a meeting of the ruling citizens, Governor Pico favored a British or French protectorate. "Is not monarchy better than anarchy?" he asked.

General Castro thought France, as a Catholic country, would be suitable.

General Vallejo strongly opposed becoming subjects of a European monarch. He favored annexation by the United States. Said Vallejo:

> It is most true, that to rely any longer upon Mexico to govern and defend us, would be idle and absurd. To this extent I fully agree with my distinguished colleagues . . . Why then should we hesitate still to assert our independence? We have indeed taken the first step, by electing our own governor, but another remains to be taken . . . annexation to the United States. In contemplating this consummation of our destiny, I

feel nothing but pleasure, and I ask you to share it . . . When we join our fortunes to hers, we shall not become subjects, but fellow-citizens, possessing all the rights of the United States and choosing our own federal and local rulers. We shall have a stable government and just laws. California will grow strong and flourishing, and her people will be prosperous, happy, and free.[8]

Loose Cannon Arrives

Consul Larkin encouraged union with the United States, and he was making progress, but his efforts were hampered by an American exploration party headed by U. S. Army Captain John C. Fremont, who found ways to exasperate the Californios. Fremont already had achieved fame as an explorer and surveyor, helping to open the American West. In 1845, he was leading a third expedition of approximately fifty civilians, each heavily armed for occasional battles with Native Americans. Larkin obtained permission for the Fremont party to winter in California before going to Oregon, and the consul provided funds for its supplies.

As will be seen in this and other instances, Captain Fremont was a rash and ambitious man who had trouble dealing with authority. He was under orders by his government to "conciliate" the Californians, but the famous "Pathfinder" and his men proved so unruly that General Castro ordered them to leave. Instead, the party camped high up on a mountain, put up breastworks, and raised an American flag. Fremont wanted the American settlers to join him, but none did. As the Californios recruited an armed force, Consul Larkin tried to keep the peace. Eventually, at Larkin's urging, Fremont left for Oregon.

Consul Thomas O. Larkin

A red-haired courier from Washington reached Larkin on April 17, 1846. This was Marine Lieutenant Archibald Gillespie in civilian clothes and posing as an invalid merchant. Gillespie arrived with memorized instructions that appointed the consul "confidential agent" for the purpose of annexing California. As confidential agent, Larkin continued encouraging union and writing articles for the Eastern press. A determined patriot, he was not deterred by whoever in Washington objected to his expenses. His consular income, Larkin complained, did not even cover the cost of the annual Fourth of July ball.

Fremont Heads Back

Traveling through Mexico by stagecoach, Gillespie had seen the Mexican army getting ready for war over Texas, and he thought war would come soon. The marine in mufti also brought some communications for Captain Fremont, most of which came from his wife and his father-in-law, the powerful Senator Thomas Hart Benton, an exponent of westward expansion. Learning that Fremont had gone to Oregon, Gillespie hired two guides and undertook a nearly 600-mile trip on horseback. Sutter warned Governor Pico that Gillespie was no invalid merchant. Upon Gillespie's arrival in Oregon, Fremont and his men immediately headed back to California.

American newspaper editors were demanding that the United States annex California in order to keep Great Britain from acquiring it. An American merchant in Los Angeles, Abel Stearns, reported to Larkin that British agents were offering to protect California if it declared independence, but that the Angelenos would strongly prefer union with the United States.[9] Many of the leading Californios, like General Vallejo, were related to Americans by blood or marriage. As evidence of British competition, on June 7 a British frigate, the HMS *Juno*, brought to Monterey an Irish priest, Father Eugene MacNamara, who said he had permission from the Mexican government to settle ten thousand Irish Catholics in California.[10] MacNamara had been in Mexico working on this project since September of 1844 (even prior to the Irish potato famine of 1845). Learning that the California capital had moved to Los Angeles, the priest headed there to see Governor Pico. Larkin asked Abel Stearns to keep an eye on him.

Surely the Mexican government would not have approved such a huge influx of foreigners, outnumbering the Californios, if it had not been dangerously in debt to Great Britain, to the extent of 50 million pesos. In former envoy Waddy Thompson's opinion, California was "literally a waif and belongs to the first occupant."

Castro's Plan for Union

Having changed his mind about France, General Jose Castro prepared a plan for declaring independence and joining the United States. He showed the plan to Consul Larkin.[11] To pave the way for a peaceful union, Larkin wanted Washington to assure prominent citizens, like Castro, employment in the new government.

In northern California, there was posted an official document ordering that land not be sold to non-naturalized foreigners and warning that Americans who did not leave California when asked to do so might be expelled at the government's convenience. Restrictive announcements were not new, but this one, combined with agitation by Captain Fremont, galvanized the American settlers. Seeing 170 horses gathered for General Castro, they decided the general was getting ready to attack them, and on June 10 they seized the animals. Nobody consulted Consul Larkin. He believed that Castro planned to use the horses in a confrontation with Governor Pico, who was raising troops in order to oust the general from his military command. Such an action by Castro would have helped the cause of union with the United States.

On June 14, thirty-three Americans on horseback captured the town of Sonoma and its arsenal. There was no resistance. They took prisoner the pro-American General Vallejo, and proclaimed an independent nation, the Bear Flag Republic. One of the insurgents was William Todd, the nephew of Mary Todd Lincoln. Todd devised a flag with the image of a bear on it. His amused comrades said the bear looked more like a pig. Today, a more handsome bear adorns the California state flag. (Todd's flag can be seen online.)

The Bear Flaggers took Vallejo to Sutter's fort, where the general asked Captain Fremont what was going on? Fremont told Vallejo he was a prisoner of the Bear Flag revolt and not a prisoner of the United States. The devious Fremont let the Bear Flaggers think the United States was behind them, but he did not permit Lieutenant Gillespie to display an American flag.[12] Imprisoned for six weeks, Vallejo was treated well and was allowed to walk around the fort until the fractious Fremont ordered no special privileges.

On July 4, Sonoma held an Independence Day fandango, and the next day Fremont took off his military uniform and put himself at the head of the Bear Flag rebellion.

Whatever Fremont did or did not do, Consul Larkin's dream of a peaceful annexation was lost. In April war had broken out between the United States and Mexico. The conflict began on the Rio Grande, and it triggered an American invasion of California. For a while, some Californios thought the reported war in Mexico was a fake excuse for the invasion.

Conquest of California

Despite its great size, California became one of history's easiest conquests. Many Californios, having no love for Mexico, were thinking about joining up with the United States or, in view of the increasing American immigration, at least were resigned to what appeared to be inevitable. In the spring of 1846, Commodore John Drake Sloat, commander of the Pacific Squadron, stood off the western coast of Mexico with orders to occupy major California ports if war broke out between the United States and Mexico. Sloat received news of hostilities on May 17, but he hesitated, perhaps recalling Commodore Jones's experience, and on June 6 Sloat reported to Washington that he was refraining from engaging in aggressive acts. For this the commodore was reprimanded and relieved. Before receiving that response, however, Sloat heard that the U.S. Navy had blockaded the Mexican port of Vera Cruz, and so he got moving and planted the American flag in Monterey. Commodore John Drake Sloat's caution contrasted sharply with that of his ancestor, Sir Francis Drake. In 1579, Drake, whose exploits earned him a knighthood, planted a flag northwest of what now is San Francisco and claimed the land as *Nova Albion*—Latin for New Britain. That name remained on the charts for 250 years.

Commodore Sloat reached Monterey on July 1 aboard the frigate USS *Savannah*. As was the custom, he prepared to salute the Mexican flag, but he did not do so since that would have embarrassed the Californio commander ashore, who said that he had no gunpowder with which to return the salute. Such was the state of California's defenses. Consul Larkin visited the *Savannah* on July 2 and received a nine-gun salute. On July 4, Monterey celebrated American Independence and coincidentally held a fiesta commemorating the patroness of the Bishopric of California. So far, the official conquest was friendly and bloodless.

Meeting Captain Fremont, Commodore Sloat dressed him down for starting a war with no authorization.

In Los Angeles, Governor Pico had little success in rounding up a Californio army. Knowing that Mexico would be no help, Pico wrote to the British vice consul in Monterey, seeking assistance from Great Britain.

Apparently the British Navy had orders to occupy the California ports if war broke out between the United States and Mexico. Admiral Sir George Seymour, in the 80-gun ship of the line HMS *Collingwood*, was patrolling the coast with fifteen warships under his command. As recorded in today's Monterey Museum, Seymour attempted to seize Monterey, but was too late. Approaching the bay on July 16, Seymour ordered the quartermaster to keep a sharp lookout for a flag on shore. Excitedly, the admiral kept asking the quartermaster what he could see. At last, a flag came into view. But it was the American flag. "Then, by God, I am too late!" exclaimed the admiral.

His project having failed, Father MacNamara departed California with Admiral Seymour. Californians suspected MacNamara of being a British agent since he did not wear clerical attire and traveled on British warships.

Most of California, including Baja California, was occupied with very little bloodshed. President Polk sent out a particularly resourceful result-getter, Commodore Robert F. Stockton, to relieve Commodore Sloat. This was lucky for Fremont. Stockton, accepted Fremont, his men, and the Bear Flaggers as the "California Battalion." Promoted to lieutenant colonel, Fremont then commanded a force of 428 men.

Commodore Robert F. Stockton

A few small battles occurred in southern California. Fifty hard-drinking Bear Flaggers (part of the California Battalion) occupied Los Angeles, and their commander Archibald Gillespie, now a captain, proved a heavy handed administrator. As ordered by Stockton, he declared martial law and established a curfew. He also prohibited gambling and broke up a fandango. The pleasure-loving Californios, feeling insulted, drove out the Americans. Los Angeles was not regained until January of 1847, with the help of U.S. Army troops under General Stephen Kearny. Kearny's men had marched overland from Kansas. On the way, they occupied Santa Fe, the capital of New Mexico, without encountering any resistance. The inhabitants were pleased to be keeping their property rights. Kearny left in Santa Fe a force of 300 to maintain order. He proceeded to California with 1,258 men.

In the California conquest, fewer than forty Americans died and fewer than ten Californios. It impressed the Californios favorably that the Americans did not massacre their enemies.

General Kearny was supposed to take over the military governorship of California, but Colonel Fremont, having been appointed by Commodore Stockton, refused to give up the position. For that Fremont was court martialed in Washington and given a sentence of dismissal from the Army. President Polk canceled the punishment, but the aggrieved Fremont resigned. The Civil War found the headstrong Fremont back in the army as a major general, and once more he shot himself in the foot. As President Lincoln strove to keep the border states within the Union, Fremont on his own initiative ordered the slaves freed in Missouri. Seeing that the political effect of this would cost him three border states, Lincoln had to relieve General Fremont of his command and cancel the premature emancipation.

Part Two

Remember the Alamo! Remember Goliad!

Like the Californios, the Americans who settled in the Texas department of Mexico could not put up with the unstable and dictatorial regimes in Mexico City. The Texans wanted a civilian government, an educational system, freedom of religion, and no tithing to the Catholic church.

They also wanted more American immigration, which the Mexican government prohibited. Some Texans were cotton growers, and they wanted to continue slavery, an institution which the Mexican government wished to abolish. In 1835, a new military government started centralizing the administration of Mexico, which for a while had enjoyed a decentralized system, and for the Texans the inevitable increase in friction was too much. In a series of battles, the Texans expelled the Mexican army from their land. In 1836, the Texans declared their independence. The news from Texas helped to inspire rebellion in California.

A contemporary view of those events in Texas has been provided by Abner Doubleday, the man popularly believed to have been the founder of baseball. Doubleday was a career army officer who during the American Civil War rose to the rank of major general. When the Mexican-American War started, he, a graduate of West Point, was a lieutenant. After retirement, Doubleday wrote a memoir titled, *My Life in the Old Army,* and he had this to say about Texas and how Americans happened to come and live there:

> In 1821 Mexico invited colonists from the United States to settle in Texas. This may seem strange to those who like myself have lived among the Mexicans and know their deep rooted dislike of foreigners. The latter were always spoken of contemptuously as "gringoes" from the verb geringar; meaning people who talk gibberish. This feeling was increased in regard to the Americans by the fact that nearly all of them were looked upon as heretics. Ever since the period referred to and until recently our people were subjected to incessant robberies and personal indignities, for which they never have been able to obtain redress of any kind. Nevertheless the scant population of Texas and the fact that it was fast becoming depopulated from the incursions of the Comache [sic], Kioways, and other nomadic tribes finally induced the Mexican government to favor emigration from the United States as a barrier to the inroads of savages. But the American colonists who responded to this invitation under Stephen Austin soon had reason to regret their action. They had always had rights and were accustomed to see them respected. They were not prepared therefore

to acquiesce in the military usurpations which were so prominent a feature in Mexican politics. The agent sent by them to the seat of government to remonstrate was seized and imprisoned, the territorial legislature was dissolved at the point of a bayonet, and orders were issued to the military commandant on the frontier of Texas to disarm the colonists, who were looked upon with great jealousy by the military satraps in power.

General Abner Doubleday

In sum, Native Americans were driving the Mexicans out of Texas, and the Mexican government wanted American settlers to come and fend them off. The settlers objected to their lack of rights, the discrimination against them, and the attempt to disarm them. How could disarmed settlers be expected to defend Mexico from hostile Native Americans?

Santa Anna's Mistake

General Antonio de Lopez Santa Anna, who also was President of Mexico, came north with an army and laid siege to some Texans who were using the Alamo mission building as a fort. In a thirteen-day siege most of the defenders were killed, and the few taken prisoner were executed. Some noncombatants survived. At another mission, the Goliad, the Mexican army was holding 303 Texan prisoners. Santa Anna ordered their execution, and the massacre took place on Palm Sunday. Santa Anna's barbaric actions proved to be a strategic error. Without those shocking and heinous events, Texas might not have been able to recruit enough volunteers to defeat the Mexican army. "Remember the Alamo!" and "Remember Goliad!" were the battle cries. Volunteers rushed from the United States. After several battles, in 1836 the Texans, under the command of General Sam Houston, won a final victory at San Jacinto.

How did the Texans do it? Santa Anna, who called himself the "Napoleon of the West," either had failed to put out sentries during the army's afternoon siesta or the sentries were not doing their job. It has been suggested that the large size of his force made the general overconfident. Perhaps it also is relevant that women called *soldaderas* traveled with the Mexican army. Late in life, the general wrote a memoir admitting that he himself was asleep when the battle began.

The Texans, approaching through woods and over a ridge, took their enemies by surprise and defeated them in a battle of only eighteen minutes. Two cannon, a gift from the people of Cincinnati, fired at the Mexican breastworks. Then the Texans charged, fired their weapons, and fell to the ground expecting return fire. One of the Texans, Manuel Flores, was still standing. "They're running!" he yelled. The rest was a matter of pursuit. General Houston, despite impatient criticism, had maneuvered around until he found the right time and place for attack.

Santa Anna quickly changed from his officer's uniform and tried to escape but was captured. As a prisoner, he wrote an order for all Mexican soldiers to leave Texas. He also signed a treaty that recognized Texas's independence and established the Rio Grande as the border. The general's life was spared. The Mexican army obeyed his order. The Mexican government refused to ratify the treaty.

Vowing to reconquer its lost territory, the Mexican government did not recognize Texan independence. Most Texans now wanted their newly established Lone Star Republic to join the United States. Mexico warned that annexation would be considered an act of war. Britain recognized

Texas's independence. *The Oxford History of Mexico* (2010 edition) adds these two comments showing how the British were still trying to prevent American expansion, as they had tried to do at Ghent:

> From the moment it had recognized Texas's independence, Britain had been pressing Mexico to do the same in order to avoid losing California [page 336].

> Britain had continued to insist that Mexico recognize Texas to avoid losing California and, in 1844, even offered a French-British guarantee of the border in exchange for Mexican recognition of Texas, but Santa Anna did not accept until it was too late. Before Santa Anna lost power in November 1844, British Minister Charles Bankhead had convinced him to recognize Texas's independence [page 338].

British Warn Mexico

The British Foreign Office feared that if Mexico and Texas went to war over annexation, the United States would intervene and end up annexing both Texas and California. To prevent American expansion, the British wanted a peaceful, independent Texas, and to that end Britain, along with France, warned Santa Anna that fighting for Texas would be a mistake. Santa Anna came to see the wisdom of an independent Texas, but he then lost power. As we shall see, Great Britain continued to lobby for Texan independence even after the U.S. Congress voted for annexation.

Many Americans opposed annexing either Texas or California. Anti-slavery Americans did not want another slave state in the Union; moreover, annexation was liable to bring war with Mexico, Britain, or both. Pro-annexation politicians warned that Britain intended to take over Texas by offering financial assistance and a military alliance against Mexico. As for the "Manifest Destiny" possibility of expanding United States territory to all the way to California, the opponents felt that such an acquisition would be the ruination of the country (but not for the cultural reasons voiced in recent times). To quote John H. Schroeder in *Mr. Polk's War*:

> With the creation of a continental empire, would come the perversion of the republican form of government and the

replacement of the federal system with an all-powerful central government, a virtually unlimited executive, and a formidable military establishment.

Have there not been such trends?

In the mid-nineteenth century, we Americans had two major political parties, the Whigs and the Democrats. In general, the Democrats favored territorial expansion, the Whigs did not. Elected President in 1844 was the Democrat James K. Polk (pronounced "poke"), who as a candidate strongly favored annexing both Texas and the Oregon Country. To his friends, Polk let it be known that he wanted to acquire California as well. Polk's territorial ambitions could have gotten us into two simultaneous wars, and in fact his timorous secretary of state, James Buchanan, predicted war. However, in dealing with Great Britain, Polk managed by diplomacy and an implied threat of force to divide successfully the Oregon Country. The United States ended up getting most of it and Canada the rest. At this time British wanted American trade, especially cotton for their mills, more than another war.

President James K. Polk

Annexing the Oregon Country pleased the non-slave states and made it politically easier to admit Texas as a slave state. However, the Texas boundary with Mexico was a problem. The customary boundary was the Neuces river, but the Texans wanted the Rio Grande, which was farther south and meandered to the northwest. That boundary had been promised to them by President Santa Anna when he was a prisoner. As another Texas argument, the Rio Grande had been the boundary in the Louisiana Purchase, which was modified in 1819 with the American acquisition of Florida.

The U.S. Congress, after much dickering, passed a resolution approving the annexation of Texas, with President-elect Polk assuring opposition senators that he would avoid war (perhaps keeping his fingers crossed). President John Tyler signed the law on March 1, just days before Polk was inaugurated. The boundary was not stated. Because of its war-making potential, mentioning a Rio Grande boundary would have prevented passage.

"Fighting Bob" Stockton

On April 2, 1845, some vague orders were given to the aforementioned Commodore Stockton, a supporter of annexation who had friends in high places. The commodore also had a reputation for exceeding his instructions. Stockton saw himself in the tradition of the British Admiral Horatio Nelson, who once during a battle, held a telescope to his blind right eye and announced his failure to see a flag signal permitting retreat. Commodore Stockton was given a squadron and told to go to Galveston, Texas, and "make [himself] acquainted with the dispositions of the people of Texas, and their relations with Mexico."

During a varied career, Stockton became a naval officer, a successful businessman, and a politician. Nicknamed "Fighting Bob" while defending Baltimore during the War of 1812, Stockton in his naval uniform was an all-purpose swashbuckler who fought pirates, intercepted slave ships (the U.S. Navy stopped more than a hundred slave ships), and dueled with British officers who, he said, disrespected the United States. He once threatened to fire cannon at a Peruvian jail holding an American; in Stockton's judgment, the prisoner was innocent. In 1821, after some failed attempts by the American Colonization Society to buy land in Africa for the founding of Liberia as a home for freed blacks, Stockton, then a Navy lieutenant, took on the job and managed to effect a purchase. The plan almost failed when the locals identified him as an officer who caught slave ships. Selling slaves was the tribe's source of income. To survive and complete the purchase, Stockton had to point a pistol at the head of King Peter, the chief.

Lieutenant Stockton was extra-good at catching slave ships. Ordered to seize ships flying the American flag, he also seized those flying the French flag since no slaver would show an American flag when an American warship was around. Figuring the courts could decide the ship's nationality, Stockton would send the suspect vessel to Boston. His interference with "lawful commerce" outraged the French government, and the case went to the U.S. Supreme Court. The defense argued that slavery was contrary to the law of nations and the law of nature. The brash lieutenant's action was upheld by the justices.

As ordered, Commodore Stockton took a squadron of four ships to Galveston, arriving on May 12. He attended a ball in his honor, and reported to Washington that nearly every Texan favored annexation.

Planning a War

Having fulfilled that mission, Stockton tried to start a war between Texas and Mexico. An accomplice in this task was Charles A. Wickliffe, a former U.S. postmaster general, who also had been sent by Polk to Galveston. He reported to the President by mail. Wickliffe hired a spy to help him investigate Mexican activities along the Rio Grande, but on the way both men became too seasick to accomplish their mission.

Commodore Stockton communicated with the President of Texas, Anson Jones, through Dr. John H. Wright, the flagship surgeon. (Building in deniability was not new with our modern CIA.) In that manner, Stockton proposed to Jones, that he, Stockton, being independently wealthy, would covertly finance a Texan army to capture Matamoros, a city on the far side of the Rio Grande. According to Stockton's plan, this would ignite a war, the United States would intervene, and Texas would have its Rio Grande boundary. President Jones stalled. Secretly, he preferred being President of an independent Texas. Helping Jones with that scheme was a British diplomat, Charles Elliot. Elliot and a French

FIRST MEXICAN-AMERICAN WAR

diplomat asked the Mexicans to approve Texas's independence on the condition that Texas reject annexation.

Was President Polk behind Stockton's scheme? There is no direct evidence. However, Wickliffe arrived in Galveston with a letter of introduction from Polk for presentation to the American envoy to Texas, Andrew J. Donelson. Stockton was exchanging letters with the secretary of the navy, George Bancroft, and certain features of the correspondence are suspect. After telling Bancroft that the Rio Grande boundary was needed for the annexation to go through, Stockton outlined a plan for military action backed by "R. F. Stockton, Esq." (has there ever been a thinner cover?):

> But it may perhaps be well for me *in this way* [emphasis in the original] to let you know how I propose to settle the matter without committing the U. States—the Major General in command of the Texas militia will call out three thousand men & "R.F. Stockton, Esq." will supply them in a private way with provisions and ammunition—[13]

Stockton later requested provisions and powder to be sent to either Pensacola or New Orleans, and Bancroft replied,

> Orders will be given to furnish powder and supplies at Pensacola on your requisitions. [George Bancroft to Stockton, June 2, 1845.][14]

If Bancroft and Wickliffe were behind the scheme, Polk must have been behind it as well. Nothing came of it, however, because the head of the Texas militia, though favorably disposed, wanted the approval of President Jones, who was not favorably disposed.

Texans Furious

With nothing but secret plans underway, it appeared to the Texan public that nothing was being done about annexation, and for his tardiness, Governor Jones was burned in effigy. Then Elliot returned from Mexico City reporting success in his mission, and on June 4 Jones announced his plan for independence. The people of the Lone Star state were furious. They wanted to be part of the United States. The Texas Congress voted for annexation, and so did the people in a referendum. The tin-eared President Jones was going to lose his job.

Amid the political machinations on all sides, the people of the United States and the people of Texas insisted on getting together, and they at last did so. The U. S. Congress passed a joint resolution on February 26, 1845. Polk was elected President because he understood the depth of the public's desire. Anson Jones did not. Unable to get himself elected to the U.S. Senate, Jones, although a rich planter, shot himself.

Mexico had been threatening war if the annexation occurred, and so it broke off diplomatic relations with the United States. Secretary of War William Marcy dispatched an "army of observation" under General Zachary Taylor. He took 1,200 men to the port of Corpus Christi on the Nueces river, and as if to signal a claim on the Rio Grande boundary, the Americans camped on the disputed side of the river, not on the side recognized as part of Texas.

General Taylor, a descendant of Mayflower pilgrims and a veteran of the War of 1812, was one of the great eccentrics of American military history. Nicknamed "Old Rough and Ready," Taylor dressed in casual civilian clothes, and he was just as informal in manner. Newly arriving soldiers might mistake the general for a farmer and enjoy a chat without discovering who he was. Reviewing his troops, the general sat on his horse sidesaddle, a leg crooked around the pommel, and often wore a straw hat. He had little formal education, but he read the philosopher Spinoza and corresponded with the poet Henry Wadsworth Longfellow. Taylor was not one to study military science. His West Point graduates helped him with that. But Old Rough and Ready was absolutely fearless.

Attempting to acquire Texas and California, the latter by purchase, President Polk sent to Mexico City John Slidell, an expansionist friend, with the title Envoy Extraordinary and Minister Plenipotentiary. As we have seen, Waddy Thompson's attempt to buy California had failed. Even before that, our very first envoy to Mexico, Joel Poinsett (who introduced the poinsettia to the United States), in the 1820s tried to buy Texas, and he arrived with an ingenious sales talk. Poinsett was instructed to mention certain practical advantages if Texas were sold: the Mexican capital then would be *nearer the center of its territories*, and the warlike Comanche tribe would be *in the United States*. A delightful prospect, with a cash payment to boot. But the Mexicans did not go for it.

Mexican Debts

Texas being independent, Polk expected to acquire that for free. If possible, Slidell was to buy New Mexico and California for cash and settlement of Mexico's debts. The debts had accumulated as a result of piracy by Mexican sailors, extortion of American businessmen by Mexican officials, and purchase of munitions from the United States during the Mexican Revolution. When Slidell's mission was proposed, the Mexican President, Jose Joaquin Herrera, said he was willing to talk about the Texas problem, but Slidell arrived with much bigger plans. It did not help that, thanks to a choice made by President Polk, Slidell arrived with an assistant whom the Mexicans heartily disliked. This was William L. Parrott, a businessman who had been pressing a claim of $690,000 against the Mexican government. The claim resulted from an illegal seizure of wine. Parrott also was one of Polk's secret agents, and he warned his employer that if war broke out between the United States and Mexico, the British navy would seize California ports in payment for debts.

To the Mexicans California may not have been attractive real estate, but it was a matter of honor. No Mexican President could accept Slidell's California proposal or even be known to think about it. Word of the American's mission leaked out and President Herrera refused to receive him. If Polk had sent Slidell to Los Angeles, he and his money would have been welcomed with a fandango.

Criticized for his moderate foreign policies and for a time imprisoned by rebellious soldiers, Herrera was ousted in a coup by General Mariano Paredes. The new President also refused to meet with Slidell, and he mobilized the Mexican army. Street crowds demanded war. Paredes talked of capturing New Orleans and Mobile. But the new President, who had fought for the Spanish in Mexico's War of Independence, sent no army to challenge Taylor. He proved more interested in re-establishing Spanish rule. Paredes also tried to obtain help from Great Britain, but according to the British envoy, Charles Bankhead, Paredes "could not find anyone trustworthy enough in Mexico to take the message and the policy was not at all popular."[15] Paredes was replaced by General Valentin Gomez Farias.

Pigeon Assignment

With the failure of the Slidell mission and the turmoil in Mexico City, War Secretary Marcy ordered General Taylor to proceed to the Rio Grande. After seven months on the Nueces, Taylor now had 3,500 men, all regular soldiers. Among them marched Lieutenant Doubleday. Another West Pointer was Lieutenant "Sam" Grant, who in the Civil War would become a military legend as General Ulysses S. Grant. In his *Personal Memoirs*, Grant recalled his experience in Mexico:

> We were sent to provoke a fight, but it was essential that Mexico should commence it . . . Mexico showing no willingness to come to the Nueces to drive the invaders from her soil, it became necessary for the "invaders" to approach within a convenient distance to be struck.[16]

Lieutenant Ulysses S. Grant

The same sort of opinion was expressed by Lieutenant Colonel Ethan Allen Hitchcock, who in the Civil War became a major general. Said his 1846 diary:

> Our force is altogether too small for the accomplishment of its errand. It looks as if the government sent a small force on purpose to bring on a war, so as to have a pretext for taking California, and as much of this country as it chooses; for, whatever becomes of this army, there is no doubt of a war between the United States and Mexico.[17]

Colonel Hitchcock and Lieutenant Grant opposed the war and believed they were on a pigeon assignment, like the American sailors in the Tonkin Gulf. Hitchcock noted the small size of Taylor's force as evidence for its pigeon status. (Compare Commodore Herrick with one outmoded destroyer.) "Whatever becomes of this army" concerned him.

As Herrera and Paredes found out, a Mexican government could not survive without attacking the Americans. The Mexicans thought of themselves as a martial people, and they were very proud of their cavalry. Still, General Farias needed more provocation.

On March 28, 1846, Taylor's little army camped on the Rio Grande across from the aforementioned Matamoros. Leaflets in Spanish informed the local people that the Americans would be there until negotiations resolved the boundary question, that the Americans had peaceful intentions, and that they would pay for the "highest prices" for any goods that they required. (Did General Taylor invent dollar diplomacy? He told Washington that "fair prices" would be paid.) The Americans raised their flag to the accompaniment of the national anthem and "Yankee Doodle." It was a stirring scene. Our men noticed, however, that the Mexican side had better musicians; they also had naked women swimming in the river. Mexican sentries kept the invaders away.

Taylor's men built around them a six-sided earthen barrier and named it "Fort Texas."

On paper the Mexican military posture looked good. Mexico had an army of 30,000 to 40,000 men, by different accounts. At one time the army consisted of 20,000 men and 24,000 officers, according to Justin

Smith, author of a two volume history of the Mexican-American War. The Mexican soldiers had gained experience in many civil wars, and the American army, totaling only 7,365 regulars, would have to operate far from its sources of supply. Considering the experience of the Spanish, British Consul Richard Pakenham estimated that with the Mexican army fighting defensively, on its own territory, the Americans would need an army of 250,000. Sniffed the London *Times:*

> The invasion and conquest of a vast region by a state which is
> without an army and without credit is a novelty in the history
> of nations.

As another handicap, the Americans soon found out that in Mexico they were susceptible to dysentery, typhus, measles, malaria, and yellow fever. During the war, American deaths caused by disease would be many times those caused by combat. But, in contrast to the War of 1812, American volunteers were plentiful and eager to fight. Mexico was disadvantaged by having an unstable government and an economy ravaged by many years of civil conflict. The Mexican peasant-soldiers did not feel much loyalty to their ever-changing government, and they were not well equipped. Their desertion rate was high. American deserters included some Irish immigrants who changed sides for reasons of religion and the inducement of land ownership. Nearly half of Taylor's men were immigrants, mostly Irish and German. General Taylor ordered his sentries to shoot anybody trying to swim across the river. Before long, two were shot. Four drowned. Father Eugene MacNamara now was in Mexico, and he was reported to be helping the Mexicans to encourage desertion among Irish-American soldiers.

In command on the Mexican side of the Rio Grande was General Francisco Mejia, who told Taylor's representative, General William J. Worth, that the Americans by their presence on Mexican territory had committed an act of war. Worth assured Mejia that his neighbors' intentions were peaceful, and he asked to see the American consul. The request was refused. Worth said the refusal was a belligerent act.

On April 11, General Pedro de Ampudia arrived in Matamoros with reinforcements. Ampudia gave Taylor 24 hours to leave the area and head for the other side of the Nueces river. Taylor replied that his instructions did not permit him to do that. Some U.S. Navy vessels were stationed off the coast, and Taylor had them blockade the river mouth. This would prevent from reaching Matamoros enough supplies to sustain Ampudia's large force. General Ampudia wanted to attack the Americans immediately, but he did not have the authority and his subordinates would not support that decision. Ampudia growled that the American Taylor was "lower than the lowest Mexican tailor."

Orders to Attack

On April 24 arrived General Mariano Arista, a sandy-haired, freckle-faced Mexican who had lived in Cincinnati, and he took overall command of the Mexican forces. Unlike Ampudia, Arista was polite, but he had orders to attack. They were dated April 4. The Mexican government had decided to fight even prior to Ampudia's arrival and the river blockade. Arista told Taylor that war was being forced upon Mexico and that hostilities had commenced. Taylor complimented Arista on his reputation for "high character," but said the responsibility for the hostilities must rest on those who begin them.

On next day, April 25, Taylor heard that Mexican cavalry had crossed the river upstream, and he ordered a detachment of 60 dragoons (the American term for cavalry or mounted infantry) to investigate. Encountering a Mexican force of 1,600, the Americans were routed with 11 killed and the rest captured. The detachment's Mexican guide survived and brought the news. This was a big enough incident to start a war. The Mexican cavalry commander, saying he did not have proper medical facilities, sent in a cart one wounded American.

It took two weeks for the news of the dragoon incident to reach Washington. President Polk was more than ready. He had been expecting conflict, and so on May 9, hours before the news arrived, the President already had persuaded his cabinet to declare war. Then the news came in, and Polk got busy writing a war message to Congress. It contained this statement about how the war started:

> On the 10th of November, 1845, Mr. John Slidell, of Louisiana, was commissioned by me as envoy extraordinary and minister plenipotentiary of the United States to Mexico, and was intrusted with full powers to adjust both the questions

of the Texas boundary and of indemnification to our citizens. The redress of the wrongs of our citizens naturally and inseparably blended itself with the question of boundary. The settlement of the one question in any correct view of the subject involves that of the other. I could not for a moment entertain the idea that the claims of our much-injured and long-suffering citizens, many of which had existed for more than twenty years, should be postponed or separated from the settlement of the boundary question.

Polk took note of his ostensible efforts to avoid the war, and he blamed Mexico for its outbreak:

As war exists, and, notwithstanding all our efforts to avoid it, exists by the act of Mexico herself, we are called upon by every consideration of duty and patriotism to vindicate with decision the honor, the rights, and the interests of our country.

Nowhere did Polk ask for a declaration of war. He asked Congress to "recognize the existence of the war." He then attached the war message to a request for funds so that anybody voting against the war could be accused of not supporting the troops.

Arista's Clever Plan

General Arista had a plan for setting up the first major battle to his advantage. By starting to cross the river downstream from Taylor's encampment, Arista forced the Americans to go and protect Point Isabel, the landing where the U.S. Navy delivered Taylor's supplies. As it happened, Arista's river transport vessels were delayed, and Taylor arrived at Port Isabel first. Then the Mexicans in Matamoros began bombarding Fort Texas. This forced Taylor to return, leaving a detachment at the port, and he found Arista's army waiting for him athwart the road.

The Mexican line spread out for a mile. It was an imposing scene, but the American regulars wanted to fight and prove their worth before the volunteer soldiers arrived. Taylor had with him at this time only

2,200 men, having left detachments at Port Isabel and Fort Texas. The ambushing Mexicans numbered about 3,700. The freckled general had played his cards well. He had forced Taylor to divide his command into three parts and if the Americans made a bayonet charge, they would be enveloped and surrounded. But Taylor had more artillery, 20 pieces compared to Arista's 12. Mexican cannon opened fire. Taylor moved his artillery in front of his line and fired back as the enemy advanced.

"Flying Artillery"

The Mexicans fought bravely, but Taylor's troops had an advantage in their "flying artillery." This was a light artillery drawn by horses. It was quickly maneuverable, and the American gunners were well trained. The Mexicans had heavy cannon difficult to move around, and their gunpowder was of poor quality. The early salvos failed to reach the American soldiers, who dodged cannon balls rolling on the ground. The larger Mexican force several times tried to flank the Americans, but quickly redirected artillery helped to fight them off. On the American side only six men were killed, the Mexicans lost an estimated four hundred. Nightfall ended the engagement.

Fatally wounded was Major Samuel Ringgold, who studied the light artillery concept in Europe, introduced it to the U.S. Army, and made improvements in the equipment. (Napoleon, originally an artillery officer, was a light artillery practitioner. "Flying artillery" was not really new, just slow to get around.) Though severely wounded, Major Ringgold refused to leave the battle. His inspiring example was much celebrated during the war, and still is commemorated in Maryland's state song *Maryland, My Maryland*.

After the battle, most of the American officers wanted to set up a defensive position and await reinforcements. "Old Zach" said no, he would attack. But in the morning the Mexicans were seen to be heading south. Apparently having learned not to put his men in an open field, advantageous for cavalry but vulnerable to artillery, Arista set up new defenses at a ravine, the whole area thick with brush and trees except for the road to Matamoros. There Arista placed some artillery. He called as reinforcements the troops which had been attacking Fort Texas. To Arista's surprise, Taylor's men came after him that very afternoon. They fought their way through the brush in small groups and engaged in hand to hand combat. This was slow going until the Americans found a path around the Mexican left and attacked the enemy artillery. Arista launched counterattacks. They failed to dislodge the Americans, and the discouraged Mexican army broke and headed for the Rio Grande. There they were met by fire from Fort Texas. Few boats were available, and at least a hundred Mexicans drowned trying to swim the river.

A little over a week later, Taylor used captured boats to cross the Rio Grande, and he occupied Matamoros without firing a shot. The Mexican army had left. General Arista was replaced and court-martialed. Somebody had to be blamed.

Washington wasn't satisfied, either. Tayor was criticized for not having crossed the river sooner and captured Arista's army. Taylor responded that he never received the pontoons that he had ordered long before. Procurement is ever frustrating. During the 1970s, before the popularization of computers, White House speechwriter Patrick J. Buchanan complained it was hard for him to get newspapers because the procurement officer could not understand why they were needed. Perhaps some procurement officer, not being a reader of newspapers, could not understand why General Taylor might want to cross the Rio Grande.

Farias as President wasn't doing any better than his predecessor, and Santa Anna, who had been in exile, volunteered to take over. Farias stepped aside.

"Old Fuss and Feathers"

General Zachary Taylor continued to command the army in northern Mexico, and General Winfield Scott, another veteran of the War of 1812, brought an army to southern Mexico. Very different from General Taylor, General Scott was a student of military science and punctilious in dress and manner. Scott was nicknamed "Old Fuss and Feathers." (Scott being another Whig, Polk got rid of him as soon as possible, despite—or perhaps because of—the general's success.) Scott's army performed the U.S. military's first major amphibious landing, with General Worth the first man on the beach, and soon captured the port city of Vera Cruz.

General Santa Anna laid an ambush for the Americans as they headed toward Mexico City, but discovering it, Scott flanked the Mexicans and routed them. When he needed more troops, he called up six thousand men guarding his supply line and lived off the land. The Duke of Wellington followed the news avidly and predicted that this gamble would end in disaster. But it worked, and the duke declared Scott's southern Mexico campaign "unsurpassed in military annals."

Although the normally laid back Californios won some battles, nowhere in Mexico did the enemy triumph. Thanks to the interception of an American message about troop movements, General Santa Anna was able to concentrate a large force that almost overwhelmed General Taylor's men at Buena Vista. Colonel John Hardin died leading a charge of Illinois volunteers who were quickly surrounded. At a critical point the Mexicans were stopped by Colonel Jefferson Davis and his Mississippi riflemen. Indispensable was Captain Braxton Bragg's artillery. On his white horse, "Old Zach" took an exposed position, with a leg crooked around his saddle pommel, and ignoring two bullets that ripped through his coat, the general shouted encouragement to his men. Taylor's victory at Buena Vista helped him to win the presidency.

When the Americans arrived in Mexico City, Father MacNamara was sheltered by British diplomats.[18]

Peace Treaty

At the end of the war, Baja California was given to Mexico, but the peace treaty gave to the United States what now are Texas, California, Nevada, Utah, New Mexico, most of Arizona and Colorado, and parts of Oklahoma, Kansas, and Wyoming. The United States forgave Mexican debts and paid $18,500,000. President Polk's representative in Mexico, Nicholas P. Trist, completed a treaty and signed it even though Polk, dissatisfied with his performance, had called him home. Polk had decided that he wanted more land than what he had told Trist to obtain. Some Democrats wanted all of Mexico. Except for a few details, however, Polk settled for what his negotiator had done. Trist was fired upon his return, and he was not able to collect his unpaid salary and travel expenses until 1871, during the administration of President

Ulysses S. Grant. Grant also helped Trist by appointing him postmaster in Alexandria, Virginia.

The treaty gave the United States responsibility for preventing hostile Native Americans from entering Mexico from Texas. This part was negated later.

Congress Complains

The U.S. House of Representatives passed a bill praising General Taylor, but referred to a "war unnecessarily and unconstitutionally begun by the United States." Zachary Taylor succeeded Polk as President, but died in office, possibly from having eaten some rotten fruit. Although a Southerner, Taylor was a staunch Unionist with enemies among the potential secessionists. A suspicion of arsenic poisoning was not confirmed in an autopsy of 1991.

President Zachary Taylor

In this brief review of the First Mexican War, it happens that most of the American army officers mentioned were Southerners, as was President Polk. (Naval officer Stockton was born in New Jersey, General Kearny in New York.) The Southern officers mentioned were General Taylor, General Scott, Colonel Davis (later to be President of the Confederacy), Major Ringgold, General Fremont, and Captain Bragg. Numerically, American Southerners have participated disproportionately in the profession of arms. Their heroic and important contributions in the Mexican War boosted the South's confidence in its ability to triumph if a Southern secession led to war.

Analysis

In monumental failures of perception and judgment, neither Spain nor Mexico would populate California or defend it. If the United States had not annexed California, Great Britain or France would have done so. The dysfunctional Mexican government needed help from American settlers even to hold Texas against hostile Native Americans.

California might have been purchased peacefully if American officials had known that the Californios were itching to be free. A consul ought to have been assigned years before Larkin was chosen. As late as 1845, purchase might have been arranged if a well funded Extraordinary Envoy and Minister Plenipotentiary, like John Slidell, had been sent to California.

Instead, President Polk, nimble and secretive, promised peace and made war. He misled the Congress and the public. Then, lacking constitutional authority to initiate war, he provoked the Mexicans until they opened fire. Here we have an example of how more responsibility for a war should be assigned to the instigator than to whoever shot first. Clearly, Polk planned and instigated the conflict.

Like Commodore Stockton, President Polk focused on winning, not on following the rules. By hook or crook, the two men were devoted to accomplishing their mission, which was to stretch American democracy from sea to sea. Stockton also believed it was his duty to end Mexico's misrule and bring the blessings to liberty to its people. He was motivated, too, by antipathy to the "haughty" British Empire. The duelist said in a political speech of 1844:

> God and nature, and inevitable circumstances, destine the United States to be the only curb or check upon the ambition of Great Britain to rule the world.

But Polk was only the latest of the land-grabbers. California's history was a competition among imperialists:

The Spanish, ignoring Britain's claim, took California from the Native Americans.

Briefly, the Mexicans took California from the Spanish.

The Californios deposed the Mexican governor and considered joining with the United States or a European power. The British were slow to attempt settling California; they sent people to Australia and New Zealand.

The Americans took California from the Californios. The territory was a ripe plum hanging by a thread.

This was the pioneer era, and the rapidly increasing American population was in an expansion mood. A non-slave state was needed to balance Texas. The Democrats promised annexation of Texas and the Oregon Country. They won the election of 1844, not the Whigs. An anti-war Whig was the Illinois Congressman Abraham Lincoln. He attributed the war to Polk's desire for "military glory—that attractive rainbow that rises in showers of blood." Lincoln did not seek reelection.

A relatively minor but real motivation for war was Mexico's refusal or inability to pay its debts. Anybody who brought up that subject in Mexico City, diplomat or businessman, was vilified. Because of debt issues, the French in 1838 bombarded Vera Cruz and landed marines to raid the city. In 1861, Mexico stopped paying interest to its foreign bond holders, and this led to intervention by the British, French, and Spanish. The French landed an army and, in response to Mexican monarchists, installed as emperor an enlightened Hapsburg.

The Emperor Maximilian reigned for three years, instituting reforms aimed at helping the poor. Following the American Civil War, pressure from the United States helped to evict the French-sponsored regime. The hapless emperor faced a firing squad, despite appeals on his behalf from European liberals such as Victor Hugo and Giuseppe Garibaldi.

An Avoidable War?

This was a war of choice, which President Polk planned and provoked.

With a decision made to acquire territory, California could have been annexed peacefully, as planned by Consul Larkin and as favored by the leading Californio generals, Vallejo and Castro. That would have saved lives and avoided much bitterness, which lasts to this day among Mexicans, who now see California as a valuable property and not just a nuisance. President Polk was impatient, and he wished to make sure that no other nation took California, which Great Britain might have done in payment of debts. The Rio Grande boundary could have been secured without going to Vera Cruz. Possibly war on that front could be been prevented altogether by sending a larger army to the Rio Grande. Taylor's army was small enough to look vulnerable; even so the Mexicans were reluctant to attack.

Useful Principles

When a President promises peace, he might not mean it.

The nation that shoots first can be less responsible for a war than an instigator who makes the conflict inevitable.

When a President puts Americans in harm's way, this can be the equivalent of initiating war. Watch out for pigeon assignments on land as well as on the sea.

A President's request for war authority should stand by itself and not be attached to other legislation.

Whatever the problem, think of diplomacy first.

With better planning the California could have been annexed peacefully, and probably New Mexico as well. With proper defenses, Texas, already annexed, perhaps could have been protected without bloodshed.

Punish rogue attempts to instigate war.

Instead, Captain Fremont was promoted.

References

1   Hubert H. Bancroft, *History of California*, volume 2, pages 450-451

2   Frances Bunsen, *Memoir of Baron Bunsen*, volume 2, page112; Michael Balfour, *The Kaiser and His Times*, page 52

3   Hubert H. Bancroft, *History of California*, volume 4, pages 296-297

4   Alan Rosenus, *General Vallejo*, page 90

5   Hubert H. Bancroft, *History of California*, volume 4, page 260

6   Alexander DeConde, *A History of American Foreign Policy*, page 193

7   Michael A. Palmer, *Stoddert's War*, 162-164

8   Joseph W. Revere, *A Tour of Duty in California*, pages 28-29

9   Harlan Hague, *Thomas O. Larkin*, page 132

10   Harlan Hague, *Thomas O. Larkin*, page 134

11   Harlan Hague, *Thomas O. Larkin*, page 138

12   Alan Rosenus, *General Vallejo*, page 135

13   Stockton to Secretary of the Navy Bancroft, May 17, 1845, George Bancroft Papers, Massachusetts Historical Society. Also see Richard W. Van Alstyne, *The Rising American Empire*, page 138.

14   *Confidential Letters, No. 1, RG 45,* Navy Department Archives, National Archives

15   John Fox, *Macnamara's Irish Colony,* page 114 (The priest wrote his name with a lower case *n.*)

16   Ulysses S. Grant, *Personal Memoirs*, volume 1, page 68

17   Ethan Allen Hitchcock, *Fifty Years in Camp and Field*, page 213

18   John Fox, *Macnamara's Irish Colony,* p. 179

CHAPTER SEVEN

Second Opium War (1856 to 1860)

War seldom enters but where wealth allures—John Dryden (1631-1700)

So far as I have been able to learn, we Americans did not participate in the First Opium War, which was fought between the British and the Chinese. On the British side, the war was managed by an aggressive foreign secretary, Lord Palmerston. Previously secretary at war for nineteen years, Palmerston was proficient in gunboat diplomacy, and his tough, result-getting policies made him popular with the British people. We Americans, although officially neutral, participated in the Second Opium War, doing so on the side of Great Britain and the opium dealers. This American war was undeclared and almost unnoticed. Yet it happened, and it has had a profound effect on our relations with China.

The Opium Wars were fought to make China allow the importation of opium and other goods, such as textiles. Most foreign trade initially was confined to one port, Canton (now Guangzhou), because the Chinese were trying to enforce their laws against selling opium, which the Chinese government called a "poison." The Chinese were ahead of the West on that subject. Opium in the United States and Britain was a legal product. Not until 1909 did the United States start passing federal laws against the drug, and its use in patent medicines was not prohibited by federal law until 1924. The drug's unhealthful effects were known. Clergymen and some conscientious politicians condemned it, but in the nineteenth and early twentieth centuries, opium was commonly used in Britain and the United States, famously by artists and writers. In 1821, essayist Thomas de Quincey published the best selling *Confessions of an English Opium Eater.* Lewis Carroll, author of *Alice in Wonderland*, reputedly found his fanciful characters in opium dreams. In fiction, Dr. Watson urged his friend Sherlock Holmes to quit using opiates, which the detective employed to entertain his powerful mind between challenging cases.

Why was it so important to sell opium to China? We Westerners wanted to buy Chinese tea, silk, and porcelain. The English, in particular, developed a great passion for tea. The Chinese government, however, was not much interested in foreign trade. In 1794, the Chinese Emperor said to a British visitor, "We possess all things. I see no value in objects strange or ingenious, and I have no use for your country's manufactures." Anything foreign the Celestial Empire deemed inferior. The mandarins running the country were Confucian intellectuals who held trade itself in low esteem and considered it a corrupting influence. Unable to sell much to the Chinese, the British usually had to pay for goods in silver. That worked for while, but soon the tea-addicted British were running short of the shiny metal. Solution: smuggle opium. To that end, the British expanded the growing of opium poppies in India. We Americans brought to China opium from Turkey. One successful American trader was Warren Delano, grandfather of President Franklin Delano Roosevelt. Americans sold furs as well.

Fast clipper ships, with narrow hulls, extra-wide sails, and guns transported the merchandise. They were called "tea clippers" or "opium clippers." Clipper sailors, handsomely uniformed, were the best paid in the world. Possibly the fastest opium clipper was the *Cutty Sark* built in Scotland. It is the magnificent windjammer pictured on bottles of Cutty Sark whiskey. In a British dialect, the "cutty sark" is a skimpy chemise, mentioned in a Robert Burns poem, and the clipper's figurehead shows a partially clad, bare breasted woman. The restored clipper is on display at Greenwich, London. The fastest public record for a clipper ship was set in 1854 by the passenger ship *Champion of the Seas* built in Boston. In 1877, it was abandoned in a storm off Cape Horn.

Clipper Ship

Triangular Trade

The British clippers brought cheap manufactured products to India for sale, loaded up opium, carried the opium to China, and there stuffed their holds with tea, silk, and porcelain. The ships were fast enough to outrun pirates and Chinese customs vessels. If becalmed, they might need their guns against pirates. As for customs vessels, they likely would shoot wide, if at all, in recompense for their bribes.

The trade balance turned around and the Chinese ran low on silver.

By the late 1830s, millions of Chinese were addicted to opium, and corruption was rampant among Chinese officials profiting from the opium trade. In 1839, the Chinese Emperor sent to Canton a mandarin dedicated to stopping this evil commerce, and he destroyed a large amount of opium stored there. The opium was kept in buildings called "factories," whose upper stories provided luxurious living quarters for the foreign traders. The mandarin's destruction of opium led to the First Opium War, and the technologically advanced British won easily. The Treaty of Nanjing in 1842 gave the British Hong Kong, opened more trading ports, and granted to the British immunity from prosecution in Chinese courts. British lawbreakers—such as drunken sailors—now would be tried in British courts. In 1844 China gave similar concessions to the Americans and the French. Chinese opium usage zoomed upward.

Negotiating the cession of Hong Kong was the British diplomat Charles Elliot, who earlier, working with Anson Jones, had tried to secure Texas's independence. Like Nicholas Trist, however, Elliot did not satisfy his government's greed and was fired. So was Elliot's Chinese counterpart. Negotiating the final Hong Kong treaty required new personnel on both sides.

Acquiring Hong Kong was a great convenience for the traders. The island was spacious and defensible, and the expatriates did not have to put up with so much harassment from Chinese officials. At the previous location, the mandarins sometimes gave hints of displeasure. When executing a Chinese opium trader the deed might be carried out in front of one of the factories occupied by the "foreign devils." The method of execution was strangulation.

Hong Kong's high quality opium was prized in the United States and Canada.

Although formerly enemies, the British and American navies had common interests in China and at times worked together. In 1855 a pirate fleet was holding seven merchant ships at an island near Hong Kong. They were rescued by the USS *Powhatan* and the HMS *Rattler*. The pirates used "war junks" equipped with small cannon. Seeing the foreign warships, many junks fled. By different accounts, ten or twenty were sunk. The pirates suffered from five hundred to eight hundred casualties, while reportedly a thousand pirates were captured. Some pirates were not Chinese. The most notorious foreign pirate was an American, Eli Boggs, who owned thirty-two war junks. Boggs ended up in a British prison. Authorities were not able to make a murder case against him.

Scarecrow Captains

The Second Opium War began after Chinese authorities on October 8, 1856, boarded a ship suspected of smuggling and piracy and arrested a dozen of its crew. Named the *Arrow*, the ship was Chinese owned, and it had a Chinese crew which was commanded, nominally, by 21-year-old Thomas Kennedy, an Irish subject of Queen Victoria. Through some legal mumbo jumbo (also described as "mystification"), it was possible for a Chinese ship owner to register in Hong Kong his vessel as British, and as the result many pirates and smugglers were protected from Chinese law enforcement by flying a British flag. These ship owners hired footloose young Britons like Kennedy, and at least one American, to make their ships look British and scare off the maritime patrols. The "scarecrow" captains normally took no part in actually running the ship.

The Chinese said the *Arrow* was Chinese and flew no flag. The British acting consul in Canton, Harry Parkes, said the ship *was* flying the British flag and so the boarding and arrests were an insult to the United Kingdom. When apprehended, the *Arrow* was at anchor in the port of Canton, and it was not a British custom to hoist the national flag in port. Nevertheless, Captain Kennedy claimed that Britain's Red Ensign was indeed aloft. To the consul, Kennedy admitted in a deposition that at the time of the arrest he was not on board. He was having breakfast on another ship with two other captains of convenience. From there, Kennedy said, he could see the flag being hauled down. It was in Kennedy's interest to say that. It pleased the consul, whose war mongering agenda will become evident, and the resulting uproar diverted attention from the activities of the *Arrow*, which, at the least, was known to have received stolen goods.

Sir Harry Smith Parkes

According to a local newspaper, the crew of a Portuguese ship near the *Arrow* said that they watched the arrest but saw no flag. The *Arrow* actually had no right to a British flag since its registration had expired, but Parkes did not tell the Chinese about that.[1]

In response to Parkes's demand, Imperial Commissioner Yeh Mingchen returned the arrested sailors, but the British consul refused to accept them since they were not returned with a public ceremony, which would cause Yeh to lose face. Parkes repeatedly lied to the commissioner asserting that Captain Kennedy was on board the *Arrow* when the flag was taken down. Parkes made a series of demands including financial compensation to the *Arrow* and a public humiliation of the Chinese arresting officer. The consul, from the beginning of his communications with the Chinese, threatened war. He wrote to his superior, Sir John Bowring, governor of Hong Kong, that the *Arrow* was boarded "while lying with her colors flying." He declared that "an insult so publicly committed must be equally publicly atoned."

War Mongering

In short, this young diplomat, though only an acting consul, worked hard at war mongering. Emphasizing the outrage of an insult to the flag, he persuaded Bowring and Admiral Sir Michael Seymour, commander of the British navy's China Station, to seize in retaliation a Chinese ship. Nobody told Admiral Seymour that *Arrow's* registration had expired. A Chinese ship was seized, but this had no effect on Commissioner Yeh's intractable position. Unable to get any action from the Canton area's British naval commander, Parkes went to Hong Kong to see again Bowring and Seymour. Bowring reported to the Foreign Office that he and Parkes met on the day of Parkes' arrival, October 20. In fact, Bowring and Parkes got together the day before, presumably to decide on how to deal with the admiral, who was not so eager as they for war. In American bureaucratic language, this is called "getting your ducks in a row." J. Y. Wong has documented the Hong Kong proceedings and other such machinations in his book *Deadly Dreams*, a detailed account of the Second Opium War published in 1998 by Cambridge University Press.

Whatever sales talk Bowring and Parkes planned, it worked. They persuaded Seymour to bombard the Chinese forts guarding Canton and also Commissioner Yeh's official residence. These acts of war necessarily would involve civilian casualties. The forts were surrounded by houses, and Yeh's residence was in the densely populated, walled city of Canton. The admiral and his ships went into action. Said one American commentator, "The brave officer, having lost an eye . . . in the Crimean War could see only one way to negotiate."

Commissioner Yeh Mingchen

There are two possible explanations for Parkes's war mongering. The first is simple. When Parkes went to see the arrested sailors, his visit was refused, and, as he claimed, one of the Chinese struck him.

The second explanation pertains to Parkes's having had a meeting in London, the previous March, with the aggressive Lord Palmerston, who recently had become Prime Minister. Parkes was scheduled to return to Canton, where he had worked at the consulate. Upon his return he was to be acting consul, and in preparation for that he was given a special meeting. Although only about twenty-seven years old, Parkes was a person of long experience in China, having lived there since he was thirteen, and he was known to the government as favoring a tough policy. He had served as an interpreter in the negotiations at the end of the First Opium War. After that Parkes helped to arrange a treaty with

Siam, and he personally presented it to the Queen. We do not know what exactly Palmerston said to the young man, but Parkes's official biographer, Stanley Lane-Pool, commented, "During that interview, Lord Palmerston played the part of Hephaistos to the consular Achilles."[2] In Greek mythology, Hephaistos was the god of fire who made armor for the warrior Achilles. So Harry Parkes returned to Canton armored by a confidential relationship with the Prime Minister. In his meetings with Admiral Seymour, did Parkes claim to represent the plans of Lord Palmerston? To persuade the admiral to commence a war, Bowring and Parkes must have made reference to some kind of authority from London.

The Master Plan

As Parkes and Bowring presumably knew, Palmerston did have some plans in mind. For several months prior to the *Arrow* incident, officials in London were scheming to open up all of China to trade, to legalize opium in China, to establish an envoy in Beijing, and to acquire other new advantages. Strongly supporting these plans was Governor Bowring, who urged action in a dispatch of July, 1856. The Foreign Office also decided to approach France and the United States and suggest joint military operations. For Britain the timing of a new war was convenient since the Crimean War had come to an end. As a correspondent for the *New York Tribune*, Karl Marx commented on Palmerston's character:

> Endowed with a restless and indefatigable spirit, he abhors inactivity and pines for agitation, if not for action. A country like England allows him, of course, to busy himself in every corner of the earth.

The Prime Minister might have been pleased to learn that his acting consul had managed to start an undeclared war, but the Parliament was not. Bowring told the Foreign Office how he had fooled the Chinese about the *Arrow's* registration, and this became public. It also came out that Admiral Seymour had been kept in the dark about that. Controversy ensued, and Palmerston argued that it was not wise to second guess the actions of subordinates. Attempting to minimize the situation, Palmerston refused to call the war a war because it had not been declared by the Parliament. (We must be reminded of President Harry S.

Truman's undeclared war in Korea, which he called a "police action.") In the Prime Minister's heated rhetoric, the Chinese were demons and the British were upholding civilization.

A different opinion was held by Lord Elgin, who in 1857 was appointed High Commissioner to China. Elgin wrote to his wife, "[The *Arrow*] is a scandal to us and is so considered . . . by all except the few who are personally compromised." William Gladstone and others in the Parliament condemned the government's actions in China as illegal and immoral. Lord Malmesbury characterized Parkes' behavior as "grotesque." The British government changed the primary focus of its complaint from the *Arrow* incident to Yeh's refusal to let its citizens enter the city of Canton, as had been provided by treaty. A flimsy complaint was replaced by one not much better since the English version of the treaty was different from the Chinese version.

Parliament passed a resolution of censure. Then the august body was dissolved, and Palmerston being wildly popular, an election returned the same government. Controversy on policies in the East continued. Another dissolution of the Parliament brought in another a new government, which also pursued the war. Later, Palmerston was brought back in time to finish the conflict and force concessions. The people of Great Britain wanted their tea and their empire.

Neutrality Compromised

Not too concerned about collateral damage, Admiral Seymour, when he bombarded Canton, included the use of Congreve rockets to spread fire. (The Congreve rocket, whose red glare was made famous by the War of 1812, was invented in India, where a rocket attack by Indians on British soldiers almost killed Colonel Arthur Wellesley, the future Duke of Wellington.) When Seymour's armed bluejackets streamed through Canton's broken wall, they were accompanied by a number of American sailors and also an American consul, who had with him a marine or sailor bearing the American flag. The consul was James Keenan, who had come to Canton from Hong Kong, his place of assignment.[3] He and his companion placed the flag on top of Yeh's house, and, according to an official report, Keenan discharged a revolver at a Chinese person.[4] Of the foreign invaders, Keenan, a veteran of the Mexican-American War, went the farthest into the city and stayed the longest. Somebody said he was "visibly intoxicated."

Very different from Keenan was the U.S. consul assigned to Canton. He, Oliver H. Perry II, had some sympathy for the Chinese. This Perry was the son of Commodore Matthew Perry, who earlier had opened Japan to American trade, and the nephew of Commodore Oliver H. Perry, victor in the Battle of Lake Erie.

Disturbed by the Navy's violation of neutrality was U.S. Navy Commodore James Armstrong. He announced American neutrality and ordered all American naval personnel back to their ships. These men had been dispatched by Commander Andrew Foote in response to a request from the chief American emissary in Canton, Commissioner Peter Parker. Parker, not having ordered an evacuation, wanted protection for American nationals in the area. Unfortunately, as Foote was returning to his ship from a conference, his boat was fired upon by the Chinese forts. The forts had been captured by the British and then abandoned.

Admiral Andrew Foote

Armstrong and Foote interpreted the firing as an insult, but considering the bravado of Consul Keenan, the Chinese action ought not to have been surprising. Foote, leading 300 sailors and marines, retaliated by attacking and capturing four forts. Methodically, the commodore used the guns of the first fort to attack the second fort, the guns of the second fort to attack the third fort, and the guns of the third fort to attack the fourth. In all 176 guns were taken and spiked.[5] Chinese killed in action were 160. Reportedly, the Americans also had to fight off 3,000 Chinese soldiers arriving at the scene. The British were impressed. But the American officer could have made his point in a more restrained manner.

One British observer decided the Chinese soldiers had great potential given better leadership, and he recommended hiring them as mercenaries.

Commissioner Parker was pleased by Commander Foote's action. He reported to Washington:

> This is the first blow that has ever been struck by our navy in China, and it has been done in a manner calculated to secure for it an important prestige in the mind of this haughty government.[6]

The details of the above actions vary a little from book to book. What is important is that American officials, both civilian and military, failed to preserve American neutrality in the Second Opium War. This embarrassing fact has been covered up. Concerning Commander Foote, the former Assistant Secretary of State James Grafton Rogers tells us that Foote "destroyed four Chinese forts during a period of melee between the Chinese and British." Rogers says nothing about a war, opium, Commissioner Parker, or Consul Keenan. Neither are those two men mentioned in a bowdlerized State Department booklet, *Right to protect citizens in foreign countries by landing forces*, published in 1912. Commissioner Parker does appear in *History of the U.S. Navy* by Robert W. Love, Jr., a teacher of naval history at the United States Naval Academy.[7]

Concerning the above events, Dudley W. Knox's *A History of the U.S. Navy* has a chapter titled unabashedly, "Supporting a Buoyant Foreign Trade," and this gives a similarly sanitized account of Commander Foote's derring-do. Knox concludes with evident satisfaction:

> The security of a valuable American trade with China was much enhanced by these operations, in which Foote had

displayed the dash and courage which was to make him more
famous during the Civil War in America.[8]

Knox's book came out in 1936. Even eighty years after the event, he
would not mention opium or acknowledge that it was wrong for the
U.S. Navy to jump into the Second Opium War without authorization
and on the side of the opium dealers.

Secretary of State Disapproves

Secretary of State William Marcy disapproved of what the Navy had
done, and he ordered an inquiry into Consul Keenan's use of the flag.
Charges were brought against the errant consul, but friends successfully
lobbied the White House for him, doing so as late as the Lincoln
Administration. Keenan, who owned a newspaper in Pennsylvania,
remained in Hong Kong until 1862 and died of an illness upon his return
to the United States. He was 38.

Commissioner Parker, an old China hand (former medical missionary),
was thick with the British old China hands, and he recommended to
Marcy that the United States join Britain in the war. As the American
contribution, Parker suggested, we could occupy Taiwan. Marcy
instructed him that the Executive Branch was not in the business of
making war. That, he said, was the responsibility of Congress. (This was
the same William Marcy who, as secretary of war, had ordered General
Zachary Taylor's "army of observation" to Mexico.) To their credit, Marcy
and President Franklin Pierce set to persuading President-elect James
Buchanan to resist British lobbying and stay out of the Opium War.

In response to British attacks, the Chinese destroyed some factories
and massacred passengers on the steam ferry *Thistle*. In Hong Kong
somebody put arsenic in bakers' bread in an attempt to kill foreigners.
There was too much arsenic for the purpose and the foreigners vomited
it up. The arsenic might have contributed to the later death of Governor
Bowring's wife.

Late in 1857, France joined in the Second Opium War. This followed the
execution of a French missionary priest. He preached in an unauthorized

area, and he was accused of aiding a rebellion. At this time missionary activities were allowed only at the treaty ports.

More joint Anglo-American actions were to come. In 1858 a British naval force bombarded forts guarding the mouth of the Peiho river, which leads to Beijing, and helping with that was the American East India Squadron commanded by the jut-jawed Commodore Josiah Tattnall in the USS *Mississippi*, a steam-driven paddle frigate. In the following year, Tattnall's squadron again provided important assistance in that area, even helping to land British troops that attacked the forts. Incidentally, in 1859 an American launch went to pick up British wounded from the gunboat HMS *Plover*, and while on *Plover*, the Americans helped the short-handed British to operate their bow gun. This has been described as the first instance in which American and British sailors fought shoulder to shoulder.

Commodore Tattnall later justified the de facto Anglo-American alliance by saying, "Blood is thicker than water." The secretary of the navy, Isaac Toucey, gave his "approbation." Presumably with the same philosophy in mind, Tattnall in 1861 joined the Confederate navy, even though he opposed secession. A British newspaper reporter found him in Savannah, Georgia, where the Confederate captain despaired of acquiring a fleet to command.

The Coolie Industry

In 1859, Tattnall's *Mississippi* landed a portion of her crew at Shanghai at the request of the U.S. consul, according to the State Department's list of military actions in foreign countries. Disorder had arisen because a French merchant ship was accused of kidnapping Chinese laborers ("coolies"). Several foreigners were attacked and one killed. James Grafton Rogers tells us that the *Mississippi* also "demonstrated," which presumably means it fired guns. Shanghai, Amoy, and Macau were notorious for shipping Chinese men and women to other countries as slaves. From this "coolie trade" the English language acquired the term "to shanghai" meaning to abduct. Probably Commodore Tattnall's peacekeeping abetted the trade.

Many thousands of Chinese were sent to the Americas, Australia, and elsewhere. Some were kidnapped. Others went voluntarily having signed contracts possibly based on misleading terms. Chinese did mining in Peru, and they helped to build the transcontinental railroad in the United States. Chinese were prized as the hardest working laborers. Recently my computer was repaired by a cheerful, rather Asian-looking young man who had immigrated from Peru; his father was retired from having been employed at the Peruvian embassy in Washington. Asked whether he was a U.S. citizen, the young repairman said, "Oh, yes!"

In 1860, Consul Perry reported that Chinese authorities in Canton had stopped three American ships about to leave the port with cargoes of coolies. The local authorities were operating under the direction of Harry Parkes, who had become the military governor of Canton. Commissioner Yeh Mingchen had been taken as a prisoner to Calcutta. When captured, he was asked the fate of some missing foreigners and responded with a long, mirthless cackle as if recalling what had happened to them. He then offered to show where the bodies were buried. In Calcutta, Yeh died because he would not eat the local food. That gave him a seventh "not." The Chinese like to number things, and in Canton Yeh was famous for the "six nots": he would not fight, not make peace, not defend, not die, not capitulate, and not run away. In Calcutta, he would not eat. What is important is that Yeh tried hard to keep opium out of China.

War Ends

The Second Opium War ended in 1860 after an Anglo-French force routed the Emperor's army and burned his summer palace. The palace was burned in retaliation for a Chinese general's having failed to respect a flag of truce. He tortured to death some members of a diplomatic entourage headed by the ubiquitous Harry Parkes. For years the Chinese had blamed Parkes for their troubles and, having this opportunity, they tortured him. Luckily for Parkes, he was released just before a message arrived from the Emperor ordering his execution. His execution, like the others, probably would have been done by a "thousand cuts." In that procedure, tourniquets were applied to keep the victim alive, and the corpse was barely recognizable.

In the agreements ending the war, the opium trade was legalized, indentured Chinese could be carried abroad, more ports were opened up, the Yangtze river was opened to traffic, foreigners (including missionaries) were given freedom of movement in the interior, Bejing accepted foreign legations, and the British added the peninsula of Kowloon to their Hong Kong territories. As an indemnity for opium destroyed and other damages, the Chinese had to fork over twenty-one million silver dollars. Palmerston and Parkes had opened up China to a big increase in trade. It was not all opium and slaves. In other commerce, the textile industry benefited the most.

One of the mandarins wrote to the Emperor:

> The English barbarians . . . are full of insidious schemes,
> uncontrollably fierce and imperious. The American nation
> does no more than follow in their direction.[9]

America's nineteenth century indiscretions have not been forgotten. In 1965, China's Prime Minister Chou Enlai said that, because of the nineteenth century opium wars, the Chinese were making sure that American soldiers in Vietnam received the very best grades of narcotic drugs; the Chinese plan was to demoralize the American army. The Chinese think long term. A Japanese expert on Chinese history once told me that, in olden times, the Chinese when building a bridge customarily used stone.

Analysis

Aggressive actions by British officials in Canton and Hong Kong started an undeclared war, and the British Parliament could do nothing about it. Prime Minister Palmerston, who had managed the First Opium War, wanted to expand trade, and he was successful in that. In his school days, Palmerston was known as a tough kid. In Parliament Palmerston distinguished himself by defending the unprovoked 1807 British bombardment of Copenhagen, which destroyed 30 percent of the city. Purpose of the bombardment was to force the Danes, who were causing no harm to the British, to surrender their fleet. The British wanted the ships on the ground that, otherwise, they might be seized by Napoleon.

The bombardment achieved its aim, and Palmerston was appointed secretary at war.

Commissioner Parker, who like the British believed in harsh measures against the Chinese, was reluctant to order the evacuation of American nationals and requested naval protection instead. Neither he nor Consul Keenan was careful to preserve American neutrality. Careless too was the secretary of state, William Marcy. Instead of just ordering an investigation of Keenan, Marcy ought to have recalled the consul immediately and made sure that everybody, including the U.S. Navy, understood that the United States was neutral. Our subsequent relations with China probably would have been much better if we had not gone to war with them.

Full of enterprising personnel and animal spirits, the U.S. Navy failed to maintain American neutrality. Infected with that spirit, and perhaps other spirits, was the U.S. consul in Hong Kong.

An Avoidable War?

American participation was unnecessary, avoidable, and pernicious. It was a rogue war initiated by subordinate personnel

Useful Principles

Stay away from other nations' wars.

Watch out for adventurism, both military and civilian, and its entangling tendencies.

Among foreign nations, make friends not enemies.

Punish those involved with rogue wars

References

[1] J. Y. Wong, *Deadly Dreams*, page 4

[2] J.Y. Wong, *Deadly Dreams*, page 82

[3] J. Y. Wong, *Deadly Dreams*, pages 6-7

[4] Te-kong Tong, *United States Diplomacy in China 1844-60*, pages 186-187

[5] Dudley W. Knox, *A History of the United States Navy*, pages 186-187

[6] Te-tong Tong, *United States Diplomacy in China 1844-60*, page 187

[7] James G. Rogers, *World Policing and the Constitution*, page 102

[8] Dudley W. Knox, *A History of the United States Navy*, page 187

[9] Alexander DeConde, *A History of American Foreign Policy*, page 231

CHAPTER EIGHT

Civil War (1861 to 1865)

Lieutenant, what shall we do?—President James Buchanan, 1861

What was our greatest national catastrophe, the Civil War, all about? The most common answer is slavery, but the leaders on both sides said that the war was *not* about slavery. President Abraham Lincoln said he had no wish to interfere with slavery. To him, secession was illegal, and secession was the chief issue. Lincoln expanded on that in a letter of August 22, 1862, which he sent to Horace Greeley, editor of the *New York Tribune*:

> My paramount object in this struggle is to save the Union, and is not either to save or to destroy slavery. If I could save the Union without freeing any slave I would do it, and if I could save it by freeing all the slaves I would do it; and if I could save it by freeing some and leaving others alone I would also do that.

Confederate President Jefferson Davis in his book *The Rise and Fall of the Confederate Government,* said slavery was the *occasion* but not the *cause* of the war. To Davis the major issues were states rights and a "systematic and persistent struggle to deprive the Southern states of equality in the Union." The slave and non-slave states, having different interests, competed for influence in all the branches of government, and the Southern states foresaw an inevitable diminishment of their power because of rapid industrialization in the North, homesteading in the West, the proposed transcontinental railroad, and the election of Abraham Lincoln. Lincoln was known to despise slavery, and the Southerners were convinced that he intended to abolish it, however much he denied that.

Whatever the exact causes of the war, it is clear that slavery was a motivating factor on both sides. A South Carolina diarist, Mrs. Mary Boykin Chesnut, capsulized the Southern position in her book *A Diary from Dixie*:

> We want to separate from them; to be rid of the Yankees forever . . . We are an unwilling bride. I think incompatibility of temper began when it was made plain to us that we got all the opprobrium of slavery and they all the money there was in it with their tariff.

Concerning the Southern cause, Mrs. Chesnut was in a position to be well informed. In 1860, her husband, James Chesnut, was the first secessionist to resign from the U.S. Senate. On April 12, 1861, Colonel James Chesnut began the Civil War by ordering South Carolina's Provisional Army to fire on Fort Sumter, a federal fort located in Charleston harbor.

Mary and James Chesnut

Secessionism

Each house of Congress appointed a committee to study the secession problem. Neither committee could decide on what to do.

As we have seen, the issue of secession had come up before, during the War of 1812, when the New England states were forced into a war with Great Britain by expansion-minded citizens in the South and West. The secretive Hartford Convention and its implicit threat of secession continued until 1815 when the war ended. The convention did not recommend secession, but it decided that *secession could be justified.* Said the New Englanders in their report:

> Whenever it shall appear that the causes are radical and permanent, a separation by equitable arrangement will be preferable to an alliance by constraint among nominal friends, but real enemies.

Consequently, the Southerners thought that the Yankees were being hypocritical in opposing Southern secession.

Other secessions: We have discussed how Texas seceded from Mexico, which refused to recognize Texas's independence, and how war followed (actually two wars). After the outbreak of the American Civil War, West Virginia seceded, successfully, from Virginia. The western Virginia counties, whose economy primarily was based on logging and mining, for long had had priorities different from those of the eastern counties, which were slave holding and agricultural. Today we have several states where people in conservative or liberal counties, feeling oppressed by their political opposites elsewhere in the state, are attempting to secede. In eleven rural counties of Colorado, for example, there is agitation to escape the dominance of urban Colorado.

Slave Empire Envisaged

Slavery was the most important issue in the presidential election of 1860, and the winner, Lincoln, was the candidate with strong anti-slavery views. Although Lincoln promised not to interfere with slavery in the South, in the past his speeches had stigmatized slavery, and he opposed its extension to new states forming in the western territories, most of which were a legacy—and a punishment, some said—from the war with Mexico. The Southerners wanted more slave states. They needed additional votes in Congress in order to maintain their political power as the free states increased in number and population. The plantation owners also wanted more land to provide work for their slaves, whose numbers were growing.

In order to forestall a split in the Union, the U.S. Congress debated several concessions to the South in legislation proposed by Senator John C. Crittenden of Kentucky, and all of the concessions were related to slavery. One of them would have prohibited Congress from interfering with the interstate slave trade. Crittenden's proposal was endorsed by thousands of people signing petitions, and *Tribune* editor Greeley believed that a large majority of the public favored it. The "Crittenden Compromise" was killed by the Republicans. It was the opinion of President-elect Lincoln that the South would never be satisfied until Northerners stopped criticizing their peculiar institution. A minority of Southerners owned slaves, but all were tarred by the criticisms of it. In the past, Lincoln said, making concessions to the South always led to more demands. He gave this example of what the future might hold:

> A year will not pass till we shall have to take Cuba as a condition upon which they will stay in the Union.

Could that have been true? Believing that slavery must expand or die, "Southern nationalists" wanted to annex the remainder of Mexico, the Spanish colony of Cuba, and the whole of Central America. They hoped to build a vast slave empire. An opportunity for acquiring Cuba had arisen in 1854, when Spanish authorities seized an American cargo ship in Havana harbor. Some Americans demanded war, and among them was Jefferson Davis, who was secretary of war at the time. Southern nationalists wanted to hurry up and annex the Spanish colony before it abolished slavery, as Mexico had done. President Franklin Pierce decided to attempt an annexation. The Administration secretly prepared a treaty for the purchase of the island, and Pierce contemplated using force if need be. In addition to expanding slave territory, another motive was to keep France or Britain from acquiring Cuba. However, the scheme leaked to the press, it was denounced as a plot of Southern slaveholders, and the unfavorable publicity caused it to be shelved.

"One South is enough," said the abolitionist Carl Schurz.

"Doughface" Buchanan

The major author of the Cuban annexation treaty was James Buchanan, whom we encountered earlier as President Polk's secretary of state. When involved with the Cuban annexation fiasco, Buchanan was President Pierce's envoy to Great Britain. Although a Pennsylvanian, Buchanan, like the New Hampshire man Pierce, tended to favor Southern interests, and that sort of Yankee was called a "'doughface," a term indicating malleability. Biographer Elbert Smith remarks in *The Presidency of James Buchanan* that the Cuban project "displayed his [Buchanan's] affinity for Southern interests." Another example was Buchanan's support of the Supreme Court's Dred Scott decision, which held that slaves were property, not citizens, and had no rights. As a result, when a slave traveled north with his master, he remained a slave. In 1860, the Southern-sympathizing Buchanan was the incumbent President as the secession movement grew in power and passion.

Southerners disliked Lincoln also because, as a Republican, he supported import tariffs, which made manufactured goods more expensive. As Mrs. Chesnut complained, this helped the industrial North at the expense of the agricultural South. The Republican platform of 1860 aggravated the North-South conflict by calling for high, protective tariffs.

President Abraham Lincoln

Abraham Lincoln, a little known Republican from Illinois, was elected President because a split occurred within the Democratic Party. The Democratic convention nominated Stephen A. Douglas, who wanted each new state to decide for itself whether to permit slavery. (Douglas, although a Northerner, owned through his wife a plantation with slaves, and he favored annexing Cuba.) Militantly pro-slavery delegates, known as the Fire Eaters, wanted a candidate unambiguously pro-slavery. They held a "rump convention" and nominated Kentucky's John C. Breckinridge, the current vice president. The nominee was pessimistic about his chances for election. He wrote to a friend, "I trust I have the courage to lead a forlorn hope." Breckinridge came in third with the popular vote and second with the electoral vote

Lincoln's Election a Southern Plot?

Critics of the Fire Eaters alleged that they deliberately split the Democratic party in order to elect Lincoln President and, in that way, spur the secession movement. (See James McPherson's *Battle Cry of Freedom*, page 213ff.)

Between President Lincoln's election in November, 1860, and his inauguration in March, 1861, seven states left the Union, led by South Carolina. The South Carolinians joyfully celebrated their independence with fireworks, martial music, and the firing of weapons. Independence was important to them in part because the slave population in their state outnumbered the white by four to three. The idea of one man one vote was not welcome in South Carolina.

The newly formed Confederacy adopted a low tariff policy, and this disturbed Northern financial interests, who feared losing their Southern customers to more cheaply priced European manufactures. Besides that, the Confederacy might put import tariffs on Northern goods. Seven Southern states having left the Union, the U.S. Congress had plenty of pro-tariff votes, and it legislated on March 2, 1861, the highest tariff in the nation's history. The importance of the tariff issue has been emphasized by Charles Adams, an historian of taxation, in his book *When in the Course of Human Events*. Said Adams:

Before the "war of the tariffs" in March 1861, the merchants, bankers, brokers, and investors in the North were all in favor of appeasing the South and allowing it to keep its "peculiar institution." Let the South have its way over slavery, if that is necessary to preserve the Union. But once it became clear, mid-March, that a low tariff was in place at Southern ports to challenge Northern commerce and even undermine Northern business and trade, the policy of "preserving the Union" then shifted from appeasing the slave owners to going to war.[1]

If the business community in New York decided for war in March, the transformation must have been a swift one. On March 16 a British journalist, William Russell of the London *Times*, arrived in New York, met with many prominent men, including bankers, and found all of them to be Democrats contemptuous of Lincoln the "rail-splitter" and sympathetic to the South. Russell was "astonished" by how calmly they viewed the "impending troubles." In his book *My Diary North and South*, Russell quoted one of the Democrats:

> The majority of the people of New York, and all the respectable people, were disgusted at the election of such a fellow as Lincoln to be President, and would back the Southern states, if it came to a split.[2]

Russell did note concern that if the Southerners seceded, they might not pay back the debts owed up North. The debts were estimated at $150 million.

Whatever was the importance of the financial issue in the North, it was very important in the South, with its debts to the North and its hope of paying less for imported goods.

Inaugural Address

On March 4, Lincoln in his inaugural address set out his policies. He assured the South that he had no intention of interfering with the institution of slavery "where it exists." He acknowledged that there was disagreement as to whether slavery should be extended to the western territories. Following are Lincoln's words; the italics are his:

> One section of our country believes slavery is *right*, and ought to be extended, while the other believes that it is *wrong*, and ought not to be extended.

The new President held that secession was illegal:

> . . . no state, upon its own mere motion, can lawfully get out of the Union . . . *resolves* and *ordinances* to that effect are legally void, and . . . acts of violence, within any State or States, against the authority of the United States, are insurrectionary or revolutionary, according to circumstances.

Lincoln recognized the right to change the Union by amending the Constitution or by rebellion:

> This country, with its institutions, belongs to the people who inhabit it. Whenever they shall grow weary of the existing Government, they can exercise their *constitutional* right of amending it, or their *revolutionary* right to dismember or overthrow it.

Military Deaths: 625,000

In the Civil War, military fatalities totaled at least 625,000, counting both Union and Confederate losses, although the American population in 1860 was less than 32 million. If in 1860 the American people had known that such a cataclysm lay ahead, they might have preferred to amend the Constitution. Among the Northerners who favored a split was Horace Greeley, who said, "If the cotton states shall decide they can do better out of the Union than in it, we insist on letting them go in peace." The journalist William Russell in conversation with Lincoln's secretary of the treasury, Salmon P. Chase, received the distinct impression that he did not oppose secession. Neither did General Winfield Scott, of Mexican-American War fame, who now was general-in-chief of the U.S. Army.

"Say to the seceded States--Wayward Sisters, depart in Peace!" Scott recommended to Secretary of State William Seward in a letter of March 3, 1861.

Abolitionist William Loyd Garrison was glad to see the "sinful" South depart.

Most Northerners did not believe war would come or, if it did, that it would be a long war. The diarist Henry Adams went so far as to say, "Not one man in America wanted the civil war or expected or intended it." That was not true in the deep South. There many assumed that the election of Lincoln inevitably meant war. In South Carolina Mrs. Chesnut observed,

> Nobody at the North, or in Virginia, believes we are in earnest. They think we are sulking and that Jeff Davis and Stephens [Alexander Stephens, vice president of the Confederacy] are getting up a very pretty little comedy.

Lincoln's Big Mistake

Like Henry Adams, President Lincoln misunderstood the situation. He believed, and said in his speeches, that the secession crisis was an "artificial" one designed by politicians. On the way to Washington, he said in Pittsburgh on February 15, 1861:

> Notwithstanding the troubles across the river, [the speaker pointing southwardly, and smiling] there is really no crisis, springing from anything in the government itself. In plain words, there is really no crisis except an *artificial one*! What is there now to warrant the condition of affairs presented by our friends "over the river?" Take even their own view of the questions involved, and there is nothing to justify the course which they are pursuing. I repeat it, then—*there is no crisis*, excepting such a one as may be gotten up at any time by designing politicians. My advice, then, under such circumstances, is to keep cool. If the great American people will only keep their temper, on both sides of the line, the troubles will come to an end, and the question which now distracts the country will be settled just as surely as all other

difficulties of like character which have originated in this government have been adjusted. Let the people on both sides keep their self-possession, and just as other clouds have cleared away in due time, so will this, and this great nation shall continue to prosper as heretofore. But, fellow citizens, I have spoken longer on this subject than I had intended in the outset—and I shall say no more at present.

Crisis "Invented"

According to Lincoln scholar Ronald Rietveld at California State University (Fullerton Lecture, April 14, 2011), Lincoln thought an "artificial" crisis was invented to intimidate the North into granting Southern demands:

> During those months of crisis, President-elect Lincoln overestimated the strength of Unionism in the seceded and non-seceded slave states and underestimated the willingness of the deep South to go to war . . . It was believed that the threats of secession were a ploy to intimidate the North into granting southern demands . . . Lincoln called the crisis artificial, and, left alone, it would dissipate by itself. Convinced that secession was a rebellion of individuals, not states, he insisted that the Union remain intact, and the states retained all their constitutional rights.

There were in fact Unionists in the South, but they were threatened and intimidated. The prominent minister Henry Ward Beecher told of how he met on a train a western Virginia farmer who, fearing for his safety, was taking a circuitous route home after voting against secession in Richmond.

In his inaugural address, Lincoln promised that there would be no violence or bloodshed unless it was forced upon the Union. But he also promised that he would hold on to the southern properties belonging to the federal government and collect taxes:

> . . . there needs to be no bloodshed or violence; and there shall be none, unless it be forced upon the national authority. The power confided to me will be used to hold, occupy, and possess

the property and places belonging to the government, and to collect the duties and imposts; but beyond what may be necessary for these objects, there will be no invasion—no using of force against or among the people anywhere.

No doubt many a Southerner thought that the Union demanding payment of its big, new tariffs would be an occasion for bloodshed.

Rebels Acquire Arms

In the last months of President Buchanan's Administration, the seceding states began taking over, without firing a shot, the federal military facilities in the South. They were helped by secret secessionists within the government. Buchanan was immobilized. As an attorney, it was his opinion that secession was illegal, but in his opinion stopping it also was illegal. In Texas, General David Twiggs handed over every one of his bases to the seceded state. Twiggs was dismissed from the U.S. Army for traitorous conduct. He then joined the Confederate Army as a major general. Buchanan's secretary of war, John B. Floyd, was a secret secessionist. He transferred weapons and property to the rebels and impeded the strengthening of federal forts. A secret transfer of 10,000 muskets was handled by a New York bank. Buchanan stopped Floyd when he tried to ship south 124 cannon. Public fury moved the lethargic President. The cannon were to be shipped from Pittsburgh, and Floyd's plan got into the press. Said the *Pittsburgh Gazette* of December 25, 1860:

The people could hardly believe so astounding a story at first; but every inquiry only confirmed the report. There is no doubt of its truth. There is the utmost activity in the Arsenal, and the steamboat, the "Silver Wave," has been chartered to convey the guns to their Southern destination.

We hear also that large quantities of the small arms at the Arsenal have been shipped South, lately, by railroad.

General Scott had wanted to prevent "acts of rashness" by putting an adequate garrison into each Southern fort and arsenal in order to prevent a "disruption of the Union." Beginning on October 29 of 1860, Scott repeatedly urged such action, but he was stymied by the fecklessness of Buchanan and the ulterior motives of Floyd, the secessionist running the War Department.

President James Buchanan

Later, it was alleged that Secretary Floyd had dispersed the Army out West so that few soldiers would be available to garrison the forts or to protect the capital when secession occurred. In fact, most of the Army *was* dispersed out West, and for adequate protection of the capital, President Lincoln anxiously waited almost two months for an adequate number of volunteers. On April 22, 1861, General Scott still worried that Washington was in "danger of being attacked on all sides." Five days later enough men finally arrived.

Secession Planned in 1855

The Buchanan Administration dispersed the Navy to the far corners of the earth, and it allowed money to be drained from the U.S. Treasury for the Southern cause. There is evidence that contingency planning for the secession had been going on for a long time. The Navy's ships were designed so as to require deeper water than existing in Southern harbors. Following is a quotation from *The Naval History of the Civil War* written by Admiral David D. Porter, who played an important role in the conflict:

the writer [Porter] was told by a Southern Senator in 1860, that, as far back as 1855, when the *"Colorado"* class of ships were built, he and others had voted to have them and all other vessels constructed of such a size and such a draft of water, that they could not enter any Southern ports; so it seems that the thought of secession had been maturing for years, and while Southern statesmen were apparently urging the building of large vessels instead of small ones, on the ground that the dignity of the Nation called for these cumbersome structures, it was really for the purpose of crippling the Government in case the Southern States should secede. In this they succeeded admirably, so much so, in fact, that these large ships were of little use in the beginning of the war, as they could enter no Southern ports, and their guns, without so doing, could not reach the opposing forts.

Having built warships too heavy to enter Southern harbors was an important factor in the Battle of Fort Sumter. It was Porter's opinion that if the Navy had had thirty shallow draft gunboats, the "rebellion would have been unable to raise its head."[3]

By the time Lincoln took office, the Confederates had seized almost all of the federal facilities in the South and had strengthened their positions. Some federally commanded forts remained in Charleston, South Carolina, and Pensacola, Florida. (Two forts on the Virginia coast remained in Union hands throughout the war.) Lincoln's attempt to retain federal properties in the South almost inevitably would lead to the outbreak of war.

Charleston was a major seaport in whose harbor might be seen dozens of ships at a time, and according to a long-established plan, the city was to be protected by four forts. They were Fort Sumter, Fort Johnson, Fort Moultrie, and one called Castle Pinckney. We are fortunate that the U.S. Army stationed at Fort Moultrie Abner Doubleday, whom we met earlier in the First Mexican-American War. He now was a captain and second in command at Fort Moultrie. After the Civil War, Doubleday wrote a book titled *Reminiscences of Forts Sumter and Moultrie*, which provides valuable information about how the war began. It reports that Secretary Floyd refused to strengthen the Union-held forts in Charleston while he sent weapons elsewhere in the South for the use of secessionists.

The Center of Secession

According to Doubleday, already in the summer of 1860, months before the presidential election, the prospect of Lincoln as President caused tension in Charleston:

> Charleston, at this period, was far from being a pleasant place for a loyal man. Almost every public assemblage was tinctured with treasonable sentiments, and toasts against the flag were always warmly applauded. As early as July there was much talk of secession, accompanied with constant drilling, and threats of taking the forts as soon as a separation should occur.

> To the South Carolinians Fort Moultrie was almost a sacred spot, endeared by many precious historical associations; for the ancestors of most of the principal families had fought there in the Revolutionary War behind their hastily improvised ramparts of palmetto logs, and had gained a glorious victory over the British fleet in its first attempt to enter the harbor and capture the city.

After the November election anti-Union sentiment was even greater, and the Charleston forts, despite requests, lacked the manpower and arms needed to defend themselves. Holding President Buchanan responsible for that, Secretary of State Lewis Cass resigned in protest, and in some cities the President was burned in effigy. Secretary Floyd had even forbidden the Charleston forts' commanding officer, Lieutenant Colonel John L. Gardner, from taking arms from the U.S. Arsenal in Charleston. When Gardner requested more men, the war secretary sent a new commanding officer.

The new commander was Major Robert Anderson, a Kentuckian whose wife's family owned slaves. The major had a reserved personality, a medium build, and fine, aristocratic features. He came from a distinguished, patriotic lineage, and going by his mother's genealogical records, he happened to be the great-grandfather of moving picture actor Montgomery Clift. Older readers might find this amusing since Clift in movie roles portrayed soldiers at war with their own side as well as with the enemy's—just like Major Anderson at Fort Sumter.

Key Men Born in Kentucky

For whatever this might signify, Robert Anderson was one of many Kentucky-born men who played key roles in the onset of the Civil War. Among them we have mentioned so far Vice President Breckinridge, Senator Crittenden, Abraham Lincoln, and Jefferson Davis. Another was Orville H. Browning, an unofficial but important Lincoln adviser to be discussed later. Besides having been born in Kentucky, all of the foregoing men had in common their participation in the Black Hawk War with Native Americans. As a colonel of Illinois volunteers, Robert Anderson mustered in Abraham Lincoln and a company of volunteers, of whom Lincoln was the elected captain. When Chief Black Hawk was captured, Anderson and Davis escorted him to the proper authorities. Anderson abhorred the Black Hawk War and was depressed by the sight of Native American women and children casualties. He rescued a wounded baby from its dead mother. Lincoln did not see action, but he enjoyed the Army life and re-upped when his short enlistment expired. As a private, the lanky Illinoisan joined a reconnaissance unit known as the Spy Battalion. Anderson mustered him in again.

General Robert Anderson

Major Anderson was not against slavery, and when appointed to Sumter by Secretary Floyd, he was serving with Senator Jefferson Davis on a commission examining the curriculum at West Point. Floyd probably thought he understood the major pretty well. It must have surprised the war secretary that Anderson, going by his principles, would turn out to be loyal and not give up his command without a fight. Doubleday's memoir gives us this appraisal of his new commanding officer and the political situation in Charleston:

> On the 21st [of November] our new commander arrived and assumed command. He felt as if he had a hereditary right to be there, for his father had distinguished himself in the Revolutionary War in defense of old Fort Moultrie against the British, and had been confined a long time as a prisoner in Charleston. We had long known Anderson as a gentleman; courteous, honest, intelligent, and thoroughly versed in his profession. He had been twice brevetted for gallantry—once for services against the Seminole Indians in Florida, and once for the battle of Molino del Rey in Mexico, where he was badly wounded. In politics he was a strong pro-slavery man. Nevertheless, he was opposed to secession and Southern extremists. He soon found himself in troubled waters, for the approaching battle of Fort Moultrie was talked of everywhere throughout the State, and the mob in Charleston could hardly be restrained from making an immediate assault. They were kept back once through the exertions of Colonel Benjamin Huger, of the Ordnance Department of the United States Army. As he belonged to one of the most distinguished families in Charleston, he had great influence there. It was said at the time that he threatened if we were attacked, or rather mobbed, in this way, he would join us, and fight by the side of his friend Anderson. Colonel Memminger, afterward the Confederate Secretary of the Treasury, also exerted himself to prevent any irregular and unauthorized violence.

Buchanan Gets an Earful

Anderson's wife, Eliza (whom he called "Eba,") was a wealthy Southerner who lived in a hotel in New York City. Although a semi-invalid, she went to Washington, confronted President Buchanan, and complained that a wild mob might attack her husband any day. Buchanan later described the experience as "painful."

When fighting the Seminoles, Anderson contracted a fever that continued intermittently the rest of his life. In Mexico, he could have gotten on the staff of General Scott, who was a close friend, but he sought a combat command and performed heroically at Molino del Rey, where he was wounded three times. Anderson was not a war lover. From Mexico he wrote to his Eba, "I think that no more absurd scheme could be invented for settling national difficulties than the one we are engaged in—killing each other to find out who is in the right." Like Major Ringgold, Anderson was an expert on artillery, and he helped to write the Army's book on the subject.

Major Anderson was determined to do his duty as a Union officer, but Captain Doubleday sometimes felt that he could have tried harder. Anderson's orders were to act strictly on the defensive so as not to provoke a war. As a religious man, he took that responsibility with the utmost gravity.

Anderson Upsets Confederate Plans

On an island close to the mainland, Fort Moultrie was easily accessible from land, and a large force could take it from that direction. Rather than look forward to a hopeless battle, Anderson on December 26, the night after Christmas, surreptitiously transferred his men and some weapons from Moultrie to the more defensible Fort Sumter, which stood in the middle of the harbor. Before the move, Fort Sumter was unoccupied since interior construction was going on. Anderson kept his plan so secret that neither the War Department nor his second in command knew about it. Here is how Doubleday got the word:

> ". . . on the last evening of our stay (December 26th) I left my room to ask him [Anderson] in to take tea with us [Doubleday and his wife]. The sun was just setting as I ascended the steps leading to the parapet and approached him. He was in the midst of a group of officers, each of whom seemed silent and distrait. As I passed our assistant-surgeon, I remarked, "It is a fine evening, Crawford." He replied in a hesitating

and embarrassed manner, showing that his thoughts were elsewhere. I saw plainly that something unusual had occurred. Anderson approached me as I advanced, and said quietly, "I have determined to evacuate this post immediately, for the purpose of occupying Fort Sumter; I can only allow you twenty minutes to form your company and be in readiness to start." I was surprised at this announcement, and realized the gravity of the situation at a glance. We were watched by spies and vigilance-committees, who would undoubtedly open fire upon us as soon as they saw the object of the movement. I was naturally concerned, too, for the safety of my wife, who was the only lady in the fort at that time, and who would necessarily be exposed to considerable danger.

Doubleday rushed to get ready for the move.

I made good use of the twenty minutes allowed me. I first went to the barracks, formed my company, inspected it, and saw that each man was properly armed and equipped. This left me ten minutes to spare. I dashed over to my quarters; told my wife to get ready to leave immediately, and as the fighting would probably commence in a few minutes, I advised her to take refuge with some family outside, and get behind the sand-hills as soon as possible, to avoid the shot. She hastily threw her wearing-apparel into her trunks, and I called two men to put her baggage outside the main gate. I then accompanied her there, and we took a sad and hasty leave of each other, for neither knew when or where we would meet again. As soon as this was accomplished, I strapped on my revolver, tied a blanket across my shoulders, and reported to Major Anderson that my men were in readiness to move.

Mrs. Doubleday found a temporary refuge, then returned to the fort to pick up the rest of her belongings. After that, she walked the beach with friends and gazed in the direction of Sumter.

Rebel Steamboats Patrol

Captain Doubleday and his men made a suspenseful transit. War had not begun, but the rebels had two steamboats available for patrolling the harbor, and their principal job was to keep Anderson and his men from occupying Fort Sumter:

> Everything being in readiness, we passed out of the main gates, and silently made our way for about a quarter of a mile to a spot where the boats were hidden behind an irregular pile of rocks, which originally formed part of the sea-wall. There was not a single human being in sight as we marched to the rendezvous, and we had the extraordinary good luck to be wholly unobserved. We found several boats awaiting us, under charge of two engineer officers, Lieutenants Snyder and Meade. They and their crews were crouched down behind the rocks, to escape observation. In a low tone they pointed out to me the boats intended for my company, and then pushed out rapidly to return to the fort. Noticing that one of the guard-boats was approaching, they made a wide circuit to avoid it. I hoped there would be time for my party to cross before the steamer could overhaul us; but as among my men there were a number of unskillful oarsmen, we made but slow progress, and it soon became evident that we would be over-taken in mid-channel. It was after sunset, and the twilight had deepened, so that there was a fair chance for us to escape. While the steamer was yet afar off, I took off my cap, and threw open my coat to conceal the [brass] buttons. I also made the men take off their coats, and use them to cover up their muskets, which were lying alongside the rowlocks. I hoped in this way that we might pass for a party of laborers returning to the fort. The paddle-wheels stopped within about a hundred yards of us; but, to our great relief, after a slight scrutiny, the steamer kept on its way. In the meantime our men redoubled their efforts, and we soon arrived at our destination. As we ascended the steps of the wharf, crowds of workmen rushed out to meet us, most of them wearing secession emblems. One or two Union men among them cheered lustily, but the majority called out angrily, "What are these soldiers doing here?" I at once formed my men,

charged bayonets, drove the tumultuous mass inside the fort, and seized the guard-room, which commanded the main entrance. I then placed sentinels to prevent the crowd from encroaching on us. As soon as we had disembarked, the boats were sent back for Seymour's company. The major landed soon after in one of the engineer boats, which had coasted along to avoid the steamer. Seymour's men arrived in safety, followed soon after by the remaining detachments, which had been left behind as a rear-guard. The latter, however, ran a good deal of risk, for in the dark it passed almost under the bow of the guard-boat *Niña*. [The other guard boat happened to be named *Clinch*, after Anderson's father-in-law, General Duncan Clinch, who was elected to Congress.] The whole movement was successful beyond our most sanguine expectations, and we were highly elated. The signal-gun was fired, and Hall at once sailed over, and landed the soldiers' families and supplies. As soon as the schooners were unloaded, the disloyal workmen were placed on board and shipped off to the mainland. Only a few of the best and most reliable were retained.

Having a new lease on life, the troops cheered as the flag went up at the massive Fort Sumter. The Irish among them bellowed three extra cheers for the Auld Sod. Three-quarters of Sumter's enlisted men were immigrants, mostly Irish with some Germans as in Mexico. In the forthcoming war, the enlistment of European immigrants would swell the ranks of the Union Army while the Confederate forces were depleted by casualties.

South Is Outraged

Anderson's movement to Sumter outraged the people of Charleston and the rest of the South. On Christmas Day, the rebels rejoiced in the thought they were going to get away clean. Now a huge fort stood in their way, and laying siege to it would have incalculable consequences. Without further delay, the South Carolina militia barged into the virtually undefended Castle Pinckney, taking it over with no shots fired. The same occurred at Fort Johnson and Fort Moultrie.

In a letter to the War Department, Major Anderson reported that he had moved his command because it was "necessary to prevent the effusion of blood." Before his letter arrived, he received a telegram from an infuriated Secretary Floyd, who already had heard from the rebels in Charleston. The following quotations are from *The War of the Rebellion: a Compilation of the Official Records*, volume one, chapter one:

> Intelligence has reached here this morning that you have abandoned Fort Moultrie, spiked the guns, burned the carriages, and gone to Fort Sumter. It is not believed, because there is no order for any such movement. Explain the meaning of this report.

Responded the major:

> The telegram is correct. I abandoned Fort Moultrie because I was certain that if attacked my men must have been sacrificed, and the command of the harbor lost. I spiked the guns and burned the carriages to keep the guns from being used against us.
>
> If attacked, the garrison never would have surrendered without a fight.

For his initiative Major Anderson would receive no praise from the secessionist in charge of the War Department. Prior to the move, Anderson had been smart enough not to seek permission. If push came to shove, he could reveal that, when he was in Washington, General Scott had discussed with him a possible need for the move. The same move also had been suggested by an Army inspector visiting Charleston.

Secretary of War John B. Floyd

Anderson a National Hero

The Buchanan Administration had established a truce in Charleston by which the rebels would not attack the federal facilities so long as they were not reinforced. Anderson argued that he did not reinforce anything; he merely had moved his command. The major became a national hero. At last, somebody had stood up to the rebels and their belligerent acts. The House of Representatives voted its approbation of Anderson 125 to 56. Cities fired salutes in his honor. Philadelphia honored him with a huge banquet, and every mention of his name drew a deafening applause. Anderson was celebrated even more because Secretary Floyd said he had disobeyed orders. General Scott recommended that the major be promoted, but the war secretary did not approve.

At Sumter Anderson had only a small fraction of the men and guns for which the fort was designed. Apparently moved again by public opinion, President Buchanan, going against his war secretary, decided to send more troops and supplies. General Scott recommended the use of a warship, but it was decided to charter a commercial ship instead. Various reasons for that have been given: that a civilian ship would be less provocative, that a warship would have too deep a draft for maneuvering in Charleston harbor, and that a fast merchant steamer well known to the Charlestonians might slip in and out of the harbor before the rebels knew what was happening.

Sumter Uninformed

The steamship *Star of the West* powered its paddle-wheels and headed south with 250 men and supplies. The uninformed men at the fort heard only rumors about the expedition, which was going to play out like a Keystone Kops farce. Following are Captain Doubleday's observations of what took place:

> We had seen a statement in a Northern paper that a steamer named the *Star of the West*, which belonged to Marshall O. Roberts, was to be sent to us, under command of Captain John M`Gowan, with a re-enforcement of several hundred men and supplies of food and ammunition; but we could not credit the rumor [one of many printed rumors; another one said there had been a mutiny at the fort and the abolitionist Captain Doubleday had been put in irons]. To publish all the details of an expedition of this kind, which ought to be kept a profound secret, was virtually telling South Carolina to prepare her guns to sink the vessel. It was hard to believe the Government would send to us a mercantile steamer—a mere transport, utterly unfitted to contend with shore batteries—when it could dispatch a man-of-war furnished with all the means and appliances to repel force by force. As the insurgents at this period had but few field-guns, and a very scanty supply of cannon-powder, the *Brooklyn* [a warship] alone, in my opinion, could have gone straight to the wharf in Charleston, and have put an end to the insurrection then and there; for we all know what its distinguished captain, Farragut ["Damn the torpedoes, full speed ahead!" David Farragut], was able to accomplish when left to his own resources.

USS *Brooklyn*, an up-to-date propeller-driven warship, if able to navigate the harbor, might well have set back the rebellion. At this time South Carolina was the only state which had seceded. Doubleday continues,

Although I had little faith in the announcement, I scanned with increased interest every vessel that approached the harbor. Soon after daylight, on the morning of the 9th, I was on the parapet with my spy-glass; for I fancied, from a signal I had observed the previous evening on a pilot-boat, that something must be coming. As I looked seaward, I saw a large steamer pass the bar and enter the Morris Island channel. It had the ordinary United States flag up; and as it evidently did not belong to the Navy, I came to the conclusion it must be the *Star of the West*. I do not remember that any other officers were on the lookout at this time. Anderson himself was still in bed. When the vessel came opposite the new battery, which had just been built by the cadets [cadets of The Citadel military college], I saw a shot fired to bring her to. Soon after this an immense United States garrison-flag was run up at the fore. Without waiting to ascertain the result of the firing, I dashed down the back stairs to Anderson's room, to notify him of the occurrence. He told me to have the long roll beaten [continuous drum roll indicating imminent action], and to post the men at the guns on the parapet. I ran out, called the drummers, and had the alarm sounded. It took but a few minutes for men and officers to form at the guns in readiness for action. The battery was still firing, but the transport had passed by [Morris island], and was rapidly getting out of range. At the same time it was approaching within gun-shot of Fort Moultrie. The latter immediately opened fire from one or two guns. Anderson would not allow us to return this fire; and the captain of the vessel, wholly discouraged by our failure to respond, turned about, and made his way back to New York. Two shots had struck the steamer, but no essential injury was done. I think the people in Fort Moultrie, who expected to be driven out to take refuge behind the sand-hills, were especially astonished at our inaction. It is very true that the Morris Island battery was beyond the reach of our guns. Still, we did not know this positively at the time; and our firing in that direction, even if ineffectual, would have encouraged the steamer to keep on its course. We had one or two guns bearing on Fort Moultrie; and as that was within easy range, we could have kept down the fire there long enough to

> enable the steamer to come in. It was plainly our duty to do all that we could. For any thing we knew to the contrary, she might have been in a sinking condition. Had she gone down before our eyes, without an effort on our part to aid her, Anderson would have incurred a fearful responsibility by his inaction . . .
>
> It was concluded to send Lieutenant Talbot to Washington with a full statement of the occurrence, and await his return with specific instructions from the War Department . . .

Possibly Lieutenant Theodore Talbot was chosen as the fort's emissary because he was the son of a U.S. Senator and familiar with the corridors of power. As described by Doubleday, Talbot was a "cultivated man" and represented well the "chivalry of Kentucky" (another Kentuckian). Apparently without realizing it, Doubleday had a clue as to why the fort was not informed of the steamship's coming:

> We now began to get out of fuel, but we still had a resource in some wooden sheds inside the fort, which had been used as a temporary shelter for cement and building materials. Our position was greatly alleviated in one respect. Owing, it is said, to the influence of Mr. Gourdin, already referred to as a leading Secessionist, and an old friend of Major Anderson, we were *allowed to receive our mails once more* [emphasis added]. After the *Star of the West* affair, they probably thought we were very harmless people, and deserved some reward for our forbearance.

Mystery Solved?

It appears that, when writing his memoir, Doubleday still could not imagine that Washington's message about the *Star of the West* had been sent by mail. That in fact is what happened, and the letter was not posted until April 5. Presumably the letter was intercepted by the authorities in Charleston, who eagerly sought information about the rumored event, and perhaps it never did reach Major Anderson. The missing missive not only provided information about the expedition but authorized Anderson to fire in its support.[4] This puts a different light on

President Buchanan, who otherwise has been notorious for his extreme passivity. But he never showed that sort of courage again. The message to Fort Sumter ought to have been carried by a special courier. Major Anderson then would have been informed, and he could have sent back recommendations.

Despite his sophistication, Lieutenant Talbot came back not knowing any more than when he had left. Doubleday again:

> On the 19th, Lieutenant Talbot returned from his visit to Washington, where, it will be remembered, he had been sent to explain the *Star of the West* affair, and ask for specific instructions, which would relieve Anderson from the responsibility, and throw it upon the Administration. The orders he brought back were to the effect that they had the utmost confidence in Major Anderson, and that they left every thing to his judgment. This was throwing the responsibility all back upon him. It was very complimentary, but far from satisfactory.

Buchanan Adrift

President Buchanan wanted somebody else to decide the question of war and peace. When young Talbot was in Washington, the commander-in-chief laid a hand on his shoulder and asked, "Lieutenant, what shall we do?"

The Charlestonians were getting more restive and they hated Doubleday, who was known to disapprove of slavery:

> Talbot stated that he had great difficulty in making a safe transit through Charleston; for while the leaders seemed to be more pacific than ever, the populace had become more violent. It was even thought necessary to send an officer with him to secure his personal safety. He brought me the pleasant information that the mob were howling for my head, as that of the only Republican, or, as they called it, "Black Republican," in the fort.

The ignominious failure of the supply effort prompted this challenge from U.S. Senator Louis Wigfall of Texas:

> Your flag has been insulted; redress it, if you dare.

Wigfall was biting the hand that fed him. He did not withdraw from the Senate until March 23, more than a week after the fall of Fort Sumter. The Texan, originally from South Carolina, was one of the Washington officials who told Charleston about the *Star of the West* plan. So did Secretary of the Interior Jacob Thompson, who was from Mississippi. Thompson then had the decency to resign. Adding Treasury Secretary Howell Cobb, who chaired the rump convention that nominated Breckinridge, half of Buchanan's cabinet was secessionist.

President Buchanan could have found in the *Star of the West* incident a sufficient cause for war if he had chosen to do so, but he had no such inclination. Northern opinion, though, was heating up, and it now was clear that the rebels would fight for Sumter. Buchanan could have sent another expedition, protected by the fort, but he did not.

At the time of the *Star of the West* fiasco, delegates of seven states were in Montgomery debating secession, and the Union's humiliation must have boosted their confidence. That was inferred by Kenneth Williams, author of the two-volume work *Lincoln Finds a General:*

> Amateur artillerymen and schoolboy soldiers had turned back a ship under the very muzzles of guns commanded by a professional officer and served by regular soldiers. Only a very unimaginative people would have failed to be aroused by the amazing success they had achieved . . . Well could have the delegates from all seven of the seceding states convene in Montgomery feeling confidence mixed with a little disdain or even contempt for the administration in Washington. But secession would not have looked so easy if Sumter's guns had replied.

Two More Secessions

Mississippi and Florida seceded immediately after the *Star of the West* incident.

Federal forts were threatened also in Florida. They included Fort Pickens located on Santa Rosa island near Pensacola and Fort Barrancas on the nearby mainland. Fort Pickens was even larger than Fort Sumter and was not occupied. Forty-seven soldiers lived in barracks at Fort Barrancas, and on January 8, as the *Star of the West* steamed southward, a group of men approached the barracks at night and were scared off by a sentry firing his gun. This perhaps was the first shot of the Civil War. A few hours later, the fort's commanding officer, Lieutenant Adam Slemmer, received an order from General Scott. At that time Slemmer had access to the commercial telegraph. The telegram ordered the lieutenant to do his "utmost" to protect his forts. Wisely, he copied Anderson. Having only forty-seven men, Slemmer moved to Santa Rosa island and occupied Fort Pickens.

Not located within a harbor, Fort Pickens was easily accessible to the Navy and much easier to defend than Sumter. The Buchanan Administration sent a fleet and two hundred additional soldiers for its garrison. But then an order came not to unload. The Administration had agreed to a truce in Pensacola. The fleet anchored and waited.

In a separate development, Secretary Floyd resigned. Buchanan asked him to resign in part because of upcoming legal troubles. He was replaced by Postmaster General Joseph Holt, a Unionist (and yet another Kentuckian).

Floyd Enabled the Confederacy

Floyd was indicted for conspiracy and fraud, having been party to an embezzlement of Native American bonds held by the government. The indictment was quashed for technical reasons, and Floyd went south to become a brigadier general in the Confederate Army. In that capacity he lost an important battle, abandoned his troops, and was fired, ending up a general in the Army of Virginia. However, as a spy and rebel agent in Washington, John B. Floyd earned an extremely significant, though little known, place in the history of espionage. Floyd's thwarting of

General Scott's plan to garrison the Southern forts made possible the creation of the Confederacy, according to the *Richmond Examiner*. The newspaper's words are quoted in Scott's memoirs:

> The plan invented by General Scott to stop secession was, like all campaigns devised by him, very able in its details and nearly certain of general success. The Southern States are full of arsenals and forts, commanding their rivers and strategic points. General Scott desired to transfer the Army of the United States to these forts as speedily and quietly as possible. The Southern States could not cut off communication between the Government and the fortresses without a great fleet, which they cannot build for years—or take them by land without one hundred thousand men, many hundreds of millions of dollars, several campaigns, and many a bloody siege Had Scott been able to have got these forts in the condition he desired them to be, the Southern Confederacy would not now exist.

President Buchanan has been criticized by historians for his passivity when action was urgently needed. He might have headed off the Civil War, at least for a number of years, and a war postponed may be a war avoided. The *Encyclopedia Americana's* article on Buchanan presents a different view:

> The nation was headed toward civil war, and he could not avert it. When war came, after his administration, Buchanan was a convenient scapegoat.

The Leaders

Nowadays, the eloquent and compassionate President Lincoln is venerated even more than President George Washington, the Father of Our Country. William Russell had a chat with Lincoln and "left agreeably impressed with his shrewdness, humour, and natural sagacity." Quoting friends, Mrs. Chesnut recorded a Southern view of the lanky rail-splitter:

> Mrs. Scott [no known relation to General Scott] was describing Lincoln, who is of the cleverest Yankee type. She said: "Awfully ugly, even grotesque in appearance, the kind who are always

at the corner stores, sitting on boxes, whittling sticks, and telling stories as funny as they are vulgar." Here I interposed: "But Stephen A. Douglas said one day to Mr. Chesnut, 'Lincoln is the hardest fellow to handle I have ever encountered yet.'" Mr. Scott is from California, and said Lincoln is "an utter American specimen, coarse, rough,[5] and strong; a good-natured, kind creature; as pleasant-tempered as he is clever, and if this country can be joked and laughed out of its rights he is the kind-hearted fellow to do it."

Confederate President Jefferson Davis was the son of a Mississippi cotton planter, who founded his plantation in 1812. Three of Jefferson's older brothers served in the Army during the War of 1812. Jefferson himself graduated from West Point, and in 1832 his commanding officer was Colonel Zachary Taylor, who assigned him to escort Chief Blackhawk. We have noted Davis's outstanding service in Mexico. He later was elected to Congress, and he became secretary of war under President Franklin Pierce. In that position Davis, ironically, worked hard at strengthening the Army which in the future he would have to fight. Elected as a senator from Mississippi, Davis argued against secession, but he maintained that every state had that right. When Mississippi left the Union, Davis planned to serve as a general in the Confederate Army, but without seeking the Confederate presidency, he was elected to it. Davis devoted his life to public service, and like most Southerners, he gave his primary loyalty to the state of his birth.

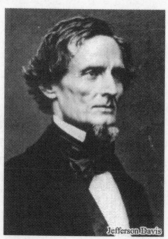

Confederate President Jefferson Davis

Browning's Master Plan

On February 17, 1861, a close friend of President-elect Lincoln sent him a letter which outlined a strategy for dealing with the seceded states. The writer was the aforementioned Kentucky-born Orville H. Browning, a Black Hawk War veteran who had served with Lincoln in the Illinois legislature, and who also had helped him become President. Browning emphasized that in any future military conflict with the seceded states it was very important that they be kept "constantly and palpably in the wrong" as aggressors, and he predicted that this would be the case with Fort Sumter:

> In any conflict which may ensue between the government and the seceding states, it is very important that the traitors shall be the aggressors, and that they be kept constantly and palpably in the wrong. The first attempt that is made to furnish supplies or reinforcements to Sumter will induce aggression by South Carolina, and then the government will stand justified, before the entire country, in repelling that aggression, and retaking the fort.[6]

Lincoln Shocked

On March 5, President Lincoln started his first day of work at the White House, and, metaphorically, the roof fell in. Secretary of War Joseph Holt brought in news from Major Anderson. It was all bad. South Carolina had cut off Anderson's access to the markets in Charleston, and the fort had provisions for only six weeks. The rebel troops had become so numerous and had installed so many cannon that it would take a force of twenty thousand well disciplined men to secure the area and supply the fort. At this time, the U.S. Army had a total of only sixteen thousand men. To save the fort, it was impossible to recruit and train enough soldiers before its provisions ran out. Holt acted as if he had been kept ignorant of the fort's circumstances, and that caused President Lincoln to doubt Major Anderson's loyalty. Yet the increasingly frustrated major had been sending in regular reports. His latest was numbered 58. Holt also had conferred personally with two of Anderson's officers. One was Lieutenant Talbot, mentioned earlier; the other was Lieutenant Norman Hall, who had visited Washington with a delegation of disgruntled South

Carolinians. Hall was in town for a month. Lincoln must have wished that, in the last four months, he had spent more time investigating the situation in South Carolina.

Like Holt, the President had been inattentive. Even back in Illinois, before he came to Washington, Lincoln had had access to excellent sources of information. He had some communication with General Scott, and even with Captain Doubleday. Doubleday was corresponding with his younger brother Ulysses, who forwarded letters to the President-elect.

For security, Captain Doubleday invented a simple code. The brothers possessed identical dictionaries, and they composed messages using two numbers for each word. One was the dictionary's page number, the other the line number. As for Fort Sumter's official correspondence, it, amazingly, went in *plain text*, and it did so by interceptable regular mail and commercial telegraph. Although Americans had used encryption as early as the Revolutionary War, in 1861 the U.S. Army's written messages were not encrypted until late in that year. As we have seen, the lack of reliable and secure communication was a disadvantage in the *Star of the West* incident. This same disadvantage continued. Since Major Anderson had not been able to communicate with the *Star of the West*, he asked for a copy of the Navy's signal book. The request went to Adjutant General Samuel Cooper, who, although born in New York, defected to the South, and Anderson never received the book.

The precarious nature of Fort Sumter made it politically all the more important to keep Fort Pickens out of rebel hands. The President right away on March 5 tried to reinforce Pickens, but his order directing "all possible vigilance for the maintenance of all the places within the military department" had no effect. Perhaps nobody equated vigilance with reinforcement; moreover, reinforcement would have broken the Pickens truce and risked war. A few days later, Lincoln found out that nothing was being done about Pickens, the order having "fizzled out" as he put it, and so on March 12 General Scott dispatched an order which was carried by steamship. The intended ship was the USS *Mohawk* as reported by the President's private secretaries, John Nicolay and John Hay, in their ten-volume work *Abraham Lincoln a History*. But *The Dictionary of American Fighting Ships* tells us that the *Mohawk* left earlier, on March 11, and did not arrive in Pensacola until May 10, a month after the war had begun:

> On 11 March 1861, *Mohawk* departed for the Caribbean, escorting supply ship *Empire City* to Havana and then Indianola, Tex. The warship proceeded to Pensacola via Havana and Key West, arriving 10 May and took up her blockade station off that port.

Conundrum Solved

In actual fact, General Scott's message reached the *Brooklyn* on April 1 almost three weeks after its reported dispatch on March 12, which would be consistent with transportation by ship—but not consistent with transportation by the *Mohawk*. There is a solution to this conundrum. Lincoln's secretary of the navy, Gideon Welles, in later correspondence mentioned that General Scott's message had been carried by the USS *Crusader*. From this we can infer that Scott was not fast enough to catch the *Mohawk* and perhaps did not wish to report that an urgent communication, already delayed once, had been delayed again. In any event, as we shall see, the second order proved no more effective than the first.

The early months of the Lincoln Administration were chaotic, and officials had conflicting agendas. Oblivious to most of this, the President devoted as much as twelve hours a day to meeting with hordes of office seekers, despite complaints in the press about this waste of time. As a lawyer, Lincoln had no experience managing a large organization. He caused confusion by ignoring lines of authority, and he did not watch carefully what was happening. Lincoln's secretary of state, William Seward, was an overbearing busybody who had plans of his own and often acted as if he were a British prime minister (his hero was Lord Palmerston). A former governor of New York, Seward was convinced that he, a rival to Lincoln for the Republican presidential nomination, would have made a far better President.

Secretary of State William H. Seward

It was Seward who, back in 1858, authored the term "irrepressible conflict" for the collision of North and South. Seward, nevertheless, bent every effort—and tried every trick—to repress the conflict he had predicted. Like Lincoln, Seward believed there was strong Unionist sentiment in the South. Unlike Lincoln, Seward opposed reinforcing the forts. He believed that a "cooling off" period would bring the seceded states back into the Union. In March, General Scott had opposed reinforcement of Fort Sumter because the rebels had built up their forces around it. After the departure of Buchanan, Scott also opposed reinforcing Pickens, perhaps because he came under the influence of his old friend Seward, who had been an ally when, as a Whig, Scott ran for President in 1852. Scott's relationship with Seward might help to explain why the general seems to have dragged his feet whenever Lincoln tried to reinforce Pickens. For example, if Scott had let it be known that his Fort Pickens message was too late for the *Mohawk*, somebody might have suggested having an officer deliver it by rail, which would have been two weeks faster than by ship.

In addition to the bureaucratic handicaps, the Administration was full of rebel spies. So was Washington society. Washington was a Southern city, and the journalist William Russell reported that most of its inhabitants would have preferred Jefferson Davis as President. Almost the entire diplomatic community in Washington, according to Russell, believed that the Union was "broken forever."

Lincoln had a potentially great asset in General Scott, who was a giant both physically and intellectually (when he kept clear of politics). Scott weighed 300 pounds and at 6 feet and 5 inches stood an inch taller than Lincoln. The general's health was poor and he spent much time in bed. But he was an encyclopedia of military lore, and the Duke of Wellington, while admiring Scott's campaign in Mexico, pronounced him the world's "greatest living soldier." The old general impressed Henry Adams as the "only military figure that looked equal to the crisis."

Scott's Strategy Rejected

If the secession came to war, Scott expected a conflict lasting two or three years. His time estimate was short, but the war might have been shorter and far less bloody if, initially, Scott's proposed strategy had been adopted. He recommended using a combination of Army and Navy forces for economic as well as military effect. Scott wanted the Navy to blockade the South, and he wanted to split the Confederacy by controlling the Mississippi river. In his plan, the Army would penetrate the Confederacy along the Mississippi in cooperation with Navy gunboats. But the general's advice was not politically acceptable. The press derided it as an "Anaconda Plan" designed to squeeze slowly the South into submission. The press rules America, and no one can face it and live, War Secretary Holt's successor, Simon Cameron, told William Russell.

General Winfield Scott

Press and public demanded a quick victory to be achieved by marching on Richmond, a little more than a hundred miles from Washington. This would require fighting through forests and across rivers, but "On to Richmond!" was a popular slogan. Among other disasters, this crowd-pleasing strategy led to the Union's two lost battles at Bull Run. Robert W. Love, author of the two-volume *History of the U.S. Navy*, has characterized as "mindless" the North's strategy of "advancing everywhere." That strategy was not always bad. Disgusted by his Army's inactivity, Lincoln issued on January 27, 1862, an order that every unit, wherever it was, undertake an advance on February 22. This order fizzled out like the one to reinforce Fort Pickens; but prior to February 22, a more energized Union Army won a few victories. Probably the Army commanders preferred to attack by surprise and feared that Lincoln's February 22 plan would leak to the enemy.

General Scott's plan for blockading seaports and Army-Navy riverine cooperation eventually helped greatly to win the war for the Union. Tributaries of the Mississippi river also were used for seizing strategic points. In 1865, the first Union soldiers to enter Richmond were based on the James river. Results would have come faster if the Army and Navy had not been slow to get organized. Secretary of the Navy Gideon Welles for a time refused to have anything to do with river warfare, and the Army had to pay for the construction of gunboats. The result was a hybrid Navy which went into service with Navy officers and Army enlisted men.[7] Various Union delays enabled the Confederacy to transfer troops to the Mississippi and fortify the bluffs of Vicksburg, Mississippi, which became the "Gibraltar of the Confederacy." The city was not captured until July 4, 1863. Said President Lincoln, "Thank God, the Father of Waters again flows unvexed to the sea."

Responsible for creating the hybrid "brown water Navy" was the ingenious Captain Andrew H. Foote, who had captured Chinese forts in the Second Opium War. Fortunately for the Union, Captain Foote and General Grant worked well together. Foote was promoted to Rear Admiral in 1862 and died of an illness in 1863.

General Scott was pressured out of his job. To be sure, the septuagenerian was not healthy enough to work throughout the war. Whenever Lincoln went to see Scott at his home, he found the general, who suffered from gout and dropsy, in an armchair with both feet in a tub of ice. Old Fuss and Feathers would pull up his great bulk with a rope attached to the ceiling and insist that the embarrassed President take his chair.

Evacuate Sumter?

Lincoln called a cabinet meeting on March 9, 1861, and stunned its members with the news of Fort Sumter's predicament. From there the word spread, even down to Charleston, that the fort had to be evacuated. Hearing of the proposed evacuation, elderly Francis Blair, who had been a close adviser to President Andrew Jackson, stomped into the White House. Angrily, Blair told Lincoln he would be impeached if he gave up the fort. One of those who spread the word about evacuation was a friend of Seward's, James E. Harvey, who formerly had lived in Charleston. Harvey will turn up again, in a similar capacity.

While the South Carolinians enjoyed a joyful spring, thinking Fort Sumter would be evacuated, Lincoln tried to figure out what to do. He worried about Major Anderson's loyalty. General Scott vouched for it, and perhaps it was he who told the President about Mary Doubleday's being in town. After her husband moved to Fort Sumter, his wife sneaked over in a boat transporting the fort's construction laborers. Because of the danger and the lack of heat (the available fuel was conserved for cooking), she left and moved to Washington. To the lady's surprise, the President called on her and asked to see her husband's letters. Mrs. Doubleday made this sacrifice for the Union. The letters seem to have been helpful.

Another question (at this late date): how real was the secessionist sentiment in Charleston? Probably Mrs. Doubleday helped there, too. But Seward, at least, still believed the pro-Union sentiment was strong. Learning of Seward's opinion, the *Times* man Russell noted with some wonderment that the secretary of state never in his life had traveled in the South outside the Washington area. Southerners often traveled in the North but Northerners did not travel much in the South, the correspondent was informed. Lincoln and Seward could have discussed affairs in the South with official representatives of the Confederacy but refused to do so. Buchanan had met with three official "commissioners." Lincoln preferred not to confer any sort of recognition on the seceded states. Seward communicated with the commissioners, but through various intermediaries. Reportedly, with no approval from Lincoln, he assured them that Fort Sumter would be evacuated. Seward also told the commissioners nothing would be done about Fort Pickens, although an order to land the reinforcements was en route. W. A. Swanberg in *First Blood*, a book about the Fort Sumter crisis, comments:

> Lincoln was against this [evacuation of Sumter] at the moment. But Lincoln was a backwoods lawyer, a newcomer in Washington with almost no experience in national affairs, and Seward seemed to have no doubts that the logic of events plus the influence of Seward would win him around. The Secretary of State dove into incredible error because of one bad mistake: he thought he could run Lincoln.[8]

Seward believed Unionists in the South would win out after a cooling off period, which he personally intended to provide.

Scouting Charleston

To obtain information on political sentiment in Charleston, Lincoln sent there two lawyer friends from Illinois. For their safety, both men traveled under pretenses. One of the friends was Ward H. Lamon, a burly gentleman who served as the President's unofficial bodyguard. Once Lamon instantly decked a man who harassed the President. Lamon was appointed marshal of the District of Columbia; he also bore the military rank of colonel. (The night Lincoln was assassinated, Lamon was overseeing the surrender of Richmond.) In Charleston, Lamon had some official business with the post office, but nonetheless a mob threatened to hang him. He was saved by an old acquaintance formerly in the Congress. Lamon sensed in Charleston no Union sentiment whatsoever.

In order to visit Fort Sumter, Lamon had to seek permission from South Carolina Governor Francis Pickens and also discussed with him the procedure for evacuation, according to Jefferson Davis's book about the Confederate government. Lamon's plan for removing fort personnel with a warship was rejected by the governor, but he accepted the proposal of a commercial steamship. It is not clear whether Lamon's discussion of evacuation had been authorized by Seward or Lincoln.

Lincoln's other investigating friend was Stephen A. Hurlbut, a native Charlestonian who had moved to Chicago. Ostensibly, Hurlbut went to Charleston to see relatives. He had excellent contacts in the city, and during his visit he learned that Charleston had only one declared Unionist. This was a highly respected attorney by the name of James J. Pettigrew. (Although opposed to secession, Pettigrew, whose name often is spelled "Pettigru," served as a general in the Confederate Army, helped to lead Pickett's charge at Gettysburg, and was mortally wounded a few days later.) Hurlbut discovered that the secessionists were very confident of success, and that they looked forward to Charleston's becoming like New York City as the trading capital of the South. After the war, Hurlbut was interviewed for an oral history by John Nicolay, mentioned earlier as one of Lincoln's private secretaries. Said Hurlbut:

> I saw two or three representative men of each class among lawyers, merchants, mechanics, and northern citizens settled there, and found only one expression among them all: and that was that there would be no war—that the north dared not or would not fight—and that secession would establish the city of Charleston as the great commercial metropolis of the South.

Seward was hard to convince. Hurlbut continued,

> The object of my mission was accomplished, and I left Charleston on Monday night, returned to Washington, and made my report to the President verbally, which he caused me to repeat in the presence of Mr. Seward. Seward still insisted upon it that there was a strong Union party in the South which would stop the movement. I told him that Fort Sumter at that time was commanded by batteries which had been erected without molestation, and that I was satisfied from my knowledge of the men that it was the intention to reduce the fort at all hazards.[9]

Buchanan's Missed Opportunity

Hurlbut warned that not only reinforcement but the mere sending of provisions would draw fire. In a postscript to his written report (an unpublished manuscript dated March 27, 1861), he recommended blockading the coast as the least warlike means of coercion. Expressing a view similar to that of Captain Doubleday, Hurlbut said President Buchanan could have stopped secession "in the bud" if he had had the Navy seize the port of Charleston. Instead, he noted,

> Treason was abetted by our own high functionaries and every impediment sedulously removed from its path.

As late as July 4, Lincoln evidently doubted that most people of the seceded states favored secession, with the possible exception of South Carolina. He said in a message to the Congress:

> It may well be questioned whether there is to-day a majority of the legally qualified voters of any State, except, perhaps, South Carolina, in favor of disunion. There is much reason to believe that the Union men are the majority in many, if not in every other one, of the so-called seceded States.

Secessionists Rule

In strong disagreement was William Russell, who as the result of his Southern travels, wrote in his book:

> To a man the people went with their states, and had but one battle-cry, "States'-rights and death to those who make war against them!"

Yet in northern Georgia many citizens opposed secession. Howell Cobb, formerly Buchanan's secretary of the treasury, had to tour the area and give fire-eating speeches.

The science of public opinion polling was badly needed.

Buchanan's inaction while federal facilities were taken over had encouraged the rebels to believe that the North would not fight. In South Carolina, Russell was told that that state *all by itself* could whip the whole of Yankeedom. In the view of many Southerners, one Southern soldier was worth three Yankees, the Union Army was full of Irish immigrants, the cowardly Yankees were afraid to duel, and for that matter, Yankees were not inclined to do *anything* unless it made money. As it happened, the war did make money for the industrial North, which prospered as the agricultural South, its cotton exports curtailed, sank into poverty.

Mrs. Chesnut remarked bitterly, "Genuine Yankees can get rich trading jack-knives."

A Plan for Sumter

Lincoln wanted to send provisions to Sumter, and shortly after the inauguration a former naval officer presented to him a plan for doing that, a plan which previously had been rejected by Buchanan. Gustavus Vasa Fox (named for a Swedish king although his family was not Swedish) suggested having warships escort to Charleston some chartered steamships which at sea would load their cargo onto chartered tugboats. The shallow draft tugboats then would sneak into the harbor at night, without having to follow the channel, deliver their cargoes in the shallow water at the fort, and escape by dawn. General Scott had supported this sort of plan during the Buchanan Administration, but now, he said, the Confederate defenses were too advanced. Naval officers were more optimistic, although doubting that the civilian tugboats would perform more heroically than the *Star of the West*. War Secretary Cameron viewed the plan, if it succeeded, as a temporary measure that would merely postpone the surrender of the fort.

Hoping to find facts that would support his argument, Fox went to Charleston. From Governor Pickens, he obtained permission to visit the fort by saying his purposes were "pacific." Fox spoke to Anderson about plans for evacuation, and tentatively mentioned his idea for delivering supplies. Anderson said the supply idea would not work: The harbor patrols surely would find the tugboats and Fort Moultrie would

169

fire thirteen cannon at the landing place. Anderson thought that his objections had settled the matter, but ignoring the major's advice, Fox gave an optimistic report to the President. Support for Fox's idea came from the gung-ho but indiscreet Captain Doubleday in a letter to his wife.

Charleston Optimistic

In late March, Major Anderson and the people of Charleston expected that the fort would be evacuated shortly. Lieutenant John Foster wrote to a friend in the city that he would be unable to visit because he was taking inventory in preparation for departure. Orders for reassignment were received by Anderson and Talbot. Talbot was to be promoted to captain and proceed to the Oregon Country. Probably somebody thought the invigorating air would cure his tuberculosis. Anderson, the highly publicized national hero, was to fill another key job. Promoted to lieutenant colonel, he would head the Army's Western Recruiting Service based in Kentucky, one of the border states that Lincoln was striving to keep within the Union. "I hope to have God on my side," said Lincoln, "but I must have Kentucky!" It will be recalled that the rambunctious General Fremont was no help with that.

Sumter worried Seward every day. He still had not persuaded Lincoln to evacuate the fort, the Southern commissioners were complaining of delay, and Seward probably saw that his scheme was falling apart. If Lincoln decided to reinforce Sumter, Seward would be branded a liar and his inability to manage Lincoln exposed. Perhaps it was in a state of panic that the secretary of state wrote a memorandum suggesting a bizarre plan: reunify the nation by declaring war on France and Spain. As an excuse for that, the French and Spanish were reported to be carrying out intrigues in Mexico and the Caribbean. In the event that this course of action would involve too much responsibility for the President, the secretary of state stood ready, he hinted, to run the nation's affairs. Seward presented the memorandum on April 1, and it may have looked like a joke, but it was absolutely serious. Lincoln decided to ignore this creative demarche. We can picture him shaking his head.

After considering for almost a month Fox's plan to relieve Fort Sumter, Lincoln on March 29 ordered that the expedition be *prepared* to depart by April 6, with the final decision yet to be made. Fox said he would need more time for the preparations. Overruling that, the President told Fox he would best fulfill his duty by *making the attempt.*

On April 4, Lincoln was shocked to read a message from Anderson saying that his provisions would run out in about a week. General Scott had talked of putting the men on half rations, but he did not send an order. And why would the men decide to go on half rations if the fort, as they believed, was about to be evacuated?

Two days later, the President was shocked again. He learned that Fort Pickens still had not been reinforced. If that weren't enough of a problem, the Southern press was reporting that the ship tasked with delivering reinforcements, the USS *Brooklyn*, had gone to Key West.

President Lincoln was learning about Washington, where, to this day, everything has to be checked and double-checked. Things tend to fizzle out. In 1952, President Truman said of his successor, General Eisenhower (paraphrasing): He will pick up the phone, say do this or do that, and he'll be shocked when nothing happens.

Union Commander Rejects Orders

As mentioned above, General Scott sent a message—by steamship—to where the fleet had been waiting since early January with two hundred soldiers on board. Since then, the rebel troops ashore had been multiplying into the thousands. The rebels were under the command of General Braxton Bragg, another hero of the Mexican War. Upon at last receiving Scott's order to disembark the troops, the commander of the Union ships refused to obey. He was Captain Henry A. Adams, not to be confused with the diarist Henry B. Adams. Captain Adams replied that the truce was still in effect and the orders for disembarkation conflicted with his previous orders from the secretary of the navy. In a matter of this importance, argued Adams, the order should have come through regular channels, which would be the secretary of the navy, not the Army commander. The captain emphasized that reinforcement would be seen as an act of war:

> No one acquainted with the feelings of the military assembled under Genl Bragg can doubt that it [the

reinforcement] would be considered not only a declaration, but an act of war.

If Scott's message had been carried by rail, the officer bearing it would have been able to explain the urgency and the President's involvement. The result also might have been different if Scott had signed the message with the President's name instead of his own name. Possibly the foot-dragging general had that in mind. Captain Adams's refusal—even "rebellion"—has been roundly condemned by historians. But he had a point. The reinforcement could provoke immediate hostilities. Did Lincoln want that?

Wisely, Captain Adams sent his response by rail. When this unwelcome message reached the capital, Lincoln suddenly saw himself in danger of losing both of the Deep South federal forts, after having promised the American people to retain those properties. Secretary Seward, who had been playing a devious game, now sought favor by volunteering to organize, secretly, another expedition for the reinforcement of Pickens.

Seward and Army Captain Montgomery Meigs got busy on that, ignoring difficulties that General Scott pointed out. The job of carrying another order through rebel territory—the *third* ordering Pickens's reinforcement—was given to Navy Lieutenant John L. Worden, a native of Westchester, New York. After getting on the train, Worden memorized the message and destroyed it.

Under pressure to save some fort, Lincoln finally decided to implement Fox's plan for aiding Fort Sumter. The White House prepared a message to Major Anderson, probably written by the President, which went out under the name of Secretary of War Cameron. The message said Fox's expedition would arrive by April 11 or 12, that the major was expected to "act like a patriot and a soldier," but authorized him to surrender the fort if he felt that this was a "necessity." Nicolay and Hay described the message as "considerate and humane" in their book *Abraham Lincoln a History*. In disagreement has been David Detzer, author of a book, *Allegiance,* on the beginning of the Civil War. Detzer interpreted the message as Lincoln "covering his backside" by putting the responsibility for the fort solely on Anderson (as Buchanan had done). In my opinion, the message could be interpreted as Lincoln telling Anderson not to take too many casualties in a battle more important for its occurrence than for its outcome. In other words, the fort itself was not important. If there was to be war, the Commander-in-Chief just needed for the South to shoot first.

Anderson Aghast

Major Anderson was aghast to learn that Fox's scheme had been approved. Believing that the expedition would fail and knowing it would mean war, he sent a letter of protest to the adjutant general's office. As always, the mail had to go through Charleston, where Brigadier General P. G. T. Beauregard, a Louisiana creole, now was the military commander, having been assigned by the Confederacy, and Beauregard's men intercepted the letter. Anderson and "Bory" Beauregard were old friends from West Point. If Anderson assumed that his friend was too much of a gentleman to open another man's mail, he was right. Beauregard gave the letter to Governor Pickens. The politician opened the letter, read it, and gave it to the press. Part of the extraordinary, bluntly written missive:

> I ought to have been informed that this expedition was to come. Colonel Lamon's remark [about evacuation] convinced me that the idea, merely hinted at to me by Captain Fox, would not be carried out. We shall strive to do our duty, though I frankly say that my heart is not in the war which I see is to be thus commenced. That God will still avert it, and cause us to resort to pacific measures to maintain our rights, is my ardent prayer.

Commented Mrs. Chesnut, "He ought to have thought of all that before he put his head in the hole."

Because Seward had promised to notify the Confederates if there were to be any change in the Charleston truce, Lincoln informed the governor of South Carolina that he planned to send provisions. The message was carried by Robert Chew of the State Department, arriving on April 8. The message was curt and unsigned. Its authenticity was attested by the presence of Lieutenant Talbot, who was known to be one of Anderson's officers. The message said provisions would be sent to Fort Sumter, and if there were no resistance, reinforcement would not be attempted. No reply was requested and Pickens offered none. The governor would not permit Talbot to rejoin his unit at Sumter. He had the two men escorted to the railroad station.

It has been commented that Robert Chew "lives in history only because of this brief moment of drama." Not so. After the war, he negotiated the purchase of Alaska from Russia, as I have been told by his great grandson, Professor John Chew. A painting at the Seward Museum in Auburn, New York, shows Secretary Seward, the Russian ambassador, and Chew, who is holding the treaty in his hand.

Again, No Surprise

Fox had meant for his plan to succeed by *stealth*, but for more than one reason, that definitely was not in the cards. Even the details were known in Charleston. A local businessman mentioned in a letter that one of the tugboats was named *Yankee*. One leak came from Seward. He again gave secret information to James Harvey, who again telegraphed Charleston. Seward always had wanted to surrender Sumter, and he was not about to give up on that.

Fox's expedition got off to a ragged start with the assigned vessels leaving at different times. Then they were delayed and scattered by a severe storm. Fox was supposed to leave New York by April 6, but he did not get underway until April 10 (according to his official report; some accounts say April 9). He steamed off with the reinforcements on the commercial vessel *Baltic*. Before he left, one of Fox's ships *already had arrived* on April 8 at the planned rendezvous point, which was ten miles off the Charleston harbor. This was the revenue cutter *Harriet Lane*, named for President Buchanan's niece. Evidently Fox was not keeping the Revenue Cutter Service up to date concerning his plans. *Harriett Lane's* arrival gave the rebels plenty of notice that Fox, the supplies, and the possible reinforcements were on the way. A rebel boat spotted the cutter, flashed signals, and not receiving the correct response, scurried into the harbor.

Harriet Lane's early arrival jolted into motion the gears of war. President Davis ordered General Beauregard to "reduce" Fort Sumter before the provisioning could be accomplished—if the fort would not surrender.

The decision was made in a meeting of the Confederate cabinet. Secretary of State Robert Toombs of Georgia was the only person to vote against the decision. He asserted that firing on the fort will "inaugurate a civil war greater than any the world as yet seen." Pacing back and forth, Toombs argued unsuccessfully, "It is unnecessary; it puts us in the wrong; it is fatal."

Davis and his cabinet must have been full of indignation. Lamon had indicated that Sumter was to be evacuated, and through intermediaries, Seward had conveyed the same information two or three times. In the last communication, though, he was ambiguous. He said, "Faith as to Sumter fully kept. Wait and see." That message was sent as Gustavus Fox and President Lincoln were planning the supply expedition. The commissioners took the message to mean that Sumter would be evacuated. Seward's defenders argue that it could have meant there would be no change in Sumter's status without first notifying the rebels, as Seward had also promised. Davis assumed the failure to evacuate Sumter represented duplicity on the part of Lincoln and his men. And this raised an important question. What about Lincoln's promise not to reinforce Sumter if the provisions were allowed to land? The commissioners had given a warning. On April 10 they sent this message to General Beauregard:

> The "Tribune" of to-day [April 10] declares the main object of the expedition to be the relief of Sumter, and that a force will be landed that will overcome all opposition.

In view of all the misinformation coming from up North, the Confederate leaders had little reason to believe anything. To quote Swanberg in *First Blood*:

> The "provisions only" story he [Davis] believed another deception, feeling sure the federals were coming with the intention of attacking and aimed to land a large force on Morris Island to take the batteries there from the rear.

In fact, War Secretary Cameron's orders were, to "deliver the subsistence" and only in the case of opposition "place both troops and supplies in Fort Sumter." Here is the actual message from Cameron, dated April 4, taken from the *War of the Rebellion* official records:

Capt. G. V. Washington, D. C.

SIR: It having been decided to succor Fort Sumter you have been selected for this important duty. Accordingly you will take charge of transports in New York having the troops and supplies on board to the entrance of Charleston Harbor, and endeavor, in the first instance, to deliver the subsistence. If you are opposed in this you are directed to report the fact to the senior naval officer of the harbor, who will be instructed by the Secretary of the Navy to use his entire force to open a passage, when you will, if possible, effect an entrance and place both troops and supplies in Fort Sumter. I am, sir, very respectfully, your obedient servant,

SIMON CAMERON
Secretary of War.

A Duel Between Friends

General Beauregard was a former student of Major Anderson's. At West Point he had studied artillery under Anderson, and the two got along so well that Beauregard became the instructor's teaching assistant. Now they would confront each other in a duel of artillery. Anderson, seeing Beauregard's emplacements, knew that the younger man had learned his lessons. Commander of the rebel navy at Charleston was Captain H. J. Hartstene, who warned Beauregard that, in his opinion, the fort could be relieved by small boats on a dark night. To prevent that, Hartstene's men anchored in the harbor two boats loaded with flammable material. If Fox's boats came at night, the fires would light them up. To handicap larger vessels, Hartstene already had removed the buoy from the main channel.

General Beauregard was ordered to demand Sumter's evacuation "at once," but he delayed, wiring back that he would get started at noon on the following day, April 11. A message was sent to hurry him. The general from Big Easy land replied that he had "special" reasons for waiting. He did not say what the reasons were. Possibly they related to setting up a new rifled cannon, very accurate and powerful, just received from London.

Major Anderson's eviction notice finally arrived at mid-afternoon of April 11. The operative part:

> . . . the Confederate states can no longer delay assuming actual possession of a fortification commanding the entrance of one of their harbors, and necessary to its defense and security.

Delivering the ultimatum in a rowboat were Colonel James Chesnut, husband of Mary Chesnut, and two more of Beauregard's aides. Anderson read the ultimatum, discussed it with his officers, and handed back a written refusal. As Chesnut left, Anderson remarked that since the fort was running out of provisions, he would have to evacuate by the fifteenth. Earlier, the major had given the same information to War Secretary Cameron. Telling Chesnut was Anderson's final attempt to clear out of Fort Sumter without starting a war, and it was a bold one. The fort commander ought not to have told the enemy his provisions were limited. Furthermore, the garrison still had a two week supply of salt pork, according to Doubleday's memoir. If Lincoln and Fox had known that the fort could hold out until April 25, there would have been more time to prepare the expedition and do a better job of it. But maybe Doubleday was wrong.

Rebels' Golden Opportunity

What a golden opportunity Anderson had given the rebels. So as not to incur the odium of firing the first shot, they could have waited until April 15 and taken the fort peaceably. However, Beauregard did not want to fight the fort and Union ships at the same time (although threatened so far only by a revenue cutter); President Davis was breathing down his neck; and the general decided that Anderson's answer was not good enough. There would have been more time if *Harriett Lane* had not arrived early.

Beauregard sought advice from headquarters in Montgomery. He was told to refrain from firing if Anderson would specify a time for the evacuation and promise not to use his guns unless fired upon. At about midnight, back to Sumter went the aides in the rowboat. Anderson woke his officers for another meeting, which took hours. Afterward, the major designated noon of the fifteenth for the evacuation. But he said he would have to open fire if ordered to do so or if the flag were fired upon—in other words, if he had to provide support for a supply vessel.

At about that time, 3 a.m. of April 13, Gustavus Fox arrived in *Baltic* at the rendezvous point. He found *Harriet Lane,* whose skipper for four days had been wondering, *Where's the Navy?* Fox 's principal firepower, the frigate *Powhatan*, was nowhere to be seen; neither were the tugboats. High winds were blowing *Yankee* to Savannah, Georgia, and *Uncle Ben* to Wilmington, North Carolina. There was supposed to be a third tug, *Freeborn*, but its owner decided he did not wish to participate. *Baltic* got stuck on a shoal and worked itself loose.

Seward Hijacks a Frigate

Both the Sumter relief expedition and the Pickens relief expedition were supposed to be secret, even from each other, and although Fox counted on *Powhatan* as the "fighting portion" of his flotilla, Seward had hijacked it for the relief of Fort Pickens. As the result, *Powhatan* left New York on April 6, three days before Fox, and nobody told Fox. The crafty Seward had promised to change *Powhatan's* destination from Pensacola to Charleston, but still wanting to surrender Sumter, he was slow about it, and he signed his message to New York "Seward" instead of "President." Commanding *Powhatan* was Lieutenant David D. Porter, later Admiral Porter. He, having one order signed by the President and a newer one signed by the secretary of state, decided to obey the President. Lincoln's orders were to guard the steamship *Atlantic* as it disembarked six hundred troops at Fort Pickens, and at this time *Atlantic* was ten miles en route. Porter hurried after the *Atlantic*.

Colonel Chesnut Starts the War

Major Anderson did not promise to refrain from using his guns until April 15, it now was April 12, and Colonel Chesnut had to decide what to do. Should he tell Beauregard about Anderson's answer? He decided not, and took upon himself the responsibility of starting the Civil War. Chesnut wrote out a response saying the Provisional Army would open fire in one hour. It was 3:20 a.m. Upon parting with his friend Chesnut, Anderson said, "If we do not meet again on earth, I hope we may meet in Heaven." Presumably Beauregard's aide acted within the scope of his orders. I have found no indication of complaint by his superiors.

We cannot know what would have happened if Chesnut had consulted again with Beauregard. James Ford Rhodes in his Pulitzer Prize winning *A History of the Civil War,* published in 1917, decided he made a mistake:

> Beauregard's aides assumed too great a responsibility in giving the order to fire the first shot; they should have referred Anderson's reply to their chief. There can be no doubt that the Confederate States would have obtained peacefully on Monday what they got by force on Sunday. If Beauregard had had Anderson's last response, he would unquestionably have waited to ask Montgomery for further instructions. The presence of the United States fleet was of course disquieting; yet the danger from this source, even as exaggerated in Beauregard's mind, could be averted quite as well by acting on the defensive, as by the bombardment of Fort Sumter. But South Carolina was hot for possession of the fort and the aides who gave the order that precipitated hostilities were swayed by the passion of the moment.[10]

Owing to stormy weather and Secretary Seward's intrigue, not much of a "fleet" actually was present, just the cutter *Harriet Lane* and the commercial steamship *Baltic.* Beauregard ought to have been informed of that, but I find no report that, after the *Harriet Lane* was spotted, any rebel craft kept a watch on the rendezvous point. Not until 7 a.m. did a third Union vessel turn up. This was the 11-gun sloop-of-war USS *Pawnee* (which formerly was commanded by Hartstene when he was in the U.S. Navy).

An explanation for Chesnut's open fire decision was found by historian Samuel Eliot Morison, who said,

... as one of them [the three aides] admitted later in life, they feared that Davis and Lincoln would shake hands and the chance of war would slip away forever.[11]

First Shot Fired

One of the foremost Fire Eaters, Roger Pryor of Virginia, late of the U.S. Congress, was offered the privilege of firing the first shot at Fort Sumter. He had urged the people of Charleston, "Strike a blow!," assuring them that this would bring Virginia into the Confederate fold. But when it came to pulling the lanyard, Pryor declined, saying he could not fire the first gun of the war. The awesome responsibility was passed to Lieutenant Henry S. Farley, a West Point graduate, who in 1863 was killed by a cannon ball. Pryor's refusal at Sumter marked the Fire Eater's second famous backing down. Earlier, he had challenged a Wisconsin congressman, John F. Potter, to a duel but withdrew his challenge when Potter chose bowie knives as the weapon. Pryor complained that knives were not a civilized weapon, and the Northern press took great delight in this incident. During the war, Pryor served in the Confederate Army and was captured as a suspected spy. He was paroled by President Lincoln. After the war, the former Fire Eater became a prosperous attorney in New York City, and as his wife gratefully noted, this would not have been possible had he fired the first shot at Fort Sumter.

The artillerymen delayed by ten minutes the first shot, the "signal shot," to be sure it was aimed well. A shell exploded over the fort. Some admirers thought the explosive pattern looked like the palmetto on the South Carolina flag.

Colonel Chesnut's wife was in bed when her husband started the war. Her diary:

> At half-past four the heavy booming of a cannon. I sprang out of bed, and on my knees prostrate I prayed as I never prayed before.

The second shot was fired by white-haired Edmund Ruffin, a longtime secession advocate who in 1860 had predicted war would begin at Fort Sumter. The war lost, Ruffin shot himself.

The bombardment of Sumter went on all day, all night, and much of the following day, for thirty-four hours. The garrison performed admirably the work of operating the cannon, assisted by the loyal construction workers. The rebels fired heated cannon balls ("hotshots") that set fire to the wooden barracks inside the fort. The installed fireproofing did not work, and flames almost blew up the store of gunpowder.

At this stage, the war was a game. Anderson and his men had friends in Charleston, and many onlookers respected them for doing their duty. Some cheered because the fort kept firing as it was enveloped by dense, suffocating smoke. Many cursed and jeered the Union ships for not helping. Not only Fox's few ships but some commercial vessels gathered outside the harbor; hence the Charlestonians mistakenly thought a large Union naval force was assembled there.

At about 1 p.m. the fort's flag was shot down and seeing that, the ever-busy Senator Wigfall thought the fort had surrendered, and had himself rowed to the island carrying a white flag. The senator arrived at 2 p.m. By that time the fort's flag had been restored, but Wigfall, asserting falsely that he represented General Beauregard, persuaded Major Anderson it was time to evacuate. Wigfall, as mentioned earlier, still was drawing pay as a member of the U.S. Senate. The fort hoisted a white flag and, following additional discussion when Beauregard's real representatives arrived, the battle was over. Wigfall's true status, or non-status, had to be explained to Anderson circuitously because of the senator's reputation as a duelist.

At the end of the bombardment, the fort's main gate, facing toward land, was partly burned. Because of the fire, the men had thrown into the sea approximately a hundred barrels of gunpowder, but some remained. Bombardment killed nobody in the fort. Nor among the rebels. The Sumter men had taken refuge in the gun enclosures. However, for the evacuation ceremony Major Anderson ordered a gun salute, and an exploding cannon killed two of his men

At about the time of the surrender, Fox's fourth ship, the USS *Pocahontas* made its appearance, ready to protect the transfer of troops from the *Baltic* to the missing tugboats.

Charleston Ecstatic

Charleston was ecstatic about the rebel victory. Much of the citizenry headed for the fort in small boats, some calling for Captain Doubleday's head. Captain Hartstene's men kept the celebrants from landing.

At his hotel in Montgomery, President Davis was not feeling well and lay down on a couch. His war secretary, Leroy Walker, addressed a crowd cheering wildly outside. Getting carried away, Walker predicted the Confederate flag would fly over the Capitol in Washington and maybe even Faneuil Hall in Boston. This undercut Davis's strategy, which was to present the North as the aggressor. The Unionists made the most of Walker's challenging words.

Why did Lincoln not evacuate the fort? War Secretary Cameron was right: Even if Fox 's plan had succeeded, the fort could not have been held for long, not within Beauregard's "ring of fire." Or it could have been starved out. For political reasons, was the relief expedition a token effort to keep Lincoln's promise to retain the forts? Was the expedition intended to provoke the Confederates into firing first? Lincoln consoled Fox with the following words:

> You and I both anticipated that the cause of the country would be advanced by making the attempt to provision Fort Sumter, even if it should fail; and it is no small consolation now to feel that our anticipation is justified by the result.

Lincoln knew the rebels would fight even if he only sent "bread to Anderson," as he put it. The Southern commissioners made that clear, according to William Russell. The *Star of the West* incident had proved it, and warnings had been given by Hurlbut and Anderson. Nicolay and Hay explained the President's thinking in their book:

> Whether the expedition would fail or succeed was a question of minor importance. He was not playing a game of military strategy with Beauregard. He was looking through Sumter to the loyal States; beyond the insulted flag to the avenging nation.

Accidental Success

Lincoln applied the strategy which had been recommended on February 17 by his Kentuckian friend Orville Browning. This came about partly by accident, as we shall see.

President Lincoln and President Davis simultaneously were planning to break the truce in Florida. But General Bragg knew that capturing Fort Pickens would not be easy. Santa Rosa island was a mile and a half from the mainland, the Union fleet was strong, and for those reasons Bragg had no confidence in making an overt assault. He suggested to Davis trying to use ladders under cover of darkness, noting that casualties would be high. Davis decided to adopt a different plan, which was bribery. General Bragg heard there was disaffection among the Union troops at Pickens and he asked for a "corruption fund." From Montgomery came a Captain Boggs with $40,000. But the bribery plan did not work.

Lieutenant Worden and his memorized message arrived in Pensacola on April 11, the day Beauregard demanded Sumter's evacuation. General Bragg gave the lieutenant permission to visit the fleet (for pacific purposes?), but heavy weather held him back for a day. On April 12, Worden finally completed his mission. The original two hundred reinforcements were still available. Before going to Key West, the USS *Brooklyn* had transferred them to the USS *Sabine*. On the night of April 12, Captain Adams dropped the long awaited men quietly on the sea side of the island. One of Bragg's boats observed what was happening but was detained by the Navy until the operation was completed. Just hours too late, Bragg received a telegram warning him to keep a man named "Worden" away from the fleet.

Powhatan and *Atlantic* arrived after the reinforcement was completed, and six hundred more men were added to the garrison. No firepower was needed.

His luck run out, Lieutenant Worden was nabbed by the rebels on the way back to Washington, and it was seven months before a prisoner exchange took place. His health was impaired, but in 1862 Worden commanded the USS *Monitor* in its epic battle with the Confederate CSS *Virginia* (formerly the USS *Merrimack*), and history's first contest between ironclad warships came to a draw. The *Virginia* later was blown up to keep the ship from falling into the hands of advancing Union forces. Giving the destruction order was Confederate Captain Josiah Tattnall, who as a commodore had fought in the Second Opium War.

Lincoln's Luck

If Lieutenant Worden had not been detained by heavy weather, war might have begun on Santa Rosa island, before the firing on Sumter, and the Confederates could have charged that Lincoln broke the truce. President Lincoln, therefore, implemented the Browning strategy partly by chance. Lincoln met with his strategist friend on July 3, 1861, and Browning in his diary recorded the President's summary of events:

> He [Lincoln] himself conceived the idea, and proposed sending supplies, without an attempt to reinforce giving notice of that fact to Gov Pickins (sic) of S.C. The plan succeeded. They attacked Sumter—it fell, and thus, did more service than it otherwise could.

Despite attacks on both forts, the Union held Fort Pickens throughout the Civil War and the Confederacy held Fort Sumter.

For months the nation's attention had been focused on the besieged but plucky Major Anderson. Five states passed resolutions honoring him. There was a stage play about him and his men. There were a song, poetry, and many other expressions of adulation. Among a huge fan mail, two letters from nephews in Kentucky said Anderson's example had slowed the secession movement in that state, which Lincoln said he "must have."

The nationwide desire to revenge the heroes of Sumter conferred a great power on President Lincoln. "At one stamp of his foot," said Henry Adams, "the President called the whole nation to arms." Among professional Navy and Army officers, more than half, like the Virginian General Scott, stayed with the Union.

But for every action there is a reaction. The Southern states interpreted Lincoln's policy on Fort Sumter as coercion, which they had warned against; and Virginia, where as recently as April 4 a convention had voted to stay within the Union, decided to secede. The Old Dominion was followed by Arkansas, North Carolina, and Tennessee. Eleven states formed a Confederate nation ranging from Texas to Virginia.

President Davis Pessimistic

With the accession of Virginia, the Confederate government moved from Montgomery to Richmond. (Mrs. Chesnut suspected that was because the hotels were better.) Jefferson Davis, when in the U.S. Senate, had argued against secession. Yet he was drafted into the Confederate presidency. Now that war had begun, he was not enthusiastic about that, either. Mrs. Chesnut had a long talk with him:

> In Mrs. Davis's drawing-room last night, the President took a seat by me on the sofa where I sat. He talked for nearly an hour. He laughed at our faith in our own powers. We are like the British. We think every Southerner equal to three Yankees at least. We will have to be equivalent to a dozen now. After his experience of the fighting qualities of Southerners in Mexico, he believes that we will do all that can be done by pluck and muscle, endurance, and dogged courage, dash, and red-hot patriotism. And yet his tone was not sanguine. There was a sad refrain running through it all. For one thing, either way, he thinks it will be a long war. That floored me at once. It has been too long for me already. Then he said, before the end came we would have many a bitter experience. He said only fools doubted the courage of the Yankees, or their willingness to fight when they saw fit. And now that we have stung their pride, we have roused them till they will fight like devils.[12]

Neither Lincoln nor Davis wanted the secession. Davis had been happily serving in the Senate, and his wife Varina loved Washington society. The Davises left Washington with heavy hearts. Departing Springfield, Illinois, Lincoln was depressed, too, but cheering crowds at the train stops brightened his mood. If the two Kentucky-born frontiersmen had gotten together to discuss the situation, could Lincoln, with his inimitable wit, have laughed and joked the country back together again?

Analysis

Both sides miscalculated. The Northerners thought the Southerners were not serious about seceding, and the Southerners thought the Northerners would not fight.

Abraham Lincoln declared secession illegal, but the Confederates thought otherwise. As they saw it, the federal government had been formed by the states for their convenience, and so why should the states be imprisoned by their agent? There was no time to settle the matter in court. The Senate appointed a committee to make a recommendation, and so did the House of Representatives. Neither committee could agree on what to do.

President Buchanan had opportunities to stop the secession and keep the peace. He could have garrisoned the forts, declared a blockade, and fired the secessionists within his Administration. The rebels would have had few weapons, and they would have seen that, menaced by the forts and blockaded by the Navy, they could not establish a separate, more prosperous nation. As a doughface and outgoing president, Buchanan was reluctant to take action. He ran out the clock.

If President Lincoln's prime objective had been to keep the peace, the obvious way to do that was to permit secession, as recommended by Horace Greeley and General Scott. However, the American people elected as President a man who was determined to regain the federal forts and preserve the Union. "This was a Caesar!" declared the novelist and historian Gore Vidal. (I happened to see that on television when Vidal was interviewed about his book *Lincoln*. Vidal earlier had written a book about the Roman Emperor Julian.) Lincoln's vow to retain federal properties in the South preceded the tariff crisis of mid-March, 1861. (The President's resolve may have been stiffened by the visit of Francis Blair, but that was on March 11 before William Russell visited New York and discovered a state of complacency.)

Lincoln knew that his attempt to relieve Sumter would bring war. The *Star of the West* incident had shown that, and he had been warned by knowledgeable persons. However, Lincoln had pledged to keep the federal facilities, and if there were to be war, it would be better for the Union if the Confederacy shot first. Nicolay and Hay said their boss was looking "beyond the insulted flag to the avenging nation." Lincoln himself confirmed that in his July 4 conversation with Orville Browning.

Some Southern writers have claimed that Lincoln deliberately provoked the war. He might have done. But the South was the first to take provocative steps and did in fact start the shooting. The rebels fired at the *Star of the West* and then at Fort Sumter. The Southerners clearly initiated the violence, and the men attacked were familiar to the people up North, viewed as heroes, and even idolized on the stage. In the public eye, Lincoln only tried to "send bread to Anderson," a national hero. Had the shooting started at Fort Pickens, with Lincoln breaking the truce, the result would not have been a galvanizing event but a subject of debate. From that standpoint, Secretary Seward, General Scott, and Captain Adams performed a valuable service by delaying the reinforcement of Fort Pickens.

An alternative to Lincoln's On to Richmond plan was General Scott's Anaconda plan. It would not have kept the peace, but it might have saved hundreds of thousands of lives.

From the standpoint of the South, staying within the Union would have kept the peace. After several states seceded, could war still have been prevented? A different strategy might have accomplished that. In order to prevent a violent response from the North, the secessionists could have been less confrontational and aggressive. Occupying the federal forts worked very well up to a point, but at Sumter and Pickens Lincoln drew the line. So why cross the line? Fort Sumter was neutralized by Southern artillery and its need for supplies. As for Fort Pickens, it could not do much harm. The eight or ten thousand Confederate troops stationed in Pensacola were not able to take the fort, and in 1862 they were withdrawn for more important duties.

The Battle of Fort Sumter brought more states into the Confederacy, and the Confederacy needed them. However, if instead, several months of tranquility had gone by, garnished with professions of friendship and offers of trade, it would have been difficult for Lincoln to raise an adequate invasion army. In that strategy the South would have had an ally in Secretary Seward, who thought a period of tranquility would bring back the seceded states. Lincoln, too, believed there was much latent Unionism in the South. If the secession continued, the Confederacy's low tariff policy might have drawn in border states.

Whether there was a war or no war, in time the institution of slavery surely would have been abolished in the United States, as it has been, almost completely, south of the Rio Grande. In today's world, slavery is invisible but not dead. Children are sold to be servants. Women and children are trapped into prostitution. Many people are enslaved for political reasons. In this hemisphere, the United States, Canada, and Colombia have the least slavery, while Haiti and Cuba have the most, according to the State Department's 2010 *Trafficking in Persons Report*.

An Avoidable War?

President Buchanan could have prevented the war by firing the secessionists in his cabinet and securing the federal facilities in the South. With the aid of Sumter's guns, Buchanan could have resupplied the fort when Charleston's defenses were weak, and he could have used the guns of the fort to prevent the emplacement of Southern artillery. Next, he could have blockaded the port to discourage the secessionists, especially those who expected to get rich by increasing traffic at Charleston. Instead, Buchanan emboldened the rebels and betrayed the Union with his do-nothing policy.

President Lincoln adopted a strategy which enabled him to bring an outraged North into the war. Whether in March or April he could have headed off the war is a difficult question.

After the war began, President Lincoln could have minimized the casualties and possibly shortened the conflict by adopting the Anaconda plan recommended by General Scott.

Useful Principles

Avoid miscalculation by collecting pertinent data.

President Lincoln underestimated secessionism in the South. President Davis understood the North pretty well. But he had the rebel presidency thrust upon him by acclamation.

The leader must be alert and keep in close touch with events when the danger of war is imminent.

On the Union side, Secretary Seward, General Scott, and numerous Southern agents had their own priorities. President Lincoln was more engaged than President Buchanan, but not enough. As soon as he was elected, Lincoln could have urged Buchanan to secure the forts and arsenals. If Buchanan were not too proud to seek advice from Lieutenant Talbot, perhaps he would have welcomed assistance from the President-elect. James Polk as President-elect had helped President John Tyler with the annexation of Texas. Lincoln, however, erred in thinking that the secession crisis was not real.

On the Confederate side, President Davis was fortunate to have telegraph lines to Beauregard and Bragg. However, he bucked the open fire decision to General Beauregard, who bucked it to Colonel Chesnut. If Colonel Chesnut had bucked the decision back up the chain of command, Fort Sumter might have been taken peacefully on April 15. Davis was pressured to be aggressive, and the secessionists believed, correctly, that the outbreak of hostilities would bring Virginia and other states into the Confederacy. Would the peaceful capture of Sumter not have done the same?

To get a clear picture of the situation, check the assumptions, especially those that are comforting.

As late as April 6, 1861, Secretary Seward told William Russell that the seceded states would voluntarily come back into the Union. President Lincoln in his July 4, 1861, address to Congress doubted that most people of the seceded states favored their separation. There were

Unionists in the South, but they were so few or so remote as to be unnoticed by the London *Times* correspondent William Russell.

The Southerners also made convenient assumptions. They overestimated their military strength, and many expected help from Great Britain. The latter Southerners were convinced that a Union blockade would be broken by the Royal Navy because British textile manufacturers needed American cotton. Russell could not talk anybody out of that.

To keep the peace, strong leadership may be required.

President Buchanan had the means but not the will to prevent secession.

The Southern leaders wanted to achieve a peaceful separation from the Union, but they failed to control their followers, and Southern hotheads delighted in projecting an offensive, belligerent image. There were countless unnecessary incidents. In Charleston, men of Fort Sumter had their provisions cut off; they even were prevented from taking to the fort tobacco they had purchased in the city. Ward Lamon, a Unionist with Southern sympathies, was threatened with hanging. In Washington, at President Buchanan's New Year's Day reception, some guests were insulting. They wore secession cockades (a knot of blue ribbons) and refused to go through the receiving line. President Lincoln's first reception was distinctly cool. The noxious Senator Wigfall was in a class by himself. Ordinarily, Southerners were noted for their good manners and hospitality, but not when a charm offensive was urgently needed.

Mitigating casualties ought to have a high priority. If there has to be war, a small war is better than a big war.

Had President Lincoln defied public opinion to go with the Anaconda strategy, he would have received shorter and fewer casualty lists.

Keep a cool head.

The public's unbridled emotion produced the On to Richmond! strategy intended to bring a quick victory. Professional military opinion was overruled.

The South, too, was bursting with over-confidence, and the Fire Eaters became irrational. An illustrative moving picture scene comes to mind. In the Bette Davis film *Jezebel*, Henry Fonda is an ante bellum Southerner concerned about the spread of malaria. He suggests draining a swamp as they do up North, and he is accused of "talkin' like a Yankee." In the duel-prone South, that was a serious matter.

References

[1] Charles Adams, *When in the Course of Human Events*, pages 62-63

[2] William Russell, *My Diary*, page 14

[3] David D. Porter, *The Naval History of the Civil War*, page 22

[4] Kenneth P Williams, *Lincoln Finds a General*, pages 26-27

[5] The book says "rouge." I assume "rough" was intended.

[6] Abraham Lincoln, "Orville H. Browning to Abraham Lincoln, Sunday, February 17, 1861"; *Abraham Lincoln Papers*

[7] James M. McPherson, *War on the Waters*, pages 70-71

[8] W. A. Swanberg, *First Blood,* page 226

[9] John Nicolay, *An Oral History of Abraham Lincoln*

[10] James F. Rhodes, *A History of the Civil War,* pages 15-16

[11] *The Oxford History of the American People*, page 611

[12] Mary Boykin Chesnut, *A Diary from Dixie*, page 71

CHAPTER NINE

Spanish-American War (1898)

All nations want peace, but they want a peace that suits them—Admiral Sir John Fisher, 1894

The Southern Nationalists' hope of acquiring Cuba as a slave state died in the American Civil War, and it was buried in 1886 when slavery in Cuba was abolished by the Spanish Cortes (parliament).

In 1894, the U. S. Congress passed another of its disaster-producing tariffs. Our lawmakers raised the tariff on sugar by 40 percent in order to help the American beet sugar industry. This impacted severely the cane sugar industry in Cuba, and amid economic distress, the Cuban people in 1895 rebelled against Spanish rule—a recurring phenomenon. Inspiring and organizing the new rebellion was the poet Jose Marti. Overall military commander was Maximo Gomez. The third major leader was an Afro-Hispanic by the name of Antonio Maceo. He, the "bronze Titan," was shot more than two dozen times in combat before receiving his fatal wounds. Of the three leaders, only Gomez survived the rebellion. Unfortunately for the people of Cuba, and for the people of Spain as well, the government of Spain was willing to commit hundreds of thousands of troops to maintain its rule.

To the Spanish the war in Cuba was a holy mission. When in the late fifteenth century the Spanish finally defeated the Moors, ending nearly eight hundred years of oppressive Muslim rule, the Spanish government, along with some private individuals, decided to invest in Christopher Columbus's plan to reach Asia by sailing across the Atlantic. Columbus never reached Asia, but his voyages resulted in founding an enormous Spanish empire, and the Spanish people interpreted their good fortune as a gift from God for their having returned Spain to Christian rule.

The Spanish government decided to maintain political stability by allowing only one religion, Roman Catholic Christianity. Moors were permitted to stay in Spain only if they converted. As mentioned earlier, many of them went to Northern Africa and took up piracy and slave trading. Also required to convert or emigrate were the Spanish Jews and the few Protestant Christians. The task of the Spanish Inquisition was to identify false converts, and punishments were carried out by the state. Those persons judged to be false converts were burned at the stake. During the severe tenure of Grand Inquisitor Tomas de Torquemada, who came from a family of Jewish converts, an estimated 2,000 people were executed, according to the *Encyclopaedia Britannica*.

Columbus explored the islands of the Caribbean thinking he was in Asia, and so, in a long-lasting error, he dubbed the inhabitants "Indians." Cuba became a profitable colony. Slaves mined gold. After the gold gave out, the slaves grew and harvested sugar cane. The slaves at first were native Caribbeans, later Africans.

No Popular Uprising

Jose Marti's troops assembled in Costa Rica and the Dominican Republic, and in February of 1895 they began landing in Cuba. Marti hoped for a general uprising, but it did not happen. A previous rebel landing in 1851 had met the same disappointment. These two disappointments foreshadowed the general uprising which did not happen in 1961, when United States-backed Cuban exiles landed at the Bay of Pigs. Their aim was to overthrow the Communist government headed by Fidel Castro. Our strategists needed more knowledge of history.

Jose Marti's rebels carried on as guerrillas, using hit and run tactics to wear down the enemy. That part of the rebellion was much like the later war in Vietnam. The Cuban rebels destroyed the sugar industry in order to make the island unprofitable to Spain. The Spanish Army destroyed crops and livestock to make life miserable for the rebels. Malnutrition and starvation resulted, but ordinary Cubans continued to support the rebels, hoping someday the Spanish army would leave.

Americans were appalled by the Spanish strategy of concentrating the rural Cuban population in unhealthful, disease-ridden enclosures surrounded by barbed wire. Rural people outside the concentration camps and fortified towns were hunted down and killed. The Spanish strategy presaged the concentration camps in South Africa during the Boer War, the gulags in the Soviet Union (initiated by Lenin and expanded by Stalin), camps in Germany and Nazi-controlled Europe (forced labor camps and death camps), forced labor camps in North Korea, camps in South Vietnam ("strategic hamlets," relatively benign), camps in Communist China (forced labor camps and, according to Cable News Network, camps for the harvesting of body organs from live prisoners).

In New York City, Jose Marti founded the Cuban Revolutionary Party, which coordinated propaganda and practical matters concerning the rebellion. This organization was better known as the "Junta." Junta propaganda exaggerated Spanish atrocities and Cuban military successes. Like the Castro refugees of the later centuries, Marti sought support from Cuban emigre communities in Florida. Cuban-American tobacco workers became an important source of funds. Solicitous of underdogs and people seeking freedom, the American public sympathized strongly with the Cuban rebels, and some Americans went there to fight. A small Ohioan, Frederick Funston, five foot five and weighing 120 pounds, felt he had it in him to be a soldier. Funston, formerly a journalist, taught himself about artillery, joined the rebels as their only artillery expert, and earned a general's rank. Spain blamed the Cuban rebellion on the United States.

In 1896, Marti and Maceo were dead, and a nearly-broke Spain was recruiting soldiers as young as fifteen. Forty-five thousand Spaniards paid a fee to be excused from military service, according to the *New York Times*. President Grover Cleveland's offers of mediation were rebuffed by the Spanish authorities, and Americans increasingly were outraged by the sufferings of the Cuban people.

Rebellion in the Philippines

Also draining Spanish manpower was a rebellion in the Philippines, which began in 1896. Again the inspiration came from a man of letters.

He was Jose Rizal, the son of a wealthy Philippine family. Rizal earned degrees from two European universities, spoke several languages, and wrote two famous novels that criticized Spanish rule. After he founded the Philippine League, an educational organization suspected of being revolutionary, Rizal was arrested and executed. In the Philippines he is honored annually by Rizal Day, a national holiday. In Cuba, the birthday of Jose Marti is a national holiday.

Unlike the American people and the U. S. Congress, who were fired up by the sensationalist press, our Presidents did not succumb to war fever. President Grover Cleveland and after him President William McKinley wanted a stable Cuba, not one up for grabs by unknown rebels or some European power. Cleveland condemned the Junta for its war mongering. In 1896, he opposed sending a warship to Havana because it might become an excuse for trouble with Spain. When in 1898 Cleveland handed over the presidency to McKinley, he predicted nothing could stop a war over Cuba. But McKinley would try. In his inaugural address he said, "Peace is preferable to war in almost every contingency."

President William McKinley

McKinley appointed as secretary of the navy John Long, an old friend who was more interested in writing poetry than running the Navy. Under political pressure, the President reluctantly appointed as Long's assistant the energetic Theodore Roosevelt, who, McKinley worried, was "always getting into rows." Roosevelt not only was eager for war but formed a pro-war coterie of influential friends including Senator Henry Cabot Lodge, Ambassador John Hay (Lincoln's former private secretary) in London, *New York Sun* editor Charles Dana, head of naval intelligence Commander Charles Davis, and Navy Captain Alfred Thayer Mahan (later Admiral Mahan). Lodge and Roosevelt differed on one point. While the senator saw commercial possibilities in Cuba, Roosevelt disdained "money-getters" and complained that commercial interests were hindering his plans. They were too concerned, he said, about the money owed to them by the people in Cuba Before the revolt, American trade with Cuba amounted to about a hundred million dollars per year. Of course, if the trade resumed, that would benefit the United States, except for the beet sugar industry, and benefit Cuba as well.

As the debate continued, even the peacenik President McKinley blasted the Cuban concentration camps as not "civilized warfare" but "extermination." But he also said, "I have been through one war; I have seen the dead piled up, and I do not want to see another." When the Civil War began, McKinley enlisted as a private soldier, and he rose to the rank of major. Now this veteran was burned in effigy for his devotion to peace. Theodore Roosevelt, it was rumored, wrote to one his friends that McKinley had "no more backbone than a chocolate eclair."

America "Needs" a War

Roosevelt was motivated not only by his natural love of combat but by certain theories. One was Social Darwinism. A boxer and physical fitness enthusiast, Roosevelt believed it important for the post-Civil War generation to prove its mettle, and this notion was so strong it overcame his concern for the welfare of our coastal cities. A few years before the Spanish War, the United States was having a row with Britain concerning Venezuela, and Roosevelt told his friend Senator Lodge,

> This country needs a war . . . but the bankers, brokers and anglomaniacs generally [favor] peace at any price.[1]

197

And to a reporter Roosevelt said,

> American cities may possibly be bombarded . . . [but] Canada
> would surely be conquered, and once wrested from England
> would never be restored.

On June 2, 1897, Roosevelt stated his philosophy to the Naval War College:

> All the great masterful races have been fighting races; and
> the minute that a race loses the hard fighting virtues, then,
> no matter what else it may retain . . . it has lost its proud right
> to stand as the equal of the best.

Cohabiting comfortably with Social Darwinism in Roosevelt's mind was a theory about the importance of sea power. In 1890, the aforementioned Captain Mahan published one of the most influential books of modern times. This was *The Influence of Sea Power Upon History*. Mahan showed how command of the sea throughout history often had been the key element in winning wars and building empires. The British Empire was an obvious case in point. Said Mahan concerning the Napoleonic Wars:

> Nelson's storm tossed ships, which the Grand Army never
> saw, were the only things that stood between it and the
> conquest of the world.

Throughout its wars with France, Great Britain, thanks to the Royal Navy, was inaccessible to the French army, was able to maintain the nation's life-giving commerce, and usually was able to land troops wherever needed. (But not at Yorktown, thanks to the French navy, which also demonstrated the importance of sea power.)

Mahan's thinking had been anticipated by John Adams, who perceived Neptune's trident as the scepter of the world. Adams wrote to the American naval hero Thomas Truxtun, who defeated *L'Insurgente*, that the "great questions of commerce and power between nations and empires must be determined by sea." He cited as like-minded four historical figures: Themistocles of Athens, Pompey of Rome, DeWitt of Holland, and Colbert of France.

Mahan Honored

Captain Mahan's supervisor advised him, "It is not the business of a naval officer to write books." But rulers and naval men the world over became the captain's disciples. After Mahan received degrees from Oxford and Cambridge, American universities raced to honor him. Germany's Kaiser Wilhelm II ordered all of his naval officers to read Mahan's book, and the Kaiser kept a copy of it at his bedside. Under the American theorist's influence, the imperialist nations sought harbors and coaling stations everywhere. Germany, unified only since 1871, had come late to the game of imperialism and was trying to catch up. Germany's construction of a navy for a time appeared to threaten Britain's naval supremacy.

Thanks to the Kaiser and his Mahanism, German warships prowled the Caribbean, inspiring still more American concern about the fate of Cuba, which Germany, it was feared, might wish to purchase from its penniless owners in Madrid. In 1897, a pair of German warships (actually school ships operated by naval cadets) visited Haiti on behalf of one Emile Luders, a part Haitian German national. Because of a shipwreck that had deposited Germans in Haiti, Germans long had been active on the island as coffee growers and merchants. Luders was jailed and deported after engaging in four duels and an altercation with the police. Overly enraged, the German government demanded a $20,000 indemnity for Luders, an apology, his readmittance to Haiti, and a twenty-one gun salute. Haiti sought help from the United States but none was forthcoming. A French newspaper commented acidly that the Americans were too busy conspiring against Spain. This was prior to Roosevelt's tenure at the Navy Department.

U. S. Navy Impotent

Further straining relations between the United States and Spain was a series of ship incidents. The first was humiliating to the American side. During the Ten Years War (a Cuban rebellion of 1868 to 1878), the Spanish intercepted an American vessel, the *Virginius*, which was carrying guns and guerrillas to Cuba. The ship's captain and fifty-two others were shot. (One might say this foreshadowed the mass executions perpetrated by Fidel Castro in the 1950s.) Another one hundred and fifty-five on board would have been executed except for a strong protest lodged by the commander of a British warship. The U.S. Navy was impotent. After the Civil War, most of the American Navy was disbanded, as had happened after the Revolutionary War. The remaining vessels, now obsolete, could have been sunk in less than an hour by two modern warships, according to Admiral Robley Evans, who was a lieutenant at the time. An American fleet assembled at Key West, but our sailors, as Evans put it, realistically could do no more than make faces at the enemy. An American naval construction program got underway in the 1880s. In the 1890s America boasted "the New Navy," a powerful force.

In 1895, a Spanish gunboat mistook an American merchant vessel for a gun runner and fired on it. Three years were required to wring an apology from Madrid. We Americans showed our good faith by intercepting more gun runners than did the Spanish navy, but our courts' lenient treatment of the captured rebels displeased the Spanish authorities.

In the fall of 1897, the situation in Cuba appeared to be getting better. A new premier took over in Spain. He promised to end the concentration camps, and he said Cuba would be given more control over its affairs. It did not help matters when the Spanish foreign minister, Carlos O'Donnell, responded to criticism by comparing the Spanish Army's harsh tactics to those of Union General William T. Sherman in the Civil War. O'Donnell did not need to add that General Sherman was an older brother of John Sherman, currently the American secretary of state

USS *Maine* Visits Havana

Early in 1898, the battleship USS *Maine* visited Havana as an intended goodwill gesture, and, because of recent riots in Havana, to evacuate Americans if need be. The visit started off fairly well. The *Maine's* captain, Charles D. Sigsbee, was treated courteously, if stiffly, by his counterparts. He noticed that the Spanish officers had polished manners but that their crews were not well trained. When Sigsbee attended a bull fight, the crowd did not look friendly, and soldiers were stationed nearby for his protection. Bullfighting, the Cubans told American visitors, was a barbaric entertainment forced upon them by the Spanish. Bullfighting was outlawed in Cuba after it became independent.

Our binational relations suddenly went from improving to catastrophic. First, the Spanish envoy to the United States angered Americans by writing a letter that disparaged McKinley as "weak and a bidder for the admiration of the crowd." The Junta somehow got hold of the letter and gave it to the press. Less than a week later, on February 15, the USS *Maine* blew up in Havana harbor. Spanish authorities did their best to rescue surviving sailors and provide other assistance. But 260 Americans died, and in the United States press and public blamed the Spanish for allegedly having planted a mine. The U.S. Navy formed a court of inquiry.

Then came a third source of outrage. As the public awaited the results of the Navy's investigation, Senator Redfield Proctor of Vermont reported on a trip to Cuba, and his description of the sufferings of people in concentration camps "made the blood boil," said the *Wall Street Journal*. Highly respected, Proctor formerly was a Civil War colonel, a secretary of war, and a governor of Vermont. He said he had no opinion on what happened to the *Maine*, and that when he went to Cuba he thought the descriptions of suffering had been exaggerated. Proctor now agreed that the suffering of the Cubans was horrendous. Concerning the people evicted from their homes to live in camps and fortified towns, he said on the floor of the Senate:

> When they reached the town they were allowed to build huts of palm leaves in the suburbs and vacant places within the trochas [fortifications], and were left to live if they could. Their huts are about ten by fifteen feet in size; and for want of space are usually crowded together very closely. They have no floor but the ground, and no furniture, and after a year's wear but little clothing, except such stray substitutes as they can extemporize.

> With large families or with more than one in this little space, the commonest sanitary provisions are impossible. Conditions are unmentionable in this respect. Torn from their homes, with foul earth, foul air, foul water and foul food, or none, what wonder that one-half have died and that one-quarter of the living are so diseased that they cannot be saved. A form of dropsy is a common disorder resulting from these conditions. Little children are still walking about with arms and chests terribly emaciated, eyes swollen

and abdomen bloated to three times the natural size. The physicians say these cases are hopeless.

Deaths in the streets have not been uncommon. I was told by one of our consuls that people have been found dead about the markets in the morning where they had crawled hoping to get some stray bits of food from the early hucksters, and that there had been cases where they had dropped dead inside the market, surrounded by food.

Ten Percent of Cubans Perished?

According to the senator, more than 10 percent of the Cuban population had perished. The Spanish Army suffered as well. Losses required the recruitment of younger and younger troops. The senator praised the work in Cuba done by Clara Barton, president and founder of the American Red Cross. As for the war, Proctor saw no actual war. He told his colleagues:

> It is not peace, nor is it war. It is desolation, misery, and starvation.

Proctor's unemotional recitation of what he saw caught fire in the press, and some commentators, pointing out that war did not come until more than two months after the sinking of the Maine, have asserted that Proctor's speech was the more influential.

Marxist revisionists claim the rebels had almost won their war when the Americans arrived to snatch victory away from them and replace Spanish colonialism with capitalist tyranny; but Senator Proctor did not perceive a rebel victory in the offing. He reported that the rebels controlled eastern Cuba, known as Cuba Libre, and the Spanish controlled the western half of the country, including Havana. Proctor traveled four hundred miles safely by train in western Cuba, observing fortified towns and camps. What he reported was an insufferable, static situation. Two previous rebellions had failed, and the Junta was seeking intervention.

Spain's top admiral, Pascual Cervera, kept warning his superiors that, for lack of funds, Spain's navy was no match for the Americans' up-to-date and well maintained warships. American wealth was demonstrated on

March 9 when the U.S. Congress, though still waiting for the court of inquiry, voted fifty million dollars for defense. No borrowing would be needed. That impressed Spain's Queen Regent Christina, and hoping to save her throne, she decided it might be a good idea to sell Cuba to the United States. There was insufficient support in the Cortes.

As the American people grappled with the horrors in Cuba related by Senator Proctor, the court of inquiry finished its investigation, and it announced on March 28 that the ship had been sunk by two explosions. An explosion under the ship bent upward the keel, and that was followed by a larger explosion inside when the forward magazines ignited. To the public, this was proof of Spain's culpability, and in Congress both parties demanded war.

Subsequent investigations have favored other possibilities, such as spontaneous combustion in a coal bunker as the initial explosion. Such fires were not unusual. The month before the *Maine* exploded, an investigative board warned that a coal bunker fire could ignite an ammunition magazine located on the other side of a bulkhead, and just a month *after* the *Maine* exploded, a coal bunker did catch fire in the USS *Brooklyn*. In 1898, the *Maine's* explosion was blamed on a coal fire by most of the naval officers in Washington. They were polled by the *Evening Star* newspaper. Among those expressing that opinion were the Navy's chief ordnance expert, Lieutenant Philip R. Alger, and the Navy's chief engineer, George W. Melville. Such publicly expressed opinions were not welcomed by Assistant Secretary Roosevelt. He fired off a complaint to the Navy's chief of ordnance, Admiral Charles O'Neil.

Rickover Investigates *Maine*

The mystery of the *Maine* was not forgotten, and in 1976 the coal fire explanation was accepted by an investigative team recruited privately by Admiral Hyman Rickover, the Navy's top expert on nuclear powered ships. Said Rickover's investigators:

> We have found no technical evidence in the records examined that an external explosion initiated the destruction of the *Maine*. The available evidence is consistent with an internal explosion alone.

As for the bent keel, the investigators said this was caused by the secondary explosion, which occurred in a place different from where the court of inquiry had thought.

In 1998, *National Geographic* published an investigation done by computer modeling. It strengthened the case for a mine, but was not conclusive

Getting back to events in 1898, Roosevelt was delighted with the court of inquiry's report. He told Washington's Gridiron Club, "We will have this war for the freedom of Cuba," despite "the interests of the business world and of financiers."

President McKinley hung back. He was negotiating with Spain, which offered an armistice in Cuba. An armistice was not enough to please the public. Only Cuban independence would bring peace was the general view in both the United States and Cuba.

A delegation from European countries met with President McKinley. Representing them, Sir Julian Pauncefote, British ambassador to the United States, said, "We hope for humanity's sake you will not go to war."

The President responded, "We hope, if we do, you will understand it is for humanity's sake."

Most Europeans Favor Spain

The Europeans favored Spain in its confrontation with the United States. However, Ambassador Hay in London wrote to Senator Lodge that if need be, we might obtain "practical assistance" from the British navy:

> I do not know whether you especially value the friendship and sympathy of this country [England] . . . it is the only European country whose sympathies are not openly against us . . . If we wanted it—which, of course, we do not—we could have the practical assistance of the British navy.

Queen Victoria did not favor the American side. Perhaps the de facto alliance in the Second Opium War fostered a spirit of back channel cooperation between the two navies.

As Secretary Seward had envisaged in 1861, having a common enemy helped to bring North and South together. In reuniting the United States, much progress already had been made. Our consul general in Havana was Fitzhugh Lee, who had been a brigadier general in the Confederate Army, serving under his uncle Robert E. Lee. Confederate General "Fighting Joe" Wheeler, who in 1865 led the last Confederate charge in Virginia, in 1898 was chairman of the House Ways and Means Committee. President McKinley asked Wheeler whether he would like to join the U.S. Army for the war with Spain? The chairman said he would. At the age of 61 Wheeler accepted a major general's commission and served in Cuba with distinction—a rare instance of a man having been commissioned general in both of two opposing armies. It reminded people of how Robert E. Lee who, at the beginning of the Civil War, had to choose between a generalship in the Union Army or a generalship the Confederate Army. Wheeler died in 1906 and was buried in a blue uniform. When Fighting Joe arrived in Heaven wearing that uniform, some commented, Stonewall Jackson must have been flabbergasted.

Patriotism burgeoned across the land. The Stars and Stripes appeared everywhere. So did volunteers. There was no shortage of them. The War Department turned down the services of former outlaw Frank James, brother of Jesse James. Frank wanted to lead a company of cowboys. Vaudeville superstar Annie Oakley offered to recruit fifty lady sharpshooters who would provide their own guns and ammunition.

Ambassador to Spain Opposes War

Let's everybody calm down, advised Stewart L. Woodford, American ambassador to Spain. On April 9, Woodford reported that the Spanish government was moving toward freeing Cuba, or at least toward an autonomy acceptable to the insurgents, as fast as it could without provoking a revolution. Woodford expected results by August 1 if only the President could persuade the Congress to be patient. A former Union general, Woodford assumed that the summer rainy season in

Cuba would halt combat. McKinley was not up to the job of persuading Congress. The emotional strain was too much. Stanley Karnow reported in *In Our Image: America's Empire in the Philippines*:

> One evening in late March he slipped away from a White House concert with an old friend, Chicago newspaper publisher H. H. Kohlsaat. They retired to a parlor, where McKinley burst into tears as he poured out his troubles: his wife's failing health, his sleepless nights, his fear of war. After the cathartic confession, he checked himself; he could not afford to collapse in this crisis.

On Capitol Hill no patience was available. The powerful Speaker of the House, Thomas B. ("Czar") Reed, was asked whether he could not control the bellicosity of the Congress. Reed said he might as well try to stop a cyclone in Kansas. On April 11, McKinley, badgered by congressional leaders and facing a cyclone of public opinion, asked the Congress for authority to demand that Spain relinquish sovereignty over Cuba, and for the authority to use the armed forces to compel Spain to do that. McKinley did not request a declaration of war. He still hoped to avoid the conflict for which most of the nation was clamoring.

Congress adopted the "Teller amendment" stating, in effect, that the United States would not annex Cuba. That was offered by Senator Henry M. Teller of Colorado. Very thoughtfully, the senator meant to prevent a continued guerrilla war, protect the beet sugar industry in Colorado, or both. In favor of the amendment, the Senate voted 42 to 35 and the House 311 to 6. Evidently few Americans wanted to annex Cuba.

On April 21, Spain severed relations with the United States. Ambassador Woodford explained, "The Army is still the controlling factor in Spanish politics" (as it was in Mexico). The Spanish army viewed the revolt in Cuba as an unholy cause aided by meddlesome Americans.

McKinley Caves

War now was inevitable. Under tremendous pressure from lawmakers, President asked the Congress to declare war. The Senate voted in favor 42 to 35 and the House 310 to 6. There was no huge margin in the Senate, but in the Lower House the influence of press and public was overwhelming. The President signed the war declaration on April 20. He ordered a blockade of Cuba and asked for 125,000 volunteers.

William McKinley was nothing like the twentieth century's war-making "imperial Presidents." Harvard University historian Ernest May commented that Mckinley led the nation into a war "he did not want for a cause in which he did not believe." McKinley was not so stubborn as John Adams. But unlike Adams, he would get reelected.

The national battle cry was, *Remember the Maine!* Some added, *To hell with Spain!*

In her diary, Queen Victoria said about the war, "It is monstrous of America." Spain's Queen Regent, Maria Christina, was her Austrian cousin.

The Spanish-American War was about Cuba, but Theodore Roosevelt, as assistant secretary of the navy, made sure the Philippines would be part of it. A few weeks after the sinking of the *Maine*, Secretary Long felt worn to a frazzle by incessant demands for war. His osteopath having acquired a new massage machine, Long decided to take some time off, leaving his assistant in charge. The secretary, it is said, expected his assistant merely to carry out the office's daily routine, but Roosevelt seized the opportunity to take several actions in preparation for war.

Among his war preparations, Assistant Secretary Roosevelt sent secret orders to Commodore George Dewey, commander of the Asiatic Squadron. Dewey's ships were spread around the Far East. Roosevelt ordered the commodore to concentrate his ships at Hong Kong and keep them full of coal. In the event of war with Spain, Dewey was to make sure the Spanish squadron in Asia did not leave that area, and he was to conduct offensive operations in the Philippines. Roosevelt was implementing a hypothetical plan on which the Naval War College had been working for years. Secretary Long never countermanded those fateful orders, which led to the American acquisition of the Philippines and the forgotten Philippine-American War, a dress rehearsal for Vietnam.

As commander of the Asiatic Squadron, Dewey ought to have been promoted to rear admiral, but he, at Roosevelt's urging, had obtained the Asiatic command by lobbying the influential Senator Proctor, a fellow Vermonter, and for spite Secretary Long did not approve the promotion. Political influence would have assisted Dewey's competitor for squadron commander if that letter of recommendation had not gotten delayed somehow in Roosevelt's office. The assistant secretary achieved his aim. He stationed in Asia a more aggressive squadron commander, an authentic Civil War hero, than otherwise would have been appointed. In his quest for conquest, Roosevelt was not a man to leave a stone unturned. Neither was Dewey. His battle preparations were exemplary in their thoroughness and initiative.

Unable to find a good supply of coal in the Far East, Commodore Dewey arranged to buy from Wales two shiploads of smokeless anthracite, prized by the world's navies. To make sure the precious cargo did not go astray, he also bought the ships carrying it. In the event of war, Dewey would not be able to use neutral harbors; hence he stationed the coal ships in a Chinese harbor which he knew to be careless in matters of international law. The Navy Department suggested a Japanese harbor, but the Japanese, Dewey knew, were even more punctilious than the British in Hong Kong. Told by the Navy Department he could not receive any ammunition for six months, Dewey, with Roosevelt's assistance, found a way to expedite a shipment. But the Asiatic Squadron still went to war without a full supply.

Admiral of the Navy George Dewey

"Impregnable Manila"

The U. S. Navy was confident of victory and the Spanish navy was not. But opinion in Europe favored the Spanish, and in Hong Kong even the navy savvy British doubted American success because of "impregnable Manila's" fortifications, mines, and warships. According to Dewey's autobiography,

> The prevailing impression even among the military class in the colony was that our squadron was going to certain destruction. In the Hong Kong Club it was not possible to get bets, even at heavy odds, that our expedition would be a success, and this in spite of a friendly predilection among the British in our favor. I was told, after our officers had been entertained at dinner by a British regiment, that the universal

remark among our hosts was to this effect: "A fine set of
fellows, but unhappily we shall never see them again."

The Spanish in the Philippines had a few more ships than Dewey, but
they were smaller and obsolete. The Americans had more and bigger
guns. For that reason, the Spanish commander, Admiral Patricio
Montojo, planned to hole up in the narrow Subic bay under the
protection of coastal artillery and other defenses. However, upon arrival
at Subic, Montojo discovered the commanding officer there had not
installed the weaponry which had been sent to him. Modern guns lay
on the ground unmounted, shore-based mobile torpedoes were not
in place, and most of the mines had been stolen by Philippine rebels
for their gunpowder content. This was not Dewey-level efficiency.
Only forty miles separated Subic bay from Manila bay, and the two
commanders had a telegraph line connecting them. Yet Montojo got
the surprise of his life.

Greatly disappointed, the Spanish admiral took his squadron to the
broad Manila bay and anchored where there was some artillery support
and relatively shallow water close to land. In that location, more
survivors of the battle could save themselves by, for example, climbing
the masts of their sunken ships.

Dewey had heard that Montojo would be at Subic. Not finding him
there, he proceeded slowly to Manila bay, timing his arrival for well after
dark. Ahead the Americans saw signaling and a rocket. The commander
at Subic had telegraphed Montojo about the American squadron's
arrival (the one thing he did right), and Montojo's men could make
out ghostly warships approaching in the moonlight. At the entrance
to Manila bay, Dewey aimed his column toward a wide channel,
Boca Grande, that was reputed to be mined. Dewey had decided the
reports of mining were a bluff, and luckily for him they were. Neither
searchlights nor fire boats greeted the invaders. The Americans tensely
expected shells to come their way, but the shore guns were strangely
quiet. The last ship in line was the revenue cutter *McCulloch*. Soot in
its smokestack suddenly caught fire, shooting up like a roman candle,
and this drew some cannon shots. Four American ships responded and
the shore battery went silent. Some of the Spanish gunners were not
even at their posts. At one battery the men were ready to fire, but the
commanding officer did not give the order. Clouds obscured the moon

just as the squadron completed its passage into the bay. In disgrace, a Spanish colonel of artillery shot himself.

Admiral Montojo had assumed the Americans would not risk navigating the harbor at night. As they were doing so, Montojo, the picture of nonchalance, was in a carriage riding back to his command. He had attended a reception hosted by his wife, according to Dewey's autobiography.

"Automobile Torpedoes"

History books portray Dewey's victory as a piece of cake, and in fact that is how it turned out. But Dewey could not be sure of that, and his passage into Manila bay might have been very different. The Spanish had failed to do a proper job of mining the bay's entrance, but guarding the channel were several modern cannon and some old muzzle loaders. The defenders' combined fire on the American ships, passing like ducks in a row, ought to have done some damage, especially if the invaders had been illuminated by flammable boats like those Captain Hartstene anchored in Charleston harbor. In a coordinated defense, Montojo could have employed gunboats, of which he had more than twenty, to harry the carefully spaced column, and in the general commotion, low-profile torpedo boats might have sunk a ship or two with their self-propelled "automobile torpedoes," the high tech weapon of the time.

The torpedo boat, a new weapon devastating at short range, in the future would achieve its successes by stealth at night or by deception in daytime. Both tactics were employed by history's champion torpedo boat skipper, Luigi Rizzo. Rizzo was a Danube ferry boat captain who in World War I joined the Italian navy and sank two Austrian battleships. As Rizzo knew, the torpedo boat's high speed was better suited to the getaway than to the approach. Why alarm the enemy with noise and a bow wave? When chased, Rizzo went top speed and dropped short-fuzed depth charges in his wake.

Considering the defenses available at Manila bay, the American entrance might have been very different. Dewey gambled on Spanish inefficiency and won.

At dawn of May 1, the invading squadron drew a few more shots from coastal artillery. Dewey, concerned about his ammunition supply, ignored them. Montojo at last was on the job, and he opened fire when the American ships hove into view. Dewey ignored those shots as well, again saving ammunition. When within range of the Spanish flotilla, the commodore gave his second in command a famous order, "You may fire when you are ready, Gridley." Shells rained on the Spanish vessels, and they were destroyed in seven hours. Neither Montojo's gunners nor the coastal artillery did much damage to the Americans, although the Spanish made several hits and one observer thought hundreds of men must have been killed. What appeared to be two Spanish torpedo boats made a suicidal dash and were demolished. It will be recalled that in daytime three boats tried that un-Rizzo like tactic in the Tonkin Gulf.

Suicidal Attack

In desperation, Admiral Montojo tried to ram the *Olympia*. The attempt was unsuccessful and half of Montojo's crew was killed or wounded, his ship destroyed. Spanish officers shot some men deserting their posts. In the Battle of Manila Bay, the Spanish suffered 161 dead, 210 wounded. Montojo survived with a wounded leg. Seven Americans were slightly wounded. One American fell dead of heat stroke, but that was before the battle. Dewey commented that the Spanish were long on valor but short on preparation.

As another item in the annals of nonchalance, it has been recorded that in the middle of the battle Dewey moved his ships out of range and ordered breakfast to be served. This is true, and the crews did eat breakfast. The men were not happy about it: "To hell with breakfast!" was their attitude. The real purpose of the withdrawal was to check the ammunition supply. Dewey had heard he was running out of 5-inch shells, a report which turned out to be incorrect.

As a result of the pause in battle, the Spanish telegraphed from Manila that the American ships, severely damaged, sought refuge behind merchant vessels across the bay. Madrid claimed victory. The erroneous Spanish reports made Dewey's achievement the more stunning when, several days later, the commodore's report reached the United States. Dewey had to send dispatches on the *McCulloch* to the telegraph office in Hong Kong.

A "Dewey craze" engulfed America. Once allegedly cowering behind merchant ships, the American officer now was idolized for his boldness, compared to Lord Nelson, and destined for the "Valhalla of great naval commanders." For a triumphal parade upon Dewey's return, there were built in New York City, of temporary material, a colonnade and a tall arch adorned with the work of twenty-eight sculptors. The hitherto under appreciated Commodore Dewey was promoted to rear admiral. Later, he jumped all known ranks to "admiral of the navy," a six-star rank still unique to him. (The five-star admirals of World War II were "fleet admirals.") The Congress awarded Dewey an ornate golden and bejeweled Tiffany sword, and it exempted him from retiring at the mandatory age. All of his crew members were presented a special "Dewey medal." An appropriation of $10,000 paid for the sword and medals. Still commemorating the Battle of Manila Bay, the USS *Olympia* is on display in Philadelphia. Impressive for its technology as well as for its history, the ship features the Navy's first ice making machine and other wonders, but it needs expensive repairs and financial assistance is being sought.

In Spain, Admiral Montojo was court-martialed and imprisoned, but later absolved. The resplendent Admiral Dewey testified as to the Spaniard's disadvantages.

Cuba Next

The warships that Spain sent to Cuba were not obsolete, but they were not ready for battle, either. With the Spanish army fighting in Cuba and the Philippines, the Spanish navy lacked funds for maneuvers, gunnery training, repairs, and maintenance. Owing to a contract dispute, one new ship did not yet have its largest guns installed. Wooden ones poked out. Some of the on board engineers were Scottish, as on the fictional starship *Enterprise*. (The Scottish engineer became a cliché in fiction). Wisely, the Scots quit when the war began.

Torpedo-launching craft were available.

The Spanish commander, Admiral Pascual Cervera, wanted to form his defense in the eastern Atlantic at the Canary islands, which he thought the Americans would want to capture and use as a base against the mainland. At the Canaries, the Spanish ships could be repaired and well supplied with coal and ammunition. Many Americans, too, assumed that the U.S. Navy would bombard the Spanish coast, and they wondered why they heard no news of this. Cervera's squadron was ordered to Cuba. He and his officers saw doom ahead. Cervera told his superiors:

> It is impossible for me to give you an idea of the surprise and consternation experienced by all on the receipt of the order to sail. Indeed, that surprise is well justified, for nothing can be expected of this expedition except the total destruction of the fleet or its hasty and demoralized return.

Crossing the Atlantic, Cervera managed to elude the U.S. Navy, and he made it into the harbor at Santiago, Cuba. There he was protected by coastal artillery and electric mines. However, blockaded by the U.S. Navy in Santiago harbor, Cervera could not prevent American troops from landing in Cuba. He missed the perfect opportunity. American troop transports carrying ten thousand men departed Key West on June 14 and, moving at only seven knots, took six days to reach the port of Daiquiri near Santiago. Since Cervera was in Santiago, the War Department planned to capture that city first instead of Havana. At night, the American troop transports, under the command of General Rufus Shafter, blazed with lights despite the Navy's warnings to dim them, and a few well placed torpedoes would have made a fiasco of the U. S. Army's Cuban expedition.

Holed up in Santiago, Cervera's squadron, except for loaning out a thousand sailors as infantry, might as well have been in the Canaries.

U. S. Army Unprepared

After years of debate about intervention in Cuba, the U.S. Army was caught flatfooted. No Theodore Roosevelt energized that organization or planned ahead. Spanish riflemen used up-to-date smokeless powder. Most American soldiers had to use old fashioned black powder, which gave away their positions and fouled their weapons. The American Army had no summer uniforms. In Cuba and the Philippines our men wore heavy blue wool. Relying on the advice of a Cuban "yellow fever expert," our generals defied conventional wisdom in thinking that it would be all right to invade Cuba during the rainy season. Medical science as yet did not know that malaria and yellow fever were transmitted by mosquitoes, and most of our soldiers soon were incapacitated by disease. There was no proper food supply. Secretary of War Russell A. Alger (a distant relative of author Horatio Alger) had to resign for buying what our soldiers called "embalmed meat." Low bidding Chicago meat packers made beef extract from meat and, for the Army to eat, shipped the pallid remainder in cans with chemical preservatives.

Navy's Advice Rejected

Like Admiral Cervera, General Shafter missed a golden opportunity. Admiral William T. Sampson advised the Army to land not at Daiquiri but at the entrance to Santiago harbor, with the site cleared first by naval gunfire. Once that area was captured, Sampson's mine sweepers could do their work, and the American warships could enter the harbor, sink the enemy ships, and command the city. Without the Spanish navy to bring men and supplies, Cuba would be conquered. Shafter decided to land at Daiquiri. The Army then fought for the high ground behind Santiago, suffering casualties from enemy fire and disease.[2] The high ground could have been cleared by naval gunfire, even from outside the Santiago harbor. Shafter himself, weighing more than 300 pounds, was not able to charge any high ground.

Admiral William T. Sampson

After his signal accomplishments as assistant secretary of the navy, Theodore Roosevelt found that job too dull, decided to join the Army, and ordered a blue uniform from Brooks Brothers. In Cuba, Lieutenant Colonel Roosevelt became famous for his participation in the Battle of San Juan Hill, as depicted by the artist Frederic Remington. It is doubtful Roosevelt actually did anything at San Juan Hill. Remington worked behind the lines and did not see the battle. It is definite that Roosevelt charged nearby Kettle Hill, leading the "Rough Riders," a regiment of eager volunteers most of whom charged on foot. All were good horsemen, but the enlisted men's horses were left in Florida for lack of space on their ship. The majority of "Riders" were cowhands, ranchers, Native Americans, Mexican-Americans, and former Ivy League athletes. The Rough Riders' war chant:

> Rough tough, we're the stuff. We want to fight and we can't get enough. Whoopee!

The Westerners at first thought Roosevelt comical with his spectacles and Harvard accent, but on horseback their leader presented an inspiring figure, and fame in combat helped him to win the vice presidency. Following the assassination of President McKinley, the Rough Rider from Brooks Brothers became President.

Colonel Roosevelt and his Rough Riders

Authorities in Madrid wanted Admiral Cervera to get out of Santiago and fight. Knowing this would result in destruction of his ships and endanger the lives of his two thousand sailors, Cervera preferred to help the Army defend Santiago, and if that failed, scuttle his ships rather than let them be captured. His captains agreed. Next came an orgy of buck passing. Not wishing to be responsible for the destruction of Cervera's fleet, the Spanish Admiralty put Cervera under the authority of General Ramon Blanco, who commanded the Spanish army in Cuba. Cervera explained his disadvantages to the general. Blanco referred the matter to General Arsenio Linares, the army commander at Santiago. Linares referred the matter to Cervera. Blanco jumped back in saying the captain of a German cruiser at Havana thought that a sortie from Santiago "could be effected without running great risks." Cervera interpreted this message as an order to leave the harbor, but said he needed the order to be *explicit* so that he would not be making a mistake. In the event of a sortie, Cervera added, he would need for Linares to send back the sailors helping the army. Blanco sought advice from Linares. Linares was facing the American army and did not want to give back the sailors.

Shafter Seeks Help from Navy

Inattentively, General Shafter allowed the Spanish to march reinforcements into Santiago, and the city's defenses then were so strong that, it was estimated, three thousand Americans might be lost in the assault. But with the added troops, the city had far too many mouths to feed. Learning that, Shafter, increasingly worried about the spread of yellow fever, wanted to let the hungry Spaniards depart unmolested and then move his men into the city. McKinley rejected that idea. Why let the Spanish escape and fight another day? Shafter then considered threatening the city with a long range bombardment by Admiral Sampson's guns. This tactic, if implemented, would tarnish the humanitarian aspect of the war, and so it had to be approved by the President. He approved.

Admiral Cervera finally decided to get going. Under pressure from the Spanish army and with the Americans threatening to bombard Santiago, Cervera planned a desperate departure. He chose a Sunday morning when fewer American ships were present, and not all had steam up for a battle. Admiral Sampson was ashore having a conference with General Shafter. The Spanish fleet's sudden emergence surprised the Americans, who were dressed in white uniforms for religious services; but commanded by Commodore Winfield Scott Schley, they overwhelmed the Spanish, anyway.

The Naval War College would have done well to keep in mind Cervera's Sunday morning tactic, which was employed by Japan on December 7, 1941.

Spanish gunnery was not bad. But the Spanish shells were not very effective because of substandard gunpowder (the same trouble Mexican artillery had in 1846). Some shells carried sawdust, which was used in practice, and a defective gun blew up. One of the large ships was slowed by its neglected bottom having been fouled by barnacles and grass. No Spanish torpedo found a target. Cervera's men made a gallant but useless effort. All the deficiencies of the Spanish ships and their equipment had been known for many months; yet little was done to remedy them.

On the American side, 1 man was killed and 10 wounded. Among the Spaniards, 323 were killed and 151 wounded. Some 1,600 Spaniards, including Admiral Cervera, were rescued by the American forces. Cervera wrote a warm letter of thanks.

With civilians evacuated, Santiago was bombarded briefly on July 10 and for five hours on July 11. Negotiations brought about a surrender on July 17. The Spanish in Cuba were isolated and without hope.

General Rufus Shafter

Admiral Sampson had another argument with the Army when it came to invading Spanish Puerto Rico. Sampson thought a naval demonstration might be enough to capture the capital of San Juan. The Army's commanding general, Nelson Miles, preferred to storm the city with troops. Luckily for the troops, San Juan decided to surrender and that ended the argument.[3] The Spanish authorities were disgusted by how, with the surrender, the Puerto Ricans went from fervently Spanish one day to enthusiastically American the next.

What About the Philippines?

Admiral Dewey recommended sending five thousand troops for the capture of Manila, and McKinley put Major General Wesley Merritt in charge of a Philippine expedition. In conversation with the President, Merritt did not find out whether he was merely to capture Manila or the entire archipelago. Later, on May 19, McKinley in writing advised the general of a "twofold purpose," which was "the reduction of Spanish power in that quarter" and the introduction of "order and security to the islands while in the possession of the United States." At the same time, according to a State Department memorandum, the native population had to show the "obedience which will be lawfully due to them [the American military]." This implied martial law. No doubt McKinley failed to imagine that his twofold purpose would require seventy thousand men and a fourteen-year war. The frustrated General Merritt was acutely conscious that different missions required different resources.

From a military standpoint, one could argue that there was a need to destroy or blockade Admiral Montojo's ships lest they cross the Pacific and do some harm, but there certainly was no need to take Manila. Nobody there threatened Cuba or the United States. Manila might be useful only as bargaining chip in the peace negotiations with Spain. Some light is provided by a note McKinley wrote to himself. It was discovered after his death:

> While we are conducting war and until its conclusion, we
> must keep all we can get. When the war is over, we must keep
> what we want.[4]

McKinley was not trying to limit the war or mitigate its effects. His idea was to expand the conflict and pick up useful territories. In for a penny, in for a pound.

"Battle" for Manila

As matters turned out, Manila, for its surrender, required only a mock assault. On the landward side, the city was hemmed in by the Filipino army, and toward the bay it faced Dewey's flotilla. There was no importation of food. Horses were being butchered. So were dogs and cats. But if like San Juan, Puerto Rico, the city surrendered without a fight, there would be courts martial when the Spanish army returned home, and so a let's-pretend battle was agreed upon. As part of the deal, the Americans kept the Filipino army out of the city. The Spanish felt they had not been conquered by the Filipinos and so were not willing to surrender to the Filipinos.

The mock battle took place on August 13. It was quite a show. Some foreign warships were in the harbor, and the event began with a British band playing Admiral Dewey's favorite march, "Under the Double Eagle," an Austrian composition. The American warships broke out their huge battle flags, took their positions, and bombarded for an hour Manila's Fort Antonio. An American skipper deliberately gave false ranges to his gunners, but the gunners corrected them and scored direct hits. There was no response from the fort, where two Spaniards were killed and two wounded. Apparently nobody told them what was happening. Equally ignorant American troops advanced into Manila meeting light resistance. Six Americans were killed and forty-three wounded. A total of forty-nine of the Spanish died. The casualties were regrettable, and perhaps could have been avoided, but having a mock battle was better than having a real battle. As we saw in the case of Admiral Cervera's doomed squadron, the Spanish were willing to take a lot of casualties in order to save their honor.

The American flag went up in Manila with Dewey's band playing the "Star Spangled Banner." The *Salt Lake Herald* headlined, "Dewey Bombards Manila and the City Surrenders."

Manila was not needed as a bargaining chip. Just a few hours before the mock battle, the war officially ended with the signing of a peace agreement in Washington. Nobody in Manila knew about that because Dewey's men had cut the cable and dispatches were still moving by ship between Hong Kong and Manila.

A Glorious Victory

The American people gloried in suddenly having become a major world power. "The nation has at a bound gone forward in the estimation of the world more than we would have done in fifty years of peace," exulted Senator Proctor. "No war in history has accomplished so much in so short a time with so little loss," said Ambassador to France Horace Porter. In Chicago, cartoonist Finley Peter Dunne's Irishmen expressed the national mood:

"We ar-re a gr-reat people," said Mr. Hennessy.

"We ar-re that," replied Mr. Dooley. "We ar-re that. An' th' best iv it is, we know we ar-re."

With the defeat of the Spanish navy, the U.S. Navy was in a position to bombard the Spanish coast, but there was no need. The Spanish knew they had lost the war. Thanks to Senator Teller and the sugar beet growers, we Americans did not annex Cuba, but we leased Guantanamo bay and took from Spain Puerto Rico, Guam, and the Philippines, paying Spain $20 million. Counting Hawaii, we now had bases and coaling stations all the way across the Pacific, a triumph for Mahanism. The war turned out to be partly humanitarian and partly Mahanian.

As a major Pacific power, the United States acquired a new neighbor and potential enemy: the Japanese Empire. Henceforth, the American and Japanese navies both would plan on that basis. Belatedly, Theodore Roosevelt came to view his territorial acquisition as the "heel of Achilles." The U.S. Navy conducted mock attacks on Pearl Harbor, and the attacks were considered successful. Unfortunately, the Japanese kept a closer watch on our navy than we kept on theirs.

Analysis

Is it not strange that Spain fought for years to keep the Philippines, Mexico, and Cuba, but would not send a frigate to preserve Spanish California? The Spanish governor of California certainly was surprised. For some reason, the Mexicans did not value California, either. They did not want to live there, and General Vallejo, after asking for two hundred soldiers, received pardoned convicts who terrorized and robbed the Californios. Some Ph.D. candidate ought to investigate the nineteenth century Spanish and Mexican attitudes toward California.

The American press and public demanded a crusade to stop the suffering "next door" in Cuba. There was indeed suffering and starvation, but the yellow press invented and exaggerated reports. The Junta helped with lurid copy and sponsored rallies around the country. The Spanish government also got boxed in by press and public, and the Spanish political concessions always came too late. After the war started, the knowledgeable Admiral Cervera could not make a prediction dark enough to discourage the demand for him to do something.

In his book *Three Centuries of Harvard*, historian Samuel Eliot Morison cited among Harvard men "three political musketeers who did the most" to bring on the war. They were Senator Henry Cabot Lodge, Navy Assistant Secretary Theodore Roosevelt, and publisher William Randolph Hearst.[5] Hearst aroused the public with sensational reporting;

he flatly blamed the Spanish for the sinking of the *Maine*. Lodge and Roosevelt, among others, browbeat Mckinley.

An anti-war Harvard man was the philosopher William James. He advised his students, "Don't yelp with the pack."

The most famous anecdote to come out of the Cuban crusade featured William Randolph Hearst and artist Frederic Remington. Hearst sent Remington to Cuba to sketch pictures of the war. After his arrival, Remington telegraphed Hearst to say that all was quiet, there was no war. Responded the publisher: "You furnish the pictures and I'll furnish the war." Historians doubt the authenticity of that exchange. But it is true that after Dewey's naval victory at Manila, Hearst's paper for three days headlined the question:

"How do you like the Journal's War?"

Already in the Civil War, we saw the power of the press, which promoted the On to Richmond strategy and ridiculed the advice of General Winfield Scott, which might have saved hundreds of thousands of lives. The press ruled America, War Secretary Cameron explained to William Russell of the London *Times*. In 1898, the press still ruled America. In Europe the press ruled, too. In Spain, it predicted that Spanish patriotism would impel its military personnel to great deeds while America's foreign mercenaries abandoned their posts. Prior to the "New Navy" of the 1890s, the U.S. Navy was known for its immigrant sailors; an early example was the Revolutionary War's John Paul Jones, a Scot by birth. Dewey's men, the admiral said in his autobiography, were 80 percent American.

The power of the pen went on. The Spanish-American War became known as the "splendid little war," an appellation often attributed to Theodore Roosevelt. Actually it was originated by John Hay, who became secretary of state in August of 1898. Hay wrote to his friend Roosevelt:

It has been a splendid little war, begun with the highest motives, carried on with magnificent intelligence and spirit, favored by that Fortune which loves the brave.

Ending the desultory colonial conflict did save the lives of many Cubans. Unfortunately, democracy and the rule of law failed in Cuba. Since independence, the island almost always has been ruled by dictators. Concentration camps still exist. For the past six decades, Cubans have been governed by the iron fists of Fidel and Raul Castro, the sons of a Spanish soldier who fought against the liberation of Cuba.

An Avoidable War?

This was a war of choice undertaken for humanitarian reasons. President Cleveland did not want it. President McKinley did not want it. Spurred by Cuban propagandists, the press and public wanted it. And they were in a hurry. Our ambassador in Madrid recommended giving the Spanish government a few months more time so that it could arrange Cuban autonomy without starting a revolution in Spain. That ought to have worked. With their inferior navy, the Spanish had no hope of winning the war. The U. S. Navy could have blockaded both Cuba and the Philippines rendering the Spanish army helpless. The Spanish could not have held out for long in either place. Unwilling to wait, we Americans declared war and the Army rushed into Cuba during the rainy season, the worst time for yellow fever and malaria.

Tropical diseases were rampant in Cuba, and typhoid ravaged camps in the United States. According to the *Encyclopedia Americana*, 5,000 Americans died from combat and disease. Combat fatalities were fewer than 400, which tells us that more than 4,600 men died of disease. Most sources report fewer than 3,000 deaths from disease but they omit disease deaths in the United States. After only forty days in the field, General Shafter requested that his entire "army of convalescents" be recalled. His men were shipped to Long Island, where they were quarantined.

Capturing hills in Cuba was not necessary. With the Navy blockading Cuba and perhaps bombarding the coast, the Army could have landed after the Spanish surrendered. For bureaucratic and political reasons, both of the American military services had to *do something*, ready or not. Recklessness prevailed and little thought was given to minimizing casualties. After the war, Roosevelt bragged that his regiment suffered the most from enemy fire.

In the Philippines, our commanders did give thought to mitigating casualties. The mock "battle of Manila" wasn't perfect, but it helped. The blockaded Spanish army surrendered. No hills had to be climbed.

The Spanish-American War was an avoidable but noble cause that could have been better managed.

Useful Principles

Watch out for the power of the press and other communications media.

Watch out for foreign lobbying organizations.

If the object is peace, do not put a war lover in a key government position.

Do not rush into war when speed is not necessary.

Do not expand a war unnecessarily.

Do not assume that each of the armed services must be given an equal role, and bear in mind that the services have been known to seek glory by inventing unnecessary tasks, as when the Air Force insisted on bombing North Vietnam.

If it comes to war, consider how victory can be achieved most easily and with the fewest casualties.

References

[1]   Henry F. Pringle, *Theodore Roosevelt*, page 167

[2]   George J. A. O'Toole, *The Spanish War*, pages 256 to 265. See also Dudley W. Knox's *A History of the U.S. Navy*, page 353.

[3]   Robert Love, *History of the U.S. Navy*, pages 399-400.

[4]   Stanley Karnow, *In Our Image*, page 108

[5]   Samuel E. Morison, *Three Centuries of Harvard*, page 413

CHAPTER TEN

Philippine-American War (1899 to 1913)

You know where a war begins, but you never know where it ends—Prince Otto von Bismarck (1815-1898)

When the news of Commodore Dewey's victory reached Washington, President McKinley had to look for a globe. "I could not have told where those darned islands were within two thousand miles," the President admitted to his friend Herman H. Kohlsaat. On another occasion the President said, "When the Philippines dropped into our laps, I confess I did not know what to do with them." He had thought only so far as Manila, which he figured might be a good "hitching post" for the Navy. McKinley devoted intense thought, consultation, and prayer to the question of what to do with the distant archipelago. In the end, he decided that the inhabitants were unfit for self-rule and prone to "anarchy." It was necessary to "educate the Filipinos, and uplift and civilize and Christianize them, and by God's grace do the very best we could by them."[1]

McKinley did not know what he was talking about. The Philippines already were a Christian country, the most Christian country in all of Asia. Catholic friars had been Christianizing Filipinos for almost four hundred years. They started before the Pilgrims landed at Plymouth Rock. As for the "anarchy," this was a tale originating with the Spanish and other foreign residents of Manila. If the President or the Congress had sent an investigator to the Philippines, he would have discovered that the Filipinos were Christian and that they were enjoying a quiet, peaceful life, thanks to the Americans' having ended Spanish rule.

But not for long would the Filipinos enjoy a quiet life, thanks to President McKinley.

At first, Admiral Dewey formed a good opinion of the Filipinos. He employed hundreds of them at the Cavite (now Kawit) island naval yard and found them "amiable," "intelligent," and "kindly disposed." Dewey reported to Washington:

> These people are far superior in intelligence and more capable of self-government than the natives of Cuba.[2]

The month after Dewey arrived, Philippine independence and a Philippine government were proclaimed by the insurgent leader Emilio Aguinaldo. After that, two of Admiral Dewey's officers investigated the new government's effect in the countryside and were very favorably impressed. Paymaster Willis Cox and Naval Cadet Leonard Sargent talked to hundreds of people in seven different provinces. Sargent reported that the Filipinos had established a quiet and orderly society that desired independence. Said he:

> It is a tribute to the efficiency of Aguinaldo's government and to the law-abiding character of his subjects that Mr. Wilcox and I pursued our journey . . . with only the most pleasing recollections of the quiet and orderly life we found the natives to be leading under the new regime . . . On one point they seem united, that whatever our government may have done for them, it has not gained the right to annex them.[3]

Dewey delayed weeks before passing on Cox and Sargent's report, and then he sent it by mail.

Dewey's Mistake

Meanwhile, Dewey had received from President McKinley a list of questions, and apparently having changed his mind about the Filipinos, he said that they would not be capable of self-government for "many, many years" and that the United States ought to keep these "valuable" islands permanently. For that purpose, he estimated, fifty thousand troops would be needed. Dewey was influenced by diplomats who told him that the Filipinos wanted to become a colony and acquire American citizenship. (Then why the fifty thousand troops?) Two of the diplomats were American, Consul Oscar Williams in Manila and Consul

General Rounseville Wildman in Hong Kong. A third was Edouard Andre, the Belgian consul in Manila. Williams and Wildman were political appointees. Williams formerly taught business law. Wildman had been a journalist.

The admiral's answers to McKinley's questions must have pleased most of the President's advisers. The attorney general, John Griggs, and the secretary of the interior, Cornelius Bliss, thought there would be commercial advantages to acquiring the islands. The secretary of agriculture, James Wilson, wanted to evangelize the population. Senator Henry Cabot Lodge and Captain Alfred T. Mahan wanted a naval base. Opposition came from the secretary of state, William R. Day. The United States, he said, was not suited to the work of colonization and it would violate the principle of consent by the governed. Contradicting himself about consent of the governed, the secretary recommended letting the Spanish remain in charge.

Business interests, although opposed to the Cuban war, anticipated expanded trade in the Orient and backed the colonization of the Philippines.

In the United States, an Anti-Imperialist League opposed annexation. The League had many distinguished members including former President Grover Cleveland, industrialist Andrew Carnegie, union leader Samuel Gompers, author Mark Twain, and the philosopher William James.

Initially, neither President McKinley nor the American people wanted to keep the archipelago. Over a period of several months, however, the feeling grew that, like the Cubans, the Filipinos needed American help and guidance. "We will do our duty," became the consensus. In that spirit, Rudyard Kipling wrote a poem, "The White Man's Burden," about the civilizing effect of colonialism, and he subtitled it, "The United States and the Philippine Islands." Kipling knew how to write a persuasive poem. But not everybody was impressed. When an African-American unit arrived in Manila, its men joked about how they were there to "take up the white man's burden."

Aguinaldo "Soft-spoken, Unimpressive"

Emilio Aguinaldo, was a handsome young man, part Chinese, and only 29 years old. Dewey described him as "a soft-spoken, unimpressive little man who had enormous prestige with the Filipino people." Impressive in appearance or not, Aguinaldo had been a capable general in the revolt against Spain, and he proudly wore a sword captured from a Spanish officer.

Before the Spanish-American War, Aguinaldo was in exile. In Hong Kong and Singapore he met with the American consuls, who, as he thought, agreed that the United States would support Philippine independence in return for Philippine assistance in the war against Spain. *Encyclopedia Americana* states flatly, "the American consul in Singapore assured Aguinaldo of Philippine independence if he became an active ally." Filipino residents of Singapore held a party for Consul E. Spencer Pratt, and he toasted their planned "republic." Pratt reported his convivial diplomacy to Washington, but Secretary Day was not pleased. He cabled, "Avoid unauthorized negotiations with Philippine insurgents." Pratt denied having done that, but he was dismissed anyway.

Pratt offered to help Aguinaldo buy arms on commission, but nothing came of his proposal. The arms job was corralled by Wildman in Hong Kong. The consul general took 17,000 pesos and delivered little merchandise. What happened to the money is not known. On the way back to the United States, in 1901, Wildman died in a shipwreck. At the State Department, he is honored on a plaque as a Foreign Service hero.

Having heard that the exiled Aguinaldo wanted to help fight the Spanish, Dewey ordered the *McCulloch* to bring him to Manila. The rebel leader arrived on May 19, and the admiral accepted him as an ally. Dewey gave the rebels captured Spanish weapons, and the rebels helped the Americans to find provisions and horses. No fool, Aguinaldo drew the line at providing maps. His men attacked Spanish posts, which had been cut off from supplies, and captured thousands of prisoners. The Filipinos occupied the large island of Luzon except for the city of Manila, which they surrounded on the land side. According to Aguinaldo, Dewey promised independence, but Dewey denied that.

Independence Ceremony

It was on June 12, 1898, that Aguinaldo declared Philippine independence. There was a solemn ceremony at his ancestral home in Cavite. From his balcony, Aguinaldo looked out at a crowd dressed in top hats and cutaway coats, many of the attendants having been educated in Europe. The host read aloud a lengthy *Act of Declaration of Independence*. He envisaged freedom "under the protection of the mighty and humane" United States. Aguinaldo had commissioned a flag and a national anthem. There was a banquet with French food and fine wines. The attendants "conducted themselves with great decorum, and showed a knowledge of debate and parliamentary law," said a correspondent.

Other than the press, the only American present was a businessman, retired Colonel L. M. Johnson. Aguinaldo wanted to have an American signature on the declaration of independence, and Johnson obliged. Admiral Dewey refused to attend the ceremony, explaining later it was "mail day." Also absent was the American consul, Oscar Williams, who presumably feared to give the event any sort of recognition. In 1902, Dewey told a Senate committee:

> I attached so little importance to the [independence] document that I did not even cable its contents to Washington, but forwarded it through the mails. I never dreamed that they wanted independence.

On June 18, Aguinaldo established a provisional dictatorship and asked for the election of delegates to a revolutionary congress. Why "revolutionary"? Nominally, Spain still owned the islands. On June 23, there was a change of plan. Aguinaldo announced a Revolutionary Government headed by himself as President. Deciding that the election of delegates was not practical at this time, Aguinaldo appointed them instead. Fifty delegates assembled at the town of Malolos on September 15. Elections were held there. The congress ratified the declaration of independence and began work on a constitution, which was enacted on January 23, 1899. This was the beginning of the Philippine Republic, later to be remembered as the First Philippine Republic.

President Emilio Aguinaldo

Asia's First Republic

A Christian nation established the first republic in Asia. The Filipinos did that without any American aid program or harangues from shuttling diplomats. We Americans ought to have been proud of our role. Instead, we went to war against the fledgling democracy and destroyed it.

When in August the insurgents were not allowed to take part in Manila's capture, this disturbed Aguinaldo and so did the increasing number of American troops. American officials said they had not agreed on Philippine independence, that they had no authority to do so, and that the President had made no decision. Earlier, Americans on the scene had said that the United States had no need for colonies, and they stressed that the United States did not intend to annex Cuba. General Thomas H. Anderson informed the anxious Aguinaldo:

> In one hundred and twenty-two years we have established no colonies. I leave you to draw your own inference.[4]

Aguinaldo had to tread carefully. He wanted independence, but he also wanted the U.S. Navy to provide protection from foreign powers. If that were not possible, he had in mind seeking help from Japan.

Germany was interested in providing a protectorate, and the American ambassador to Berlin encouraged that ambition. He was Andrew D. White, the founding president of Princeton University (formerly the College of New Jersey), now a politically appointed ambassador. In conversation with the German foreign minister, the amiable White was receptive to discussions when the German showed an interest in the Philippines, and Washington tried to rein in its erring envoy.[5]

Dewey versus German Navy

Britain and Germany often kept a warship or two in Manila's spacious harbor. Perhaps thanks to Ambassador White, soon the Germans had floating around more firepower than Dewey, and their ships appeared to be unacquainted with the rules of blockade. Without seeking permission they went on mysterious errands and did not like to be boarded for identification. The German commanding officer appeared to be getting very friendly with the Spanish, and the Filipinos began to worry about a resumption of Spanish rule. Increasingly irritated, Admiral Dewey tried hinting his displeasure. Finally, he threatened to fire on any ship that failed to stop when requested and stated that he was ready for war if need be. He did all that without consulting Washington. In a meeting of the three local naval powers, Dewey's position was supported by the British. The Germans decided to cooperate, and after a while most of them left. Dewey disliked the Germans and predicted war with them.

The German navy's clumsy attempt to gain influence in the Philippines was the work of the mercurial Kaiser Wilhelm II, who had fired Chancellor Otto von Bismarck, Europe's most talented and forceful statesman. The retired Bismarck happened to take his last breath as the kaiser's warships were exasperating Admiral Dewey. But Ambassador White's encouragement must be remembered as well.

Although Dewey professed little confidence in the Filipinos' ability to govern themselves, he recommended giving them as much participation in their government as possible. This idea was slow to take hold. The Army, not the Navy, would manage land operations. The Army was accustomed to fighting Native Americans, and many of its personnel were inclined to see the Filipinos in that way. In particular, that was true of the commanding general, Elwell Otis. An insomniac as the result of a

Civil War wound, Otis worked long hours at a desk at the Malacanang Palace, which formerly was occupied by the Spanish governor. The portly general was not one to go out and view operations in the field.

President McKinley did not make known his plan for annexation until after the peace treaty with Spain was signed on December 10, 1898. The delay made it easier to get the treaty signed.

The First Shot

Filipino and American soldiers were stationed near each other around Manila. On the night of February 4, 1899, an American sentry, William Grayson from Nebraska, shot a Filipino who mocked the order to halt and did not stop. Two of the dead man's companions also were shot. Possibly all three Filipinos were just drunk, but the incident grew into a general conflict. The Nebraskan blamed General Otis for what happened. He said Otis's "damned bullheadedness" put American troops in disputed territory.

As bullets flew, Aguinaldo, through intermediaries, offered a truce and suggested establishing a buffer zone. From his palace, General Otis, who never had met the Philippine leader, would not agree. His meetings with residents of Manila had persuaded him that the Philippine army was collapsing. Otis sent word to Aguinaldo: "Fighting, having begun, must go on to the grim end."

By failing to meet with the genuine native leader and giving credence to unrepresentative individuals in Manila, General Otis furthered a tradition of self-deception by "ugly Americans" that would flourish all over Asia. We Americans naturally have preferred to deal with the local person who "wears a tie and speaks English," and these people, though helpful, often have led us astray.

Undeclared War

What was called the "Philippine Insurrection" was not declared as a war by the U.S. Congress. Neither was it authorized explicitly, although the Congress provided funds. James Grafton Rogers described the

Philippine hostilities as a "continuation of the Spanish War," but that was not true because, as Rogers also noted, a treaty of peace had been signed with Spain. In dealing with related financial questions, federal courts decided a "war" existed. By hindsight, there was erosion of Congressional authority, but it did not seem that way at the time.

If the Congress had followed proper procedure by debating a declaration of war, the lawmakers would have had to name the enemy, and might have noticed the existence of the Philippine Republic. Listing reasons for the war would have been difficult since there were none.

Optimistic Reports

As happened later in Vietnam, the commanding general wrote optimistic reports, and the news correspondents disbelieved them. Most of Otis's fellow officers regarded him as incompetent. As for the enlisted men, they decided that the war made no sense, but they wanted to win it before going home. Again, that was like Vietnam. Unlike Vietnam, the American commander was able to censor the news; he controlled the cable, now repaired. To get around that, the reporters had to send reports by ship to Hong Kong.

General Elwell S. Otis

American officers were handicapped by a lack of policy guidance from Washington and by the President's confusing orders. After the capture of Manila, General Merritt, still dissatisfied with his instructions, transferred out and was replaced by General Otis. McKinley could not picture what was happening. He assumed the Filipinos would understand America's benevolent intentions and fall into line. He ordered the Army to occupy the port of Iloilo, *but without risking a fight*. Not knowing what to do, the invasion force baked in the sun on transport ships for six weeks until the operation was called off. (But they did not have to wait as long as the Union troops off Pensacola.) The American gunboat *Petrel* obtained the surrender of the island of Cebu. Assistance was rendered by the British gunboat *Pygmy*, as if to repay a debt from the Second Opium War. General Otis protested the Navy's action, saying that the occupation of Cebu would divert some of his troops. Elsewhere, naval gunfire helped the Army by destroying Filipino strongpoints.

Otis's wartime command did not last long. In May, 1900, he was replaced by General Arthur MacArthur. He was a fierce critic of Otis and the father of Douglas MacArthur, who in World War II became a five-star general.

Aguinaldo Captured

The official end of the war, as declared by President Theodore Roosevelt, came in 1902 following the capture of Aguinaldo in 1901. Aguinaldo swore allegiance to the United States and that ended the First Philippine Republic. The former guerrilla founded a Veterans of the Revolution organization to arrange veteran pensions and help the men to obtain land. After the declared end of the war, Filipino resistance continued until 1913. Resistance actually increased in the Muslim area known as "Moroland."

Masterminding the capture of Aguinaldo, done as an undercover operation in insurgent territory, was the adventurous Frederick Funston. After the United States declared war on Spain, Funston joined the U.S. Army as a colonel, having organized the 20th Kansas Volunteers, and rose to the rank of brigadier general. In one of his Philippine exploits, Funston earned a Medal of Honor. Why did Funston care about freedom for the Cubans but not freedom for the Filipinos? Perhaps the whole time he just wanted to fight. In the Philippines he was known for his harsh tactics.

General Frederick Funston

General Funston was commanding San Francisco's Presidio when the 1906 earthquake struck. Although martial law was not declared, the general took over the city, ordered looters to be shot, and with dynamite blasted swaths of buildings to stop the fire. Like Fighting Bob Stockton, Funston and Dewey showed extraordinary initiative. President Woodrow Wilson planned to have General Funston command the American Army in Europe during World War I, but the self-taught artillery expert suddenly died of a heart attack.

Admiral Dewey recommended that a civilian commission administer the Philippines. President McKinley appointed two civilians along with General Otis and Admiral Dewey. The two military men did not get long and stayed away. American governors-general began to be appointed in 1901. In 1907, an elected Philippine legislature was established, and in 1916 the ruling commission was replaced by an elected senate. The nation now had a bicameral legislature. In 1935, a new government was organized with a Filipino president, and following a delay caused by

World War II, full independence was granted on July 4, 1946. Aguinaldo ran for President but lost to Manuel Quezon, a fiery popinjay, who had been an Aguinaldo aide. Aguinaldo assisted Quezon as an adviser on the Council of State.

Humanitarian Labors

While the U.S. Army fought guerillas in the bush, it also performed humanitarian labors, beginning in Manila. The long besieged city was in deplorable condition with garbage everywhere. Soldiers cleaned sewers, reopened schools, and provided many other kinds of help. They held English classes, making friends among the island people. In time, American civilian teachers established English as a common language—a great convenience for an archipelago with more than a hundred native tongues. During the period of territorial rule, the Philippine death rate was cut in half. Free trade with the United States transformed the economy. Originally, the Philippine revolution was directed at Spanish friars who had acquired great wealth and oppressed the peasants. Spain became a target because it supported the friars. The United States bought some of the friars' land and distributed it to sixty thousand former tenants.

President Manuel Quezon, trying to build a national spirit among the dwellers of seven thousand tropical islands, expostulated, "Damn the Americans! Why don't they tyrannize us more?"

There had been plenty of oppression in terms of war fatalities. The guerillas lost more than 12,000 killed, and the Philippine Constabulary (on the side of the Americans) 2,000. American fatalities totaled 4,165, mostly from disease.

In *A History of American Foreign Policy*, Alexander DeConde summed up the Philippine-American War:

> [The United States] used more troops than in the Spanish war, expended six hundred million dollars, and sacrificed over four thousand [American] lives. Americans found their soldiers resorting to brutal repressive measures, just as the Spanish had done in Cuba. They too used forms of

torture and concentration camps to break the spirit of the insurrectionists.[6]

Would we have won this war if it had been televised?

Analysis

"If old Dewey had just sailed away when he smashed that Spanish fleet, what a lot of trouble he would have saved us," McKinley commented ruefully after his second war began.

Public opinion swung toward annexation. President McKinley could have shaped public opinion differently if he had known more about the Philippines. Alternatively, McKinley could have stood on principle, refusing to govern a people without their consent.

What was the point of going to war with the people of the Philippines? There was some concern that the islands might be seized by another power, either Germany or Japan. Britain also might have taken "our Philippines." Rather than go to war, the United States could have made a deal in which it acquired Subic bay as a port, like Guantanamo in Cuba, in return for providing naval protection. This would have saved much blood and treasure for both the Filipinos and the Americans. It ought to have satisfied Captain Mahan, who said we needed a Philippine base to protect our commerce.

A true imperialist, President Theodore Roosevelt in 1908 recognized Japan's seizure of Korea and Manchuria in return for Japan's recognition of the American acquisition of Hawaii and the Philippines.

The Philippine-American War served to acquire a base for American naval power in the western Pacific, but that did not prevent the Japanese invasion of 1941. The American defenders were imprisoned for the duration of the war. Their commander, General Douglas MacArthur, escaped in a torpedo boat saying famously, "I shall return." He did so, and the 1944-1945 Philippine campaign became yet another bloody conflict. MacArthur's critics have argued that in 1944 our recently established naval supremacy had enabled us to bypass the archipelago, as we had bypassed many other Pacific islands held by the Japanese.

An Avoidable War?

Like the war with Spain, the Philippine-American War was a war of choice. There was no need for it. We could have skipped the war, which was based on misinformation, and proceeded to work constructively with a friendly, democratic government.

Useful Principles

Follow proper constitutional procedure.

Respect self-determination.

Require diplomats to learn about the areas where they are stationed. Do not hire dilettantes seeking cushy jobs.

Our diplomats in the Far East knew little about the Philippines. They all were political appointees. Career diplomats might have served us better. Oscar Williams was a former professor at Rochester Business University. Ohio Senator Joseph Foraker had asked McKinley to give Williams a consular post. The President said he had available only a place "somewhere away around on the other side of the world . . . [he] had not time to look it up." That was fine with the professor. In fairness to Williams, he helped Dewey by forwarding information about Manila's defenses. Singapore Consul E. Spencer Pratt is listed as having been "non-career" in the State Department's records. As we have seen, consuls Pratt and Wildman were eager to make an extra buck by dealing in arms.

If you do not want a war, do not put troops of antagonistic nationalities next to each other in a disputed territory.

We saw in Mexico how that works out.

What looks like a short war can end up a long war involving long-term ramifications.

Who in 1898 could have imagined that helping Cuban rebels would bring about fourteen years of war in the Philippines, followed in the 1940s by the need to defend this unnecessary conquest, and that followed by a campaign to reclaim it? After all that effort, we freed the Philippines as soon as possible. But we signed a mutual defense treaty in 1951.

References

1   Susan K. Harris, *God's Arbiters*, page 14
2   Stanley Karnow, *In Our Image*, page 114
3   Ivan Musicant, *Empire by Default*, page 584
4   Stanley Karnow, *In Our Image*, page 121
5   William R. Braisted, *U.S. Navy in the Pacific*, pages, 39-42
6   Alexander DeConde, *A History of American Foreign Policy*, first edition, page 354

CHAPTER ELEVEN

Second Mexican-American War (1914 to 1917)

I am going to teach the South American Republics to elect good men—President Woodrow Wilson, 1913

As in the case of the Second Opium War, probably few people today have heard of our second war with Mexico, although nine moving pictures have been made about its circumstance, the Mexican Revolution. Perhaps the best known film was "Viva Zapata!," which was written by John Steinbeck and starred Marlon Brando. The Mexican Revolution of 1910 to 1920 became a civil war and cost a million lives. The American involvement was peripheral. It resulted from President William H. Taft's "dollar diplomacy" and President Woodrow Wilson's "missionary diplomacy." Taft wanted Mexico to be a good place to do business. Wilson wanted to spread democracy and good government.

President Woodrow Wilson

American companies invested heavily in Mexico, in mining, oil, railroads, rubber, and telegraph lines. This modernized Mexico's economy, but most of the population derived little or no benefit. As in Cuba and the Philippines, a revolution was instigated by a man of letters. He was Francisco Madero, a wealthy young man educated in France and the United States. In France, Madero developed a passion for "spiritism" and came to believe himself a medium who could draw wisdom from the deceased. In the United States, he studied business and agriculture.

Back in Mexico, Madero improved the lot of his tenant farmers. Then, guided by spirits, he wrote a book advocating replacement of the nation's dictatorial President, Porfirio Diaz, who had been ruling the country since 1876. The book incited a revolt in 1910, and after some adventures, Madero was elected President in 1911. He received almost 90 percent of the vote. One of the Mexican generals helping Madero was Emiliano Zapata, who in southern Mexico was leading a peasant revolt for land reform.

An Ineffectual President

More philanthropist than executive, Madero as President proved indecisive, and his lack of interest in land reform antagonized Zapata. In 1913, Madero was ousted by General Victoriana Huerta in a bloody coup. One of Huerta's backers was the American ambassador, Henry Lane Wilson, who acted without orders from Washington. An appointee of President William Taft, Ambassador Wilson perceived Madero as a leftist "lunatic" bound to hurt business. Huerta's men executed Madero, and this infuriated the Mexican people. The spirit medium had been a weak leader, but he was honestly elected, and he had wanted to give poor Mexicans a better life. The Emperor Maximilian also had wanted to give poor Mexicans a better life, and he too was executed. So was Emiliano Zapata.

The coup occurred during the administration of President Taft's successor, Woodrow Wilson, and he refused to recognize Huerta's dictatorship, saying privately, "I will not recognize a government of butchers."

General Venustiana Carranza rebelled against the Huerta regime and declared he would re-establish constitutional government. Wilson sent an emissary to suggest Huerta's resignation, but the dictator vowed to oppose any attempt by the United States to interfere with Mexican affairs. Favoring neutrality for the United States, Wilson forbade the export of arms to either side in the ongoing Mexican civil war. Nonetheless, he soon considered sending troops to help Carranza, but the latter did not want them. Carranza did want arms and Wilson allowed their shipment.

Next came the Tampico Affair. Several American sailors and one officer went ashore in Tampico, a port controlled by Huerta, to buy petroleum fuel. They had no Spanish interpreter and were arrested for being in a prohibited zone. Learning of the arrest, the area's Mexican commander released the sailors, who were held for only one hour and a half. He also sent an apology to Rear Admiral Henry T. Mayo, who commanded the American squadron off Tampico. Another apology was forwarded by General Huerta. Commented Alexander DeConde in *A History of American Foreign Policy*:

> The apology might have ended any further difficulty if Wilson had not decided to use it as a means to overthrow Huerta.[1]

To make up for the arrest, the admiral demanded a 21-gun salute to the American flag. Huerta specified that a return salute would be needed. No salutes occurred.

Congress Authorizes Force

President Wilson, saying there had been a series of such incidents, asked the Congress for permission to employ force against General Huerta and his followers, redressing the wrongs done to the United States, but, as he said, *with no force used against the Mexican people*. This was like President McKinley telling the Army to occupy the Philippine port of Iloilo but without risking a fight. Wilson was talented as an orator, but his utterances often were more visionary than practical.

To evade Wilson's arms embargo, the Remington Arms company decided to send guns to Huerta in a German freighter, and hearing of that, Wilson ordered American forces to occupy the ship's intended destination. The intended destination was Vera Cruz, Mexico's biggest port, population 60,000. There was a fight. Some of Huerta's men resisted, aided by local civilians. American fatalities numbered 22 and Mexican fatalities approximately 165, the latter owing chiefly to naval gunfire. Wilson was appalled. A newspaper cartoon showed the President and a sailor standing in a cloud of gun smoke, with the sailor assuring the Commander-in-Chief that he never fired at the Mexican people, only at "one Huerta." After marines and armed sailors landed in whaleboats and secured the port, the U.S. Army took over with General Frederick Funston in command.

All of Latin America was outraged by the invasion. Even Carranza had to denounce it. A London newspaper termed the American action "medieval." The German freighter unloaded its cargo at a different port, which also was controlled by Huerta.

The day after Vera Cruz was seized, the Congress authorized the use of armed force. The occupation of the port continued from April to November. No gun salute was received. However, the occupation weakened Huerta by diverting more of his troops to that area.

President Wilson felt he was not making any progress in Mexico and complained of being stuck in a "blind alley." Argentina, Brazil, and Chile offered to mediate. Under pressure, Huerta resigned. General Carranza captured Mexico City, but one of his generals, Francisco "Pancho" Villa, revolted and replaced him. Wilson decided to support Villa. But Carranza made a comeback, and the embarrassed Wilson decided to be neutral.

Pancho Villa's Revenge

Pancho Villa resented the American recognition of Carranza's government, and having decided to be the man who defeated the Americans, Villa took sixteen American engineers from a railway train and murdered them. Then he invaded Columbus, New Mexico, killed nineteen more Americans, and burned the town. The American people demanded action. With the permission of Carranza's government and the backing of another congressional resolution, Wilson sent into Mexico General John J. Pershing with several thousand troops. They were ordered to attack Villa's forces but not Carranza's. Villa eluded the Americans. More troops were sent after Villa attacked the town of Glen Springs, Texas. The increasing size of the American force alarmed Carranza. After a shooting incident with Carranza's soldiers, the Mexican President demanded an American withdrawal. Wilson called out the National Guard. American and Carranza's troops clashed again at Carrizal.

General Francisco "Pancho" Villa

Fifty thousand American civilians were residing in In Mexico, and they suffered from anti-Americanism caused by Wilson's invasions. Many lost their property and took refuge back in the United States. The U. S. Consulate in Ensenada had to be rescued. We now had seventy-one ships in Mexican waters.

In 1916, President Wilson secretly was planning war with Germany, and he decided to pull out of Mexico. The last American troops came home in February of 1917. Mexico now had a new constitution and Carranza was President. But the civil war went on for another three years. General Alvaro Obregon drove President Carranza out of Mexico City, and Carranza later died of gunshot wounds.

What to do with four of Carranza's men who shot American soldiers in a Texas border town? Locally they were convicted of murder. The Texas Criminal Appeals Court reversed that decision, saying the

Mexicans were fighting a war and so the jurisdiction was federal. But the U. S. Government had not declared a war; neither had the Mexican government. The appeals court decided, nevertheless, that a state of war existed.[2]

Analysis

President Taft wanted to make Mexico safe for investment and President Wilson wanted to make it safe for democracy. Neither succeeded. The Mexicans did what they wanted to do. Continuing in that vein, in 1938 the Mexicans nationalized foreign-owned oil properties, and for years their oil was boycotted by the United States, Great Britain, and the Netherlands. Nationalization has not proved an efficient way to run the Mexican oil industry, and at this writing the Mexican government is beginning to bring back private expertise.

President Wilson obtained congressional authority for his invasions.

An Avoidable War?

The second Mexican war was avoidable, did a lot of harm, and poisoned our relations with Mexico and the rest of Latin America. President Wilson kept the war going until he was about to enter World War I.

Useful Principles

Do not invade countries unnecessarily.

The Tampico Affair should have stayed in Tampico.

When dealing with a foreign country, be mindful of the need for competent translation.

In time of civil war, sailors were landed in Tampico to do a job. They perhaps did not know about the prohibited zone and would not have been able to read a sign if there had been one. Matters escalated from there.

Translation often is a problem even at the highest levels of diplomacy. In 1963, during the Cold War with the Soviet Union, President John F. Kennedy went to Berlin to express his support for West Germany, and he did so by declaring, *"Ich bin ein Berliner,"* meaning "I am a Berliner." What Kennedy said was correct German, and the crowd's response was enthusiastic. However, if Kennedy had known that to Germans the word *Berliner* also referred to a jelly-filled pastry, he surely would have chosen a different way to express his support.

Almost a half-century later, our translating ability had not improved. Secretary of State Hillary Clinton met in Geneva, Switzerland, with Russian Foreign Minister Sergei Lavrov, and to symbolize the peace overtures she and President Barack Obama were making, Mrs. Clinton presented to Lavrov a symbolic "reset button" labeled in English and in Russian.

"We worked hard to get the right Russian word. Do you think we got it?" Clinton asked with a big smile.

"You got it wrong," was Lavrov's blunt response. "This says *peregruzka,* which means "overcharged."

When, for a high profile event, a one-word translation can be so difficult, what misunderstandings take place on a day to day basis?

References

1   Alexander DeConde, *A History of American Foreign Policy*, first edition, page 433
2   Fred L. Borch, "Mexican Soldiers in Texas Courts, 1916," *The Army Lawyer*, November, 2012

CHAPTER TWELVE

World War I (1917 to 1918)

Part One

The United States must be neutral in fact as well as in name . . . we must be impartial in thought as well as in action—
President Woodrow Wilson, 1914

When in 1914 the "Great War" or "World War" began in Europe, we Americans wanted to be neutral. "Let's stay out of it!" was the common cry, and we were pleased when President Woodrow Wilson declared American neutrality. Wilson was a former president of Princeton University and a former governor of New Jersey. He was scholarly and eloquent. He was experienced in politics. As in the case of the Mexican Revolution, however, he was not neutral.

Psychologically, President Wilson was a deep-dyed Anglophile. All of his grandparents were British, having emigrated from England and Northern Ireland. He had studied the British constitution, he admired Great Britain's cabinet form of government, and he was steeped in English literature, especially the poetry of William Wordsworth. The President had spent some vacations in England's beautiful lake country, where Wordsworth had lived and drawn inspiration for his poetry. The son of a Presbyterian minister, Wilson also loved Thomas Gray's "Elegy Written in a Country Churchyard." On the lighter side, the President stored in his memory a great number of Irish limericks.

Continental Europe the President knew relatively little about, but he always had detested Germany. That he told British Prime Minister Lloyd George in 1919:

> I have always detested Germany. I have never gone there. But I have read many German books on law. They are so far from our views that they have inspired in me a feeling of aversion.[1]

Shortly after the Great War began, President Wilson met with the British ambassador, Sir Cecil Spring-Rice, and as reported by the ambassador, Wilson expressed not only a preference for the Allied side but a state of alarm, saying that if German military prowess overcame the Allies, it would be necessary for the United States to "give up its present ideals and devote all its energies to defence, *which would mean the end of its present system of government* [emphasis added]."[2]

Probably knowing Wilson's interest in literature, Spring-Rice mentioned the Wordsworth sonnets written during the Napoleonic wars. The scholar-President, his eyes becoming moist, responded that he knew the sonnets by heart and had them in his mind all the time. The ambassador remarked, "You and [British Foreign Secretary] Grey [another Wordsworth devotee] are fed on the same food and I think you understand." No doubt with satisfaction, the diplomat cabled London that as far as England's interest was concerned, the President had an "understanding heart."

Foreign Secretary Sir Edward Grey shared Wilson's aversion to Germany. As a negotiator he had found the Germans too peremptory in manner. It might be worth noting that the flutist Sir James Galway had a similar personality conflict with the Germans and managed to solve it, according to what I have heard him say in a radio interview. The Irish virtuoso was invited to join the prestigious Berlin Philharmonic and refused. Asked why, Galway explained that the musicians struck him as brusque and impolite. The orchestra members then treated Galway very nicely, and he spent the next eight years with them. Afterward, in his soloist career, Galway affectionately referred to the Berlin Philharmonic as "my old band."

A True Neutral

Unlike President Wilson, Secretary of State William Jennings Bryan truly favored neutrality, and from the beginning he hoped the war would end in a stalemate. A victory for either side, he feared, would stoke so much resentment that it would lead to another war.[3]

Bryan was right about that.

Secretary of State William Jennings Bryan

To President Wilson, however, an Allied victory was the only desirable outcome, and in practice, as opposed to announced policy, Wilson favored the Allies (Britain, France, and Russia) over the Central Powers (Germany, Austria-Hungary, and Turkey). After three years of aiding the Allies short of going to war, he went the last mile, leading the United States into the European conflagration.

Next, Wilson fought for establishing the League of Nations in order to keep the peace. League members had to accept a moral obligation to defend each other from aggression, and not enough senators would agree to that. Opponents saw the organization as a device to draw America into more European wars, becoming involved with European vindictiveness and secret treaties. The League was founded, but

America did not join. Wilson nevertheless received a Nobel Peace Prize, and scholars have ranked him as one of our ten greatest Presidents.

Leaving all that aside, did it make any sense for the United States to enter World War I?

Critics of the American Entry

For us Americans World War I was a war of choice, and some commentators have considered our participation a huge and far-reaching mistake. An early postwar critic was the socialist John Kenneth Turner, who offered this harsh observation in his book *Shall It Be Again?*

> Having pronounced for a peace without victory in January [of 1917], Wilson went to war in April to destroy the opportunity for such a peace, and to postpone for two years the realization of a peace of any kind.[4]

Harry Barnes, professor of historical sociology at Smith College, in 1929 termed the American entry an "unmitigated disaster for both America and the world." In his weighty volume *The Genesis of the World War* Barnes explained,

> It was the ever brighter prospect of American intervention which encouraged the Entente [the Allies] to reject the peace proposals of Germany, President Wilson and the Pope. American intervention unnecessarily prolonged the War for two years, with all the resulting savagery, misery and increased economic burdens. It made possible the abomination of Versailles, which has postponed the beginning of European readjustment for a decade and produced almost as much loss, misery, and hatred as the War itself. The desolation and despair brought about in Europe by the prolongation of the War is what established Lenin in Russia and Mussolini in Italy.[5]

Had he seen the future, Barnes could have added that the war established Adolf Hitler as well as Vladimir Lenin and Benito Mussolini.

Another critic was Charles Tansill, professor of history at Johns Hopkins University, who said in his 1952 book *Back Door to War*:

> If we had not entered the war in Europe in 1917, World War I would have ended in a stalemate, and a balance of power in Europe would have been created. Our intervention completely shattered the old balance of power and sowed the seeds of inevitable future conflict in the dark soil of Versailles.[6]

In the opinion of the critics, it would have been much better if World War I had ended in a stalemate, as Secretary Bryan had hoped, with the soldiers climbing out of their trenches and heading back home. Instead, nearly two million fresh and eager American troops went over there and changed the world—not for the better. The old ruling houses of Germany, Austria-Hungary, and Russia fell along with their evolving, partly democratic governments. They were replaced by Communist and Fascist totalitarian regimes hostile to the democracies. The "war to end war" and "make the world safe for democracy" destroyed budding democracies, gave birth to regimes that murdered millions in cold blood, and made almost inevitable World War II.

Winston Churchill's View

Another critic turned out to be the British statesman Winston Churchill, who, when serving in Britain's World War I cabinet, strove to bring America into the war. In 1936, Churchill had changed his mind. He said bluntly that we Americans ought to have stayed home and minded our own business, according to William Griffin, publisher of the *New York Enquirer* and a member of the United States-Polish Arbitration Commission. Griffin was in London at the time, and he was invited to Churchill's apartment for a talk.

Churchill, a Conservative member of Parliament whose mother had been a famous American socialite, wanted to know what Americans were thinking about Great Britain, whether there were any controversial issues? Griffin replied that the American people would be pleased if Britain paid back the five billion dollars it had borrowed from the United States during the World War. Churchill agreed the debt should be paid, but he said four billion and nine-hundred million of it ought to be deducted for expenses from the time the United States declared war until the time American troops were in action. The United States, Churchill argued, was a partner during that time and so was liable for half of the expense. Griffin expressed his astonishment at this opinion, and pointed out that, with interest on the alleged American debt, we Americans would end up owing Britain money.

"Such a settlement would not be very fair to the United States," protested the American, "in view of the fact if we hadn't entered the war, England would have lost the war, the British Empire would have broken up, and today England would be ruled from Berlin."

Churchill disagreed. He said that in 1917 he was very enthusiastic about the American declaration of war, but he now saw that it was a mistake. He explained,

> If you hadn't entered the World War, we would have made peace with Germany early in 1917. Had we made peace then there would have been no collapse in Russia followed by Communism, no breakdown in Italy followed by Fascism, and Germany would not have signed the Versailles Treaty, which has enthroned Nazism in Germany. In other words, if America had stayed out of the war, all of these "isms" wouldn't today be sweeping the Continent of Europe and breaking down parliamentary government, and if England had made peace early in 1917, it would have saved over one million British, French, American, and other lives.[7]

Following from that premise, not only World War II but the Cold War, the Korean War, and even America's anti-Communist war in Vietnam grew from what Professor Tansill called the "dark soil of Versailles." The results were even worse than what Secretary Bryan had feared.

Churchill's Prophecy

In Churchill's opinion, the United States had a good reason for going to war in 1915, when a German submarine sank the *Lusitania*, a British passenger liner with Americans on board, but not in 1917. Griffin responded that next time we Americans will know better and stay home. Churchill disagreed with that, too. Prophetically, he said,

> You may want to stay out of it, but the long arm of world events will reach right around the American Continent, and the United States will be dragged in, and you will find yourselves fighting shoulder to shoulder with us in common defense of our democratic institutions.

The discussion lasted about one hour. According to Griffin, Churchill offered to put his thoughts into an article if Griffin would buy a series of ten articles at five hundred dollars each. The publisher was willing to buy only one article, and so none was purchased.

Griffin met with some other prominent Europeans, including David Lloyd George, who had been a British Prime Minister during the World War, and Albert F. Lebrun, the current President of France. Lloyd George said that if the United States in 1914 had had a bigger navy, as Theodore Roosevelt recommended, no power would have harassed our ships and we could have avoided war. Had we been truly neutral and had built up our army, he added, we could have forced peace on the warring nations by threatening to throw our weight against the recalcitrant side. We actually would not have had to send any soldiers to France, said the tough old Welshman.

President Lebrun of France said his country was not paying its debts to the United States because the Germans were not paying their reparations to France. Griffin noted that France was loaning money to some Eastern European countries. That did not sway the French President. In lieu of cash, Griffin suggested giving to the United States France's new passenger ship SS *Normandie,* the biggest, fastest and most luxurious passenger vessel of the time. Lebrun responded the ship was too important to French pride.

Lebrun made this interesting assertion: "France at the present time is doing quite a bit for Americans." By that he meant France was awarding decorations to American individuals from time to time. And they are greatly appreciated, he said. After an American receives a rank in the Legion of Honor, he is inclined to perform another service for France and seek an upgrade. Awarding these honors, Lebrun contended, ought to please the American people. Griffin surprised the French President by saying it was unconstitutional for an American to accept such an award if it were not approved by Congress. The publisher explained that the recipient might put the interests of the decorating country ahead of the interests of his own country. Lebrun seemed not to have thought of that.

In 1938, Griffin discussed his meeting with Churchill when testifying to the Senate Naval Affairs Committee. At the committee hearing, Griffin opposed going to war but espoused Lloyd George's idea: build a navy big enough to scare off any would be attackers.

Another World War Looms

In the summer of 1939, another war in Europe appeared imminent, and on July 3 an anti-war weekly newspaper, *Social Justice*, reviewed the Griffin-Churchill discussion of 1936. This was extremely inconvenient for those Americans who were inclined to support Britain in a new war. In opposition to them were the "isolationists," who feared that President Franklin D. Roosevelt already was making secret agreements. As evidence of such agreements, the isolationists pointed to the sale of aviation equipment to Britain, the lending of more money to Britain, a combined American and British naval demonstration at Singapore, and the transfer of American battleships to the Pacific while the British patrolled the Atlantic and Mediterranean.

Probably the isolationists remembered the geographical division of naval power that preceded World War I. At that time, the British made an arrangement with the French by which the British navy patrolled France's northern and western coasts, countering the German navy, while the French patrolled the Mediterranean, countering the Austro-Hungarian and Italian navies. In 1939, it looked as if the United States already was countering the Japanese navy in the Pacific as the British countered the German and Italian navies in the Atlantic and Mediterranean.

Shortly after the *Social Justice* article appeared, Churchill called it a "vicious lie" and claimed that he never had met Griffin. Senator Lynn Frazier provided evidence in Griffin's favor. He put into the *Congressional*

Record of October 21, 1939, a photostatic copy of the telegram which invited William Griffin to visit Churchill. Griffin defended himself by saying that Churchill did not disavow the interview in 1936 when the gist of it appeared in the press or in 1938 when he gave the same information to the Senate's Naval Affairs Committee.

Griffin brought a million dollar libel suit against Churchill. The case did not come up until 1942 when the United States was at war and Churchill was Britain's Prime Minister, leading his embattled nation in its "finest hour." Churchill answered to the lawsuit by admitting that he was interviewed by Griffin, but denied having said it was a mistake for the United States to have entered World War I. The Prime Minister also denied that he had called Griffin's article a "vicious lie." In 1942, Griffin, as a leader of the Keep America Out of War Committee, was under indictment for sedition, charged with conspiracy to lower the morale of American armed forces, and he could not go to London and appear in court. Since Griffin did not appear in the British court, his lawsuit was dismissed, and he was ordered to pay the defendant $103.85 in court costs. The *New York Times* reported the case on October 22, 1942 (page 13). Sedition charges against Griffin and forty-one other anti-war Americans eventually were dropped.

World War a Bonanza

When in 1914 the First World War began, President Woodrow Wilson announced that the United States would be neutral like the peripheral states in Europe, such as Spain and Denmark, but we Americans faced a great commercial temptation. Our economy happened to be slowing down, and the war, a sudden bounty, provided an opportunity to export vast amounts of war materiel and foodstuffs. There was no law that prohibited American citizens from trading with belligerents. Stock in Bethlehem Steel rocketed from $33.75 per share to $600 and General Motors stock from $78 to $750. With European manpower in uniform and not on the farm, American agriculture benefited greatly as well.

J. P. Morgan bank became Britain's exclusive purchasing agent, collecting a commission on all goods. On Wall Street it was said that J. P. Morgan, Jr., made more money in two years than his father had made in his entire life. Cooperation between Morgan and its major client was so close that British servicemen in civilian clothes went to work at Morgan's offices.[8] The bank's American employees were unabashedly pro-British. "We did not know how to be neutral," said one of them.

Unlike the neutral nations in Europe, we supplied arms to the Allies, and this was a controversial decision. At the State Department, the Allies had a staunch advocate in Counselor Robert Lansing, who was such an Anglophile that he took lessons in how to affect an English accent.[9] Lansing worked hard at justifying the arms exports. He even invoked humanitarian grounds. The counselor argued that a peaceful nation having no arms industry ought to be able to import arms when needed, and from that sentiment Lansing derived a general principle that neutral nations ought to be able to ship arms to belligerent nations. Lansing was an uncle of the famous Dulles brothers: Allen W. Dulles, first civilian head of the Central Intelligence Agency, and John Foster Dulles, secretary of state during the Eisenhower Administration.

Only the Allies could buy large amounts of goods from the United States. The British navy effectively blockaded Germany by declaring a "war zone" in the North Sea. By international law this was illegal since a legal blockade had to be conducted near the enemy's ports, which the German navy was strong enough to prevent. The British blockade also was extraordinary for declaring foodstuffs contraband. This violated the London Declaration of 1909, which Britain had signed but not ratified. Like Britain, Germany normally imported most of its food. First Lord of the Admiralty Winston Churchill, as he put it, intended to "starve the whole population—men, women, and children, old and young, wounded and sound—into submission."[10] Germany protested the foodstuff embargo as illegal and retaliated by declaring a war zone around the British isles. German submarines then attacked British merchant ships in addition to warships.

The Royal Navy cut Germany's undersea cables so that in the American press Allied propaganda enjoyed a great advantage. In the United States, Britain's chief of propaganda and espionage was William Wiseman, who kept in close touch with President Wilson and Colonel Edward Mandell House, Wilson's close friend and adviser. (Wiseman later mentored William Stephenson, who succeeded to Wiseman's role in World War II.)

Kaiser a "Man of Peace"

During the war, British propagandists did a remarkable job of painting the German leader, Kaiser Wilhelm II, as a bloodthirsty monster. In this they were aided by the Kaiser's habit of wearing a uniform, making bombastic speeches, and keeping his mustache turned up fiercely at the ends. However, Wilhelm, although possessing reputedly the strongest army in Europe, had kept the peace there, except for conflicts in the Balkans, since 1888. Before the war, that important service was acknowledged in the press. In Britain on October 17, 1913, the *Evening News* commented,

> We all acknowledge the Kaiser as very gallant gentleman whose word is better than many another's bond, a guest whom we are always glad to welcome and sorry to lose, a ruler whose ambitions for his own people are founded on as good a right as our own.

Former President William H. Taft told the *New York Times* of June 6 and 8, 1913:

> The German Emperor has been for the last quarter century the greatest single individual force in the practical maintenance of the peace of the world.

On July 28, 1914, the *New York Times* expressed hope that war in Europe could be avoided and said,

> ... the sober-minded statesman of Europe, and above all the Kaiser, are not men of blood but men of peace

On the same day, the *New York Sun* said,

> For more than a quarter of a century the German Emperor, the master of the most tremendous and most effective military organization that ever existed, has worked persistently and successfully for the peace of Europe.

Kaiser Wilhelm II

Once the war began, British propagandists controlled the news, invented atrocities, and made the Kaiser the most reviled man on earth. The press carried phony stories about Germans stealing valuables from churches, raping nuns, and cutting the hands off Belgian children. The *New York Herald* blared, TOURIST SAW SOLDIER WITH BAGFUL OF EARS. Reporters in Berlin tried to evade the British censor by filing stories in the neutral Netherlands, but the cable went through London. Some American correspondents protested that their work was "suppressed, mutilated, or delayed" by the British censor. British propagandists enlisted the patriotic services of distinguished authors, including H. G. Wells, Rudyard Kipling, and Arthur Conan Doyle. They put together a mailing list of 260,000 influential American men and women.

German Blockade

To save torpedoes and follow international law, German U-boats, when finding a British merchant vessel, preferred to surface and give the crew an opportunity to disembark in lifeboats. Then the submarine crew would sink the ship with planted bombs or gunfire. However, on orders from the British Admiralty, British commercial vessels began flying neutral flags and trying to ram the surfaced U-boats. Innocent-looking "Q-ships" with hidden weapons fired on surfaced U-boats, and their marines seldom took prisoners, according to a book published by the U. S. Naval Institute Press.[11] Germany, therefore, announced that neutral ships might be sunk without warning unless they had made arrangements with the German government. The new German policy was called "barbaric" and "uncivilized."

Americans complained of British actions, too. The British intercepted our mail, flew American flags on their ships, and seized and searched American officials. Cargo often was delayed and searched, and this proved an advantage to British commercial competitors. So did reading the American mail. Interference with the mail even Lansing condemned as "reprehensible," in his memoirs.

In a letter to American diplomat Henry White, naval historian and commentator Admiral F. E. Chadwick said that most American naval officers supported Germany and Austria-Hungary rather than Britain and France. They all had studied the War of 1812. It was Chadwick's opinion that "England is the true devil in the whole business." Chadwick wanted to speak out against the pro-Allied press, but President Wilson had ordered all active and retired officers to refrain from publishing comments on the war. Admiral Mahan favored Britain, but he died on December 1, 1914.

America's Power to Decide

Somehow I never heard this in high school or college, but we Americans had it in our power to decide who would win the war or whether there would be a draw. The belligerent nations were desperate for our products. Without industrial and agricultural imports from the United States, the Allies would have lost the war. Germany, lacking this access, and facing American troops, did lose the war. Sir Edward Grey, British foreign secretary during the first half of the conflict, admitted in his memoir *Twenty-Five Years*:

> After Paris had been saved by the Battle of the Marne, the Allies could do no more than hold their own against Germany; sometimes they did not even do that. Germany and Austria were self-supporting in the huge supply of munitions. The Allies soon became dependent for an

adequate supply on the United States. If we quarreled with the United States, we could not get that supply. *It was better therefore to carry on the war without blockade, if need be, than to incur a break with the United States about contraband and thereby deprive the Allies of the resources necessary to carry on the war at all or with any chance of success* [emphasis added].[12]

American Benedict Crowell, who was an assistant secretary of war during the conflict, in his book *America's Munitions, 1917-1918,* told of how the Allies "molded their military programs in reliance" on American supplies adding, "Failure of supply meant disaster."

In negotiations with Britain, President Wilson held the high cards. According to Grey, he could have stopped the illegal British blockade. Instead, he allowed that and other British offenses to continue.

American businessmen complained strongly about the British blockade, but along with Wilson's quiescence, the British had their wily friend Counselor Lansing in the State Department. An old hand at international law, Lansing also was an expert pettifogger. He appeared to protest the blockade while at the same time he obscured its illegality with complicated questions. By his own admission:

> The notes that were sent [to Britain] were long and exhaustive treatises which opened up new subjects of discussion rather than closing them in controversy . . . It was done with deliberate purpose. It ensured continuance of the controversies and left the questions unsettled.[13]

A Strange Sequel

In other words, having a hidden agenda, the State Department's top lawyer helped the British navy to block and regulate American commerce. Was that not a strange sequel to the War of 1812?

Secretary Bryan did not choose Lansing as his counselor. Bryan had opposed Lansing's promotion, on the ground that as a junior employee he had been "guilty of impropriety in receiving financial benefit from commercial interests." Senator Elihu Root arranged Lansing's appointment with President Wilson. Root was a former secretary of state and a pro-British opponent of neutrality.

Counselor Robert Lansing

Another extreme Anglophile was our ambassador in London, Walter Hines Page, a former journalist and publisher. When Washington protested the British navy's stopping of American merchant ships headed for neutral ports, Page told Foreign Secretary Grey that he disagreed with Washington, and he helped Grey to write a rejoinder.[14] The blockade of neutral ports continued.

The extent to which the Allies became dependent on the United States came as a surprise. Mistakenly, most of Europe's leaders had thought that modern, highly destructive weapons would bring about a short war. They did not expect a long war of attrition. The Franco-Prussian War of 1870-1871 was over in less than a year. So was the Spanish-American War of 1898. The Russo-Japanese War of 1904-1905 lasted eighteen months, but that required sending ships and men half way around the world. In 1914, the Europeans surely would have tried hard to keep the peace if they had known how long and destructive the conflict would be. Before the war, the French army estimated that it would need 13,600 75-millimeter shells per day. By 1915, the French were firing 150,000 such shells per day. The French began the war with 2,500 machine guns. By the end of the war, they had deployed 314,000.

American Money Needed

We Americans not only supplied the Allies with foodstuffs and munitions, but loaned them the money to buy them. Far from being neutral, we both financed and supplied the Allied war effort.

A German, Dr. Heinrich Pohl, commented on how the Central Powers' war effort was being thwarted by the United States. Said he:

> Germany finds herself in the position of a warrior, hemmed in on all sides, whose enemies are all aiming at his heart. Every time this warrior succeeds in disarming the foe most harmful to him, every time the warrior strikes the sword from the hand of the enemy, a so-called neutral comes running from behind and places a new weapon in the hand of the defeated foe.

President Woodrow Wilson held the whole world in his hands. He could have brought about an Allied victory, a Central Powers victory, or a stalemate. He could have asked both sides to stop fighting. If the British refused, he could have cut off or reduced their supplies. If the Germans refused, he could have threatened to join the war on the side of the Allies. However, our President, while talking about neutrality and peace, helped the Allies, stretched out the war, and enabled the Allied victory—along with the disastrous Versailles treaty.

The Dark Soil of Versailles

As Professor Tansill pointed out, additional conflict grew from the "dark soil of Versailles." How did that soil get so dark? There was a little known factor in this baleful process: The Great War did not actually end when the Armistice was signed on November 11, 1918. The Allies continued using their strongest weapon—the blockade. The blockade was so effective that many Germans and other Europeans were starving before the Armistice. In August of 1917, an American named Lang left Germany through a neutral country and reported that people were dropping in the streets, faint from hunger. Lang himself had lost fifty-five pounds. Up to December of 1918, 763,000 people had died as a result of the blockade, according to the National Health Office in Berlin. From then until April another 100,000 Germans died, according to other studies. Dog meat was called "blockade mutton."

Following the Armistice, the blockade actually tightened because the Allied navies no longer needed to look for submarines. With the German navy sequestered, British warships could concentrate on making sure "not a loaf of bread" got through, as one writer put it. They even invaded the Baltic to stop the fishing. In Germany, the sight of starving children hurt the morale of the occupying British troops, and they asked to be sent home. In March of 1919, General Sir Herbert Plumer sent the following message to higher command:

> Please inform the Prime Minister that in my opinion food must be sent into this area by the Allies without delay . . . The mortality amongst women, children, and sick is most grave and sickness due to hunger is spreading. The attitude of the population is becoming one of despair, and the people feel that an end by bullets is preferable to death by starvation.

The Allies damaged the German economy by seizing railway equipment, coal mines, and livestock. Said an indignant American attending Versailles conference:

> The Germans were made to deliver cattle, horses, sheep, goats, etc . . . A strong protest came from Germany when dairy cows were taken to France and Belgium, thus depriving German children of milk.

Friendly Nations Starve

Not only Germany but all of Europe east of the Rhine was in a state of famine, according to the London *Daily News* of March 13, which quoted Lord Henry Cavendish at a meeting about famine relief. According to the paper, Cavendish said,

> The people of Rumania, Serbia, Russia, Bohemia, Bulgaria, Syria, Armenia, Austria, and Germany were all starving,

267

and unless something was done to relive their necessities thousands, if not millions, would die of hunger.

The Allies were not only maintaining a blockade against nations with whom we are technically at war, but were actually by closing the Adriatic ports preventing food from reaching the Jugo-Slavs, Czecho-Slovaks, and Serbians—nations who had stood by us and whom we had liberated. It was high time that this horrible and calculated brutality should cease. Food was a far more effective weapon to control Bolshevism than the futile armies which we were maintaining in Russia.

Irrationally, the Allies wanted to starve Germany, destroy its economy, and at the same time force it to pay for the war. To keep food away from the Germans, their neighbors had to be starved as well. The plan was to force Germany to confess it had started the war and agree to pay reparations.

Winston Churchill perceived the folly of what was happening, and he cited the rise of Bolshevism as a reason for ending the blockade. On April 11, 1919, Churchill warned, at a private club luncheon, that if Germany were not fed it would collapse into Bolshevism and "not only will there be no indemnity [war reparations] but we shall ourselves be impoverished, and our trade revival will be paralysed by the increasing disorder and ruin of the world." Churchill wanted Germany kept alive as a cash cow and productive, capitalist economy.

Beginning in April a limited amount of food was allowed into Germany, but it was sold at such high prices that that the lower economic class and even some of the middle class could not afford it.

A "Monstrous" Treaty

As the famine continued month after month, the Allied peace delegates were wining and dining at the Trianon Palace hotel in Paris. The leading figures were Prime Minister Georges Clemenceau of France, Prime Minister David Lloyd George of Britain, and President Woodrow Wilson of the United States. Wilson wanted to lift the blockade, but he was thwarted by Clemenceau and George. The American President was eloquent when it came to giving speeches, but he was not skillful in debate. The Allies slowly hammered out a treaty that Churchill condemned as "monstrous" and "malignant." Most resented by the Germans was the "war guilt clause." Here is the text of that:

> The Allied and Associated Governments affirm and Germany accepts the responsibility of Germany and her allies for causing all the loss and damage to which the Allied and Associated Governments and their nationals have been subjected as a consequence of the war imposed upon them by the aggression of Germany and her allies.

In an idealistic Fourteen Point proposal, which helped Wilson to receive the Nobel Prize for Peace, the President had promised the Central Powers "peace without victory" because "only a peace between equals can last." Wilson had no power to implement that plan. Once the Allies were rescued, the President lost his bargaining power. Now, instead of a noble Fourteen Point prospect, our former enemies were confronted with a vindictive treaty that they could not refuse. The European Allies wanted money, territory, revenge, and, on top of all that, an admission of German guilt. I shall take up later the question of how the war began.

On May 7, 1919, the German foreign minister, Ulrich von Brockdorff-Rantzau, having been brought to Versailles, was given an opportunity to speak. He did not mince words. Brockdorff-Rantzau admitted that Germany had some responsibility for the war's having come to pass, but he said that for him to confess that Germans were the only ones responsible "would be a lie," and he charged that hundreds of thousands of people had been killed by the blockade since Germany asked for the armistice. Said the German foreign minister:

> I ask you when reparations are demanded not to forget the armistice. It took you six weeks until we got it at last, and six months until we came to know your conditions of peace . . . The hundreds of thousands of noncombatants who have perished since November 11 by reason of the blockade were killed with cold deliberation after our adversaries had conquered and victory had been assured to them. Think of that when you speak of guilt and punishment.[15]

The conferees were intensely displeased, some said outraged, by what the German foreign minister had to say. Wilson thought it the "most tactless speech" he had ever heard.

On June 28, Germany signed. It was the fourth anniversary of when a Serb had assassinated Austria's Archduke Ferdinand, the event which ignited the war.

On July 4, the Manchester *Guardian* printed a letter from one William Robertson on how an experienced American nurse broke down at the sight of the "skeletal-like body" of an old woman, and how in country districts "90 percent of the children were rickety." The blockade continued until July 12 when Germany was allowed to import raw materials and export manufactured goods. Malnutrition lingered for another year; in December of 1919 starvation was reported in Vienna.

The conferees at Versailles were not Lincolnesqe figures favoring "malice toward none" and "charity for all." Clemenceau and Lloyd George were politicians who during the war required enormous sacrifices from their peoples, and in secret treaties not involving the United States, they agreed to exact as much in compensation and revenge as possible. They also insisted upon having their innocence established by the "war guilt clause." As Winston Churchill had predicted in 1901, "The wars of peoples will be more terrible than those of kings."

It often has been explained that President Wilson had to go along with the Europeans in order to obtain their help in establishing a League of Nations to keep the peace. Not sharing Wilson's optimistic vision of the future was France's commanding general, Marshall Ferdinand Foch, who uttered an oracle:

This is not a peace. It is an armistice for twenty years.

Exactly twenty years. In September of 1939, Germany and the Soviet Union invaded Poland, reclaiming lost territories. Britain and France then declared war on Germany.

During the peace conference, Americans were disgusted by the Europeans' secretive and grasping behavior. In 1921, Republican Warren

G. Harding was elected President, and spurning Versailles, he made separate treaties with the Central Powers.

Origin of Nazism

Concerning the European blockade, Herbert Hoover, America's official "food administrator," warned,

> Nations can take philosophically the hardships of war. But when they lay down their arms and surrender on assurances that they may have food for their women and children, and then find that this worst instrument of attack on them is maintained—then hate never dies.

Hoover got that right. Said *Vorwarts*, a German socialist newspaper:

> Treaties based on violence can keep their validity only so long as force exists. Do not lose hope. The resurrection will come.

The "resurrection" came with Adolf Hitler and the National Socialist Party. In his early days as a political speaker, Hitler's most effective and dramatic speeches recounted the Treaty of Versailles.

Belgium suffered even though it had fought against Germany. With great difficulty, Hoover squeezed food shipments through the blockade into Belgium, the British Admiralty objecting that food going to that country would end up in Germany. In his battles with the Admiralty, Hoover sought help from Secretary Grey, advising him, "It would be a cynical ending [to the war] if the civil population of Belgium had become extinct in the process of rescue."[16] According to the Hoover biographer Richard Smith, the importunate food administrator "found few friends among the mighty, but his picture appeared in millions of Belgian homes." Hoover's efforts were much admired by Americans, too, and in 1929 he was elected President of the United States.

The Cover-Up

The postwar blockade and its effects have been well covered up. Examining history textbooks, I find little or nothing on that subject despite its historical importance. *Encyclopaedia Britannica* says civilian deaths attributable to World War I amounted to 13 million from all causes but does not say whether that includes postwar deaths. *Britannica* says military deaths totaled 8.5 million. *Encyclopedia Americana* mentions the continuing blockade, but just barely. It tells of post-Armistice insurrections in Germany and comments,

> All of these difficulties were increased by the Allied blockade,
> which, continuing throughout the period of treaty-making,
> brought much of the population to the point of starvation.

That is better but inadequate. The "treaty-making" went on for eight months, and "to the point of starvation" is ambiguous. In 1942, the Hoover Library published a book titled, *The Blockade of Germany After the Armistice, 1918-1919* by Suda Lorena Bane. The book is composed largely of official documents, and fifty-two pages of it are about "Policies on Censorship." This helps to explain why so little is known. Failure to obey censorship regulations could incur a fine of 5,000 francs and six months' imprisonment.

Disarmed and starving, Germany signed the treaty because of its desperate need for food and because the Allies were preparing to resume military operations.

Part Two

Nothing in particular started it—Woodrow Wilson, 1914

How did the war begin? Who started it? At first, it seemed that an accumulation of colonial rivalries, commercial resentments, grudges from previous wars, and fears of aggression generated so much heat that Europe burst into flames. One could argue that, as in Agatha Christie's *Murder on the Orient Express*, the whole cast was in on it. President Wilson said on October 26, 1914:

> So far as I can gather, nothing in particular started it [the war], but everything in general. There had been growing up in Europe a mutual suspicion . . . a complex web of intrigue and spying, that presently was sure to entangle the whole family of mankind in its meshes.[17]

That sort of talk made the Allies "frantic with rage," his friend and adviser Colonel House was warning Wilson as late as November of 1916. The Allies blamed the war on German militarism. After the United States entered the war in 1917, President Wilson fell into line. Said he in a Flag Day speech of June 14, 1917:

> The war was begun by the military masters of Germany.

After the war, he apportioned the blame differently.

The Agatha Christie theory has its merits, but perhaps we should consider a different literary comparison. Readers of Homer's *Iliad* are familiar with how, during the Trojan War, the mortals fought with each other on the plains of Troy while the gods on Mount Olympus actually decided how things were going to be. Could that have been the situation on Planet Earth before and during the Great War? Did a few willful people on high shape events according to their desires while ordinary folk fought with each other and tried to survive? If so, who were these modern Olympians?

Confrontation of Alliances

In 1914, the political situation in Europe was inherently dangerous. Two heavily armed alliances confronted each other, and this made it possible for any local conflict to become a world war. On one side was the Triple Alliance of Germany, Austria-Hungary, and Italy. Facing it was the Triple Entente of Britain, France, and Russia. The French word *entente* means "accord" or "understanding," and the British leaders claimed that the Triple Entente was *not a military alliance*. They lied about that because the people of Britain did not want to get involved with a new Franco-German war.

The Triple Alliance was founded in 1882 by German Chancellor Otto von Bismarck as a defensive measure against France, which had lost the Franco-Prussian War of 1870-1871. (The German Empire Bismarck in 1871 organized under Prussian leadership from dozens of little German states.) France, Bismarck assumed, at some point would wish to retake the two provinces, Alsace and Lorraine, it lost in the war; these border provinces had been seized by France in the seventeenth century and held until 1870. Bismarck strongly opposed the provinces' annexation by Germany as an endless source of trouble, but he lost the political battle. As a countermeasure to French hostility, Bismarck made a secret "reinsurance" treaty with Russia, so that Germany would not have to fight on that front.

Bismarck aimed to preserve the status quo. Kaiser Wilhelm II, who had an English mother and admired the British Empire, wanted colonies, but the professional military did not. American writer G. J. Meyer has presented this unconventional view of the German militarists:

> The Junkers [Prussian noblemen] were never expansionist imperialists . . . What they wanted was the little world of their forebears, and every new stage of growth, of expansion, made that world less sustainable. Even the expansion of the army, unavoidable in the arms race that gripped the great powers . . . deeply troubled many traditionalists. Just as for a good Junker the only acceptable army officer was an East Prussian of acceptable family background, the only dependable recruit was an ignorant and docile East Prussian farm boy.[18]

To the Junkers, city dwellers were strange beings with radical ideas. Colonel Erich Ludendorff, later to become Germany's top general, in 1913 was expelled from the general staff because he, expecting war, lobbied to expand the army by six corps. There were not enough Junker officers available for that big an army, and Ludendorff's superiors did not want to commission so many outsiders.

It is true that, for historical reasons, Germany had an exceptionally militarized culture. In 1913, however, Britain, France, and Russia spent more than twice as much on armaments as Germany and Austria-Hungary. Their population was double as well,[19] and according to the *Encyclopaedia Britannica*, in 1914 the Allied armies numbered 3.186 million men and the Central Powers armies only 2.35 million. (Being neutral at that time, the

Italian and Turkish forces are not included. Italy later joined the Allies and Turkey the Central Powers.) As we shall see, the Russian and French leaders, in private, appeared eager to fight.

The Kaiser Takes Over

Kaiser Wilhelm II fired Bismarck in 1890 over domestic issues; the Kaiser was more liberal toward labor. The new Emperor let the Russian treaty expire. Wilhelm II was related to the Czar of Russia, he thought this familial relationship could keep the peace, and he feared that exposure of the secret treaty would harm relations with Great Britain. (The treaty favored the Russian navy's access to the Turkish straits connecting the Black Sea to the Mediterranean, and this would have irked the British.) Later, the treaty did get into the press.

In 1902, Russia formed an alliance with France. Shocked, the Germans saw that in any future war with France they would have to take on the Russians as well, and fight on two fronts.

Another of the Kaiser's post-Bismarck mistakes was to reject an alliance with Great Britain. The British, after decades of having no allies, a period of "splendid isolation," decided that going it alone was "dangerous" (Queen Victoria's term), and so, concerned about Russian intentions in the Far East, the cabinet sought an alliance with Germany, the nation that Russia feared most. Presciently, the Kaiser's English mother, Victoria, urged him to embrace this "world saving idea."[20] Her son rejected the offer, reminding the British that the Russians maintained a very large army aimed at Germany. As another impediment to the alliance, the British wanted Germany to help defend India, while the British would not agree to defend Germany's ally Austria-Hungary. Finally, there was an old grudge. The Prussian King Frederick the Great made an alliance with Britain which was betrayed by a new government formed in London, and the Germans decided that democracies did not make reliable allies.

Had Germany and Britain been able to negotiate a mutually advantageous alliance, modern history would have been very different.

As one of his idiosyncrasies, the Kaiser feared that the peoples of Asia would become powerful and eventually engulf Western civilization. He coined the term "yellow peril." In 1900, the German envoy to Beijing was killed in the Boxer Rebellion The ambassador's heart literally was cut out and eaten by a Muslim captain in the Manchu army. Earlier, two German missionaries had been murdered. Along with the United States and other nations, Germany sent troops to rescue the foreigners, and to a departing German unit, the excitable Kaiser said in an impromptu speech:

> When you come upon the enemy, smite him. Pardon will not be given. Prisoners will not be taken. Whoever falls into your hands is forfeit. Once, a thousand years ago, the Huns under their King Attila made a name for themselves, one still potent in legend and tradition. May you in this way make the name German remembered in China for a thousand years.

That explosion of fury was the origin of the World War term "Huns" for the Germans.

Kaiser Proposes an Alliance

Too late, the Kaiser changed his mind about a British alliance. When his grandmother Queen Victoria lay dying in 1901, he rushed to the bedside, showed genuine grief, and briefly won the hearts of England. In this atmosphere of family intimacy, the Kaiser proposed to his uncle, the new King, Edward VII, an alliance. The Kaiser's reasoning:

> I believe there is a providence which has decreed that two nations which have produced such men as Shakespeare, Schiller, Luther, and Goethe must have a great fortune before them; I believe that the two Teutonic nations will, bit by bit, learn to know each other better, and that they will stand together to help in keeping the peace of the world. We ought to form an Anglo-Germanic alliance, you to keep the seas, while we would be responsible for the land; with such an alliance, not a mouse could stir in Europe without our permission, and the nations would, in time, come to see the necessity of reducing their armaments.[21]

Wilhelm returned to Germany in an ebullient, Anglophilic mode even wearing civilian clothes, not his normal practice, as he had done in Britain. Notice, however, that when the Kaiser listed great Teutons, only one was British. Having no talent for diplomacy, he did not think to include John Milton or Isaac Newton.

The newly proposed Anglo-German alliance did not materialize. Germany offered two different plans, but Britain decided to counter Russia with a Japanese alliance. The negotiations ended in a public quarrel about the Boer War and the British policy of forcing people into concentration camps. The Germans felt a responsibility for the Dutch of South Africa, as the Russians felt a responsibility for the Slavs in the Balkans. The Boers in 1913 erected in the city of Bloemfontein a monument memorializing the deaths in concentration camps of approximately twenty-seven thousand women and children.

Besides the row over the Boer War, popular novels fantasizing German invasions of England fueled distrust of Germany. There were at least seventeen of them. Admired for its literary merit, as a sailing novel, was *The Riddle of the Sands* by Erskine Childers.

Russia Lights a Fuse

In 1903, Russia lit a fuse that led all the way to the explosive rivalries of 1914. King Alexander of Serbia was assassinated by a group of Serbian army officers headed by Colonel Dragutin Dimitrijefic, who was in the pay of the Russians.[22] Trying to escape, the King, by one account, hung from a window sill until his fingers were chopped off with a saber. Next to assume the throne was the pro-Russian King Peter of a rival family. Colonel Dmitrijefic became head of Serbia's military intelligence, and with funds from Russia, he propagandized and plotted industriously against the Austrians. For that purpose he already had a terrorist organization, later known to members as the "Black Hand." Serbian terrorists, however, killed at least twenty people by the time the war began in 1914.

While the Black Hand with Russian help was trying to undermine the Austro-Hungarian Empire, in Turkey the Kurdish and Armenian minorities with Russian help were trying to undermine the Ottoman

Empire. (This led to the Armenian genocide, beginning in 1915, in which the Turks massacred at least one million Armenian Christians.)

Colonel Dragutin Dimitrijefic

Kaiser Wilhelm in 1908 again sought friendship with Britain by recalling instances of his having given assistance to British foreign policy, but in the process he offended the British and other nationalities as well. Exasperated by the German invasion novels, Wilhelm told London's *Daily Telegraph*, "You English are mad, mad as March hares. What on earth has come over you that you harbor such suspicions against us?" Britain's distrustful attitude he took as a "personal insult." The Kaiser even provoked the far off Japanese, justifying his naval expansion by saying there might be trouble with Japan. The public reaction was so bad that in Germany there were calls for the Kaiser's abdication. Bureaucrats and military men gained influence at his expense. Yet the Foreign Office bureaucrats also were at fault for not revising the text of the interview when they had the opportunity. Perhaps their misfeasance was an intentional grab for power, but a leading German businessman, Albert Ballin, dubbed the German Foreign Office a "preserve for aristocratic incompetents."

In another circumstance, Prince Max of Baden wrote to Princess Daisy of Pless:

> Poor William (English for Wilhelm), he means so awfully well, and everything he does is intended for the best, and still he is so completely destitute of tact that everything turns out exactly opposite to what he intends.

In her diagnosis, Daisy, a Welsh lady married to one of Germany's richest noblemen, compared the Emperor to an actor: "effusive, voluble always striving for effect." Theodore Roosevelt, another master of bluster, described Wilhelm as "jumpy." Perhaps relevant to the Kaiser's lack of emotional stability was his having been born with a short and useless left arm, which he tried to conceal. The British Foreign Secretary Sir Edward Grey had a physical problem, too. He was gradually going blind and would leave office in 1916.

Daisy, Princess of Pless

In 1904, Great Britain began a special friendship, the Entente Cordiale, with France. Agreeing on spheres of influence, the British let France have Morocco, and the French let the British have Egypt.

Three Agendas Unite

King Edward VII personally took a hand in forming the Triple Entente of Britain, Russia, and France. During the Russo-Japanese War, Edward went to Copenhagen and met there with the Russian envoy to Denmark, Count Alexander Isvolsky. They discussed the possibility of Russia and Britain forming an accord. After the war, which Russia lost, the alliance of Russia and Britain was implemented in 1907 by Isvolsky, who had become Russia's foreign minister, and Sir Edward Grey. As mentioned above, Britain already had an accord with France, which was allied with Russia.

Sir Edward Grey and Count Alexander Isvolsky

Presto! the Triple Entente. Everybody in the Entente had a secret agenda. The British wanted to counter the growing power of Germany, which was expanding its navy along with its military and industrial might. The French foreign minister, Raymond Poincare, was native to Lorraine, and his burning ambition in life was to retake for France the lost provinces of Alsace and Lorraine. The Czar of Russia needed some kind of foreign policy success to make up for the loss of his war with Japan; he wanted to gain control of Constantinople (now Istanbul) and the Turkish straits.

With the straits open, the Russian Black Sea Fleet could access the Mediterranean. The lack of that access had been a handicap during the Russo-Japanese War, although a few armed ships actually sneaked through in disguise. Russia also needed the straits open in order to export grain, its chief source of income, and even commercial passage was liable to be closed during Balkan wars. As another objective, the Russians wanted Austrian Galicia, an oil-producing territory on the Russian side of the Carpathian mountains.

Foreign Minister Isvolsky decided that in order to accomplish all of the Entente's objectives, a *European war would be needed.* He referred to the projected war as "European complications." As part of a general war, France and Russia could make their land grabs, and Germany would be weakened.

Obviously, the linkage of France, Russia, and Britain threatened Germany, and in 1912 this was made explicit in a telegram to the Czar sent by his new foreign minister, Sergei Sazonov. Foreign Minister Poincare, said Sazanov, reminded him that:

> According to the letter of the treaty of alliance only an attack
> on Russia by Germany could be ground for the fulfillment by
> France of her obligations towards us.[23]

In other words, an attack on Russia by a country other than Germany, such as Austria-Hungary or Japan, would not provide an excuse for France to invade Alsace and Lorraine. For the French to achieve their aims, there had to be a war with Germany, and France would not help Russia if the latter were attacked by any other country. With that understood, Sazanov made plans for a seizure of the Turkish straits.[24]

Top Secret Planning

Ostensibly, the Triple Entente was just a friendly association, as the British leaders told Colonel House.[25] Actually, on a top secret basis there was military planning from the beginning. The plans were detailed and meticulous including, for example, a supply of forage for British horses in France. Few in the British government knew about these plans. The obligations involved seem not to have been on paper and rather vague.

Colonel Edward M. House

The existence of any military obligation on Great Britain's part was routinely denied in Parliament by Foreign Secretary Grey and Prime Minister Herbert Asquith. At the Admiralty, Churchill even denied that "any naval agreement" resulted in the French fleet's patrolling the Mediterranean while the British fleet stayed near France in home waters,[26] although these deployments were plain to see. The press was skeptical and questions kept arising. As a result, Grey told his Russian and French counterparts that Britain needed to "keep its hands free"— but added that if Germany came to dominate the Continent this would be "disagreeable." In reference to relations between Britain and France, First Lord Churchill in 1912 advised Grey and Asquith:

> Every one must feel who knows the facts that we have the obligations of an alliance without its advantages and, above all without its precise definitions.[27]

In the face of all the public denials, how could the French and the Russians feel assured of British help in a war with Germany? The British historian Niall Ferguson has commented with wry humor: "They were relying on nothing more than Grey's *private* [emphasis in the original] undertaking as a Wykehamist [graduate of the ancient Winchester College prep school], a Balliol man [a graduate of the even more ancient Oxford University], and an angler" (Grey had written a book about fly fishing). The Entente's secret planning and preparations went on for seven years and in such detail that, although publicly denied, the alliance acquired a moral force. As Grey's colleague Sir Eyre Crowe advised him on the critical day of July 31, 1914:

> The whole of the Entente can have no meaning if it does not signify that in a just quarrel England would stand by her friends.[28]

Why the Secrecy?

The secrecy gives us reason to doubt that the Entente was meant to be defensive. How could the Entente deter attack if its military component were not known? It could not—*and it did not*. But if the alliance were publicly acknowledged, it would have been rejected by the British Parliament and public. In short, this clandestine, wobbly alliance was not well designed for the purpose of deterring an attack. The alliance's military effectiveness hinged on Grey's personal word, which he denied in public, and the Germans quite reasonably believed that the British would want to stay out of a war over the Balkans. Indeed, the people of Great Britain did not even want to fight for France. They would have to be tricked into doing that.

I am reminded of a scene in the moving picture *Dr. Strangelove*. American bombers, launched by a demented Air Force general, were heading for the Soviet Union, and the Soviet ambassador to Washington revealed that the American attack would trigger a Doomsday Machine designed to destroy with radioactivity all human life on Earth. The Soviets, explained the ambassador, had built the lethal machine as a comparatively cheap method of deterrence. And it might have worked, pointed out the saturnine Dr. Strangelove, *if the machine had not been kept secret*. "Why didn't you tell the world?" he asked.

Soviet leaders must not have seen that film. In real life, they in 1985 completed a secret "Dead Hand" system to launch missiles automatically if the Soviet leadership was decapitated by an American strike. One of the designers, Colonel Valery E. Yarynich, argued that keeping the system secret made it pointless.[29] As a young rocket officer, Yarynich had been shaken by his experience in the Cuban Missile Crisis of 1962. In his last years, he attempted to persuade the United States and Russia to scrap their hair trigger launch alert systems.

Fighting Over Scraps

Bismarck had warned about the Balkans and the fierce rivalries there. A perennial problem was the breakup of the Ottoman Empire and who would get which piece. In 1908, Austria-Hungary annexed Bosnia and Herzegovina, partially Slavic territories which it had been administering since 1878. This angered the Russians as protectors of the Slavs. Germany dissuaded the Russians from going to war, but Foreign Minister Isvolsky, who in Russia was blamed for the annexation, bore a grudge against Austria, and he made a speech in which he advised the Balkan states to federate, thus provoking the Austrians. The irate Isvolsky also provided aid to Austria's enemy, Serbia, which wanted to expand its territory by expelling Austria from the Balkan peninsula. In 1909, Isvolsky made a secret military agreement with Bulgaria which implied war as the solution to the Balkan problems. Said Isvolsky:

> The realization of the high ideals of the Slav peoples in the Balkan peninsula, which are so close to Russia's heart, is only possible after a fortunate issue of the struggle of Russia with Germany and Austria-Hungary.[30]

Isvolsky plotted with Foreign Minister Poincare to make war with Germany (and therefore also with Isvolsky's hated Austria), and he helped the revanchist firebrand to become President of France, according to the German historian Friedrich Stieve, who studied Isvolsky's autobiography and the official Russian documents made public by the Bolsheviks after the Russian Revolution. In 1910, Isvolsky, having been blamed for the 1908 annexation, left his position as foreign minister and moved to Paris as ambassador. There he could work more closely with Poincare. After his arrival, the new Russian envoy was dismayed to see that the younger generation in France was losing interest in reclaiming Alsace and Lorraine. Something had to be done about that.

At Isvolsky's request, the Russian government provided 300,000 francs for the bribing of newspapers to help Poincare get elected President. Along with assisting that project, the bribes did much to neutralize the pacifists, leftist radicals, and others opposed to the alliance of France and Russia. With Poincare's election, the press noted a new spirit of patriotism and revanchism. The French army quit planning with a defensive strategy and began planning with an offensive strategy.[31] Outside of France, Isvolsky put on his payroll Gabriel de Wesselitzki, a Serbian-Russian journalist who was president of London's Foreign Press Association. Isvolsky was pleased by how well Wesselitzki's writing and lecturing sowed discord between Russia and Germany.

War Warning Requested

Isvolsky on January 29, 1913, telegraphed St. Petersburg to say that the alliance was firmly in place, good for the seven years of Poincare's presidency. Concerning the possibility of war breaking out, Isvolsky said that Poincare wanted advance notice so that the French government could prepare public opinion. Apparently, Russia, having a blank check, was expected to initiate the war. Reported Isvolsky to St. Petersburg:

> As he [Poincare] put it, it is of the greatest importance to the French government to have the opportunity of preparing French public opinion in advance for participation in any war which might break out over the Balkan question. That is why the French government asks us not to take any separate action which might result in such a war without a prior understanding with France.[32]

Why would Russia be the one to start the war? An easy place to start a war was the Balkans, and troubles in the Balkans affected Russia, not France. Furthermore, Russia was in a hurry. The Turks had ordered five super-battleships from foreign shipyards, and by the summer of 1914 two of them would be nearing completion. Once these "dreadnoughts" entered the Black Sea, Russia would have no hope of grabbing the Turkish straits.

Poincare made it possible for the Russians to borrow money for railways needed to transport their troops to the border with Germany. Stieve details other actions that Isvolsky took to encourage the onset of war. For example, he saw to the dismissal of the French ambassador in St. Petersburg, a man peaceably inclined. The new ambassador was Theophile Delcasse, a Germanophobic expansionist who had helped to arrange the alliance of Britain and France. Part of Delcasse's new job was to facilitate the railway construction and encourage other kinds of military preparedness.

In 1925, Sir Edward Grey in his autobiography remarked,

> The impression made by what has since come to light about his [Isvolsky's] doings as Ambassador at Paris is far from favourable.[33]

Grey did not mention specifically what Isvolsky was doing.

Spark Needed

A European tinderbox having been prepared, only the right spark was needed to ignite a conflagration. Sparks were bound to be available. War had been predicted as early as 1888 by Bismarck, who said, "One day the great European War will come out of some damned foolish thing in the Balkans." Later he predicted that Germany's "crash" would come twenty years after his death, which turned out to be 1918.

Already in the early 1900s sparks were flying in Morocco. Two different crises there had the Germans and French sending troops to their border. Germany wanted an "open door" policy in Morocco, consciously imitating the American policy on China. France wanted to control Morocco by means of a protectorate, which it finally achieved, thanks to decisions at multinational conferences. One conference was held at the Spanish port city of Algeciras, overlooking the Strait of Gibraltar, where the British mounted what probably was history's most impressive non-lethal naval demonstration. A British fleet pulled into the bay, and at night, with Gibraltar looming in the background, one hundred and forty searchlights beamed columns of light into the sky. One might call that a celebration of Mahanism as well as an attempt to intimidate the Germans.

In that same year, 1906, Britain revolutionized naval warfare by building the HMS *Dreadnought*, the first of the all-big-gun super battleships. Technical advances in gunnery had made it possible to achieve accuracy over a range of several miles, and so rifled guns of 12-inch diameter and more began to predominate. This advance rendered obsolete Britain's existing fleet of battleships, and that provided Germany an opportunity to rival British sea power by constructing "dreadnoughts." The ensuing naval race between Britain and Germany has been cited as a major cause of World War I. Little attention has been given to Russia's more urgent concern about losing its naval dominance of the Black Sea.

Royal Friction

As another facet of the precarious European situation, the heads of state had interpersonal difficulties. The royal leaders were related, but there was friction among them and family feuds endangered the peace. "Nicky," the Czar of All the Russias, felt that he was patronized by his cousin "Willy," the Emperor of Germany, who, in turn, felt that he was patronized by his uncle "Bertie," England's Prince of Wales. In 1901, Bertie became King Edward VII, and in 1910 he was succeeded by cousin "Georgie," King George V. Willy regarded Georgie as a nice but uninformed country gentleman. Their royal upbringings did not prepare well the younger generation for leadership. Bertie was a glutton and a playboy, Wilhelm excitable and vain, Nicky weak and fatalistic. Georgie normally was not much involved.

In the Kaiser's opinion, if his grandmother, Queen Victoria, had been alive, she never would have allowed the royal cousins to go to war with each other. In short, the matriarch left the scene and the squabbling children took over.

Standing: Czar Nicholas II and his cousin the Prince of Wales, later Edward VII
Sitting: Czarina Alexandra, her baby Grand Duchess
Olga, and Queen Victoria. 1896

More Predictions

After Bismarck's, there came more predictions of war. In 1906, Admiral Sir John ("Jackie") Fisher, Britain's first sea lord (equivalent to the American chief of naval operations), told Edward VII that war with Germany would come in 1914. In that year, he said, the expansion of Germany's Kiel canal would be completed and dreadnought-sized battleships could transit between the Baltic Sea and the North Sea. Fisher liked and respected the Kaiser (a "wonderful man") as a fellow Mahanist.[34] But he resented how German businessmen took advantage of the Pax Britannica to market their goods around the world. In 1907, Fisher recommended the Royal Navy eliminate Germany's growing fleet as it had bombarded Copenhagen in 1807. His suggestion was rejected.[35] But Fisher, known to be a friend of the King, threatened the Germans in public,[36] and the possibility of getting "Copenhagened" weighed on German minds.

It annoyed the British that Germany held the speed record for passenger ships crossing the Atlantic. In 1907, the British regained that supremacy with the steamship *Lusitania,* nicknamed the "greyhound of the sea" for its 25-knot top speed, which was unprecedented for a passenger liner. So much was published about the *Lusitania's* speed and magnificent accommodations, comparable to those of a first class hotel, that two hundred thousand people turned out to watch the liner's maiden departure. Passenger ships were a glamorous and important form of technology in those days.

Probably having talked to Admiral Fisher, a U.S. Navy officer, Commander William S. Sims, predicted war for 1914. He recalled later:

> In December, 1910, I submitted a report to the admiral commanding my division, which stated that, having discussed the subject with military men of Great Britain and France, the consensus of opinion was that war would come in four years.[37]

The French, too, were expecting war in 1914. Was Fisher trying to build an informal alliance? If so, he had picked the right man. Sims was an Anglophile and a brilliant, up-and-coming officer.

Unification or Death

Colonel Dimitrijefic founded the Black Hand in 1911. Informally it was called the Black Hand; the formal name was "Unification or Death." The conspirators' goal was to unify all the Balkan Serbs in a Greater Serbia. The members initially were army officers. Added in time were lawyers, journalists, and university professors. Membership increased to about twenty-five hundred, and the Crown Prince was a financial supporter. The society was outraged by Austria-Hungary's annexation of Bosnia-Herzogovina, and in 1911 Dimitrijefic allegedly ordered the assassination of Austria's Emperor Franz Josef. This failed. Next, the colonel assigned a man to kill the Austrian governor of Bosnia-Herzogovina. This also failed.

During the period 1912-1914 two Balkan wars took place. No world war resulted because Germany and Italy restrained Austria-Hungary from taking part. Action by Austria-Hungary in the Balkans would have risked war with Russia, which also had to be restrained.

As an attempt to mitigate troubles in the Balkans, ambassadors of six powers met in London from 1912 to 1914. The six were Britain, France, Germany, Austria-Hungary, Russia, and Italy. In 1913, the Russian ambassador, Count Alexander Benckendorff, warned St. Petersburg that France, Russia's ally, might be seeking war:

> I get the feeling, almost the conviction, that of all the Powers France is the only one which, not to say wants war, at all events would see it without regret . . . To use a familiar expression, France is "on her hind legs again." Rightly or wrongly, she has complete trust in her army; the old ferment of exasperation is once more at work, and France might very well believe that the circumstances are more favourable to-day than they are ever likely to be in the future.[38]

France was concerned about the future because Germany's population was growing faster, just as Germany was concerned about the future because of the rapid growth of Russia's population. Apparently Benckendorff was not in on the Isvolsky-Poincare plot. This is understandable. He was born in Estonia (one of the Baltic nations then part of Russia), and his family was ethnically German. Many high positions in the Russian government and army were held by Baltic Germans, a tradition going back for nearly a hundred and fifty years. The Germans' prominence was much resented by the "real Russians." After the Great War began, one of the real Russians at court told the French ambassador, Maurice Paleologue, "After the war we'll wring the necks of the Baltic barons." The Frenchman advised moving carefully on that, and he was asked, "Do you think we Russians cannot govern ourselves?"

In 1912, Foreign Minister Sazanov reported to the Czar that Britain had promised France an expeditionary force in case of war. Britain was to send a hundred thousand men to Belgium in order to repel a German advance there which was anticipated by France's general staff.[39] In the event of war, both the Germans and the French planned to make use of Belgian space.

Lusitania Prepared for War

Another prediction of war came from Winston Churchill. In February of 1913, the head of the Admiralty called to his office Alfred Booth, chairman of the Cunard Line, and handed him jaw-dropping news: War was expected to break out in September of 1914. At that time, said

Churchill, the Germans will have completed their dredging of the Kiel canal, and the annual continental harvests will have been completed. It was necessary, therefore, to modify ten Cunard ships for service as warships. One of the first to be converted was the *Lusitania*.

Booth had to do as Churchill wished because the British government had helped to finance the Cunard vessels on condition that they be made available to the Royal Navy as needed. *Lusitania* went into dry dock at Liverpool with Cunard announcing that the latest design of turbines was to be installed. That story did not hold up. On June 19, 1913, the *New York Tribune* reported that the ship was being equipped with high powered naval guns. Some investigators have agreed that guns were installed while others say not. According to the latter, the Royal Navy decided that the greyhound burned too much coal to be patrolling as a cruiser, and so the ship was reconfigured as a cargo carrier with hidden compartments to hold shells and other munitions. By all accounts, there were installed revolving gun mounts.

After the modifications, the first class liner was not well balanced and no longer provided first class comfort. The ride was "lively" and the ship tended to "corkscrew." This disturbed Captain Daniel Dow who, prone to seasickness, was known as "Fair Weather Dow."

In 1913, British intrigue in Turkey forced Germany to make concessions about its construction of a Berlin to Baghdad railway. The British feared the extension of German influence in the Middle East and perceived it as a threat to their dominance of India. The railroad company already had several Frenchmen on the board; now it had British representation as well.

President's Alter Ego

In 1913, Colonel House visited London and met with Foreign Secretary Grey. Wilson called House his "alter ego" and employed the moderately rich Texan as an unpaid, unofficial super-ambassador. House collected only expenses. In Washington, the colonel had for his quarters two rooms within the White House. The alter ego got along well with Wilson's wife, but she died, and Wilson's second wife was not so friendly. House was not a colonel in the sense of having had a military career.

The governor of Texas had made him an honorary colonel of the Texas militia in return for political assistance. When House tried to explain the "geographical colonel" custom to a pair of German generals one finally seemed to understand, the other remained "befuddled."

In London, House sought Grey's cooperation in taking care of some problems in Panama and Mexico, and he discussed with Grey his and Wilson's desire to organize a league of nations for keeping the peace. House and Wilson were concerned about the brinkmanship that had been going on in the Balkans and North Africa, and they wished to set up a permanent structure for debating and resolving disputes. In contrast, the British leaders were getting ready to fight.

House advised Grey that if Germany attacked the Triple Entente, President Wilson might render Britain a very great service.[40] House was favorably impressed by Grey and forged a working relationship with him.

Sir Edward Grey, Britain's longest-serving foreign secretary, was generally admired for his eloquence and erudition. In personality, Grey was the consummate diplomat. He charmed Wilson as a devotee of the poet Wordsworth, Theodore Roosevelt as a bird loving naturalist, and House as a man of "high character." (General Taylor, as we know, complimented Mexican General Arista on his "high character." When did that term disappear from American usage?) House was surprised to learn that Grey never had visited Wordsworth's lake country. Also surprisingly, Grey had spent almost no time in Continental Europe—just as the American Secretary of State William Seward had not traveled in the South. Britain's foreign secretary was a country gentleman who wrote books about fishing and birding (*The Charm of Birds* was a best seller), and he hied to his bucolic estate whenever possible.

American Code Broken

House's relationship with Grey was closer than he knew. The honest-looking Wykehamist was reading the coded messages that House and Wilson sent to each other in their private code. Other European leaders probably did the same; it was technically possible to monitor the undersea cables. At this time, the U.S. Government had no code breaking facility and, knowing little of cryptology, had insecure communications. After the war began in 1914, this weakness was discovered by Herbert O. Yardley, a young telegraph clerk employed by the State Department. Formerly a railroad telegrapher in Indiana, Yardley now worked in the State Department's telegraph office, where he rubbed shoulders with high officials such as Secretary of State William Jennings Bryan. As President Lincoln had done, Bryan often visited the telegraph office to see what was happening. Yardley liked Bryan but viewed him as a bumbler and helped with his spelling. One of Yardley's anecdotes about Bryan concerned Henry Wilson, our coup-promoting envoy to Mexico. After Bryan sent him a telegram of congratulations, Wilson ordered him to retract it.

In his spare time, the young Hoosier, a born genius, taught himself code breaking, and one night, for practice, he attacked a message from Colonel House, who was in Berlin. In only two hours the telegrapher was reading the colonel's confidential report. Yardley recounted the experience in his book, *The American Black Chamber*, published in 1931. Said he:

> Colonel House must be the Allies best informant! No need to send spies into Germany when they have Colonel House's reports of interviews with the Emperor, Princes, Generals, industrial leaders . . .

> I am trembling with my great secret but what can I do with it? I can inform my superiors. But what then? The President holds advice in contempt. Besides, this would put him in a very bad light, and adverse criticism he will not tolerate. He would have some one's head and that head would be mine for presuming to read his secret dispatches. I have other uses for my head. I touched a match to the sheets of paper and destroyed the ashes. Let the President and his confidential agent continue their comedy.[41]

The supercilious telegrapher would have been even more amused if he had seen the letter of introduction that Wilson gave House for his European mission. Wilson wanted the belligerents to exchange views on how to end the war, and the letter emphasized the colonel's importance as a *confidential* channel of communication. In the spring of 1915, the

British did House a favor, and themselves a favor, by giving him a British code to use when communicating with Secretary Grey.[42] I have found no indication that House took the hint as it might have pertained to his other communications.

Lieutenant Herbert O. Yardley

When in 1917 America entered the war, Yardley sold his services to the Army for a second lieutenant's commission, and he built a code breaking unit with nearly two hundred people employed. Yardley's efforts included espionage. To find out about one foreign code book, he employed an attractive society woman. (The female sex also distinguished itself in cryptanalysis. Born in little Geneseo, Illinois, Agnes Meyer Driscoll became a leading American cryptanalyst, served in both World Wars, and retired from the National Security Agency in 1959.) Yardley's unit, MI8, was funded in part by the State Department, and in 1929 Secretary of State Henry L. Stimson closed it down saying, "Gentlemen do not read each other's mail." (As we know, some gentlemen, like General Beauregard, might not, but others, like Governor Pickens, certainly would.) The Stimson anecdote commonly is told when somebody reviews the history of American code breaking, but there is another explanation for the shutdown. Stimson was Catholic, and he did not seem pleased when Yardley mentioned that he was reading the Vatican's messages. Unemployed in the Depression,

Yardley needed book royalties to support his family. Stimson had brought about a major security breach.

Shaw's Plan for Peace

In letters to newspapers published in 1913 and early 1914, the dramatist and social critic George Bernard Shaw pondered how to prevent a European war. Here was one of his ideas:

> We should tell Germany that if she carried out her *well known military programme of attacking France lest France should attack her first* [emphasis added], we should throw ourselves on the side of France . . . we should at the same time assure Germany that if France attacked her we should throw our armaments on the side of Germany.[43]

> Nobody ventured to tackle that proposal in public. In private it was said that such a declaration might provoke war. I was strongly of the opinion that the absence of a declaration of some positive sort was far more likely to end in a war.[44]

Assuming one wished to keep the peace, Shaw's recommendation surely would have been better than having two heavily armed blocs, each with elaborate military plans, nervously watching each other and vulnerable to the spread of some local conflict. That point was made in cabinet discussion by member John Morley, who resigned just before the war began. He said in his resignation:

> Grey has more than once congratulated Europe on the existence of two great confederacies, Triple Alliance and Triple Entente, as healthily preserving the balance of power. Balance! What a beautiful euphemism for the picture of two giant groups armed to the teeth, each in mortal terror of the other, both of them passing year after year in an incurable fever of jealousy and suspicion![45]

As the year 1914 opened, the Russians were planning a conflict more than local. Foreign Minister Sazanov on January 6 sent a memorandum to the Czar in which he proposed European "complications" that would lead to Russia's acquisition of the Turkish straits and the dividing up of Turkey by the Triple Entente. A week later, the Russian army's high command said it was ready to fight Germany and Austria-Hungary and that it expected help from France and Great Britain. On February 21 the Russian parliament appropriated 102 million rubles for strengthening the Black Sea fleet, an obvious threat to the straits. (The foregoing events are covered in detail by the American historian Sean McMeekin in his *The Russian Roots of the First World War*, pages 31-32.)

Durnovo's Forecast

A prominent Russian opposed to war was Peter Durnovo, a former member of Imperial Council. As a young man he planned to become a professor of theoretical mathematics, but his family thought that not a proper occupation for the member of a noble family and so he became a bureaucrat, rising to head Russia's gargantuan secret police organization, the Okhrana. Later he was appointed minister of the interior (and happened to be the last of those to die of natural causes). In February of 1914, Durnovo foresaw war and in a letter to the Czar he recommended a way in which to avoid it. The Bolsheviks after seizing power found the letter and published it.[46] Following were some of the salient points:

1. Russia's alliance with France and England makes war inevitable. England is losing out to Germany in terms of commerce and industrial production, and England fears the increasing size of the navy being built to protect Germany's rapidly growing seaborne commerce. Concluded Durnovo:

    > England cannot yield without a fight, and between her and
    > Germany a struggle for life or death is inevitable.

(In 1910, Princess Daisy of Pless wrote in her diary that it made her "sad" to see how "laziness" and "inferior education" produced inferior British products. "Germany is always ahead," sighed the British expatriate.)

2. England needs an alliance with Russia because it does not have enough manpower to defeat Germany. Neither does France have enough manpower. Therefore, the brunt of the war will fall on

Russia. (When Russia left the war in March of 1918, American troops had joined the Allies.)

3. The needs of Russia and England conflict. Germany is a food-importer and Russia's best customer for agricultural goods. Russia therefore benefits from a prosperous, fast-growing Germany, which England does not want. A war-impoverished Germany would not be a good customer. (Notice that in pre-Communist days, Russia was a food exporter; overall, the economy was growing at a hefty 10 percent rate. As in Mexico, however, the new wealth was not trickling down enough, and the people were restive.)

4. A defeated Germany could not compensate Russia for the cost of the war. Durnovo explained,

> Defeated in the interest of England, the peace treaty will not afford Germany the opportunity for sufficient economic recuperation to cover our war expenditures, even at a distant time.

(We have seen what happened at Versailles.)

Russia could take some Polish territory from Germany, Durnovo noted, but Russia already had enough trouble with its own Poles.

5. Russia is not well prepared for war. Military reverses will be blamed on the government and endanger the monarchy. In the event of defeat, "social revolution in its most extreme form is inevitable." (Durnovo certainly hit the mark there.)

6. An alliance with Germany would be more advantageous to Russia than the present alliance with France and England.

It is not known whether the Czar read Durnovo's letter. He continued the alliance with France and Britain, which made the Germans feel encircled by enemies.

Durnovo decided the United States was fundamentally hostile to Germany and might come into the predicted war in order to obtain German colonial holdings. Durnovo was half right about that. We

Americans came into the war, but we got nothing out of it except casualty lists, a lot of bad debts, and much disillusionment. Correctly, Durnovo said Japan might enter the war to gain territory. Japan was one of fifteen nations that gained territory; it acquired Germany's Far Eastern and Pacific island holdings. The Japanese performed for the Allies a rarely mentioned but useful service. They sent seventeen warships to the Mediterranean for the protection of Allied shipping.

Peter Durnovo

After the war, President Wilson changed his mind again about the cause of the conflict. In a speech of September 5, 1919, he echoed Durnovo:

> Is there any man or woman—let me say, is there any child—
> who does not know that the seed of war in the modern world
> is industrial and commercial rivalry?

Naval Race Ends

The naval race was over by 1914, although not everybody knew it. The British were building warships so fast that the Germans, encumbered by the need to maintain a large army, could not keep up. As Churchill later noted, "naval rivalry . . . had ceased to be a cause of friction."[47] In 1914, the Triple Entente had forty-three dreadnoughts, Germany only twenty. In case of war, the Kaiser's dreadnoughts were likely to be blockaded and useless.

Churchill early in 1914 wanted to open secret negotiations with his opposite number in Germany, Admiral Alfred von Tirpitz, in order to "end the unwholesome concentration of fleets in home waters," so that the two navies would not be almost confronting each other. Churchill was overruled by Secretary Grey, who said the negotiations would give rise to wild rumors.

Frustrated as a peacemaker, Churchill continued his war preparations. In March he told the House of Commons that "some forty British merchant ships had been defensively armed." After war was declared on August 4, *Lusitania* went back into dry dock and might have acquired guns at that time. We do know the ship again ended up with more space for cargo. Guns or no guns, the luxury liner then was carried on Cunard's books as an "auxiliary cruiser," and it was under Admiralty control. If the *Lusitania* sailed with no guns installed, this ought to have been made clear to the public. The people on board might have been saved if the U-boat commander had felt sure the ship was unarmed. U-boat commanders allowed time for debarkation when possible.

German auxiliary cruisers were interned by American authorities, but not the British ones.

House Sees Kaiser

Clearly, in 1914 Europe was at a perilous juncture. In the spring, Colonel House went over and visited Berlin. Because House was a "colonel," he was invited to the *Schrippenfest*, an annual event at which the Kaiser and top military officers dined with outstanding soldiers. House later had a meeting with the Kaiser, who impressed him as having "all the versatility of [Theodore] Roosevelt with something more of the charm, something less of the force." The Kaiser complained that Secretary Grey could not understand Germany because he had never been to the Continent [almost true].[48] Wilhelm emphasized that his country was getting rich, did not need war, and that the Americans, British, and Germans ought to draw together because they were kindred peoples and "the only hope of advancing

Christian civilization." One might say that, basically, we have that now with NATO. The Kaiser's British mother would have been pleased.

House warned the Kaiser that Britain feared the growing German navy [49] (probably true as reported in the popular press and, as we shall see, perhaps true in Grey's mind). The German leader responded that his country needed a navy big enough to counter both France and Russia, and the current building program would be enough for that.

House and the Kaiser enjoyed an animated conversation that went on for half an hour. The Empress sent people to warn the two that House needed to catch a train. The Kaiser barely paid attention to the warnings, and after the last one, the effusive Emperor talked another ten minutes. In his diary, House recalled,

> By this time, I had said all I cared to and was ready to leave myself; therefore I stopped talking and was very quiet in order to indicate that I, at least, was through. This had the desired effect and we bade each other good-bye.[50]

With his concern about travel arrangements, did House miss an important opportunity? After the war, the German-American writer George Viereck visited the deposed Emperor, who was in exile, and Wilhelm told him,

> The [1914] visit of Colonel House in Berlin and London almost prevented the World War. [51]

Itchy Trigger Fingers; House's Prediction

In May of 1914, the two armed camps were getting itchy trigger fingers. The German chief of staff, General Helmuth von Moltke, warned the German foreign minister, Gottlieb von Jagow, that with respect to Russia time was working against Germany because Russia had a huge and growing population and was building up its military forces. It was suspected that Russia planned to attack in 1916. A "preventive war" was needed, said Moltke, and German policy should aim for that. Similarly, as we have noted, the French felt threatened by Germany's increase of population and industrial might. On May 29, House while in Berlin sent to President Wilson a prediction:

> Unless some one acting for you can bring about a different understanding, there is someday to be an awful cataclysm. No one in Europe can do it. There is too much hatred, too many jealousies. *Whenever England consents, France and Russia will close in on Germany and Austria"* [emphasis added].[52]

Now the President's alter ego was sounding like Durnovo. Possibly the Kaiser read that disturbing message, sent from Berlin, and possibly so did Secretary Grey.

The shuttling alter ego arrived in London on June 9 bursting with news and opinions, but he had to wait more than two weeks to see the foreign secretary. "Here they have their thoughts on Ascot, garden parties, etc., etc." he grumbled. At last, on June 27, House had lunch with Grey and Ambassador Page. House suggested that Grey, the Kaiser, and he get together at Kiel, where soon the opening of the enlarged canal would be celebrated. "But this was not gone into further," House said in his diary. In other words, the suggestion fell flat. House warned Grey that the atmosphere in Germany was very tense and "some spark might be fanned into a blaze." The colonel also informed Grey that the Kaiser was waiting for any encouraging news that he, House, might send from Britain.

Grey's not approving Churchill's proposed trip to Berlin and House's proposed gathering in Kiel were crucial mistakes if we go by an opinion expressed after the war, in 1920, by Lloyd George. The war, said Lloyd George, was something into which the nations of Europe "staggered and stumbled, perhaps through folly, and *a discussion, I have no doubt, would have averted it* [emphasis added].[53]

That was quite a change from what Lloyd George had said during the war, on August 4, 1917:

> [We are fighting] to defeat the most dangerous conspiracy ever plotted against the liberty of nations, carefully, skilfully, insidiously, clandestinely planned in every detail with ruthless, cynical determination.[54]

By 1925, even Poincare soft-pedaled German war guilt. He said,

> I do not claim that Austria or Germany in the first place had a thought-out intention of provoking a general war. No existing documents give us the right to suppose that at that time they had planned anything so systematic.[55]

In 1914, a parley at the summit was sorely needed. Foreign Secretary Grey, however, did not want that. He and Churchill would stay at home.

The Right Spark

Bismarck had expected some "damned foolish thing in the Balkans" to spark a great European war. And so it did. The first shot was fired on June 28, 1914. It was fired in Sarajevo, the capital of Bosnia, and the shooter was a Serb who had been recruited by Colonel Dimitrijefic and his Black Hand terrorists. The Serbo-Russian fuse had burned to its destination. Nineteen-year-old Gavrilo Princip assassinated Archduke Ferdinand of the Austro-Hungarian Empire, and this set in motion a train of events that, two months later, culminated in World War I, a conflagration from which, according to columnist George Will, the "world has not yet recovered and from which Europe will never recover."

Gavrilo Princip

Princip's family was extremely poor, and after failing a school entrance examination, he tried to join the Black Hand, but was rejected for membership because he was too small and too weak. However, the organization assigned the teenager, along with seven other young men, a special one-time mission. Armed with six hand bombs and four pistols, their job was to assassinate the archduke, who was expected to visit Sarajevo. Apparently Dimitrijefic had learned that, for a high profile assassination, putting one man on the job was not enough. He presumably recruited idealistic young amateurs so that he could disavow any connection in case of their capture. As an additional security measure, Princip and the others were ordered to end their own lives by taking cyanide of potassium. Possibly all of them, like Princip, were afflicted with tuberculosis.

Some of the potential assassins were smuggled from Serbia into Bosnia by means of the Black Hand's "underground railroad." Little Princip was among them. He and the other assassins were deployed along the route of the archduke's motorcade. One of the gang threw a bomb that bounced off the archduke's automobile, some of the youths failed to act, and then came Princip's opportunity. The archduke's open car happened to stop where the armed Serb was standing. He pistol-whipped a spectator to get him out of the way, then fired several shots at the car. The bullets killed the archduke and his wife Sophie, Duchess of Hohenberg. Seeing his wife was hit, the archduke cried, "Sophie, Sophie, don't die. Live for the children!"

Cyanide Fails

Princip was seized and beaten up. He swallowed the cyanide, but the pill was too old and failed to kill him. After the assassination, mobs attacked Serbian citizens and businesses. Besides Serbs, there lived in Sarajevo Muslim Turks and Christian Croats. The Black Hand's Greater Serbia was bound to include ethnic minorities, just like the Austro-Hungarian Empire. In 1999, President William Clinton ordered the bombing of Serbs to stop their alleged ethnic cleansing.

Princip apologized for accidentally having killed the duchess. He died in prison in 1918, of tuberculosis. Princip's bones, once hidden, now are interred in Serbia along with those of some other Serbs exalted as heroes.

The Austrians asked Serbia to investigate the assassination. The Serbian foreign minister demurred saying that the assassination had nothing to do with his country. This was far from true. Princip was a Serb, and Dimitrijefic was head of Serbia's military intelligence. (But to this day, as I see in newspaper commentary, it appears that most Americans think Princip acted alone.) The enraged Austrians, being in possession of Princip and the bomb-thrower (his cyanide reportedly did not work, either) were able to arrest all but one of the designated assassins, find out what they knew, and roll up the underground railroad. Like Princip the bomb thrower was consumptive.

Serbia's Prime Minister Pasic supported the killing of the Serbian King in 1903, but he did not favor killing the Archduke Ferdinand because he feared it would provoke a war with Austria-Hungary. Pasic made a half-hearted attempt to prevent the assassination and failed.

According to one theory, the terrorist society knew that Ferdinand, in line to become Emperor, would be a more liberal ruler than Franz Josef, and might wean the Serbs away from their separatist tendency. Alternatively, it has been suggested that the Black Hand's aim was to incite war between Serbia and Austria-Hungary in the hope of starting a war between Russia and Austria-Hungary. In fact, Russia did go to war with Austria-Hungary, ostensibly on behalf of Serbia. If that is what they wanted, the Russians in supporting the Black Hand got their money's worth.

Okhrana Involved?

The Austrians sought help from Russia with their investigation but of course received no cooperation. The Russians for years had encouraged Serbia's anti-Austrian activities, and Colonel Dimitrijefic kept in close touch with the Russian military attache in the Serbian capital of Belgrade. The Austrians perhaps knew or suspected that the Black Hand was a front for Russia's Okhrana. The Okhrana was known to implement covert operations everywhere in Europe and even in the United States. The Russian spy agency was a master of false flag operations.

A Friendly Celebration

News of the assassination reached the Kaiser while he was attending the celebration at Kiel. Dreadnoughts and other large ships now could transit the canal with a saving of nearly three hundred miles. Celebrating along with the German navy were the crews of four British battleships and three cruisers. Historian Sir Martin Gilbert described the event:

> Officers and men of both navies exchanged enthusiastic compliments as they went on board each other's ships to enjoy the pageantry. Together they stood bareheaded at the funeral of a British pilot killed in an air accident during the festivities . . . [British embassy Counselor Sir Horace] Rumbold recalled . . . "I could not fail to be impressed by the great cordiality which existed between the German and our sailors."[56]

At Kiel, the American ambassador to Germany, James W. Gerard, dined with the Kaiser and Admiral Tirpitz who, according to Gerard, were "most enthusiastic" about their meetings with House. Unfortunately, Secretary Grey and Colonel House were not present. What might have been the result if those two had joined in the festivities? Or if Churchill had been there?

Contributing to the general cordiality ought to have been the end of the naval race. Germany was building only one dreadnought that year while Britain was building three. Nevertheless, two years after the get-together in Kiel, German and British sailors would be blowing each other to bits at the Battle of Jutland.

The great confrontation took place in the North Sea near Denmark. Admiral Nelson with his wooden ships used to go for point blank range, sometimes his cannon bumped into the enemy vessel. A century later, in 1916, dreadnoughts at Jutland fired shells at ranges of five to seven miles. The Germans tried to decoy a British force into an ambush, but the British, being in possession of a German naval code book, ambushed the Germans instead. The code book had been retrieved from a German cruiser run aground in Russian waters. The British, as in 1812 when fighting the United States, got the worse of the battle with respect to casualties and ships sunk. Again, however, their upstart opponent, having fewer ships, could not afford its losses. After Jutland, the German surface navy gave up its goal of operating in the Atlantic, and bored dreadnought men volunteered for U-boat duty. Would the outcome have been different if the stranded German cruiser had destroyed its code book? Probably not. According to Yardley, the British had an agent in the German Admiralty copying code books.

Another Blank Check

With the Black Hand's having succeeded in assassinating a high Austrian official, the Austro-Hungarian government in Vienna determined to teach the Serbs a lesson. What about danger from Russia? The Kaiser's Foreign Office judged France and Russia not ready for war, and Wilhelm believed his cousin the Czar would not sympathize with the Serbian killers of royalty. The Czar, after all, had proclaimed twelve days of mourning for the archduke. Nonetheless, the Kaiser promised to back up Austria-Hungary if need be, and he urged the Austrians to strike quickly at the Serbs, before the Russians could get organized.

After presenting his "blank check" as it came to be known, the Kaiser went on his annual three-week summer cruise in Norwegian waters. To cancel the cruise, it was thought, would add unnecessarily to the sense of crisis. By the same reasoning, several high German officials went on vacation, including the foreign secretary, who enjoyed a honeymoon. The British foreign secretary, Grey, went fishing. Ambassador Gerard planned to sail for the United States in August. Complacency ruled.

Our affable Texan, Colonel House, waited in London for an encouraging word that he could send to Berlin, and on July 3 he finally was asked to write to the Kaiser about Britain's hope for peace. Grey said he himself did not want to send anything official or in writing for fear of offending the French and Russians. This raises a question. Why would Britain's hope for peace offend the French and the Russians? Because they wanted a war? House wrote a letter and sent it on July 7. When the letter arrived in Berlin, the Kaiser, predictably, was on his Norwegian cruise, and House's peace initiative had come to naught.

On July 14, the German businessman Albert Ballin was in London, and he discussed with Churchill the possibility of limiting a war if it came about. Ballin understood the network of alliances. Germany, he said, if it had to fight France, might be willing to take no French territory except in the colonies. Would that condition keep Britain out of the war? Churchill was noncommital. On July 29 the same proposal was telegraphed from Berlin and was rejected by the British cabinet.

First Lord Churchill on July 15 supervised a "test mobilisation" of the Fleet, which he had been planning since the autumn of 1913. As Churchill said in *The World Crisis*, "The entire Royal Fleet Reserve and all the Reserve officers were to be mobilised and train together for a week or ten days."[57] The test mobilization, said Churchill, was "incomparably the greatest assemblage of naval power ever witnessed in the history of the world." The first lord was getting assembled and ready for war the greatest naval force in world history, and this was the result of a plan he had made in the autumn of 1913, when expecting war in 1914.

House Heads Home

With travel arrangements again taking precedence, Colonel House sailed for the United States on July 21.

Like the Kaiser, former Prime Minister Asquith after the war said House's efforts had almost borne fruit. An American correspondent asked Asquith whether he had not gotten tired of House thrusting himself into British affairs (the view of Ambassador Page). The response:

> At this Asquith struck the terrace with his cane and said there would have been more of breath and life if the plans of Colonel House had been acted upon.[58]

In January of 1916, House wrote in his journal:

> I have always felt that the war might possibly have been avoided if they [the British] had acted with expedition.

House regretted that the British in June of 1914 had "delayed" his proposal "looking toward a better understanding with Germany."[59]

A Party in Petersburg

To firm up his alliance with Russia, President Poincare went to St. Petersburg and met with the Czar. Beginning on July 20, it was a three-day visit featuring martial music and a review of 70,000 soldiers. At a dinner banquet, Ambassador Paleologue chatted with the Grand Duchess Anastasia. (This was not Anastasia the Czar's youngest daughter but the wife of Grand Duke Nicholas, who would command Russia's army in the war.) According to the Frenchman's memoir, the grand duchess told him exultantly, "There's going to be war... There'll be nothing left of Austria... You're going to get back Alsace and Lorraine [she displayed a box of soil from Lorraine]... Our armies will meet in Berlin... Germany will be destroyed." Grand Duchess Anastasia was a princess from Montenegro. She and others talked about the forthcoming war as a duel between Germanism and Slavism. There was an air of confidence among the Russians. Ambassador Benckendorff, it will be recalled, reported on how confident were the French back on their "hind legs again." In St. Petersburg this was apparent when Poincare treated the Austrian ambassador rudely.

While the Czar and Poincare met in private, Paleologue sat and waited with the Czarina Alexandra. The Czarina looked "worn out" and "strained." The ambassador stopped a band performance that was shattering the lady's nerves. For Poincare's visit, the bands were playing French marches such as the *Marche Lorraine*. A war between Germany and Russia could not turn out well for the Czarina. She was born a German princess.

In 1918, the Bolsheviks would execute the Czar and his entire family.

Austria Focuses on Serbia

The Austrians kept their focus on Serbia. But they were slow to act. The Hungarian part of the Dual Monarchy had to agree with the plan. On July 23, Vienna at last sent an ultimatum to Belgrade. It contained fifteen demands. Among them: Eliminate terrorist groups and suppress anti-Austrian publications. The Austrian Council of Ministers fully expected that Serbia would reject the demands and war would follow. They assumed, or just hoped, Germany would keep Russia out of the war.

Hearing of the ultimatum, Foreign Minister Sazonov was reputed to exclaim, *"C'est la guerre Europeene!"* (It's a European war!). Sazanov might not actually have said that, but the Ministry of Finance on July 24 decided to withdraw all of the Russian government's funds deposited in Berlin.

Surprisingly, Serbia on July 25 agreed to all but two of the fifteen demands, and for the rest it suggested making use of the International Court of Justice at the Hague. That is what the Austrian envoy was told in the morning. Shortly afterward Serbia received Russian assurance of backing in case of war, and at 3 p.m. the Serbs began mobilizing their army. At 6 p.m. President Pasic in a complicated note reneged on what he had said in the morning. Immediately the Austrian diplomats burned their codebooks and left for home.

On the same day, Russia, with French backing, secretly began mobilizing against Austria. That involved the navy and more than a million men in the army. As part of the Russian mobilization procedure, as planned back in 1913 (when Churchill was planning his test mobilization) Russian officials were to *mask the war preparations with negotiations in order to allay the enemy's fears*. (The foregoing information is reported in Sean McMeekin's book *July 1914: Countdown to War*, published in 2013.)

Masking Ploy

Presumably to allay German and Austrian fears, Sazonov recommended to the British ambassador holding a conference in London, like the previous Balkan conferences, and on July 26 that idea was passed on to Foreign Secretary Grey. Grey approved. Not interested in a multilateral conference, Germany wanted the Austrians and the Russians to negotiate on the Serbian problem, keeping the conflict local.[60]

While the Kaiser gazed at Norwegian fiords, Bethmann-Holweg tried to keep bad news from him. After returning from his cruise, the Kaiser at last read Serbia's response to the Austrian ultimatum, and (did he read the right one?) thought it was a great diplomatic victory for Austria. He decided to mediate for peace and wrote a memorandum to that effect. He sent the memorandum to Austria by courier, and before it arrived the Austrians had declared war on Serbia. Hearing that, Wilhelm rebuked his Chancellor, "You have got me into a fine mess!"

In Vienna the public was overjoyed by the prospect of finally taking action against the treacherous Serbs. Almost all of the American press sympathized with Serbia, describing it as an underdog being bullied by an empire. Exceptional was the Birmingham *Age-Herald*. It said the Serbs would have to be "completely subjugated" or Austria would "never be safe from their plottings."

Shots Are Fired

Austrian gunboats on the Danube river shelled a railroad bridge and a fortress at Belgrade.

First Lord Churchill on July 29 sent his First Fleet to war stations in the North Sea. As described by Churchill, there went "eighteen miles of warships running at high speed and in absolute blackness through the Narrow Straits." The German ambassador, Prince Karl Max Lichnowsky, learned of the deployment and protested it as a provocation

The Kaiser's younger brother, Prince Heinrich, back home from visiting England (he was a popular figure there), reported that, according to King George, Britain would stay out of war. The Kaiser's men were skeptical, but Wilhelm said the word of a king was good enough for him. In St. Petersburg, the German ambassador was Count Friedrich Pourtales, and he according to Paleologue, desperately strove to find some kind of compromise with Sazanov. Sazanov refused to agree that Serbia had anything to do with the assassination, and he would not allow any action against Serbia. Pourtales insisted that Germany had to support its ally. Failing in his efforts, Pourtales was distraught and his eyes brimmed with tears.

The Czar on July 29 secretly ordered general mobilization of Russian arms, knowing this was tantamount to declaring war on Germany. Then, having received a conciliatory telegram from the Kaiser, the Czar changed his mind and canceled the order saying, "I will not be responsible for a monstrous slaughter!" On July 30, Sazonov talked the Czar into signing another mobilization order arguing that Germany was making war inevitable. To make sure that this new order was final, the foreign minister told the army's chief of staff, "Now you can smash your telephone!"

Europe's fate was sealed.

As in the case of the partial mobilization, the Russians kept their general mobilization order secret. On July 31, however, Pourtales found out what was happening and sent the news to Berlin. The Kaiser then ordered a pre-mobilization which canceled all leaves and put the railroads under military control.[61] Outmanned, outgunned, and having to fight on two fronts, the Germans needed to move fast. Knowing that, the Russians had done their best to steal a march.

Kaiser's Peace Effort

The Kaiser had erred in thinking the Czar would not defend the regicidal Serbs. As another disappointment, he learned that a week had gone by since the Russians had started mobilizing. Nevertheless, the Kaiser on July 31 made a final attempt to preserve the peace. He telegraphed his cousin Nicky, in English, and sent a copy to cousin Georgie in London. First, he pointed out that the Czar had asked him to mediate the dispute between Austria and Serbia at the same time the Russians began their mobilization, thus making the mediation "illusory." Then said the Kaiser:

> The responsibility for the disaster which is now threatening the whole civilized world will not be laid at my door [he was wrong about that]. In this moment it still lies in your power to avert it. Nobody is threatening the honour or power of Russia which can well afford to await the result of my mediation. My friendship for you and your empire, transmitted to me by my grandfather on his deathbed, has always been sacred to me and I have honestly often backed up Russia when she was in serious trouble especially in her last war. The peace may still be maintained . . . if Russia will stop the military measures which must threaten Germany and Austria-Hungary.

In response, Nicky thanked Willy "heartily" for his mediation, but said that it was "technically impossible" to reverse the mobilization.

Russia began laying 3,200 mines in the Baltic Sea.

The war "already was a decided thing" after July 25 (when Russia's partial mobilization began), according to what was said in 1921 by General Sergei Dobrorolsky, formerly head of Russia's Mobilization Department. Dobrorolsky added that the telegrams sent afterward between Berlin and St. Petersburg merely set the stage for an "historical drama." (Christopher Clark, *The Sleepwalkers*, page 486).

Germany now faced its great fear: war on two fronts, east and west. In preparation for that dire possibility, the army had a plan which had been prepared by the army's late chief of staff, General Count Alfred von Schlieffen, a classic tall and monocled Prussian. Sometimes, perhaps to make a point, he would twist the monocle. In 1906, the year of his retirement, Schlieffen finished designing a strategy in which Germany would invade and neutralize France quickly, then turn and deal with the much larger Russian army in the east. It was assumed that the Russian steamroller would take six weeks to get moving, and in that time France could be dealt with. In order to deal with France quickly the Schlieffen plan required circumventing French fortifications with a flanking movement through Belgium. Although supposed to be secret, the basic Schlieffen plan was known in European foreign offices. Even George Bernard Shaw knew something about it.

With speed being essential to the Schlieffen plan, the Russians, as noted above, were careful to mobilize first and attempt to lull the Germans with negotiations. Presumably requesting the Kaiser's mediation was part of that.

Germany Declares War on Russia

France began general mobilization on August 1, calling up a million men. Belgium mobilized, too. Not having received a favorable response concerning the Russian steamroller, Germany started general mobilization and declared war on Russia. On August 3, Germany declared war on France. In most of the world, Germany appeared guilty of having started the war, even though among the great powers it had been the last to mobilize.

The French ambassador in London, Paul Cambon, anxiously tried to find out whether Britain would honor Grey's secret commitment to his country. Cambon reminded the foreign secretary that France's northern and western coasts were open to attack since, by agreement, the French fleet patrolled the Mediterranean. Grey promised naval assistance, but no help on the ground. "They are going to desert us!" Cambon despaired. Shocked upon hearing of the naval pledge, four members of the British cabinet resigned. Evidently, like Benckendorff in Russia, they were not in on the secret "conversations." Two of them were talked back into the cabinet, the other two remained outside. One of the two remaining outside was John Morley. Grey was juggling problems in the air the way Bismarck used to do.

Belgium Invaded

On August 4, the German army invaded Belgium on its way to France, as the French had expected, and Britain sent an ultimatum to Berlin. The plight of "brave little Belgium" provided Grey an excuse to help France. In Britain, neither the public nor the Parliament knew that Grey and Asquith had promised to defend France. The commitment was based on seven years of planning so secret that military officers did the secretarial work. Few Britons were willing to get involved in a war between the Germans and the French, and nobody cared about the Serbs. But saving nearby Belgium appeared an important and noble cause, even though the country was in bad odor because of its exploitation of the Belgian Congo. The late King Leopold II's ruthless harvesting of rubber and ivory had cost the lives of an estimated ten million Africans,[62] one of history's forgotten holocausts.

The invasion of Belgium was the publicly acceptable casus belli for which Grey had been waiting. Seeing a lamplighter working in the dusk he remarked, "The lamps are going out all over Europe, we shall not see them lit again in our lifetime." Probably the pensive secretary had his dimming eyesight in mind as well.

Learning of Britain's decision for war, Admiral Tirpitz shocked his colleagues by blurting out, "All is then lost!" Tirpitz knew that the Royal Navy, overall, was twice as big as his. Even before the British troops began to arrive, the Germans were outnumbered on both fronts. Assuming a short war, General Moltke thought the small British army could be dealt with. In time, however, the British and French empires would contribute vast resources. India alone would send a million men.

The Kaiser was despondent: "If only someone beforehand had warned me that England would take up arms against us!" Actually, both of the last two ambassadors to London had done just that, but both were considered too Anglophilic to be trusted. In 1912, Ambassador Count Paul-Wolff Metternich had been sacked for predicting war by 1915 because of the Kaiser's naval plans. His successor, Lichnowsky, did not help his credibility by accepting, in June of 1914, an honorary degree from Oxford University. Lichnowsky was the first German ambassador to receive this honor since Baron von Bunsen. Bunsen was a prominent scholar, but Lichnowsky was not even a college graduate, and in Berlin Lichnowsky's honor was viewed as a payment for his Anglophilia. (Ambassador Page, a scholar of ancient Greek, also received a degree.)

The Kaiser said he could not believe the English would gang up on fellow Teutons with the French and the Slavs. His generals felt otherwise.

On August 5, the French ambassador to Berlin, Jules Cambon, remarked to his British colleague, "There are three people in Berlin tonight who regret that war has broken out; you, me, and Kaiser William."[63]

Isvolsky's Triumph

In Paris, the overjoyed Ambassador Isvolsky declared, *"C'est ma guerre!"* (It's my war!). Grey in his autobiography discounted the boast on the ground that Isvolsky was just an ambassador and no longer Russia's foreign minister.[64] But a French Socialist politician, Jean Jaures, asked a group of newspapermen, "Are we going to unleash a world war because Isvolsky is still furious over . . . the Bosnian affair?" Jaures was referring to how Isvolsky lost his job as foreign minister because of Austria's annexation of Bosnia. That evening, Jaures was shot to death.

The assassin was an appropriately named ultra-nationalist, Raoul Villain, who was incarcerated until 1919. A jury then acquitted Villain of the charges against him. Having reportedly inherited money, the assassin fled France and hid on the Spanish island of Ibiza. There in 1936 he became a casualty of the Spanish Civil War.

Belgium refused to allow the German army to pass, although the Germans promised to pay for any damages, and so the Germans began shooting their way through the smaller country. Enormous siege guns destroyed the Belgian forts.

France had a relatively simple "Plan 17." Primarily it called for an all-out plunge across the Rhine and on to Berlin. *Attack!* was the French motto, and the French believed that their fighting spirit, their elan, was greater than that of the Germans. With the Germans going one way and the French going the other, Western Europe was to become like a revolving door. The French and British together planned to help the Belgian army stop the German advance through Belgium. The British Empire's well seasoned troops proved to be excellent shots.

The chain reaction of war declarations continued. Austria-Hungary declared war on Russia, Serbia on Germany, France on Austria-Hungary, Britain on Austria-Hungary, Japan on Germany, Austria-Hungary on Japan and Belgium. The Japanese had had their mutual defense treaty with Britain since 1902.

Russian War Minister Vladimir Sukhomlinov wrote in his diary, "It seems that the German wolf will be quickly brought to bay: all are against him."

Although a member of the Triple Alliance, Italy did not help its comrades. The Italians had a secret non-aggression treaty with France. In 1915, the Italians, having been promised some Austrian territories, entered the war on the side of the Allies, thus opening a third front against the Central Powers. In time, twenty-four countries comprised the Allies. Bulgaria joined the Central Powers, hoping to regain some territory from Serbia.

After a decade of crises and brinkmanship, some in the belligerent populations rejoiced at the emotional relief provided by war. Patriotic young Parisians smashed into German shops and yelled, "On to Berlin!" Some celebrations occurred in London and St. Petersburg. In Berlin, crowds sang "Deutschland Uber Alles" and Lutheran hymns. Patriotic socialists marched in the streets with their red flags. Just before Germany declared war, Ambassador Page wrote to President Wilson:

> I detect even in English opinion an acquiescence, almost a satisfaction, that war between England and Germany is certain. They feel that it must come some time—why not now and have it over? It is better to have it when Germany will have other enemies than England in the field than at some time when England might alone have to fight Germany—better, too, when the responsibility for starting it lies at Germany's door.[65]

As Durnovo had said, Britain lacked the manpower to tackle Germany by itself. Britain was lucky enough—or clever enough—to have allies with bigger armies.

Grey Culpable?

Although the press and the Entente governments managed to fasten the war guilt on Germany, in retrospect some observers maintained that Britain was in a position to control events and that Secretary Grey, in particular, was at fault for letting the war come to pass. We have Woodrow Wilson's opinion on this subject. In 1919, the President was a sadder but wiser man, and sounded more like Durnovo than his usual Anglophile self. On September 4, the President said in Columbus, Ohio:

> I did not meet a single public man who did not admit these things, that Germany would not have gone into this war if she had thought Great Britain was going into it.

One such public man was Bonar Law, who served in the British cabinet. Said Law on July 18, 1918, in the House of Commons:

> It has been said—and I think it is very likely true—that if Germany had known for certain that Great Britain would have taken part in the war, the war would never have occurred.[66]

The Marquess of Lansdowne, who had been the British foreign secretary from 1900 to 1905, wrote to Lord Loreburn in 1919:

> The war might have been avoided if Grey had been in a position to make a perfectly explicit statement as to our conduct in certain eventualities.[67]

Grey himself did not know for certain. He had to tell the cabinet members about the secret plans, which he had been denying, and then he had to persuade them to go along. His desire for peace was called into question by Charles Trevelyan, a Liberal MP. Trevelyan encountered the foreign secretary just after the Austrian ultimatum to Serbia, and recalled later:

> So obvious was it that he [Grey] disliked the idea of neutrality that I got extraordinarily uncomfortable, without knowing what it all meant.[68]

Was this the same peace-loving foreign secretary of whom Colonel House thought so highly? Grey, anyway, did not make clear British intentions soon enough. Diplomats kept after him, trying to find out what Britain would do in case of war. Lichnowsky in telegrams to Berlin had been expressing the *opinion* that Britain would go to war for France, but that was not a welcome message in Berlin, and Lichnowsky lacked credibility.

The Kaiser hoped that King George's assurance of peace was valid, and on August 1 there came from Britain more good news. After a conversation with Grey, Lichnowsky telegraphed that Britain would stay neutral if France were not attacked. To the Kaiser that was wonderful news. He ordered champagne and wired his acceptance of the British offer. Then came a telegram from King George, written by Grey, which said Lichnowsky's report was based on a misunderstanding. So had been Prince Heinrich's report. Two putative misunderstandings had given the Germans false hope and slowed them down.

House Blames Kaiser's Ineptitude

In Colonel House's opinion, the Kaiser in 1914 neither wanted war nor expected it. House wrote in his diary on April 15, 1915:

> It is clear to me that the Kaiser did not want war and did not actually expect it. He foolishly permitted Austria to bring about an acute controversy with Serbia, and he concluded that by standing firm with his ally [Austria], Russia would do nothing more than make a vigorous protest, much as she did when Austria annexed Bosnia and Herzegovina. The rattling of the scabbard and the shining armor were sufficient in that case and he thought they would be in this, for the reason

he did not believe Great Britain would go to war concerning such a happening in the Southeast . . . he thought Germany's relations with England had improved to such an extent that she would not back Russia and France to the extent of making war with Germany.[69]

Originally, it was not Germany but Serbia that brought about an "acute controversy" in the Balkans. It seems likely that Russia at least planned or permitted it, and the Kaiser responded with his usual clumsiness.

House blamed Germany for making the war *possible*. Said he:

> Germany has been in the hands of militarists and financiers, and it has been to conserve their selfish interests that this terrible situation has been made possible.

German industrialists, however, were developing southern Russia and they wanted good relations with that country. In Britain, business interests opposed war. Although German exports were increasing their market share, British exports were *still growing*. According to Ambassador Gerard, after the sinking of the *Lusitania*, "many commercial magnates" gathered in Berlin to oppose war with the United States. They were "aghast" at the possibility. American monied interests, of course, benefited from the war.

For the Germans as well as the Belgians, the invasion of Belgium proved disastrous. It brought Britain into the war, and it helped to dramatize the Germans as bullies. As noted by Tuchman, France also planned to invade Belgium, but arrived later. The salvation of France depended on getting there second as the good guy, not first as the bad guy. Belgian resistance slowed the German advance. The British sent an army to Belgium, and Flanders fields became a no-man's land. The Allies and the Germans fought great battles at Ypres (which the British called "Wipers") and Passchendaele, as they tried to reach the U-boat base at Ostend.

War of Attrition

Germany's invasion of France did not go as planned. General Moltke failed to make the right flank strong enough, even though when

General Schlieffen died in 1913, his last words were, "Remember to make the right flank strong." Moltke succumbed to the temptation of advancing his left flank, although the left flank was supposed to retreat and draw the French away from the main action. Like Bismarck, Schlieffen was followed by inferior talent. Moltke got his job because his uncle had won the Franco-Prussian War, and because he was a fraternity brother of the Kaiser. While Schlieffen, following the death of his wife, concentrated laser-like on his work, Moltke maintained a variety of non-military interests, including Christian Science, painting, the cello, and the works of Goethe.

The German offensive bogged down at the Marne river, and both sides dug trenches across Belgium and northeastern France. Machine guns, fast-firing field artillery, and barbed wire enforced a static situation punctuated by mass, suicidal attacks. By January of 1915, generals on both sides had decided that the war on the Western Front was a military stalemate and a war of attrition. A war of movement continued in the east, where the Germans won significant victories over the Russians. As explained earlier, Germany's biggest problem was how to stop the torrent of supplies flowing from the United States to Britain and France. That could be done only with the submarine.

Another Futile Message

Not long after the war began, Chancellor Bethmann-Hollweg sent an American journalist to Secretary Grey with a message. The journalist, Raymond Swing, was recruited by a Canadian friend of the chancellor, the baroness von Schroeder. The message said that after the war Germany would pull out of Belgium and guarantee Belgium's independence, but that Germany would want an indemnity for having been forced into war. Swing doubted that mentioning an indemnity would be a good idea, but the baroness explained that the message had to include an indemnity in case the German generals found out about it. Bethmann-Hollweg, she said, was protecting himself and Grey would be "smart enough" to see that. The young man went to London and met with Grey, who, red-faced and "with a kind of high moral fury," rejected the indemnity. Britain, declaimed Grey at length, was fighting for a world of international law in which men "did not scheme for war."

Swing reported the negative result to Bethmann-Hollweg, who listened without comment.[72]

What was that all about? Possibly, with House having left Europe, the Kaiser was still seeking a back channel to Grey. He and Bethmann-Hollweg always had sought good relations with Britain, while the German generals viewed the British as unwelcoming to their friendship. The young reporter later reproached himself for not having tried to persuade Grey that he, Grey, was in a position to encourage the moderates in Berlin.

Grey's Rationale

In his memoir *Twenty-Five Years*, Grey stuck to the wartime line. He stated that in 1914 he did not believe war inevitable, and he strove to prevent it. However, said Grey:

> Germany was deliberately aiming at world predominance . . .
> Her object was first the hegemony of the continent and then
> predominance over Britain.[73]

Grey presented no evidence for that opinion, said John Morley in a cabinet meeting.[74]

In the view of German militarists, said Grey, Europe was an armed camp, war was inevitable, and 1914 was a good time for an "offensive-defensive" war, what we today would call today a pre-emptive war. Grey did not really expect the balance of power to keep the peace.

In *Twenty-Five Years* Grey also said,

> The real reason for going into the war was that, if we did
> not stand by France and stand up for Belgium against this
> aggression, we should be isolated, discredited, and hated;
> and there would be before us nothing but a miserable and
> ignoble future.[75]

He argued that France would have lost the war and

> We should have been isolated; we should have had no friend
> in the world; no one would have hoped or feared anything
> from us or thought our friendship worth having.

> We should have been discredited, should have been held to
> have played an inglorious and ignoble part.[76]

In time, said Grey, war would have been forced on Britain when the German fleet was ready and

> We should have been found dispirited, half beaten before the
> war began.[77]

A Long Term View?

Was Grey looking far into the future when German industrial might could produce a navy much larger than Britain's? While that may have been a possibility, how would going to war in 1914 prevent it? As a long term strategy, Britain could have made friends with Germany or formed an alliance with the United States. Both actually have happened in response to the growing might of Russia.

In a letter of August 4 to Ambassador Page, Grey said he wanted Britain to continue as a "first class state." In sum, Grey, as predicted by Durnovo, was determined to maintain Britain's pre-eminent status. The purported concern about the Kiel canal might have been just the insiders' cover story or excuse for plans and preparations.

If in Great Britain the people did not want war, the financial magnates did not want war, and the Admiralty did not want war, who did want war? Just the New Imperialists?

If Secretary Grey wanted peace, why did he devote his career to nurturing alliances with France and Russia, making secret promises of support, when their leaders were bent on achieving territorial gains by means of war? We have noted British predictions of war and their preparations for it. We have found more evidence of the French and Russians seeking war than of the Germans doing so.

After the shooting started, George Bernard Shaw decided that Germany was "lured to attack,"[78] according to John Kenneth Turner. I have found no other source for this quotation. If true, here was another allusion to Grey as an expert angler.

Part Three

Tumulty, from the very beginning I saw the end of this horrible thing; but I could not move faster than the great mass of our people would permit—Woodrow Wilson, 1917

As mentioned earlier, German submarine commanders tried to save torpedoes and follow international law by warning the merchant ships, letting their crews scramble to lifeboats, and then sinking the ships with shellfire or by planting bombs. As head of the Admiralty, Winston Churchill made that impossible. He put arms on merchant ships and ordered them to attack any U-boat they saw. If not armed, the ship was to ram the U-boat at high speed. Large rewards were promised. Several skippers were prosecuted for obeying U-boats instead of attacking them. Britain also outfitted "Q ships," innocent looking vessels which carried concealed guns and looked for submarines. Germany, therefore, began sinking ships without warning. This was condemned in the press as barbaric and illegal. Privately, Admiral Fisher said he would have done the same thing.

The most famous and provocative of the ship sinkings was that of the *Lusitania*, which in 1915 was torpedoed off the southern coast of Ireland. Considering the history and circumstances of what took place, it is hard to escape the conclusion that the luxurious liner, with almost two thousand people on board, had drawn a pigeon assignment, bizarre as that may seem. As noted above, the ostensibly civilian passenger liner actually was an auxiliary cruiser under the control of the British navy. It secretly carried munitions and Canadian troops in civilian clothes, which legally made it fair game for the U-boats. After the war, Churchill in *The World Crisis* admitted that the *Lusitania* carried "a small consignment of rifle ammunition and shrapnel shells weighing 173 tons."[79] New York Customs Collector Dudley Malone told President Wilson that "practically all her cargo was contraband of various kinds."[80] Churchill reported, incorrectly, that all of the people aboard the ship were "non-combatants."

Spies at the Docks

The German government had spies at the New York docks and knew all about the loading of munitions and troops. The German Embassy in Washington tried to warn Americans that the ship could be a target for attack, but the warning somehow was delayed until the day of sailing.

The Cunard line had had a close relationship with the British government since 1840. In 1902, the government financed with a low interest rate loan the construction of the *Lusitania* and her sister ship the *Mauretania;* the government also promised to provide regular funds for the ships' maintenance. In return, as mentioned earlier, the Cunard line was to make the ships available at any time for use by the Royal Navy. Some features of the original construction anticipated service as a warship. The Admiralty specified that all engines, boilers, steering gear, fuel, and vital controls be placed below the waterline to keep them safe from shell fire, as was done when building warships. Below the waterline, however, that equipment, including the boilers, was vulnerable to attack by torpedo.

In September of 1914, the Royal Navy had three cruisers patrolling in the North Sea off Yorkshire, and because the ships were slow, obsolescent, and manned by inexperienced crews, the Fleet jokingly referred to them as the "live bait squadron." Learning of that, Churchill ordered that the patrol be canceled. Later, he visited the *Lusitania* in dry dock along with the ship's proud designer, Leonard Peskett, and in reference to the towering vessel Peskett remarked, "The navy hasn't anything like her."

"To me," said Churchill, "she is just another 45,000 tons of live bait."[81]

The very next day, the three obsolescent cruisers were sunk by a German submarine, and the press reported that the trio had been known as the "live bait squadron." At first the public blamed Churchill for the disaster, but investigators decided that the Admiralty staff was to blame for having delayed in canceling the patrol. Apparently Churchill's order, like so many of President Lincoln's, fizzled out.

Lusitania's Important Job

On October 3, 1914, Cunard's Alfred Booth had a meeting at the Reform Club with Secretary of the Admiralty Sir William Graham Greene (uncle of the novelist Graham Greene). Greene informed Booth that Cunard ships were to continue running between Liverpool and New York, and that on trips to Liverpool the Admiralty had priority for use of the ships' cargo space. Booth protested that in wartime there were not enough passengers, the line was losing money, and he would prefer to lay up the ships for the duration of the war. Greene nixed that idea. He said the *Mauretania* could be laid up, but not the *Lusitania*. The government would continue *Lusitania's* maintenance subsidy, pay for the cargo space, and guarantee the ship's insurance. Booth was to prepare the greyhound to sail as soon as possible. It had a "very important job to do."

Irked, Booth wrote to his cousin George Booth: "In essence, Sir William took me into *my own club* and ordered me to be a high grade 'contrabandist' in the National Interest." In American law it was not legal to carry passengers and explosives in the same ship.

Although it was not legal, during the war British liners routinely carried both passengers and munitions. They hid the munitions and filed false manifests. All that was done with the connivance of two American officials. They were Lansing at the State Department and Dudley F. Malone, the collector of customs in New York City. Also involved was a Boston blue blood, Charles P. Sumner, who was Cunard's manager in New York. When Sumner first learned of this illegal activity, he was shocked and refused to allow munitions aboard the *Lusitania*, which then made an empty trip. British intelligence decided the New York manager must be in the pay of the Germans. Cunard doubled Sumner's salary, and he offered no more protests. A British naval attache moved into Cunard's New York office to keep an eye on things.

Lusitania's Dangerous Route

Before the *Lusitania* met its fate, there was plenty of submarine activity on its route, and the ship soon had a close call. In January of 1915, Germany's U-21 sank three merchant ships off Liverpool. No lives were lost. The crews were allowed to disembark, and the ships were destroyed by the placement of bombs. Continuing its voyage, the U-21 had an opportunity to sink the *Lusitania*—with Colonel House on board, planning to meet with European statesmen. Luckily for House and his fellow passengers, the submarine had only one torpedo left, and the skipper decided to save it for his homeward journey.

The colonel noticed something peculiar: His ship hoisted an American flag. When he asked about that, House learned that Captain Dow was concerned about submarine attack and he raised the American flag for protection. British ships did that on secret orders from the Admiralty, i.e., First Lord Churchill. As noted above, there was another secret order: Upon spotting a surfaced German submarine, *Lusitania* was under orders to ram it at high speed. In the case of U-21, this would have been done while the passenger ship was flying the American flag. The Germans knew about Churchill's orders. The men of U-21 discovered a copy on one of the three ships it sank off Liverpool.

Having hoisted the stars and stripes, the greyhound ran as fast as possible to Liverpool without stopping to pick up a pilot. According to House, Captain Dow said that if the ship were torpedoed it would remain afloat for at least an hour, unless the boilers were hit.

Wilson's Weak Protest

The false flag tactic, while increasing safety for British ships, had the effect of reducing safety for American ships, since this made it difficult if not impossible for the Germans to distinguish one nationality from another. The State Department protested the *Lusitania's* use of the American flag. So did the Germans. The British Foreign Ministry blandly explained that the flag was hoisted at the request of American passengers. An American journalist cracked wise, "Britannia not only ruled the waves but waived the rules." To quote Patrick O'Sullivan, author of *The Lusitania*:

> The effect of Churchill's new policies meant that all merchant ships including Q ships and neutrals were indistinguishable in view of the misuse of flags, a policy which caused massive loss of life and played havoc on the high seas.[82]

With a serious protest, President Wilson could have stopped all that.

As one cause of Captain Dow's alarm, he was informed by radio that two Cunard passenger steamers "having valuable cargo" had been ordered to the Irish port of Queenstown (now Cobh) to be kept safe from submarine attack. Admiral Oliver wrote on the wireless page, "Deflected into Queenstown on account of 2 seventy-ton guns on board for R.N. [Royal Navy]." The huge 14-inch diameter gun barrels, made by Bethlehem Steel, were not mentioned on the ships' manifests, but passengers saw them lying on the open decks. Four American passengers complained to the State Department about being held incommunicado at Queenstown for two days and also about the presence of the gun barrels. One would think the observation of seventy-ton gun barrels ought to have settled any question of whether British passenger ships carried munitions. It did not. Robert Lansing received the complaint and initialed it, but he evidently did not pass it on to Secretary Bryan or the neutrality officials in New York.[83] Possibly Lansing did his duty by informing the President since the two shared the secret effort to help Great Britain as much as possible.

Notice that the liners had to be protected because of their "valuable cargo," not because innocent passengers were on board.

How to Embroil the U.S.

When in 1915 Germany announced its British isle war zone, Winston Churchill perceived an opportunity to bring the United States into the war. He wrote to Walter Runciman, president of the Board of Trade, urging him not to raise insurance rates for neutral shipping. That way, Churchill explained, we can provide the Germans more targets and perhaps embroil the United States in the war. Said Churchill's letter of February 12, 1915:

> It is most important to attract neutral shipping to our shores, in the hope especially of embroiling the United States with Germany. The German formal announcement of indiscriminate submarining has been made to the United States to produce a deterrent effect on traffic. For our part, we want the traffic—the more the better; & *if some of it gets into trouble, better still* [emphasis added]. Therefore, do please

furbish up at once your insurance offer to neutrals trading with us after February 18.The more that come, the greater our safety & the German embarrassment.[84]

Urging that insurance rates be held steady, an insistent Churchill wrote three letters in five days. To him, American ships were live bait.

On February 20, *Lusitania* departed Liverpool, and the next day U-30 sank two merchant ships within ten miles of the luxury liner. On its return trip from New York, *Lusitania* carried 100,000 gallons of diesel fuel, and a freighter was torpedoed nearby. To guard *Lusitania* (or maybe its valuable diesel fuel), the Admiralty sent two destroyers and a Q ship to Liverpool bay.

That trip was enough for Fair Weather Dow, whose nerves understandably were getting frayed. Dow informed Alfred Booth that he did not want to be responsible for a ship combining civilian passenger service with military duties. Churchill saw nothing wrong with using women and children as shields for the transport of flammable oil and munitions, and Dow was replaced. Two captains were assigned. The real captain was William Turner, nicknamed "bowler Bill" because of his favorite headgear, and the extra captain was John Anderson, designated "staff captain." Turner previously had skippered a Cunarder bearing gun barrels. He was a good seaman, but since he was a man of few words and disliked passengers ("a lot of bloody monkeys"), Staff Captain Anderson was assigned to chat with VIPs at the "captain's table" as bowler Bill took his meals on the bridge.

House Called to Berlin

As the *Lusitania* tragedy began to unfold, Ambassador Gerard, on March 6, 1915, reported to House that the German foreign secretary, Gottlieb von Jagow, hoped that House would visit Berlin. Gerard commented he saw "no prospect of peace now," but that the "military general staff" was "in favor of accepting a reasonable peace proposal."[85] This was more encouraging than anything House had heard in London. In Berlin, however, House met with many officials and other important persons without achieving any progress. Peace discussions might bring down the government, he was told. In London, House had heard many complaints about the United States not entering the war; in Berlin, he heard many complaints about the United States trading with the Allies. House deplored it that every belligerent government gave unrealistic hopes to its people while painting the enemy as a malignant monster.

In London, House found the British not receptive to plans for peace. The public was in a fighting mood, and the press baron, Lord Northcliffe, threatened to run House out of the country if he kept up his peace mongering.

As a suggestion, President Wilson and the "assistant President," as some called House, wanted both sides to stop their blockades. This "freedom of the seas" plan would help American exports, and Germans favored it since it would enable their access to American goods. As one might expect, the British did not like the idea.

What made Wilson and House think otherwise?

British Code Breaking

An important part of the *Lusitania* story is Room 40, a secret location where the British decoded German communications. This was set up by Rear Admiral Henry Oliver, head of British Naval Intelligence. He recruited a variety of brainy civilians including mathematicians, German linguists, a theologian, a stock broker, a school headmaster, and so forth. They knew little or nothing of cryptology but were willing to learn. To do their job, the boffins had to learn navy jargon as well. (A warship does not "sail," it "proceeds.") Several kinds of German code book were acquired during 1914, and with that assistance Room 40 achieved great success in deciphering radio communications. When Admiral Oliver learned that a ship was in danger, he would suggest countermeasures. For example, Oliver, knowing the presence of U-30 off Ireland, suggested diverting two ships to Queenstown to await destroyer escort. The two ships were carrying mules and horses for the army.

Every day a summary of Room 40 intelligence was sent to Winston Churchill, first lord of the Admiralty.

Room 40 learned that the German Admiralty was tracking *Lusitania*. U-boats were advised when the ship was expected to reach Liverpool and when it was expected to leave. Because of a message intercept, Oliver delayed Captain Turner's departure by ten days. The ship then, so far as we know, made an uneventful trip to New York. But for some reason the crew suffered from "low morale," and upon arrival several members went ashore never to return. Staff Captain Anderson had to recruit more hands, paying extra money.

Like a warning from the gods, there came on March 28, 1915, a sinking that prefigured the tragedy of the *Lusitania*. A submarine, U-28, torpedoed the British cargo and passenger ship *Falaba* off the coast of Wales. The torpedo detonated explosives in the cargo, and the ship sank with the loss of 104 lives. One American happened to be among the fatalities. He was Leon C. Thrasher, a young mining engineer from Massachusetts. The American press headlined the incident a "massacre" and an "act of piracy." Secretary Lansing condemned it as a "flagrant violation of international law" and inferred that Germany wanted war with the United States.[86] Secretary Bryan received a different version of the *Falaba* sinking. The American consul in Plymouth, England, interviewed survivors and learned that the U-boat ordered the ship to stop and allotted some time for people to debark. During the debarkation *Falaba's* captain radioed for help, and the submarine fired a torpedo when patrol craft were approaching. President Wilson decided perhaps no action was necessary.

Wilson's Peculiar Policy

Secretary Bryan realized that another such tragedy could occur again, on a bigger scale, and he recommended warning Americans not to travel on British ships. The President refused, saying that American citizens *had a right to travel on belligerent ships with impunity, even within a war zone*. Where did he get that idea? From Lansing, who for many years had practiced in the field of international law. In fact, there was no such international law. Lansing's interpretation defied both accepted law and common sense. Professor Alexander DeConde has commented:

> According to international law, those who traveled on belligerent ships, since a ship was part of a nation's territory

329

for jurisdictional purposes, could properly look to the belligerent government for protection. Yet, the United States came to adopt the policy that its citizens had the lawful right to travel in safety on British ships and could turn to their own government for protection of that right.[87]

Professor Tansill said Lansing's erroneous opinion would have shamed a novice:

> He [Lansing] was quite familiar with American precedents and practices, and it is quite mystifying that at one of the great crossroads of American history a presumably competent lawyer should give the President and the Secretary of State a legal opinion that would have shamed a novice.[88]

A lawyer serves his client. As we have seen, during the Vietnam War, State Department lawyer Leonard Meeker provided false evidence in support of the President's right to make war. And, today, just try to ask the State Department where is that evidence?

Tansill decided that Lansing was responsible for America's entering the war in Europe:

> It is thus clear that America drifted into war in 1917 either because the chief legal adviser in the Department of State made fundamental errors of interpretation which a mere student of international law would have easily avoided, or because the adviser wanted a war with Germany and therefore purposely wrote erroneous opinions.[89]

Wilson's policy, encouraged and enabled by Lansing, was bound to lose lives and build public sentiment for war. As secretary of state, Bryan has been described as "inept," but with his common sense in the White House, we probably would not have gone to war.

Wilson's Motivation

President Wilson was a minister's son who became a militant missionary for democracy and good government. He tried by force to reform Mexico. He went to war in Europe to make the world safe for democracy and to save civilization as well. These causes gave him many opportunities to make spellbinding speeches, as his father had done in the pulpit. But his methods were unrealistic and impure. He envisioned an immaculate invasion of Vera Cruz. He did not warn Americans about traveling on British ships. Lindley Garrison, Wilson's first secretary of war, decided that Wilson was a man of high ideals but no principles. Clemenceau quipped: "He talks like Jesus Christ and he acts like Lloyd George."

In addition to the President's evangelistic psychology, was there considerable pressure coming from some quarter? Wilson was beholden to financial interests that promoted his election. They wanted him to approve establishment of the Federal Reserve Bank, which he did in 1913. In 1915, Wilson had to prepare for a reelection campaign in the following year.

As another possible source of pressure, what about blackmail? According to his biographers, Wilson was guilty of at least two adulterous affairs, and one of them was used against him. The intent was to keep the pro-British Wilson in office by delaying or stopping his second marriage. The President's first wife, Ellen Axson Wilson, happened to die in 1914 as the war in Europe began, and less than a year later the President met and began courting a widow, Edith Bolling Galt. In 1915, he wanted to marry Mrs. Galt, but House and Lansing feared that a marriage so soon would hurt Wilson's chances for reelection. They told the President that one of his former lovers was talking about their romance and showing people his letters; for that reason it would be better to delay the wedding rather than to stir up a scandal. The former lover, Mary Ellen Hulbert, possessed eight years of correspondence. Wilson and his fiancee stood firm, however, and the wedding took place in December of 1915. Going by this example, Wilson was not one to be deterred by scandal. The former lover made no trouble, and as a favor to Wilson's widow, the letters were purchased in 1928 by the financier Bernard Baruch. It is understandable that the new Mrs. Wilson never liked her famous boarder Colonel House.

President Wilson, his second wife Edith, and Colonel House

Zeus at Work

Wilson biographer Louis Auchincloss decided that President Wilson, as he said in his war message, believed it necessary to join the Allies in order to save civilization. (By contrast, some Oxford dons signed a statement that said, with Germany leading the world in the arts and sciences, going to war with that country was "sin against civilization.") Henry Adams, like the Germans, found Wilson incomprehensible. Adams described the President as "a mysterious, a rather Olympian personage and shrouded in darkness from which issue occasional thunderbolts."

Wilson's private secretary, Joseph Tumulty, recorded a simple explanation for Wilson's attitude. When the President was criticized for being tough on Germany while going easy on British offenses, Wilson explained,

> I will not take any action to embarrass England when she is
> fighting for her life and the life of the world. Let those who
> clamour for radical action against England understand this![90]

Basically, Wilson was English, like Page and Lansing. Durnovo had that figured out. And from the beginning, Wilson feared that Great Britain would lose the war, as he implied in conversation with the British ambassador.

Leaving aside the matter of motivation, we have seen how unrealistic were the Administration's views. Lansing argued that Germany wanted war with the United States. Wilson and House hoped they could persuade Britain to give up its blockade without applying any pressure. The notion that Americans had a right to travel safely in belligerent ships through a war zone we could classify as just one more of the Administration's cockamamie ideas. However, Wilson compounded that error by not stopping the illegal shipments, keeping them secret, and never warning passengers of the danger. Such extraordinary behavior makes it difficult not to wonder about motivation.

Guns on *Lusitania*?

On April 11, 1915, a German spy, Curt Thummel, reported to the German naval attache in New York City that he had seen four guns on the *Lusitania,* and he described their hiding places. The naval attache requested photographs. A chance acquaintance of the spies, Neil Leach, was a young Englishman who had worked as a tutor in Germany. In New York City, Leach visited an uncle, and the uncle, for the young man's return to England, arranged for him a well paying job as a steward on the *Lusitania.* Writing to his mother, Leach told her not to worry since the ship was "exceptionally fast and carried several copper colored cannon." It is not clear whether Leach saw the weapons himself or merely heard about them from Thummel. Leach went down with the ship.

As head of naval intelligence, Admiral Oliver was replaced by Captain William R. "Blinker" Hall, who, according to Ambassador Page, was the "one genius that the war has developed . . . all other secret service men are amateurs by comparison." A man of medium size, Hall had red hair, blue eyes, and an intense "presence." The embassy's contact with Hall, Edward Bell, viewed him as "a perfectly marvelous person but the coldest-hearted proposition that ever was.—he'd eat a man's heart and hand it back to him." The nickname "Blinker" came from a facial tic that made Hall's right eye open and close like a ship's signal lamp. His daughter blamed the tic on malnutrition when the captain was a boy. He had been sent to a Dickensian sort of military boarding school, where, as in ancient Sparta, boys as part of their training were expected to obtain food by theft. A nearby turnip field provided one opportunity.

Codebreakers' Secret of Success

Room 40's success owed much to Oliver and Hall's mistrust of government officials' ability to keep a secret (a recurring scandal in Washington, where secret operations often are publicized for political gain). According to Yardley, Hall would pass important information to Edward Bell, who was good at keeping secrets, but not to Ambassador Page. Bell kept Page informed of the essentials. Hall once sent a German code book to Washington emphasizing that this was for Yardley's *personal use* and not a gift to the U.S. Government. How could Hall have respected American security procedures? His staff could read anything we transmitted. Our security was so bad that when Yardley borrowed a code book at the American Embassy in London, it was handed to the flabbergasted American by a British employee.

Meanwhile, Ambassador Page was intensely frustrated by his cablegrams getting "leaked" to the press, as he assumed, by the State Department headquarters. At least five times Secretary Bryan assured Page that he had fixed it so that there would be no more leaks. Those assurances having proved worthless, Page put confidential information only in personal letters. Commented Burton J. Hendrick, the editor of Page's *Life and Letters*:

> This state of affairs in Washington explains the curious fact that the real diplomatic history of the United States and Great Britain during this great crisis is not to be found in the archives of the State Department, for the official documents on file there consist of the most routine telegrams . . . but in the Ambassador's personal correspondence with the President, Colonel House, and a few other intimates.[91]

Perhaps it helped British propaganda to plant some of the ambassador's correspondence in the press. That would have been William Wiseman's job, if not that of Robert Lansing. Possibly the Germans had access as well. As a poignant sidelight on Page's trouble with unremitting leaks, he complained in a letter to House that whenever a leak occurred, "I have to go with my tail between my legs and apologize to Sir Edward Grey." Luckily for Grey, Page died before Yardley's book came out.

By the time junior officer Yardley visited London, Captain Hall had become an admiral. To our prodigy from Indiana, this illustrated the difference between the American attitude toward code breaking and the European attitude.

Hall Lures U-Boats

One of Hall's projects affected the *Lusitania*. He planted disinformation to the effect that the British were going to invade the part of Germany bordering Denmark (Churchill and Fisher did propose such a plan) and for that purpose troop ships would be departing from southern and western England. The Germans acquired this "intelligence" on April 24, and as one might expect, they, anticipating D-Day, dispatched all available submarines in response. Whatever Hall's purpose might have been, one result was the stationing of U-20 in the path of the *Lusitania*. If the big liner had slipped past that predator, at least one more would have been lurking on the way to Liverpool, which served as *Lusitania's* home port.

Admiral William R. ("Blinker") Hall

During the period April 28 to May 1, U-30 sank six ships off the southern tip of England. International law was followed in each case. In addition, U-30 on May 1 torpedoed but did not sink the American tanker *Gulflight* being escorted by two British patrol craft. Seeing an American flag on the stern, U-30 broke off the attack. Still touting the idea that Germany wanted war with the United States, Secretary Lansing asserted that the *Gulflight* incident was "a determined effort to affront the United States" and cause a "rupture of diplomatic relations."[92] However, the British Admiralty decided that U-30 had acted within the law because being escorted by patrol craft nullified the ship's right to a warning. *Gulflight* did not want to be escorted. The patrol craft insisted on it because they suspected that the American vessel was refueling German submarines. Again, Wilson decided no action was necessary.

Like Secretary Bryan, George Viereck, a German-American poet and the founder of a pro-German weekly, *The Fatherland*, thought Americans should be warned against traveling on British ships. "Sooner or later," Viereck told his friends, "some big passenger boat with Americans on board will be sunk by a submarine, then there will be hell to pay." Persuaded by Viereck, the German Embassy decided to warn the public about travel on Allied ships. The plan was to have a paid notice appear in fifty newspapers on April 24, a week before the next sailing of the *Lusitania*. But nothing appeared in print until the day of sailing.

According to Colin Simpson, author of the highly regarded book *Lusitania* (see "The SS Casus Belli" in the *Times Literary Supplement* of November 3, 1972), publication of the warning was delayed by the *New York Sun* and the U. S. State Department.[93] Looking for a story, a *New York Sun* editor telephoned Cunard manager Sumner, who assured him that the greyhound was faster than any submarine. Next, the *Sun editor* called the State Department. Although it was not the State Department's responsibility to offer legal advice, the duty officer said that the content of the warning might be libelous and suggested calling the German Embassy in the morning for verification. (Simpson did not know whether the duty officer consulted anybody of higher rank, as duty officers often do.) With that caveat, the *Sun* called the United Press news service, which advised newspapers nationwide to hold up on publication.

The German Warning to Passengers

Again according to Simpson, on April 26 there were two men in Washington, D.C., who were concerned about the almost two thousand people who were going to sail on the *Lusitania*. They were an odd couple: Secretary of State William Jennings Bryan and German sympathizer George Viereck. After learning that the embassy's warning had been blocked, Viereck managed to obtain a meeting with Bryan and inform him that the *passenger liner* on all but one of its wartime voyages had carried munitions and so was liable to be attacked. Right now at Pier 54, said Viereck, six million rounds of ammunition were being put on board. With a telephone call, Bryan cleared the German warning for publication. Bryan promised to see President Wilson about issuing an official American warning, but none was issued.

More days went by. The embassy's notice finally appeared on May 1, the day of the ship's departure. This was a Saturday, the day when passenger ship advertisements normally appeared, and when sending out its warning, the embassy had asked the newspapers to place it near them.

The *New York Times* reported that the text had been received "last night" by "newspapers throughout the country." The *Times* said it had called

Sumner, who found it difficult to believe the warning came from the German Embassy. He explained that recently efforts had been made to annoy his company and make its passengers uncomfortable. Sumner remained skeptical even when the *Times* reminded him the warning did no more than restate the already known German policy concerning Allied ships. On the question of safety, Sumner said he had "no fear of submarines whatever." In the danger zone, he explained, "one may say there is a general system of convoying British ships."

Counselor Lansing saw the notice in the *Sun* and, as the *Lusitania* steamed toward its doom, he expressed indignation about the Germans having slipped something into the American press without the State Department's approval. In a memorandum to Secretary Bryan, Lansing declared the paid notice "highly improper," "impertinent," and "insolent" (Carlton Savage, *Policy of the United States*, page 304).

Senator Risks Impeachment

After the United States went to war, Senator Robert La Follette revealed the truth about the *Lusitania's* cargo, and he urged the Congress to state war aims that might lead to a negotiated peace. In the Midwest "Fighting Bob" spoke to cheering crowds. To the senator it made no sense to risk war in order to uphold an American's alleged right to travel unharmed on a belligerent ship carrying arms in a war zone. He compared that to camping near an arsenal in France. La Follette's fellow senators were enraged by his oratory, yelled in his face, and wanted to impeach him. Also demanding La Follette's expulsion was Nicholas Murray Butler, president of Columbia University. Customs Collector Malone told senators the truth about the *Lusitania's* cargo, and the impeachment was quietly dropped.

Lusitania's Departure

Having heard of the German Embassy's warning, members of the press and a newsreel team besieged the *Lusitania's* gangway with questions about whether the ship was safe. Passengers noticed the excitement and learned the cause of it. Charles Sumner again said the greyhound was so fast that no submarine could catch it. Sumner did not mention that, to save coal, fewer boilers were being fired so that the ship's top speed had been reduced from 25 to 21 knots. Captain Turner arrived in his bowler hat, and a passenger from Virginia asked him whether there was any danger. Turner responded, "There always is danger but the best guarantees of your safety are the *Lusitania* herself and the fact that wherever there is danger, your safety is in the hands of the Royal Navy." Turner was able to reassure the Virginian with confidence because he had been informed that a naval escort, Cruiser Squadron E, would await him at the southern tip of Ireland.

Despite the submarine activity on the liner's regular route, no change in course was ordered. If the ship were rerouted, it logically would have sailed around northern Ireland, where no submarine sinkings were reported. Recently mines up there had been cleared. In New York, Turner was given various kinds of anti-submarine advice compiled by the Admiralty, and the captain later said there were so many documents he could have "papered the walls with them." One advised him that submarines do not operate near land; another said the ship should keep away from coasts and headlands. Travelers heard that within the war zone the ship would be convoyed.

Apparently trying to decide whether to stay on board, many passengers asked the staff not to unpack their bags. In the end, almost everybody made the wrong decision. One lady changed her mind because a friend at Cunard informed her that the ship was under the control of the Admiralty.

Last-Minute Passengers

At the last minute, the British naval attache, Captain Guy Gaunt, brought sixty-seven men and two women from another ship and put them aboard the *Lusitania*. One of the new passengers, Mr. R. Matthews, asked for volunteers to help transfer cargo, and a surprising number of young men offered their services. None of this group survived the sinking. Matthews's body washed up ashore, and although in civilian clothes, he was identified as a captain in the Sixth Winnipeg Rifles. No doubt Captain Matthews's riflemen were the "volunteers" who helped to transfer cargo. Among the captain's personal belongings was a slip of paper saying that Mrs. Matthews had won the Ladies Potato Race.

Before *Lusitania* departed, there were discovered on board three non-passengers with a camera, and they were locked in a cell. This was illegal and the men never emerged.

Tickets Discounted

To increase bookings, Cunard reduced its rates so that the ship sailed with more passengers than usual since the war began. Three of the most prominent passengers were millionaire Alfred Vanderbilt, impresario Charles Frohman (producer of *Peter Pan),* and British actress Rita Jolivet (of French descent). Of the three, only Ms. Jolivet survived. As the ship sank, Frohman stood at the rail with a cigar and quoted Peter Pan, "To die will be an awfully big adventure." Vanderbilt promised to find a life jacket for a woman holding a baby. Unable to do that, he fastened on the anxious mother his own life jacket, although he could not swim. He and Frohman found some more jackets and fastened them on wicker "moses baskets" holding babies. In the tumult of the sinking, the jackets came loose.

Although promoted to chief of the naval war staff, Admiral Oliver continued personally to safeguard ships with the use of Room 40 intelligence. On May 2, Oliver kept the battleship HMS *Orion* in port because of danger from U-boats. *Orion* left on May 4 with an escort of four destroyers and was ordered to keep a hundred miles off the southern Irish coast, a sensible precaution considering the half dozen ships recently sunk. The U-30 had been so active that the Admiralty, according to its official history, thought there was a "whole pack of U-boats who were presumably lying in wait for the *Lusitania*." Oliver also shepherded carefully the HMS *Gloucester* and the HMS *Jupiter.*

Ambassador Page wrote to his son on May 2, "If a British liner full of American passengers be blown up, what will Uncle Sam do? That's what's going to happen."[94]

On May 5, Churchill was about to depart for France and Admiral Oliver caught him in the map room. Cruiser Squadron E's HMS *Juno* (steam frigate, not the *Juno* that carried Father MacNamara), said Oliver, was not suitable for anti-submarine duty without escorts and suggested that, instead, destroyers be sent from the Welsh port of Milford Haven. The Admiralty signaled *Juno* to abandon her escort mission and head for Queenstown. *Lusitania* was not informed. No destroyers were assigned to escort the *Lusitania*. The ship now was the responsibility of Admiral Sir Charles Henry Coke in Queenstown. Coke had four torpedo boats, but their standing orders were to sweep mines around the approaches to Queenstown harbor. At a given time the admiral could put to sea about eleven other small craft to cover 385 miles of coastline.

Another Whistleblower

Present at the conference in the map room was Commander Joseph M. Kenworthy who had no opportunity to speak and apparently was invited only because, at Churchill's request, he had written a paper on the political effects of an ocean liner being sunk with American passengers on board. Kenworthy later wrote a book in which he judged the German submarine campaign foolish and futile, and he presented a carefully worded explanation for the fate of the *Lusitania*:

> Futile because British shipping had only to disguise itself as neutral. And foolish because it was especially obnoxious to the Americans who had to use British shipping both for passengers and freight.

> The British did not retaliate in kind and no neutral ship was ever sunk by a British mine or submarine. There was no need for it and *they knew a trick worth two of that* [emphasis added]. They let a test case go before the court of public opinion. The *Lusitania* steaming at half-speed [incorrect] straight through the submarine cruising ground on the Irish coast was incontinently sunk . . . Over a hundred Americans were drowned. The warnings given them before sailing . . . in no way mitigated the intense indignation of American opinion.[95]

To Commander Kenworthy, it would appear, the *Lusitania* had been a pigeon serving as a guinea pig.

First Lord of Admiralty Churchill and Admiral Fisher

On May 5, U-20's captain, Walther Schwieger, spotted a sailing ship, the *Earl of Lathom*, near a well known Irish landmark, a headland known as Old Head of Kinsale. Schwieger let the crew disembark and sank the ship with planted bombs. Proceeding eastward, Schwieger next tried to torpedo the *Cayo Romano* but missed, and his intended victim high-tailed it for safety to Queenstown. Although the Admiralty had known about U-20 for several days, it did not inform Admiral Coke. U-20's victims brought news of the sinkings, which Coke relayed to the Admiralty.

Still patrolling the Irish coast, Schwieger on May 6 surfaced and fired his gun at a British steamship, the *Candidate*. This is a little surprising since, after his previous voyage, Schwieger had to get his periscope repaired because a steamship tried to ram him. The crew of the *Candidate* abandoned ship and Schwieger launched a torpedo. The torpedo exploded but failed to sink the ship. Going aboard, the German sailors were surprised to find operational guns protected by sandbags. U-20 finished off the ship with shellfire. Because of the *Candidate's* armament, Schwieger now was in a more cautious mood. On the evening of May

6, he spied the *Centurion* and fired a torpedo at it. The ship did not sink. Schwieger fired another torpedo, and after one hour and twenty minutes the ship disappeared beneath the waves. The crew survived.

Clearly, the pride of Britain's passenger fleet was heading into danger. Patrick Beesly, in his book *Room 40* about British code breaking, wrote a chapter about the *Lusitania*. He "found reason" to suspect that Turner requested permission to change course and proceed around northern Ireland instead of southern Ireland, but he could not be sure because much of the ship's wireless correspondence was missing.[96]

At noon of May 6, the Admiralty warned all ships of submarine activity "off Fastnet." Fastnet was (and is) a rocky islet, topped by a lighthouse, near the southwestern tip of Ireland. Fastnet was called "Ireland's Teardrop" because it was the Irish emigrants' last glimpse of their homeland. Forty miles from there *Lusitania* had been scheduled to make its rendezvous with Cruiser Squadron E. However, Captain Turner had to slow down in order to pass through the Fastnet area after dark, making sure all of his exterior lights were turned off. The squadron, he assumed, would turn up at dawn.

Knowing the *Lusitania's* schedule, Admiral Coke in Queenstown was alarmed by the U-20's running rampant. At 7:50 p.m. on May 6 he warned Captain Turner: "Submarines active off the south coast of Ireland." *Lusitania* was heading into where putatively a "whole pack of U-boats" awaited it, but the Admiralty seemed unconcerned. First Lord Churchill was in France, Captain Hall was dining at Greenwich, and Admiral Oliver was at a club. Left in charge at the Admiralty was Admiral Fisher, 75, who was in poor health. Fisher had major disagreements with Churchill, especially about the failing Turkish straits (Gallipoli) campaign, and relations were strained.

Destroyers Available

Captain Turner told his passengers there had been a submarine warning, but he reassured them, "On entering the war zone tomorrow, we shall be securely in the care of the Royal Navy." At this point, Admiral Oliver, with his Room 40 intelligence, had had nearly two weeks to figure out what to do about U-20 and its threat to the *Lusitania*. He had shown commendable concern for the *Orion* and for two ships carrying horses and mules. He was keeping *Juno* out of harm's way, likewise *Gloucester* and *Jupiter*. What about the *Lusitania*? What about the destroyers he had recommended for convoying the pride of Britain's passenger fleet? There were four new destroyers, capable of steaming at 29 knots, at the port of Milford Haven, where they had arrived on May 5 after ferrying Irish troops. The destroyers did not budge.

During the night *Lusitania* proceeded through fog sounding its foghorn. The fog did not clear until late in the morning of May 7. Captain Turner scanned the horizon for his warship escort but saw none.

King Asks About *Lusitania*

On the morning of May 7, Colonel House and Foreign Secretary Grey went to see the King and on the way they stopped at Kew Gardens to view the almond blossoms. No doubt because the newspapers were headlining recent sinkings and the German warning to the *Lusitania*, the two men, wrote House in his diary, "spoke of the probability of an ocean liner being sunk, and I told him if this were done, a flame of indignation would sweep across America, which would in itself probably carry us into the war." An hour later, House was chatting with King George who also had on his mind the possibility of an ocean liner being sunk. The King wondered, "Suppose they should sink the *Lusitania* with American passengers on board . . ."[97]

Alfred Booth read in the morning newspaper about U-20's depredations, and, having a low opinion of the Admiralty (a fact evident in his personal correspondence), he hurried to the office of Liverpool's chief naval officer, Admiral Sir Harry Stileman, and urged that something be done about his famous passenger ship. Booth left the office thinking Stileman would divert the liner to Queenstown, and his cousin George Booth arranged by telegram to meet one of the passengers there. The passenger was Paul Crompton. He, his wife, their six children, and a nanny were returning to England from Philadelphia. None of the party survived. Probably George Booth planned to meet the Cromptons in Queenstown and advise them to use other transportation.

Admiral Coke called the Admiralty and requested permission to divert *Lusitania* to Queenstown. He could not get a definite answer.

Schwieger, well to the east of *Lusitania*, sighted one of Coke's patrol boats off Queenstown harbor. Getting low on fuel, Schwieger decided to end his patrol and head home. That route, westward around Ireland, took him toward the oncoming *Lusitania*. Admiral Coke ordered his largest patrol craft, the yacht *Scadaun*, to look for submarines in *Lusitania's* path.

Captain Turner was in a quandary. His route called for him to enter the St. George's channel between Ireland and Wales, but the Admiralty said a submarine was operating near the south end of the channel. What to do?

Having crossed the Atlantic by dead reckoning, Turner needed to take his bearings in order to determine his exact location. He moved a little closer to Ireland to find a landmark. The Admiralty had ordered the ship to arrive at Liverpool at high tide rather than arrive too early and wait around in a dangerous location. (Wasn't the south end of St. George's channel a dangerous location?) In compliance, *Lusitania* slowed to a stately 18 knots, although the ship's speed was supposed to be its protection. Lifeboats hung over the sides ready to be lowered if need be. This was a perilous situation.

At noon Schwieger was submerged and he heard propellers throbbing above him. Rising to periscope depth, Schwieger viewed the HMS *Juno* heading in the direction of Queenstown. U-20 had found the proposed convoy, a single ship, but couldn't get a shot at it. Schwieger continued westward.

Captain Turner received a coded message which, he thought, ordered him to Queenstown. He turned landward so quickly that several passengers lost their balance and the galley was shaken up. Actually, the message was intended for a tugboat whose code name, MFA, coincided with *Lusitania's* radio call sign. The Admiralty did not order *Lusitania* to Queenstown.

At 1:20 p.m. Schwieger stood in his conning tower and saw smoke off the starboard bow. Soon he could make out four funnels heading toward the coast. Schwieger submerged and kept watch. According to

U-20's records, the four-funneled ship had to be either the *Lusitania* or the *Mauretania*, both armed cruisers used for carrying troops, according to German intelligence, whose spies were loading the Cunard ships in New York.

Turner recognized a lighthouse on a rocky bluff. The sea-washed prominence was Old Head near the town of Kinsale, the area where Schwieger had sunk the *Earl of Lathom*. The landmark was a good place for a U-boat to find some traffic. *Lusitania* now was twenty five miles from Queenstown. Turner had to navigate his ship along the coast and into the Queenstown harbor without a tug or a pilot, and he had to find the only channel that was swept daily for mines. He decided to take four bearings on the lighthouse to get his exact position. The ship turned eastward and steamed on a straight line. No convoy was in sight.

Lusitania Torpedoed

When *Lusitania* turned eastward, broadside to the westward bound submarine, that gave U-20 an opportunity to attack. Schwieger speeded up to shorten the range and loosed a torpedo at the distance of 700 meters (44/100 of a mile). Bubbling up from the underwater missile, a white trail sped toward the leviathan. It was spotted by lookout Thomas Quinn in the crow's nest, and he shouted to the bridge. Captain Turner ran to the starboard side as the torpedo exploded in a great spout of water. Schwieger noted in his log, "Shot strikes starboard side right behind the bridge." The torpedo struck slightly forward of where Schwieger had aimed, and so he lowered his estimate of the ship's speed from 22 knots to no more than 20 knots. Schwieger's log recorded two explosions:

> The explosion of the torpedo must have been followed by a second one (boiler or coal or powder?). The superstructure above the point of impact and the bridge are torn asunder, fire breaks out, smoke envelopes the high bridge. The ship stops immediately and heels over to starboard quickly, immersing simultaneously at the bow. It appears as if the ship were going to capsize very shortly. Great confusion is rife on board . . . some boats, full to capacity, are rushed from above,

touch the water with either stem or stern first, and founder immediately . . .

After the torpedo exploded, Turner, according to his later testimony, heard a "second rumbling explosion" (like explosives being destroyed). Seeing the bow dip downward, Turner knew the ship was doomed.

Circling around the stricken liner, Schwieger saw that the sharp starboard list prevented lowering boats on the port side. The list was caused by the two explosions and by water filling the longitudinal bulkheads used for coal storage, which was a navy specification. The navy assumed the coal would protect the boilers from gunfire. The effect of underwater torpedoes perhaps was not considered. The hatches of the longitudinal bulkhead were hard to shut because of coal debris, and so the starboard compartment filled rapidly with water. Water rushed also through open portholes. At the formal inquiry, the saloon steward said he gave orders to close the portholes as he left the area.

Amazingly, one of the world's biggest ships vanished beneath the sea in a mere eighteen minutes. Of the 1,962 persons on board, 1,201 perished, including 128 Americans. The official number of fatalities, 1,198, did not include the three imprisoned spies. Had those unfortunates completed their mission, it might have changed the war.

Lusitania was many times the size of the *Candidate*, which for its demise required a torpedo plus gunfire, and the *Centurion*, which, although struck by two torpedoes, remained afloat for an hour and twenty minutes. The Admiralty insisted that two torpedoes were fired at *Lusitania*, that was the generally accepted story of the time, and Churchill repeated it in *The World Crisis*.[98] Schwieger in his log said that he fired only one torpedo. He also said that in a wireless message reporting the sinking.

Explosive Guncotton

As for what kinds of explosive were aboard the *Lusitania*, six hundred tons of explosive guncotton were delivered to New York on April 26 in care of Britain's purchasing agent J. P. Morgan.[99] The pyroxyline kind of guncotton explodes in contact with the salts in seawater. A manifest presented to a *Lusitania* hearing in New York listed forty-six tons of aluminum powder, an ingredient of explosives which can itself explode, like coal dust, if jostled into a cloud. Artillery shells, allegedly empty of explosives, were on board.

Schwieger in his log expressed surprise at the amount of traffic along the coast, considering all the recent sinkings. "It is inexplicable," said he, "that the *Lusitania* was not routed via the North Channel" (around northern Ireland).

Juno was dispatched to pick up survivors, but it was called back by Admiral Fisher for fear of its getting torpedoed. First rescuers on the scene were local fishing boats. Admiral Coke from his base sent "everything that could float."

Captain Turner survived. When the water reached the bridge, Turner grabbed an oar and a chair floating by; in two hours he was found by a lifeboat.

The American people were shocked and infuriated by the *Lusitania* tragedy. The German Embassy's published warning, rather than mitigating the deed, was taken as evidence of evil intent. Of course, our citizenry did not know that Cunard liners routinely carried munitions and troops, using innocent passengers as human shields. Most people could not imagine such a thing. Neither did the public know that the Germans had tried to publish their warning a week early in fifty newspapers. Unlike the British, the Germans were not good at getting their message out.

House Expects War

On the evening of May 7, Ambassador Page received news bulletins about the sunken ship, and the news grew progressively worse. As the bulletins came in, Page was hosting a dinner party. This was a send-off for Colonel House, who was returning to the United States. With a sinking passenger liner as the chief topic of conversation, the party turned out to be a somber affair, with the guests talking in whispers.

Churchill was absent. He had begged off saying that, after finishing his business in France (arranging Italy's defection), he wanted to spend some time with General Sir John French. The Admiralty's first lord was suspected of seeking an army command (like Roosevelt in 1898). George Booth attended the dinner, no doubt worried about the Crompton family. Present also were Secretary Grey; Captain Hall, surely keeping mum about his disinformation trick; the foreign editor of the London *Times;* and John C. Bigham, first viscount of Mersey, who was invited at the request of Colonel House. Lord Mersey had headed the *Titanic* inquiry in 1912. He now was in charge of the *Falaba* inquiry, and he next would chair the *Lusitania* inquiry.

As the dinner guests expressed their views on the tragedy underway, House predicted the United States would go to war within a month. Although House had dinner with two of Britain's most knowledgeable officials, his next letter to the President evinced no knowledge of munitions or troops having been aboard the sunken liner.

American ambassadors in Berlin and Brussels expected war soon and prepared to close their premises. Ambassador Page cabled Washington on May 8, 1915:

> Official comment is of course reticent. The freely expressed unofficial feeling is that the United States must declare war or forfeit European respect. So far as I know this feeling is universal. If the United States come in, the moral and physical effect will be to bring peace quickly and to give the United States a great influence in ending the war and in so reorganizing the world as to prevent its recurrence.[100]

Page went on in that vein, trying to shame or coax the President into declaring war. The British press did the same. According to Yardley, Page's telegrams sometimes became so heated that his staff destroyed them before transmission; otherwise, the ambassador would have been fired.

Page thought American entry into the war would end it "quickly." Actually, after our entry that took one year and a half. Page also was too optimistic concerning America's ability to reorganize the world. The President was going to be severely disappointed.

Too Proud to Fight

Wilson refrained from going to war. Explaining his non-violent stance to a group of naturalized immigrants, the President said he was "too proud to fight":

> There is such a thing as a man being too proud to fight. There is such a thing as a nation being so right that it does not need to convince others by force that it is right.

To his disappointed private secretary, Joseph Tumulty, Wilson explained that, although at the moment it would be easy to get a declaration of war, he was "not sure whether the present emotionalism of the country would last long enough to sustain any action I would suggest to Congress . . ." Why? Because the truth about the *Lusitania* might come out?

Allied soldiers began referring to artillery duds as "Wilsons."

The British press was greatly disappointed that the United States did not declare war, and it continued to be disappointed, as well as scornful, after future sinkings. Concerning the *Lusitania*, Wilson did send an extraordinarily harsh note to Germany. Bryan tried to make it softer. Behind his back, Lansing succeeded in making it harsher. (Lansing played dumb as to how a different note happened to be written. Yardley, who wrote a book about poker, thought that the secretary with his blank face would have made an excellent poker player.) As when President Lincoln sent a curt note to Governor Pickens, Wilson omitted the normal civilities of discourse. He insisted on the right of American citizens to travel on "unarmed" British ships. Nothing was said about traveling with soldiers or munitions.

Lansing asked the Justice Department for an opinion on the American position, assuming the *Lusitania's* cargo had contained munitions. The answer was totally unfavorable. The department replied that the British would have violated the Passenger Act, which provided penalties of fining and imprisonment; that Britain had erased the distinction between merchant ships and warships; that Germany had a right to sink the ship; and that international law did not protect American passengers from harm. The Justice Department volunteered that, during the

Russo-Japanese War, the British had advised their citizens not to travel on belligerent vessels. It is not known whether Lansing passed this information to Secretary Bryan or to the President.

In any event, Bryan again wanted to warn Americans not to travel on British ships. Wilson again refused saying that the danger now was "fully known." Actually, the danger was not fully known since the public still did not know about the illegal military duties carried out by British passenger ships.

The President suffered "many sleepless hours," he told Tumulty.

Germans Justify Sinking

In their response to Wilson's complaint, the Germans deeply regretted the loss life and offered compensation. But they justified the submarine's action on the following grounds:

1. The *Lusitania* was an auxiliary of the British navy.
2. It was armed.
3. The British government had authorized the use of false flags.
4. British ships were ordered to ram or otherwise destroy a challenging U-Boat.
5. The *Lusitania* carried munitions.
6. The ship carried Canadian soldiers.

Bryan proposed investigating the German allegations. Wilson did not want to do that. He told the Germans they were "misinformed" and that he was "contending for nothing less high and sacred than the rights of humanity." After that disingenuous response, how could the President pretend to be an honest broker for peace?

Like Captain Dow, Secretary Bryan had had enough of playing games with peoples' lives. On June 9, rather than sign another note to Germany, he resigned as secretary of state. Lansing replaced him. Wilson and House wanted Page to have the job, but they decided that Page was too conspicuously pro-British; there had been criticism of that in the press. Secretary Lansing believed that Germany was bent on world domination, that war with Germany was inevitable, and a stalemate ought not to be allowed. Lansing planned accordingly.[101] Since the American people were against war, there had to be a "process of enlightenment," which "covered a period of almost two years"—in other words, from the time of Lansing's appointment to the declaration of war. [102]

On the day Bryan resigned, Colonel House left England on an American ship, and it was convoyed by two destroyers. With the *Lusitania's* having been provided no convoy at all, House's destroyers evoked speculation in the British press concerning the importance of his mission and the dispatches he might be carrying. In his diary, House said he had thought the destroyers would patrol at a distance and not be so noticeable.

Cover-Up Underway

In Britain, the *Lusitania* cover-up was barely underway when in the middle of May both Churchill and Fisher left the Admiralty. Churchill was replaced by the politician Arthur Balfour, a former Prime Minister who was innocent of naval lore.

The cover-up took the form of a routine official inquiry, which was organized by the Admiralty and the Board of Trade. The authorities had to conceal the cargo of munitions, the Canadian soldiers, the canceling of escort, and the internal explosion. Captain Turner was upset and disgusted. He had to be kept quiet. It helped the government that Ernest Cowper, a Canadian newspaperman who survived the sinking, told the *New York Times* the submarine launched two torpedoes loaded with poison gas, although Cowper himself claimed to have seen only one torpedo track. The Canadian praised the skillful lowering of lifeboats, which in reality was a bloody fiasco with loaded boats foundering and crashing into each other. Cowper claimed to having seen U-20's conning tower, even though the attacker was submerged.

With the *Lusitania* under official investigation, the British press by law was not allowed to discuss causes of the sinking. Instead, the press played up acts of heroism and other human interest stories. The Admiralty wanted to blame the tragedy on the civilian Captain Turner, who it decided must have been bribed by the Germans (like Sumner, the Boston blueblood). Admiral Fisher, who could have prevented the sinking, wanted the treasonous Turner arrested no matter what the result of the inquiry. After Fisher and Churchill left the Admiralty, it forwarded an inaccurate and misleading report to Lord Mersey. The prosecution implied that Turner was in the pay of the enemy, and it made a very selective presentation of evidence. As an example of the latter, thirty-five American survivors gave depositions to the American consul in Queenstown, and none of them was allowed in evidence. No doubt the Americans wanted to know what happened to the promised convoy.

The naval officers representing the government did not acknowledge Turner's need to fix his position after crossing the Atlantic. They told Mersey that one of the world's biggest passenger ships ought to have entered St. George's channel, between Ireland and Wales, after dark, without knowing its exact location, and despite the report of a submarine's presence.

Germans Blamed, Turner Cleared

Two merchant captains and a submariner on the board of inquiry found no fault with Captain Turner's performance. Only Admiral Sir Frederick Inglefield voted against the skipper. The Admiralty sent Mersey a letter pressuring him to censure Turner. In his verdict, Mersey let the Admiralty get away with its hiding of the truth, but he drew the line at blaming and vilifying bowler Bill, who impressed him as an honest seaman. The verdict:

> The Court, having carefully enquired into the circumstances of the above mentioned disaster, finds, that the loss of the said ship and lives was due to damage caused to the said ship by torpedoes fired by a submarine of German nationality whereby the ship sank.
>
> In the opinion of the Court the act was done not merely with the intention of sinking the ship, but also with the intention of destroying the lives of the people on board.

The court admitted there were 5,000 cases of small arms cartridges on board, but said they were 50 yards away from where the "torpedoes struck." There were no other explosives on board, said the court, and no troops.

Following the *Lusitania* case, Mersey waived his fee, and he wrote to Prime Minister Asquith, "I must request that henceforth I be excused from administering His Majesty's justice."

"The *Lusitania* case," Mersey told his children, "was a damned dirty business."

Perhaps intending to defy and reproach the Admiralty, Cunard gave Turner another ship, which also was torpedoed, and after the war promoted him to commodore. When Churchill blamed Turner in *The World Crisis* for the *Lusitania* sinking,[103] the retired seaman to escape obloquy moved to Australia for eighteen months.

Captain Schwieger died in 1917 when his new submarine, U-88, hit a mine. Forty percent of Germany's U-boat men died in the war.

President Wilson and Secretary Lansing must have felt greatly relieved by the success of the *Lusitania* cover-up since they, sharing responsibility for the great loss of life, had failed to enforce the law and had not warned the public about taking passage on British ships. (There was judicial precedent for carrying cartridges, though not such a large number of them.)

The *Lusitania* tragedy had a profound effect upon American public opinion. For most Americans the Central Powers now were clearly the "bad side" in the war. But most Americans still did not want to take up arms. Just the opposite of the situation in 1812, some citizens in the Northeast were feeling belligerent but few in the Midwest or South. Farmers saw no need for war, and in the Midwest German-Americans and Scandinavian-Americans were skeptical of the Allies. As in 1812 and 1898, war hawks pressured the President. Among them were Colonel House, Theodore Roosevelt, Elihu Root, Ambassador Page, and Secretary Lansing. At the time, former Senator Root was president of the Carnegie Endowment for International Peace. Not much pacifism had rubbed off onto him.

Allegations of Conspiracy

The Kaiser told Ambassador Gerard the British deliberately put the *Lusitania* in danger. In 1936, the American historian Samuel F. Bemis raised a question about that in his *A Diplomatic History of the United States:*

> One might well wonder whether the British government purposely exposed to attack the *Lusitania* and other British passenger vessels carrying American citizens, in order to lead the Germans on to a rash act which might bring the United States into the war.[104]

To the author of *Room 40,* published in 1982, it was most significant that nothing was done to ensure the liner's safe arrival. Beesly decided there was a conspiracy:

> I am reluctantly driven to the conclusion that there *was* [emphasis in the original] a conspiracy deliberately to put the *Lusitania* at risk in the hopes that even an abortive attack on her would bring the United States into the war. Such a conspiracy could not have been put into effect without Winston Churchill's express permission and approval.[105]

Beesly had been an intelligence officer in the Royal Navy.

Northcliffe Sways Opinion

The prediction that America would lose European respect if it did not declare war was accurate. In the Allied nations we Americans were viewed as slackers in the defense of civilization. Two principal causes of that attitude were our non-violent reaction after the sinking of the *Lusitania* and the propaganda drumbeat of the press, especially the Northcliffe newspapers. Albert Harmsworth, Lord Northcliffe, owned the London *Times* and also a chain of newspapers featuring yellow journalism. Northcliffe articulated his attitude to an American historian:

> Much as I like the Americans, for a people who have boasted of their freedom and democracy, I had never expected to

behold on their part so craven a spirit of submission. So far as exercising real independence of judgment and action with respect to the war is concerned, I can think of only one people with whom to compare the Americans, namely, the Chinese.[106]

The insulting Northcliffe was a man of such power that he probably knew the *Lusitania* carried munitions. But he was a propagandist from way back. Since 1896 his periodicals had been inciting hatred and fear of Germany. Northcliffe published one of the novels warning of German invasion. *The Invasion of 1910* described a future German attack on Britain by soldiers disguised as waiters, clerks, hairdressers, and bakers. The book sold very well in both Britain the United States. The author, William Le Queux, in 1914 believed that German agents were after him for "rumbling their schemes," and he pestered the police, vainly, for protection.

Northcliffe had an ulterior motive, according to the American military historian Thomas Fleming:

> The real reason for Northcliffe's hate campaign was economic, not military. For more than a decade, Germany had been challenging England as a competitor in the world marketplace. British economic power was in decline everywhere. Between January and June 1914, Germany's exports and gross national product had exceeded England's for the first time. Senator La Follette cited this competition as the real reason for the slaughter in Europe. George Bernard Shaw said the same thing . . . Ultimately, Woodrow Wilson himself would admit this dolorous truth.[107]

Admiral Chadwick in a letter of May 16, 1915, warned President Wilson:

> Never in our history was there greater need for caution; never was there greater need for all the serpent's wisdom. English diplomacy is a deep and subtle game of which our people in general are as ignorant as kittens.[108]

A few weeks after the *Lusitania* sinking, Germany secretly ordered its U-boats not to attack passenger liners without warning, but one did so on August 19. U-24 torpedoed the small British liner *Arabic*. There were forty-four fatalities including three Americans. The *Arabic* skipper said he was zig-zagging as a torpedo defense, and the U-boat skipper said he thought the ship was trying to ram him. The *Arabic* incident was smoothed over when Germany made known its new rules. On September 18, Germany ordered that all U-boat attacks be preceded by a warning. That being too dangerous, the German navy for a time stopped all U-boat attacks around the British isles.

Henry Ford's "Flivvership"

A major anti-war figure was Henry Ford, the automobile manufacturer. In December of 1915, Ford chartered a ship and took a large number of peace activists to Scandinavia and Holland to organize conferences on how to stop the war. The project was ridiculed in the press, which had become strongly pro-Allied because of the *Lusitania* tragedy and the propaganda efforts of William Wiseman. The peace ship was called the "flivvership." That was a play on "flivver," the current slang term for an automobile.

Following Ford's departure, President Wilson sought an increase in the nation's standing army. "Preparedness" now was his theme. Wilson's cabinet still complained about British interference with American trade. The Royal Navy would not let American goods into Holland or Scandinavia. Cotton growers were especially indignant. To the cabinet the President made his position clear. "Wild beasts" were the problem:

> Gentlemen, the Allies are standing with their backs to the
> wall, fighting wild beasts. I will permit nothing to be done by
> our country to hinder or embarrass them in the prosecution
> of the war unless admitted rights are grossly violated.[109]

Early 1916 found Colonel House touring Europe again. Now famous for his convoys, when House booked passage, the line was besieged by people who wanted to travel on the same ship as the well-protected colonel. On this trip House was not seeking peace but advice on when the United States might best enter the war. At a meeting with high ranking British officials, House was asked "what the United States wished Britain to do?" The colonel replied with utter frankness:

> The United States would like Great Britain to do those things which would enable the United States to help Great Britain win the war.[110]

In Berlin, House was told the Germans were willing to pull out of Belgium and France, but wanted an indemnity. The British said that such a deal would cement German dominance on the Continent.

House Underwrites Allies

House was far from neutral. Wilson's alter ego assured the French and British that the United States would come into the war if it looked as if the Germans were going to win—or *even if there were no improvement.* House did this although privately he estimated that 90 percent of the American people were against war. On February 7, 1916, House met with the Prime Minister of France, Aristide Briand, and his adviser Jules Cambon (whose brother Paul was the French ambassador in London). House reported to Wilson:

> It was finally understood in the event the Allies had some notable victories during the spring and summer, you [Wilson] would not intervene; and in the event the tide of war went against them or remained stationary, you would intervene. This conversation is to go no further than between Briand, Cambon, and myself, and I promised that no one in America should know of it excepting yourself and Lansing.
>
> I told them I had had a similar conversation in England and that there it would go no further than a group composed of the Prime Minister, Sir Edward Grey, Balfour, and Lloyd George.[111]

House in a Hurry

House wanted the Allies to ask for American intervention, and he was in a hurry for that. A note of February 17, 1916, in his diary:

> I am trying to force early action by making both England and France feel that they run the risk of losing our support entirely unless they act quickly.[112]

Wilson's biographers tell us that he struggled to keep America out of the war. Yet House, the President's alter ego, worked hard to wangle an invitation and reported regularly on his progress. When it finally came time to ask the Congress for a declaration of war, Wilson did so "reluctantly," according to the *Encylopedia Americana*.

House and Grey agreed that early intervention was desirable. Like two gods on Mount Olympus, they decided it would be better for the United States to come into the war now rather than let the war go to a "complete victory" won just by the Allies. House gave to Wilson this explanation:

> We both [Grey and House] think there is *more to gain for Great Britain* [emphasis added] by the President's intervention now, than there would be if the Allies won a complete victory a year from now. He [Grey] believes, as I do, that the good which would come by having an active working arrangement between Great Britain and the United States in the settlement of the world's affairs, and *the number of lives which would be saved by immediate action* [emphasis added] rather than deferred action, would more than offset a complete victory.[113]

What lives would be saved by "intervention now"? Not American lives. Like Ambassador Page, Colonel House had lost track of his job. His job was to represent the United States, not Britain, and the people of the United States did not want to fight in Europe, just as the people of Britain had not wanted to fight in Europe. Like Ambassador Page, House presented a rosy vision of an "active working arrangement between

Great Britain and the United States in the settlement of the world's affairs." Grey the expert angler had found a tempting lure.

House believed,

> if the Allies were completely victorious, Russia, Italy, and France would undoubtedly make demands and do things Great Britain would not approve, and which would not be in the interest of permanent peace.[114]

House was convinced that if the United States entered the war, we, with Britain as our partner, would make peace with reasonable and just conditions. Actually, only a stalemate could have done that.

House and Grey suggested a way in which to speed the war entry. The Allies would propose a conference with the Central Powers, and if the results were not favorable to the Allies, the United States would enter the war. Seeing this scheme on paper, Wilson inserted the word *probably,* so that the United States "probably" would enter the war. Presumably he had the congressional war-making prerogative in mind. Grey and his colleagues did not like the alteration, and the "House-Grey Memorandum" was dropped.

Durnovo Again

In House's diary of February 21, Durnovo received yet another vindication. The Texan and Lord Loreburn were discussing what kind of speech the latter should make in the House of Lords. House advised him:

> that England should cease stating through her press and public men that this was a war of annihilation, both of the German nation and German trade.[115]

A "high note" was needed, said House. Better to say it was a war to

> prevent a few selfish individuals from plunging the world into
> war for their own purposes. I thought if he would strike this
> high note it, would hurt militarism in Germany and would
> make clear the purposes of the Allies.

Of course, it sounded much better to blame the war on German militarism than to blame it on the German ability to compete in the marketplace.

Buoyed by his "working arrangement" with the foreign secretary, the colonel was having a fine time in England. He was well received by leaders of the government and other prominent persons; they confided in him almost as if the soft-spoken little Texan were a British aristocrat. A former lord chancellor, Sir Robert Reid, told House that in 1914 he was surprised to learn that the Triple Entente involved a moral obligation to defend France. Reid personally never was in favor of forming such an alliance, which, he said, was promoted on the sly by a faction known as the "new imperialists." The New Imperialists believed in spheres of influence and economic domination. Among them were Grey, Asquith, and Lloyd George. House wished that the forceful Lloyd George would become Prime Minister, which later he did.

Wilson Decides for War

Meanwhile, President Wilson, who was going to run for reelection as a peace candidate, had decided in favor of war, and he sounded out some congressmen on that. What came to be known as the "Sunrise Conference" was scheduled on February 21, 1916, and it began at 7:30 a.m. in order to avoid the attention of the press.[116] The President told three Democratic leaders of the House of Representatives that if the United States entered the war, it could be over in six months, and he needed the Congress's cooperation. All three congressmen protested vigorously, saying they would fight against a declaration of war. Alternatively, Wilson said, if we break off relations with Germany, they will declare war on us. The congressmen did not like that idea, either. The American people, they knew, wanted peace.

President Wilson batted down two proposed measures for avoiding war. One came, oddly, from Secretary Lansing. Perhaps feeling guilty about the *Lusitania*, he wanted British merchant ships to disarm so that the German submarines could give warning of attack. That idea did not please the British. They wanted to continue arming the merchant ships, and they needed German "frightfulness" on the sea in order to depict the enemy as a "Frankenstein" monster. House and Page argued strongly against Lansing's uncharacteristically humane proposal and killed it.

In Congress there was a move to warn Americans not to travel on belligerent ships, and it was thought that a resolution to that effect would pass by a 2-1 margin. But it failed. Wilson sent to Capitol Hill his most influential cabinet members, and they persuaded the Congress to "stand by the President in this time of crisis." Instead of ending the crisis, the Congress decided to live with it (vote in the Lower House: 275-135).

On March 24, a submarine, UB-29, fired a torpedo at what might have been a troopship but turned out to be the *Sussex*, a French cargo and passenger carrying vessel. *Sussex* did not sink as reported, but fifty people died either from the torpedo's explosion or from jumping overboard. President Wilson threatened to break diplomatic relations with Germany, and the *New York Herald* demanded war. Peace with honor no longer was possible, said Northcliffe's *Daily Mail*. But the crisis passed after Germany pledged not to sink ships without warning unless they attempted to escape or offer resistance. The pledge was contingent on the British obeying international law. Wilson was satisfied for the moment.

"He Kept Us Out of War"

In May of 1916, President Wilson, seeking reelection, began campaigning on the slogan, "He Kept Us Out of War" (Wilson's defenders stress that he *personally* did not make use of the slogan). Wearing his pacifist hat, Wilson announced that the United States was willing to join any "feasible association of nations" to safeguard the world against injustice and aggression. This helped to inspire the peace groups, but it did not suit the fighting mood in Britain, and some newspapers criticized it as an election year ploy. The British press and public urged "victory or death." They would not be dissuaded by the Battle of the Somme's 420,000 British casualties.

Wilson's opponent, Republican Charles E. Hughes, responded to the "He Kept Us Out of War" slogan by saying there was no reason to go to war. "You could not get this country into war" he said, "without making the most inexcusable blunders."

Ambassador Page went to Washington during the summer and for six weeks lobbied the Administration for war. According to Lansing, Page worried about what his British friends would think if he did not succeed. Another of Lansing's observations:

> Mr. Page was also critical of the fact that Bernstorff was permitted to remain in Washington and indicated that the British people considered our government the victim of German intrigue and that they wondered whether a government so easily deceived could in the future be trusted.[117]

Our ambassador must have been very unhappy in London.

Page knew that President Wilson wanted to take part in the peace negotiations, and he warned that, according to British officials, belligerents never invite a neutral to take part in such negotiations. That might have been Page's strongest argument.

In September of 1916, as the Somme kept grinding away, the Germans let Wilson know they wanted to end the war and hinted that, in the absence of a truce, they would commence unrestricted submarine warfare. Consonant with his ideals, Woodrow Wilson now had a credible opportunity to stop a World War and save hundreds of thousands if not millions of lives. Wilson decided to wait until after the election.[118]

New Imperialists Oppose Peace

In Britain, David Lloyd George became war minister and in September he scotched the grass roots peace movement almost completely. He did that by giving an interview to an American journalist, Roy Howard, who wanted to know whether a negotiated peace was possible. Lloyd George disparaged that idea, saying the Allies must fight to the finish and go for a "knockout blow." That was exactly the attitude of the jingoistic Northcliffe press. It was Lord Northcliffe himself who had advised Howard to seek the interview, and Howard suspected that Northcliffe made a phone call to smooth his path. Commentators inferred that Lloyd George, by giving the interview to an American reporter, was telling President Wilson to stop his peace mongering. Allegedly in retaliation for Lloyd George's impertinence, Wilson for a time slowed the financing of British purchases.

Lloyd George's "knockout blow" was applauded by the British press, and Secretary Grey followed up by demanding a "fight to the finish." The New Imperialists were in full cry.

After his reelection in 1916, Wilson, with the anti-war American people supporting him, ought to have been ready to negotiate peace, and the patient Ambassador Bernstorff, on instructions from Berlin, again urged him to do so. But the month of November went by with no action, although as Wilson knew, the Kaiser was under pressure from the generals to undertake unrestricted submarine warfare. That idea was popular among the German people, who were short of food and tired of the war. However, sinking American ships would bring the United States into the war, and the Kaiser, already fighting twenty-four nations, did not want that, Lansing and his unrealistic ideas to the contrary.

Viewing President Wilson as the "great vacillator," the Kaiser and his Prime Minister, Bethmann-Hollweg, went ahead with their own peace initiative. Taking advantage of the military situation having turned in their favor, Germany and its allies on December 12 announced their readiness to "enter immediately upon peace negotiations." A week later Wilson announced his plan. He asked all the belligerents to state their terms for peace and he offered to mediate. The Germans responded that they wanted a conference of belligerents. The Allies said they wanted a German withdrawal from France and Belgium and payment for all damages incurred. They said the German response was "devoid of substance" and a "maneuver of war" rather than "an offer of peace." The Allies wanted total victory, with cash payments to boot, and they knew that if they appeared likely to lose the war, the Americans would come to their rescue.

Wilson's Self-Defeating Strategy

No conference came about, and Wilson saw no way to proceed. With their past commitments to France and Britain, Wilson and House had sabotaged the peace movement. As Professor Barnes said, we were offering an "ever brighter prospect of American intervention."

Agreeing with the Allied view, of course, was Ambassador Page, who warned the British that the Kaiser's offer was a "pig in a poke." Page's views were such that Wilson said he was "really an Englishman, and I have to discount whatever he says about the situation in Great Britain." (Probably even Wilson did not expect that, upon his death, Page would be honored by a plaque at Westminster Abbey.) During the war, neither Britain nor the United States employed a proper ambassador. Spring-Rice hobnobbed with the Republicans, and the Democrat Wilson found more congenial the spy William Wiseman. Colonel House's favorite among the belligerent ambassadors was the German Bernstorff. He alone, said the colonel, had a "sense of proportion." It was a classic case of politics making strange bedfellows.

The December peace appeal having failed, the Kaiser was forced to approve unrestricted submarine warfare, which was announced on February 9, 1917, to commence on February 18. The delay gave ships en route time to find safety. The Kaiser's ally, Prime Minister Bethmann-Hollweg, left the cabinet, and Wilhelm became a "shadow emperor" as the militarists took charge. A religious man, the Kaiser prayed and studied Hebrew. He blamed the war on a conspiracy organized by his cousin Bertie.[119] His generals blamed Sir Edward Grey. At Versailles, the new German government said the war originated in Russia.

Wall Street Wants War

As Kaiser Wilhelm was pressured to authorize unrestricted submarine warfare, President Wilson was pressured to enter the war. Wall Street was for it. The Allies had run out of credit, and American industrialists wanted the U.S. Government to finance the Allies' purchases. In addition, the industrialists correctly saw gargantuan profits implicit in America's gearing up for the European conflict. Said the *Philadelphia Ledger* of March 22, 1917:

> Briefly stated, Wall Street believes that war is just one move ahead. And Wall Street is glad that it is so. The financial district here is unqualifiedly for war as soon as it can be declared. "It is a good thing for the country," one trust president declared . . . Only a few of the men thus interviewed were willing to have their names mentioned; their enthusiasm for war, however, was too real to be misunderstood.

In later years, books with titles like *Merchants of Death* and *Warhogs* were written about how the government was swindled out of incredible sums by its World War I vendors. World War II spending was more efficient, thanks to Senator Harry S. Truman and his investigative committee, popularly known as the Truman Committee. Truman's valuable work made him President Roosevelt's choice for the vice presidency. During World War II, however, nobody stopped major corporations in the United States from trading secretly with Germany through neutral countries. We even shipped ball bearings, an essential part for airplanes and tanks, as thousands of Allied bombers tried to destroy heavily defended ball bearing factories in Germany. Bearings manufactured in Philadelphia moved on Panamanian-registered ships to German factories in South America. Meanwhile, American war production suffered from a shortage of the precious little globes of steel.[120]

Wall Street's Good Luck

Luckily for Wall Street, a new German foreign secretary, Arthur Zimmerman, made a foolish mistake. He sent a telegram to his embassy in Mexico saying that if the United States and Germany went to war, Germany would be willing to fund a Mexican invasion of the southwestern United States. The message also suggested that Mexico form an alliance with Japan. Admiral Hall gave the decrypted message to Second Secretary Bell. He and many of the American public thought it was a forgery perpetrated by British intelligence until Zimmerman himself owned up to what he had done. The American people were shocked, even though the Zimmerman proposal was about as realistic as the Wilson-House plan for freedom of the seas. The *Washington Post* called Zimmerman's idea "sheer lunacy." Tending to get overlooked was the proposal's being contingent on war breaking out between the United States and Germany.

In Mexico, President Carranza rejected Zimmerman's brainstorm. Carranza was finally getting the last American troops out of Mexico. He knew that German forces could not cross the Atlantic, and that German money would not help him since his arms would have to be purchased from the United States. Nothing would have come of Zimmerman's idea if Hall had not given the message to Edward Bell. To keep secret their code breaking ability, the British pretended that a decoded copy of the message had been acquired in Mexico.

Predictably, the U-boats added to American fury by sinking three of our ships, and the *Chicago Tribune* declared the United States "must go to war." Churchill was getting his wish. On March 31, Edward G. Lowry, a former journalist then with the State Department, returned from a trip to Kansas and Missouri. He reported that the people there did not want war but would follow the President.

Wilson's War Message

On April 2, President Wilson delivered a lengthy and eloquent war message to Congress. The American objectives, he said, were not to seek material gain but to enforce our rights and destroy an autocratic government. With "civilization itself seeming to be in the balance," the President urged, "The world must be made safe for democracy." Wilson advised the Congress to declare that a state of war existed and "employ its resources to bring the Government of the German Empire to terms and end the war." Congress complied on April 6. The House voted 373 to 50, the Senate 82 to 6. Most of the opposition came from the Midwest and West.

President Wilson beat Prime Minister Palmerston in how fast he could move from one war to the next. After the Crimean War came to an end, Palmerston needed seven months to get the Second Opium War going. Wilson timed operations so that there was only one month of peace between the Second Mexican-American War and World War I.

Returning to the White House from Capitol Hill, the President said to his private secretary, Joseph Tumulty:

> Tumulty, from the very beginning I saw the end of this horrible thing; but I could not move faster than the great mass of our people would permit.[121]

President Wilson sometimes was neutral in word, but never in thought or deed.

He also said to Tumulty:

> As I told you months ago, it would have been foolish for us to have been rushed off our feet and to have gone to war over an isolated affair like the *Lusitania*. But now we are certain that there will be no regrets or looking back on the part of our people.

If the truth about the *Lusitania* had come out, there certainly would have been regrets and looking back.

The Allies greeted the long sought American declaration of war with unbridled joy, but a few days later they were hit with a wet blanket. The chairman of the Senate Appropriations Committee, Thomas S. Martin, a Democrat from Virginia, announced, "Congress will not permit American soldiers to be sent to Europe." Just a naval war was good enough for Senator Martin.

Wanted: Men, Men, Men

Just naval assistance was nowhere near good enough for the Allies. Delegations hurried over from Britain and France. The British one was headed by a new foreign secretary, Arthur Balfour. Among the French arrived Marshall Joseph Joffre, the "hero of the Marne," the river where the German right wing halted its advance. The Allies explained they were in a precarious situation, they had suffered four million casualties, and they needed, as Joffre put it, "men, men, men." Joffre asked President Wilson to send at least one American division immediately.

We did not have a division. The regular army, unprepared as in 1898, consisted of less than 130,000 men organized in small units, scattered around, and lacking heavy equipment. Portugal had a bigger army than we did. America was protected by its oceans as Britain was protected by the English Channel. The most popular American song of the time was, "I Didn't Raise My Boy to Be a Soldier." Disappointed British agents reported that the American public had little interest in going to war. Joseph Tumulty gave a similar report to the President.

Willing to help, the French said they would let us copy their airplanes and weapons if we paid them royalties in advance.

To generate patriotism and anti-German sentiment, Wilson obtained an appropriation of a hundred million dollars, and his propaganda effort was amazingly successful. A Committee on Public Information recruited seventy-five thousand lecturers who gave patriotic talks in theaters, churches, everywhere a crowd could be found. Many German-Americans were beaten up. One was lynched. George Viereck was driven from his house by a lynch mob. An anti-war demonstration by Irish-Americans encountered bayonets and twenty men were arrested. Some people were jailed for "sedition." A Bulgarian was shot. A poster depicted Germany as a giant gorilla cradling in his arms a slim, half-naked blonde. (Was this the inspiration for *King Kong*?) Hollywood produced films like *The Kaiser: The Beast of Berlin*. Audiences were allowed to hiss the Kaiser. Sometimes the audience got so out of hand, trashing the theater, that the police had to come and restore order.

Wilson had predicted correctly, "Once lead this people into war and they will forget there ever was such a thing as tolerance." Wilson forgot, too. He asked the Congress for authority to censor newspapers. The Congress refused.

Conscription raised an army of three million, and George M. Cohan fired up the recruits with his catchy composition, "Over There" ("And we won't come back 'til it's over over there!")

As in 1898, the U.S. Navy was ready to go, even though the Chief of Naval Operations, Admiral William S. Benson, was an Anglophobe who opposed the war. "We would as soon fight the British as the Germans," he told Captain William S. Sims, the Anglophile mentioned earlier as having predicted the war.[122] Benson sent Sims as liaison to London, telling him this was in spite of Sims's Anglophilia rather than because of it. Always ahead of the game, Sims departed before war was declared, in civilian clothes, and with a false identity. By the time he arrived, America had entered the war, and Sims could put his uniform back on.

It was a timely arrival.

Sims Saves Britain

First sea lord now was Admiral Jellicoe, who had commanded the British fleet at Jutland. He told Sims his biggest secret: the German blockade was working so well that Britain had only a three-week supply of grain and unless something was done, the nation could not hold out past November 1.[123] Sims was astounded. He requested from the United States the immediate dispatch of the maximum available number of destroyers and other anti-submarine craft. At first, the Navy Department thought its top Anglophile was exaggerating and sent only six destroyers.

Admiral William S. Sims

Despite enormous losses, the British Admiralty did not favor convoying merchant ships. British naval officers, who talked in fox hunting metaphors, preferred to go out and hunt for the U-boats, and the merchant captains feared running into each other at night. Sims joined forces with the officers that recommended convoys, and Prime Minister Lloyd George approved. Departing May 10, a trial convoy sailed successfully from Gibraltar to Britain, and after some more trials, convoying became a regular and very successful procedure.[124]

Britain was saved from starvation when only six American destroyers had arrived. By July 5 thirty more destroyers reached Queenstown. What a welcome spectacle that must have been. American soldiers would cross the Atlantic with absolutely no losses to U-boat attack. The biggest troop carrier was the *Lusitania's* sister ship *Mauretania*.

Sims persuaded the British to let the U.S. Navy lay a mine field in the North Sea. The British had a mine that did not work well. A 250-mile field, using electric mines made in the U.S.A., proved effective at destroying submarines and impairing the morale of German submarine crews. As another means of foiling U-boats, the convoys varied their routes instead of adhering to the traditional sea lanes. This useful suggestion and others came from a consulting group organized by the inventor Thomas Edison, who perhaps wondered why his help was needed.

On July 4, American soldiers held a parade in Paris. The raw troops did not march well and many of their uniforms did not fit, but they were greeted rapturously. One old sergeant said he never before had been kissed by so many pretty women.

Churchill wrote of the American troops:

> The impression made upon the hard-pressed French by this seemingly inexhaustible flood of gleaming youth in its first maturity of health and vigour was prodigious . . . . As crammed in their lorries they clattered along the roads singing the songs of the new world at the top of their voices, burning to reach the bloody field, the French Headquarters were thrilled with the impulse of new life . . . Half trained, half organized, with only their courage and their numbers and their magnificent youth behind their weapons, they were to

buy their experience at a bitter price. But this they were quite ready to do.[125]

French Army Mutinies

The French army badly needed encouragement. A recent offensive planned by a French general, Robert Nivelle, had been expected to win the war, but it failed with 187,000 French and 130,000 British casualties. The Germans saw it coming and deployed a lot of new machine guns. Nivelle's offensive became a repetition of the Somme. Optimism turned to despair, and revolts broke out in more than half the French divisions. Some protesters bleated like sheep on their way to the front; an entire division arrived drunk and lacking its weapons. During the war as a whole, 23,385 French soldiers were convicted of "indiscipline," and an indeterminate number were executed, either on the spot or after a court martial.

The French mutinies were one of the best kept secrets of the war. Raymond Swing heard about them from a Polish agent he met through leftist friends. Having agreed to send Colonel House any important information he found, Swing gave a report to the American Embassy in Paris for transmittal, and he insisted the report be sent even though his embassy contact disbelieved it. In Washington, House did not believe the report, either. The embassy had attached a disclaimer, saying that the Swing was known to associate with untrustworthy elements of the left. Evidently our diplomats were associating with untrustworthy elements of the right. The first person to break the news publicly was Winston Churchill in his postwar book *The World in Crisis*.[126]

A new French commander, General Henri Petain, for long a favorite with the men, drove around promising better food, no more sour wine, and more leave. When the American commander, General John Pershing, met Petain, the latter looked as glum as Admiral Jellicoe. "I hope it is not too late," said the French general.[127] House had warned the Allies not to delay seeking help until they were on the ropes. Certain of their American bailout, they delayed anyway, hoping for a "complete victory" on their own.

General John J. ("Black Jack") Pershing

In June of 1918, the Prime Ministers of France, Britain, and Italy asked President Wilson to send enough troops to bring the American strength to one hundred divisions. That level of strength never was reached, but the arrival of 1.8 million Americans made it possible for the Allies to stop the German offensives of 1918, which were intended to win the war before most of the Americans arrived.

When General Joffre said he wanted "men, men, men," that is exactly what he meant. General Pershing was under constant pressure from the British and the French to mix the American troops into British and French units, as extra cannon fodder. The last thing Pershing wanted was to put Americans into a foreign outfit liable to mutiny. He fought hard to maintain the integrity of the American units and some measure of independence. This was not easy because the unprepared American army had to borrow a lot of equipment, and it relied on British ships for transport across the Atlantic. The Allies repeatedly tried to get Pershing fired, but in a burst of common sense, President Wilson stood behind him, as he had promised to do.

Prince Max Replaces Kaiser

While in June the Allies were seeking millions of American troops, in Germany a new foreign secretary decided that the war was unwinnable and that Germany should propose a truce. For that bit of perspicacity, he was dismissed. The Reichstag, however, voted for peace, and in September the generals decided the war was hopeless. Princess Daisy's friend, Prince Max of Baden, became Chancellor. To please the Allies, Baden oversaw a transition to representative government, and amid Bolshevik revolts, he pressured the Kaiser into abdicating. Wilhelm spent the rest of his life in Holland. There he resided in a mansion formerly the home of actress Audrey Hepburn's mother, the Dutch baroness Ella van Heemstra. The exile took out his frustrations chopping wood, becoming known to his detractors as the Woodchopper of Doorn.

The American troops distinguished themselves in action, taking part in two dozen battles. The Marine Corps and Army suffered heavy casualties stopping the German advance at Belleau Wood. Of great importance was the American role in clearing out the well defended Argonne forest. Captain Harry S. Truman lost twenty pounds in that campaign. General Pershing said the Argonne offensive "stands as one of the great achievements in the history of American arms."

American Casualties

In World War I, the American military services suffered approximately 117,000 deaths and 204,000 wounded. Was it worth it to make a novel statement about wartime travel on belligerent passenger ships? Or to preserve Colonel House's cordial relationship with the British aristocracy? Or to found the League of Nations? As for the illegal blockading of merchant ships, both Germany and Britain did that. With their dominant surface navy, the British were advantaged by not having to sink any American vessels. We enabled the Allied victory, but would a stalemate not have been better?

General Pershing opposed the Armistice, which took effect on November 11, 1918. He believed that the German army soon would be surrounded and forced to surrender. Instead, the Germans marched home unmolested. Contributing to the onset of World War II, there arose a legend that the German army was never defeated but was "stabbed in the back" by civilian revolts, which did happen. After the war, the ill-fated Weimar democracy was handicapped by its association with the "November criminals" and the Versailles treaty. The man who signed the treaty, Mathias Ertzberger, was assassinated.

In 1922, the exiled Kaiser published *The Kaiser's Memoirs*, in which he accused the Allies of having planned the war.[128] Three of twelve contentions: The Entente powers began hoarding gold in April of 1914 while Germany continued exporting both gold and grain until July, even to the Allied powers. In March of 1914, claimed Wilhelm, Russia's General Sherbatsheff told the Russian War Academy that war was inevitable. The war probably would break out in the summer, said Sherbatsheff, and "Russia would have the honour of launching the attack." This fits with the Isvolsky telegram of January 29, 1913, reporting that France needed advance notice of the war's commencement in order to "prepare public opinion." As a third contention, the Kaiser said that his army in supposedly neutral Belgium discovered that before the war the British had stashed there bilingual maps of the terrain and "great stores" of army overcoats.

Analysis

We Americans can be proud that in 1914 we tried to prevent a World War. For years the approach of the war was visible to knowledgeable observers, at least to those in the Entente, to a few Americans such as Commander Sims, and to the out-of-favor Colonel Ludendorff. Was the Kaiser among them? Not according to Colonel House. Yet in world opinion, the German Emperor was convicted of having planned and instigated the monstrous event. Planning he was not good at. He let the secret treaty with Russia lapse, for fear of its exposure, and then, as he explained to House, Germany always had to be ready to march on a moment's notice.

In 1914, according to the Kaiser, Germany was getting rich and did not need war. The British historian A. J. P. Taylor agreed with that saying,

In fact, peace must have brought Germany the mastery of Europe in a few years.[129]

In this century we have seen the Germans bail out financially their neighbors. Such is the mastery of Europe.

We Americans also can be proud of our military effort, which has been under-appreciated by historians. The Yanks did not just come in at the end of the war and deliver the "coup de grace." The Allies were not merely "hard pressed and war weary." When the Americans arrived, the British were headed for starvation and the French were mutinous. The Allies' on-the-ropes status was top secret at the time and largely has remained unknown. (A 1957 moving picture *Paths of Glory* depicted the execution of French mutineers, but only four of them.)

It is understandable that President Wilson and Colonel House could not prevent or stop the war. As for their attempts to make peace, they bungled that by promising the Allies America would fight for them if need be. Minding our own business would have been better. In that case, according to Winston Churchill, the Allies would have made peace early in 1917, and possibly a million lives would have been spared. Agreeing with Churchill, the historian A. J. P. Taylor said,

> Things went so badly for the Entente in 1917 that they would have been glad to accept a compromise peace on German terms, if it had not been for the prospect of American aid on an ever-increasing scale.[130]

Sending American troops to Europe enabled the Allies to crush Germany and inflict upon it the Versailles treaty, which resulted in World War II and the pernicious "isms" that Churchill complained about. Fascism was one, Communism another. Hitler's holocaust killed six million people. Communist holocausts have killed scores of millions.

Most directly responsible for the war was Serbia, a client state of Russia. The two nations' security people were in frequent contact, and money flowed from Russia. In the interest of peace, Britain and France could have demanded that their Russian ally restrain Serbia and its terrorist organizations. In 1846, the British were perceptive enough to warn

Mexico that a war with the United States would cost them California. Surely the Balkan tinderbox, with its continual crises, deserved more attention from the British than Mexico.

To be sure, the Germans supported Austria's chastisement of Serbia. Unfortunately for the Central Powers, and perhaps everybody else, Austria could not get the job done before the Allies organized their opposition. The Allies had been planning for many years, and the Austrians were handicapped by needing Hungary's reluctant cooperation.

Motives

If we look for motives, Russia wanted Constantinople, the Turkish straits, and Austrian Galicia. When the war began, most of the Russian army actually headed for Galicia instead of Germany, to the consternation of their hard-pressed allies on the Western Front. The French and British were incensed again when Russia announced its intention to reunite historical Poland "under the scepter of The Czar." This and the invasion of Galicia undercut the Allies' effort to portray their actions as defensive. In November, 1914, the Czar confided to Paleologue that he planned to dismember Austria and Germany, annexing some parts of the latter. Paleologue must have been reminded of the Grand Duchess Anastasia's predictions. The greedy monarch also said that he would seize "European [western] Turkey" along with Constantinople and the straits.

Great Britain's motive, according to Grey (and Durnovo), was to retain its preeminent status in Europe. (Did it not occur to Grey that if the war went as planned, Russia would dominate Europe?) In Germany, General Moltke wished to forestall a possible Russian invasion in future years, but the Kaiser and Admiral Tirpitz did not want to risk war with Russia's ally Great Britain. According to President Wilson (and other public men) the Germans would not have gone to war if they had known the British would do so. The French government, headed by the Lorrainer Poincare, was determined to retake Alsace and Lorraine.

President Wilson wanted to prevent the war. When it came, certain groups, notably bankers and industrialists, were able to make a great deal of money dealing with the Allies. However, the Allies ran out of credit, Wall Street wanted the U.S. Government to pitch in with financing, and after going to war, the American taxpayers were stuck with billions in British and French debts which are unpaid to this day. Germany paid off its reparations debt in 2010. Supplying the American military was another great source of income for American companies, and many of the charges were exorbitant. Presumably Wilson was under pressure from Wall Street to get into the war, but he wanted to do so, anyway.

By January, 1915, generals on both sides perceived the war as a stalemate. It was the "wild beasts" (Wilson's term) of Germany, specifically the general staff, who wanted to end the conflict, according to Ambassador Gerard. He sent that report in March of 1915. Both sides had been surprised to see that the war was not going to be short. The German leaders knew that they were disadvantaged in a contest of attrition, but they feared that talking peace would topple the Kaiser's government. By the autumn of 1916, the Germans were ready to take that risk. The British and French preferred to keep on fighting. They had a security guarantee from the United States, provided free of charge.

Amateurs at Work

Wilson and House were amateurs in international power politics. Euphemistically, Professor Tansill commented that President Wilson was "not familiar with the formulas of a far flung empire." Wilson and House were duped by the British into thinking that as a participant in the war the United States would have great leverage at the peace conference. To the contrary, after receiving from the people of Europe a tumultuous welcome as the savior of the Allies, Wilson discovered that the Allies no longer needed a savior and that he was just an obstacle to the secret plans that they had made. The embittered President apparently blamed House, for in 1919 their association came to an end. The two never saw or spoke to each other again. In preparation for the presidency, Wilson ought to have devoted less time to Wordsworth and more time to British military history, including the bombardment of Copenhagen and the opium wars. American schools tend to neglect military topics, but they remain relevant to world affairs.

The Germans were inept, too. Peterson in his book *Propaganda for War* commented,

> Starting with the invasion of Belgium and ending with the Zimmerman note, the Germans committed a series of blunders which were simply incomparable. New to the field of world power, they [the Germans] had no appreciation of the fact that their acts had to be governed by political expediency.[131]

Repeatedly, the Germans made the same sort of mistake that the Confederates had made in Charleston. They put themselves in the wrong, doing so as a matter of "military necessity." The world-straddling New Imperialists had a better appreciation of politics and public relations.

In 1914, the unified German state had been in existence for only forty-three years. Situated between the French and the Slavs, the Germans as a people had learned to defend themselves militarily, and Napoleon Bonaparte had taught them a need for unity and nationalism. The unifier, Bismarck, had a talent for diplomacy, but in general Germany's aristocracy was not skilled in world politics. Compared to the British, the Germans were provincials needing to learn the world's ways. So was the crew around President Wilson, with their simple ciphers. The German communications were vulnerable as well. During the lead up to war, the Russians kept tabs on the Central Powers by decrypting Austrian messages. The Russians might have known more than the Germans about what the Austrians were doing.

The Germans were trying to learn about the wider world. Many Germans went to British universities. Visitors to Berlin were surprised by how many high-ranking Germans spoke English and had English wives or English-speaking wives. The Kaiser had an English mother. In addition to the prince of Pless, two other princes had British wives. The German diplomat killed in the Boxer Rebellion had an American wife. So did Ambassador Bernstorff. Bethmann-Hollweg, whose son went to Oxford, liked to attend dinners given by the baroness von Schroeder, who although Canadian, was known in Berlin as the "American baroness." The Kaiser might have achieved an alliance with Great Britain if he had not been so admiring and imitative, seeking colonies and a big navy. Ironically, he was an Anglophile. So was Bethmann-Holweg.

According to Wilson and other "public men," Sir Edward Grey could have prevented the war. Did Grey and his allies on the Continent construct the Entente with its secret plans in order to keep the peace or to wage a war? We have discussed their motives for war, and we have taken note of the prewar planning session and pep rally at St. Petersburg.

Despite their world-straddling sophistication, the British and French got gulled by the Russians, who proved more interested in grabbing territory than in fighting the Germans. Neither did the Russians fulfill their promise of helping with the Turkish straits campaign, which was undertaken for Russia's benefit. In the end, Russia collapsed, and the British and French, with American help, won a Pyrrhic victory.

An Avoidable War?

For the United States the war was one of choice. The American people wanted peace. Behind the scenes, President Wilson and his assistants engineered war with encouragement from war hawks like Elihu Root, Theodore Roosevelt, and the money men on Wall Street. As mentioned earlier, Wilson told Tumulty: "from the very beginning I saw the end of this horrible thing; but I could not move faster than the great mass of our people would permit." Needed was a "process of enlightenment," co-conspirator Lansing said in his memoirs. In short, Wilson, while making a show of wanting peace, secretly bent his efforts toward making war.

Great Britain could have avoided the war, according to British historian Niall Ferguson. In 1998, he published a highly praised 563-page analysis of the conflict titled *The Pity of War*. The British leaders erred, says Ferguson, in thinking that Germany's intentions were "Napoleonic," and if Britain had remained neutral, the war and its aftermath would not have been so bad, even if Germany had won. As for who was to blame for starting the hostilities, Ferguson blames Germany. Germany, he says, gambled on war in 1914 because financially it was not able to keep up with the arms race, on land or sea. We have noted General Moltke's fear that Russia rapidly was gaining strength.[132] *The Pity of War* mentions Count Isvolsky briefly in connection with Russia's desire for control of the Turkish straits and Austria's annexation of Bosnia.[133]

TWELVE AMERICAN WARS

Sean McMeekin in *July 1914: Countdown to War* recounts in detail the hectic summer of 1914 and concludes that the Russians and French were far more eager to fight than the Germans, who, being outmanned and outgunned on both fronts, "went into the war kicking and screaming as the Austrian noose snapped shut around their necks" [in other words, obligated to defend their ally]. Great Britain's role McMeekin sees as having been one of "blindness and blundering, not malice."[134]

On the other hand, perhaps Colonel House was right when in May of 1914 he wrote to President Wilson, "Whenever England consents, France and Russia will close in on Germany and Austria." If we assume that Grey gave his consent in December of 1913, this would have given France time to prepare public opinion. It would explain Russia's war preparations in January, Durnovo's warning in February, General Sherbatsheff's speech at the War Academy in March, Grey's keeping Churchill away from Tirpitz, Grey's delay in seeing House upon the latter's return from Berlin, Grey's scotching of House's suggestion for a get-together in Kiel, the Franco-Russian summit in St. Petersburg, and why Trevelyan, "without knowing what it all meant," noticed that Grey obviously "disliked the idea of neutrality."

The Gang on Olympus

Perhaps it would be more fair, and more instructive as well, to assign responsibility to individual persons rather than to whole nations— whose peoples normally are as duped and powerless as the Americans of 1917. In popular opinion, the culprits of 1914 were Kaiser Wilhelm and Gavrilo Princip. The Kaiser, however, had dropped out of the naval race, and he attempted to avoid a general war. Princip was just a pawn in the hands of Colonel Dimitrijefic. Paid by the Russians, the colonel colluded for years with Russian military attaches, who did the bidding of their government.

This brings us to Foreign Minister Sazanov, who worked in concert with Ambassador Isvolsky. In France, Isvolsky recruited as an ally the irredentist Raymond Poincare, and bribing the French press, Isvolsky not only got Poincare elected President of France but reawakened the French passion for Alsace and Lorraine.

After the Archduke Ferdinand's assassination and Austria's belated response, Sazanov pushed the weak-willed Czar Nicholas into ordering secret mobilizations. That triggered General Schlieffen's contingency plan, which provided Secretary Grey an excuse to bring the British Empire into the war.

"*C'est ma guerre!*" declared Ambassador Isvolsky, and within hours the perceptive, anti-war Socialist Jean Jaures was shot to death.

The last Olympian to weigh in was President Woodrow Wilson. He, with the reluctant backing of the American people, decided, as if he were Zeus on Mount Olympus, which side would be victorious.

Useful Principles

International war-making conspiracies are not beyond the realm of possibility.

In American English *conspiracy theory* is a derogatory and dismissive term, but people conspire nonetheless. The ill-fated Czarina Alexandra was acutely aware of that.

Balance of power is not enough to keep the peace.

Somebody might engineer a clash, for example, with an assassination or by offering weapons to an uncontrollable third party (as the Soviets sent missiles to Cuba).

If you want to deter a war, do not hide your deterrent.

Why was it so difficult for the Soviet rocket expert, Colonel Yarynich, to explain that?

If you want to win the game, don't give away your chips.

This principle would seem obvious, but for sentimental and cultural reasons President Wilson over-identified with the British. Wilson's generous policy left little in the way of bargaining power, and Lloyd George boldly took advantage of that, even criticizing his benefactor by implication.

In a crisis situation, check out the claims made by the governments.

One way to check the claims made by a government is to find out what its opponents have to say. Do not reject their claims out of hand. The German allegations of munitions and troops aboard British passenger liners were true, and the truth if made known, might have kept America out of the war.

World War I was another of those situations in which the Congress needed its own investigative capability. Senators were furious when Senator La Follette told them the truth about the *Lusitania*. Logically, they ought to have been furious with President Wilson, not with Senator

La Follette; but Wilson already had tricked the Congress into declaring war, and as war fever rose across the land, our lawmakers did not want to tell the public, "Oops! We made a mistake. Sorry about your boys having to face machine gun fire."

Overnight, the whole U. S. Congress went from being duped to being complicit.

> *If possible, use economic power to keep the peace or mitigate a war.*

The British and French depended on American goods, but President Wilson was loath to employ this leverage. Possibly he was constrained by the financial interests or pressure from other sources. Woodrow Wilson was no Winston Churchill.

> *Watch out for bias.*

Unabashedly pro-British and pro-war, Ambassador Page and Colonel House failed that test. So did Secretary Lansing, without even going abroad. Most important, President Wilson failed. He could not be objective when it came to the country with the culture he loved.

> *Follow the money.*

Financial and business interests wanted American involvement in World War I and they benefited greatly from it.

> *Remember Bismarck's admonition, "You know where a war begins, but you never know where it ends."*

Post World War I arrangements in the Middle East haunt us to this day.

After an unexpectedly long war, Europe was financially and psychologically exhausted. World War II grew from World War I's bitter aftermath, along with Fascism and Communism. Aggressive Communism produced the Soviet domination of Eastern Europe and the Korean War. Communism combined with anti-colonialism intensified the Vietnam War. The world might have been more manageable if Churchill and House had gone to Kiel. With all his faults, Churchill was a man to get things done.

References

1   Jim Powell, *Wilson's War*, page 149

2   Charles C. Tansill, *America Goes to War*, page 27

3   Richard Hofstadter, *The American Political Tradition*, page 198

4   Kenneth Turner, *Shall It Be Again?*, pages 238-239

5   Harry E. Barnes, *The Genesis of the World War*, pages 648-649

6   Charles C. Tansill, *Back Door to War*, page 9

7   *Social Justice*, "U.S. Entry in World War Cost 1 Million Lives, says Churchill;" page 4; July 3, 1939

8   Colin Simpson, *The Lusitania*, page 50

9   Leonard Mosely, *Dulles*, page 38

10 H. C. Peterson, *Propaganda for War*, page 83

11 Mitch Peeke, *The Lusitania Story*, page 46

12 Edward Grey, *Twenty-Five Years*, volume 2, page 107

13 Leonard Mosely, *Dulles*, page 35

14 Edward Grey, *Twenty-Five Years*, volume 2, page 110

15 Charles L. Mee, Jr., *The End of Order*, page 216

16 Richard N. Smith, *An Uncommon Man*, page 86

17 Kenneth Turner, *Shall It Be Again?*, page 189

18 G. J. Meyer, *A World Undone*, page 158. See also Brendan Simms, *Europe the Struggle for Supremacy*, page 286.

19 Brendan Simms, *Europe: The Struggle for Supremacy*, page 294

20 Miranda Carter, *George, Nicholas and Wilhelm*, page 210

21 Giles MacDonogh, *The Last Kaiser*, page 252

22 C. L. Sulzberger, *The Fall of Eagles*, page 202

23 Friedrich Stieve, *Isvolsky and the World War*, page 105

24 Brendan Simms, *The Struggle for Supremacy*, page 290-291

25 Edward M. House, *The Intimate Papers*, volume 1, page 263

26 Niall Ferguson, *The Pity of War*, pages 78-79

27 Winston S. Churchill, *The World Crisis*, volume 1, page 116

28 Arthur Ponsonby, *Falsehood in War-Time*, page 37

[29] David E. Hoffman, "Valery Yarynich, the man who told of the Soviets' doomsday machine" (*Washington Post*, December 20, 2012, page A27) See also Hoffman's book *The Dead Hand*.

[30] Friedrich Stieve, *Isvolsky and the World War*, page 16

[31] A. J. P. Taylor, *The Struggle for Mastery in Europe*, page 486

[32] Friedrich Stieve, *Isvolsky and the World War*, page 134

[33] Edward Grey, *Twenty-Five Years*, volume 1, page 165

[34] Robert K. Massie, *Dreadnought*, page 407

[35] John Fisher, *Memories and Records*, volume 1, page 35

[36] Miranda Carter, *George, Nicholas and Wilhelm*, pages 268, 285, 303

[37] John Kenneth Turner, *Shall It Be Again?*, page 188

[38] Friedrich Stieve, *Isvolsky and the World War*, page 151

[39] Arthur Ponsonby, *Falsehood in War-Time* (The falsehood was Britain's public denial), page 33

[40] Jennings C. Wise, *Woodrow Wilson*, page, 140

[41] Herbert O. Yardley, *The American Black Chamber*, page 22

[42] Edward M. House, *The Intimate Papers*, volume 2, pages 54 and 128 (footnote)

[43] George Bernard Shaw, *Agitations*, page 172

[44] George Bernard Shaw, *Agitations*, page 173

[45] John Morley, *Memorandum on Resignation*, page 7

[46] Thomas Riha, *Readings in Russian Civilization*, volume 2, pages 465ff

[47] Niall Ferguson, *The Pity of War*, pages 85-87

[48] Edward M. House, *The Intimate Papers*, volume 1, pages 261-262

[49] Edward M. House, *The Intimate Papers*, volume 1, page 255

[50] Edward M. House, *The Intimate Papers*, volume 1, page 257

[51] George S. Viereck, *The Strangest Friendship in History*, page 55

[52] Edward M. House, *The Intimate Papers*, volume 1, page 249

[53] Arthur Ponsonby, *Falsehood in War-Time*, page 59

[54] Arthur Ponsonby, *Falsehood in War-Time*, page 58

[55] Arthur Ponsonby, *False hood in War-Time*, page 59

[56] Martin Gilbert, *The First World War*, page 15

[57] Winston S. Churchill, *The World Crisis*, 1931 edition, page 98

[58] Louis Auchincloss, *Woodrow Wilson*, page 67

[59] Edward M. House, *Intimate Papers*, volume 2, page 131

[60] Luigi Albertini, *The Origins of the War of 1914*, volume 2, pages 391-394

[61] Sean McMeekin, *July 1914: Countdown to War*, page 309

[62] Thomas Fleming, *The Illusion of Victory*, page 49

[63] Michael Balfour, *The Kaiser and His Times*, page 355

[64] Edward Grey, *Twenty-Five Years*, volume 2, page 276

65 Burton J. Hendrick, *The Life and Letters of Walter H. Page*, volume 3, pages 128-129

66 Arthur Ponsonby, *Falsehood in War-Time*, page 41

67 Cameron Hazlehust, *Politicians at War*, page 41

68 Cameron Hazlehust, *Politicians at War*, page 44

69 Edward M. House, *Intimate Papers*, volume 1 page 281

70 Edward M. House, *The Intimate Papers*, volume 2, page 14

71 John Morley, *Memorandum on Resignation*, page 5

72 Raymond Swing, *Good Evening!*, pages 53-56

73 Edward Grey, *Twenty-Five Years*, volume 2, page 29

74 John Morley, *Memorandum on Resignation*, pages 3-4

75 Edward Grey, *Twenty-Five Years*, volume 2, pages 15-16

76 Edward Grey, *Twenty-Five Years, volume 2*, page 37

77 Edward Grey, *Twenty-Five Years*, volume 2, page 38

78 John Kenneth Turner, *Shall It Be Again?*, page 193

79 Winston S. Churchill, *The World Crisis*, 1923 edition, volume 2, page 334

80 Carlton Savage, *Policy of the United States Toward Maritime Commerce in War*, pages 335-337

81 Colin Simpson, *The Lusitania*, page 30; Simpson consulted the private papers of the Booth family. Churchill was referring to displacement tonnage. Often *Lusitania's* size is given as 32,500 tons, which is gross tonnage.

82 Patrick O'Sullivan, *The Lusitania*, page 37

83 Colin Simpson, *The Lusitania*, page 70

84 Papers of the First Viscount Runciman deposited at the library, University of Newcastlle-upon-Tyne. For a secondary source, see Cameron Hazlehurst, *Politicians at War*, pages 188-189

85 Edward M. House, *The Intimate Papers*, volume 1, pages 391-392

86 Charles C. Tansill, *America Goes to War*, pages 253-254

87 Alexander DeConde, *A History of American Foreign Policy*, first edition, page 449

88 Charles C. Tansill, *Back Door to War*, page 8

89 Charles C. Tansill, *Back Door to War*, page 9

90 Joseph Tumulty, *Woodrow Wilson as I Know Him*, page 231

91 Burton J. Hendrick, *The Life and Letters of Walter H. Page*, volume 2, pages 8-9.

92 Tansill, Charles C., *America Goes to War*, pages 263-264

93 Colin Simpson, *The Lusitania*, page 91

94 Burton J. Hendrick, *The Life and Letters of Walter H. Page*, volume 1, page 436

95 Strabolgi, Joseph M. Kenworthy, *Freedom of the Seas*, page 72

[96] Patrick Beesly, *Room 40*, page 105

[97] Edward M. House, *Intimate Papers*, volume 1, page 432

[98] Winston Churchill, *The World Crisis*, volume 2, pages 333-335

[99] Colin Simpson's *The Lusitania*, has several references to guncotton.

[100] Burton J. Hendrick, *Life and Letters of Walter H. Page*, 1925, volume 3, page 239

[101] Robert Lansing, *War Memoirs of Robert Lansing*, pages 18ff

[102] Robert Lansing, *War Memoirs of Robert Lansing*, page 25

[103] Winston S. Churchill, *The World Crisis*, 1923, volume 2, pages 334-335

[104] Samuel F. Bemis, *A Diplomatic History of the United States*, page 610

[105] Patrick Beesly, *Room 40*, page 122

[106] Harry E. Barnes, *The Genesis of the World War*, page 614

[107] Thomas Fleming, *The Illusion of Victory*, page 49

[108] Charles C. Tansill, *America Goes to War*, page 313

[109] Richard Hofstadter, *The American Political Tradition*, page 258

[110] Edward M. House, *The Intimate Papers*, volume 2, page 124

[111] Edward M. House, *The Intimate Papers*, volume 2, page 164

[112] Edward M. House, *The Intimate Papers*, volume 2, page 194

[113] Edward M. House, *The Intimate Papers*, volume 2, page 195

[114] Edward M. House, *The Intimate Papers*, volume 2, pages 194-195

[115] Edward M. House, *The Intimate Papers*, volume 2, pages 192-193

[116] Charles C. Tansill, *America Goes to War*, pages 467-468

[117] Robert Lansing, *The War Memoirs of Robert Lansing*, pages 166-173

[118] Alexander DeConde, *A History of American Foreign Policy*, page 456

[119] Michael Balfour, *The Kaiser and His Times*, page 351

[120] Charles Higham, *Trading with the Enemy*, pages 116-129

[121] Joseph Tumulty, *Woodrow Wilson as I Know Him*, page 257

[122] Samuel E. Morison, *The Oxford History of the American People*, page 862

[123] Byron Farwell, *Over There*, page 71

[124] Stephen Howarth, *To Shining Sea*, pages 308-309

[125] Byron Farwell, *Over There*, pages 19-20

[126] Winston S. Churchill, *The World in Crisis*, 1931 edition, page 727

[127] Byron Farwell, *Over There*, page 90

[128] William II, *The Kaiser's Memoirs*, pages 251-259

[129] A. J. P. Taylor, *The Struggle for Mastery in Europe*, page 528

[130] A. J. P. Taylor, *The Struggle for Mastery in Europe*, page 558

[131] H. C. Peterson, *Propaganda for War*, page 51

[132] Niall Ferguson, *The Pity of War*, pages 442-444.

[133] Niall Ferguson, *The Pity of War*, page 147

[134] Sean McMeekin, *1914: Countdown to War*, pages 404-405

CHAPTER THIRTEEN

Afterthoughts

Do you not know, my son, with how little wisdom the world is governed?—Count Axel Oxenstierna (1583 to 1654).

The above quotation perhaps is the most famous left to us by a Swede. It struck a chord, and why not? As the historian Edward Gibbon said, "History is indeed little more than the register of crimes, follies, and misfortunes of mankind." Question is, can we learn from history? Or as Santayana feared, must we repeat our crimes, follies, and misfortunes again and again?

Since the founding of our nation, approximately 1.2 million American military personnel have died in our wars, and now our civilian population is threatened as never before by terrorism and weapons of mass destruction. I hope awareness of the history and the principles in this book will help to save lives. Some parts of our history the reader probably has found surprising. I certainly did. When I began the research, I labeled the computer file "War Prevention" and began investigating, from war to war, how the shooting started and how it might have been prevented. Some might regard that sort of procedure as superficial; I call it reverse engineering. To give a few examples, we learned something by examining the military deployments of 1812, General Taylor's "Army of Observation" in 1846, and the patrol of the destroyer *Maddox* in 1964.

Let us categorize the twelve wars which have been discussed here.

Unavoidable Wars

There were three unavoidable wars: the Quasi-War and the two wars with Barbary pirates. They all occurred early in American history when we were militarily weak.

> *Weakness invites aggression.*

A *misperception* of weakness inspired Southern over-confidence and brought about the Civil War, which could have been avoided if President Buchanan had taken the needed precautionary measures. In 1962, President Kennedy believed it important to prevent a misperception of weakness. After the Cuban missile crisis, Kennedy commented that Soviet missiles in Cuba had affected the appearance of the balance of power and that "appearances affect reality."

> *A misperception of weakness inspires belligerence or aggression.*

> *It is important for the President and his Administration to project strength.*

There might not have been a Cuban missile crisis if President Kennedy had not failed to do that in his Vienna meeting with Premier Nikita Khruschev. I am again getting beyond our twelve wars, but I think it important to mention that there might not have been a Korean War if the Truman Administration had not twice indicated that South Korea was outside our perimeter of defense.[1] Truman's successor, Dwight Eisenhower, had a record of accomplishment and a personality that projected strength in a quiet, inoffensive way.

Avoidable Wars

There were nine avoidable wars: War of 1812, First Mexican-American War, Second Opium War, Civil War, Spanish-American War, Philippine-American War, Second Mexican-American War, World War I, and the Vietnam War. We have two more major lessons:

> *Going by past experience, a recommended war probably is avoidable and would be a mistake.*

Bearing that in mind, our decision makers ought to make sure they know what they are doing. By his account, Secretary of Defense Robert McNamara visited South Vietnam repeatedly without learning that bombing North Vietnam would bring the North Vietnamese army into the war. Then the decision to bomb was made because the Air Force wanted it and because our leaders hoped that bombing North Vietnam would stop the guerrilla war in South Vietnam. McNamara would have done better to stay at home and read a book. Or talk to Bernard Fall. McNamara and Johnson were very intelligent men. They were, for political reasons, too eager to go to war, thinking they could defeat the enemy by brute force. The Joint Chiefs even considered nuclear weapons as an option.

> *While military weakness invites attack, military strength or other advantage can inspire belligerence or aggression.*

Military strength encouraged most of the avoidable wars, as in the war with Spain, which presented an opportunity to put our splendid New Navy to work. What we believed to offer a strategic advantage, Great Britain's war with France, encouraged the War of 1812.

The Mechanics

The Spanish-American war was demanded by the press, public, and Congress to the point of overwhelming President McKinley.

Four wars were engineered by presidents with help from interested persons and groups. They were the War of 1812, the First Mexican-American War, World War I, and the Vietnam War.

President Buchanan's inaction brought about the Civil War.

Impulsive subordinate officials entangled us in the Second Opium War.

The Philippine-American War resulted from President McKinley's ignorance and General Otis's "bullheadedness." Another factor was the desire to expand trade in Asia, which could have been done without a war. Mahanism stressed the need for naval bases and coaling stations.

President Wilson apparently engineered by himself the Second Mexican-American War. This was a case of missionary diplomacy. The son of a Christian minister, Wilson wanted to be an evangelist for good government.

Rogue Wars

Ever since 1945 we have worried about a nuclear war being started by some demented or fanatical military officer. Moving pictures have been made about that. Looking back we can see that non-nuclear rogue wars have occurred without the perpetrator's having been demented, although in China one perpetrator, the Hong Kong consul, reportedly was inebriated. Some Navy men got carried away by zeal in the Second Opium War, and Commodore Tatnall by his admission heeded the call of race.

Also fitting the rogue category was the California portion of the First Mexican-American War. The ambitious Captain John Fremont tried to start a war in California and failed. Fremont tried again and succeeded. But the California conflict would have started with or without Fremont. Commodore Sloat had his orders and Commodore Stockton was on the way. It is debatable whether the Philippine-American War was a rogue war. General Elwell Otis made the shooting inevitable by accident or design, and then he rejected a truce. President McKinley was not seen to punish Otis, but the general's command continued only four months after the war began.

In Texas, Commodore Stockton probably did not go rogue but had instructions from President Polk.

> Rogue actions must be prevented by proper discipline and respect for law.

As a rule the American military have been good about following civilian leadership. Presidents are more likely to ignore the Constitution. But if unchecked, the military are liable to find cause for more action than necessary as, for example, in the Philippine War and the bombing of North Vietnam.

Trigger Effect

An unappreciated source of danger is the *trigger effect of a contingency plan*. Suppose the President's national security team plans to bomb Country X if it mines a certain shipping channel. To start a war with Country X, somebody in the American national security establishment merely has to plant a few mines. Alternatively, if the contingency plan is not kept secret, a foreign power could plant mines in a false flag operation.

The Schlieffen plan was a contingency plan, and the Germans failed to keep it secret. Secretary Grey knew about it, and in the event of war, he counted on Germany's invasion of Belgium to rouse the British public in support of defending France and Russia. (Yet in Grey's mind, as he told Raymond Swing, he was "fighting for a world of international law in which men did not scheme for war.")

President Lyndon Johnson had a plan known to national security personnel, and, to carry that out, he urgently wanted the Congress to pass his Southeast Asia Resolution. For that purpose the Tonkin Gulf incidents were set up by the 303 Committee. The committee ordered gunboat operations to coincide with the De Soto patrol, and planned to continue these picador-like raids after the August 2 battle. It also was the committee's responsibility to supervise the CIA's air raids on North Vietnamese territory. From what we have learned of the 303 Committee and its clearance procedures, it seems likely that the President was directly involved.

On a subordinate level we have the "secret team" that the late Air Force Colonel L. Fletcher Prouty wrote about.[2] Colonel Prouty was chief of special operations under the Joint Chiefs of Staff during the Kennedy Administration, and he conducted liaison with the CIA. Prouty provided hardware and other support for the agency's paramilitary operations. His successors are in a good position for inventing crises and armed clashes. Attacks can be fabricated. In 1971, an Air Force general wanted to bomb certain targets in North Vietnam but could not get permission. Permission was obtained by claiming falsely that the intended targets had fired on American reconnaissance planes.[3]

Contingency plans present temptation to war mongers both foreign and domestic.

Originally, President Wilson and Colonel House had the right idea: Engineer peace, not war. After the World War started, they could have forced it to a draw. For both purposes, they lacked the necessary confidence and experience in power politics. With their promises of help if needed, Wilson and House encouraged the Allies to keep fighting instead of making peace. From Wilson's own words, as reported by Joseph Tumulty, the President from the war's beginning expected to get into it.

Look for ways to engineer peace.

Elect presidents with experience in international relations and a record of accomplishment.

Moral Judgments

The Spanish-American War was demanded by press and public, and that pressure, generated by moral outrage, was compared to a "cyclone in Kansas." Plenty of men wanted to go and fight, and even some women. Two Presidents opposed that war. Trumping President McKinley's anti-war efforts was a circulation battle between William Randolph Hearst's *New York Journal* and Joseph Pulitzer's *New York World*. But let us not forget the jingoistic efforts of Theodore Roosevelt and his friends. Roosevelt was influenced by Mahanism and Social Darwinism. Swayed by all this zeal, President McKinley persuaded himself that fighting Spain and colonizing the Philippines were the right things to do.

Jingoism and moral outrage are a powerful combination.

Yet a well informed moral decision can be the best. President Adams thought so when he made peace with France. Secretary of State William R. Day was correct in saying that the United States had no right to colonize the Philippines. President Wilson thought he did the right thing by invading Mexico, but then was appalled to discover that Mexican civilians were being killed.

*Do not ignore the voice of conscience, but be well informed
about the risks and circumstances.*

Economic Power

Congress passed a high, secession-provoking tariff two days before
Abraham Lincoln was inaugurated. A high tariff on sugar brought about
economic distress and revolution in Cuba, and that led to the Spanish-
American War. American economic power determined the outcome
of World War I. Ironically, the United States, the world's economic
powerhouse, was defeated by an economic factor in Vietnam. Our
policy makers could not see the importance of land reform.

*Economic policies can promote either peace or war, victory or
defeat. The economic factors are not always obvious.*

Importance of History

The history of an area is important but easily overlooked. Not
knowing the history of the Vietnamese people and their opposition
to French rule, our policy makers assumed that Vietnam was a puppet
of international Communism. This was their fundamental mistake.
Studying the Philippine War would have taught our leaders much about
what they were up against in Vietnam.

When in 1961 President John F. Kennedy, his generals, and the CIA
planned the Bay of Pigs landing in Cuba, which failed, they mistakenly
assumed the invading Cuban exiles would be assisted by an uprising.
Kennedy invited an historian to sit in on the planning, but although the
historian opposed the operation, he evidently did not call attention to
the nineteenth century landings that erroneously anticipated popular
uprisings.[4] Curiously, the CIA's Intelligence Branch, which might have
known some Cuban history, was not officially consulted because it had
no "need to know."[5] That level of security did not apply in Miami, where
invasion talk enlivened the bars.

Examine the history of the problem area.

Consult the persons most knowledgeable about the area.

New Presidents Vulnerable

Every new and relatively naïve President presents a secret team, or other pressure group, an opportunity to sell its pet project. President Madison succumbed to the war hawks and their predictions of an easy victory in Canada. Thanks to Theodore Roosevelt, President McKinley got stuck with a contingency plan for the Philippines that the Naval War College had been working on. People left over from the Eisenhower Administration sold President Kennedy on the Bay of Pigs invasion of Cuba. Kennedy was especially vulnerable because as a presidential candidate he had been calling for stronger action against Communist Cuba. The Kennedy Administration handled well the Cuban missile crisis, but as an unfortunate result, the next President, Lyndon Johnson, put too much faith in President Kennedy's "best and brightest," and marched the nation into Vietnam.

New Presidents are especially vulnerable to war mongering.

Realpolitik

Presidents Polk, Wilson, and Johnson duped the Congress and the American people. President Johnson followed two Presidents who temporized on Vietnam. They all did what was expedient. President Eisenhower accepted the rigged elections. President Kennedy sent twelve thousand soldiers as "advisers" and initiated the "strategic hamlet" program. President Johnson saw no way to turn back.

Realpolitik is not necessarily practical.

Presidents Are Fallible

Presidential ignorance brought about the Philippine War. President McKinley simply did not know what he was doing. Neither did his cabinet. Thanks to Senator Teller and the beet sugar industry, it was decided that the Cubans could govern themselves; but that did not apply to the Filipinos. History has told the opposite story. Today the Philippines have a functioning democracy. Cuba is a totalitarian state ruled by the sons of a Spanish soldier who fought against Cuban independence.

Although exceptionally able individuals, our Presidents are human, and they are prone to error, misjudgment, and overweening ambition. Yet we depend on them to deal with many different kinds of problem. Lincoln was distracted by politically important patronage responsibilities, especially during the Sumter crisis. Presidents today are distracted by smoldering problems and violent flare-ups all over the world. President Eisenhower from his military experience knew the importance of having a chief of staff to run things, and as President he appointed one. Presidents now have legions of advisers and helpers, but the inmost circle tends to specialize on domestic politics with too much emphasis on the next election, presidential or congressional. As the result, foreign policy and military operations often are guided by short-term domestic political considerations. Sensitive information often is leaked to make the Administration look good and obtain votes. This destroys sources and can be fatal to the people who gather information.

There needs to be more cooperation and consultation between the Executive and Legislative branches.

Senator Fulbright observed that the Executive routinely dismisses advice from Congress, assuming the lawmakers have nothing of value to contribute. But the White House tends to become too insulated, and the Congress can provide different points of view based on its varied sources of information. In 1916, leading congressmen opposed entering World War I, but President Wilson was certain that he knew better. During the Vietnam War, Secretary of State Dean Rusk met on national television with the Foreign Relations Committee and Chairman Fulbright courageously said,

If the Vietnamese want to be Communists, just like the Yugoslavs, I don't know why we should object to it.

As an advocate Rusk was highly skilled, and in the public's perception, he crushed Fulbright and his criticisms with a scornful hint of disloyalty. To paraphrase slightly, Rusk asked his critic, *Can you not find something wrong with the North Vietnamese?*

In debate, Fulbright was "overmatched," as one commentator remarked.

On policy, however, the senator was right, and years later, as the Vietnam War went from disastrous to catastrophic, Rusk calmly and persuasively provided reasons to march ahead. Talk show host Thomas Braden commented, probably with some truth:

> Every time I hear Dean Rusk, I feel very reassured.

Skill in debate is a major factor in public affairs. So is skill in hiding one's agenda. Rusk and Johnson complemented each other.

Independent Research Needed

As noted a number of times, the Congress needs its own investigative capability. The Executive Branch's contentions need to be verified, and it would help if in crisis situations the Congress could present advice based on its own independent research. Some investigations would be easy, as in the case of Vietnam. According to General Powell, one could have learned enough just by reading a book by Bernard Fall. That was Senator Gruening's experience, too. Concerning the Philippines, it would have been most helpful to read the report from Admiral Dewey's investigators, who finished it before the war began. Unfortunately, Dewey sat on the report and, following that delay, sent it by mail. Meanwhile, Dewey's erroneous opinion was what Washington wanted to hear. The admiral lived on the USS *Olympia*. His contact with the terrestrial world was pretty much confined to a daily carriage ride along the shore and visiting the base at Cavite. Yet he was viewed as an expert on the scene.

> *The man on the scene is not necessarily an expert on the scene.*

> *An Administration consensus can be isolated from reality. In matters of great importance, an independent view is needed.*

Usurpation

Presidents believe it important—and even their duty—to preserve and expand their power, and this mindset is encouraged by their staff members, who like to empower themselves and augment their responsibilities. In other words, the White House has a built-in tendency to usurp power. Somebody is sure to tell the next President, erroneously, that the War Powers Resolution in the absence of emergency gives him ninety days to run wild militarily without getting a congressional authorization. He also will be told, erroneously, that the Commander-in-Chief has an inherent right to initiate war on his own authority. That is what kings had, and that is something the nation's founders tried to prevent.

As might have happened in the case of President Obama and Syria, a false interpretation of the constitutional war power could result in a constitutional crisis with the President going to war even though the Congress voted against it. Depending on the circumstances, this sort of crisis could bring about lawsuits, impeachment, lack of discipline in the military, violent conflict, or even a coup de tat. In addition to domestic violence, the Vietnam War with its imperfect authorization brought about disaffection of the youth, the widespread use of narcotic drugs, a general subsidence of social norms, and a loss of confidence in our institutions. We still see the effects of that.

> *Presidential candidates ought to be questioned on their understanding of the constitutional war power. So should appointees to the federal judiciary and appointees to head the State Department and the Defense Department.*

Deception often rules. We have seen how in Britain a few men in the cabinet secretly planned for many years, and secretly obligated their country, to help France and Russia in a war with Germany, even though the British people were known to oppose such a policy. As France and Russia took the lead in ordering mobilization, they counted on secret promises of British help. At the last minute, the entire British Empire was drawn into a ruinous war by the New Imperialists' pretended concern for Belgium, which then was blockaded and starved along with Germany.

In the United States, the sinking of the *Lusitania* was presented in such a way that President Wilson could allege a need to save civilization, which ironically had been a British rallying cry in the Second Opium War. As Secretary Bryan and a German sympathizer tried to save the passengers and crew, Counselor Lansing's phony legal argument enabled them to be used as human shields.

> *Executive usurpation and deception are constant hazards, even when the President adopts a high moral tone.*

Challenges

The War Powers Act, as Fulbright and I predicted, has not prevented any wars. Neither has the congressional power of the purse been able to do that. If a military action seems unjustified, the two powers ought to be employed together as a one-two punch with impeachment held in reserve. One successful impeachment could go a long way. But our lawmakers would need the fiber of John Adams and the absence of congressional gridlock. Better it would be to keep up with and anticipate the President's thinking. At that stage it is easier to influence events.

This is not to say that American power will not be needed. Since 1945 Europe has enjoyed a remarkable era of peace thanks to the United States, and American forces have kept the peace in Korea since 1953. Japan has been safe under our umbrella and so has Latin America. These are extremely important achievements, although probably few Americans are aware of them. Roving television interviewers discover among our citizens an amazing lack of knowledge concerning American history and foreign policy.

A position of military supremacy encouraged President George W. Bush to invade potentially aggressive Iraq, but his Administration lacked the skills needed to reorganize Iraq peacefully and had to face massive guerrilla resistance. The same occurred in Afghanistan.

> *A limited expedition, as in the case of President H. W. Bush's First Iraq War, can be more practical than to attempt regime change and cultural change.*

Russia, China, and North Korea remain possible sources of aggression. At this writing Russia has annexed Crimea and threatens the rest of Ukraine. In 1950, during the Korean War, China invaded and annexed Tibet. Now China has started to build a big navy and wants to extend its territory to the islands of its maritime periphery, islands that are claimed also by Japan and several South Asian countries. Our security treaties with Japan and the Philippines could bring us into conflict with China over some uninhabited rocks. The disputed islands problem calls out for negotiation by diplomats and arbitration by international law, which has a long history of dealing with disputed islands. In the past their coveted resource often was guano for fertilizer; now it is potential oil deposits. Currently, China ignores a Philippine request for adjudication at the UN International Court of Justice, and it has declared an "air defense zone" covering some islands claimed by Japan. Commercial aircraft respect the zone, having no choice; American military aircraft zoom through. This does not bode well.

North Korea and its nuclear weapons threaten that country's area and, with long range missiles, possibly even American territory. Iran, a sponsor of terrorism, denies an interest in nuclear weapons but evidently plans to produce them.

Most directly concerning the United States is the spread of Islamic radicalism, which threatens Americans overseas and at home. Palestine, with its never ending struggle over land, remains a tinderbox after half a century of "peace process."

No doubt American influence and even American power will be needed in some places to keep the peace and engineer peace. We must use our power wisely and sparingly with proper regard to the Constitution and American interests.

The Danger in Owning Nuclear Weapons

Unless stopped by its Chinese ally, North Korea probably will continue to develop nuclear arms until this dysfunctional, mendicant state implodes like the Soviet Union. Nations like North Korea and Iran ought to consider the downside to having nuclear weapons. They will be suspect if some terrorist sets off a nuclear device; and the victimized state, not knowing the source of the attack, is liable to err on the side of inclusiveness when it responds. North Korea and Pakistan both could be blamed for the same explosion.

All nations, especially those with nuclear weapons, share a need to prevent nuclear terrorism.

International Cooperation

It would help greatly to keep the peace if the peoples of the world would cooperate on defusing crises and undertaking projects that promote prosperity, human rights, and a healthful environment. As a possibly hopeful sign, Russia's President Putin has told of his Christian faith, and he wears a cross that had belonged to his mother, as we have seen in his bare-chested photographs. Is Putin's cross a symbol of faith or is it just another appurtenance of the Czarist empire that he apparently wishes to resurrect? In China Christianity is spreading so rapidly that, it has been estimated, by 2030 there could be 247 million Chinese Christians—more than in any other country.

So far President Putin has been making the same mistake as Czar Nicholas II. He would rather steal territory than improve the lot of his people. China, too, is bent on expansion, and as we have seen, a nation planning to increase its territory is likely to bring about war. To help keep the peace, the United States needs to be strong militarily and make skillful use of its diplomatic and economic powers. For that purpose a prosperous and fiscally responsible America is needed.

Beneficial would be a multiplicity of joint projects. The United States and China have agreed to reduce the use of super-greenhouse gases (hydrofluorocarbons) in refrigerators and air conditioners, and they hope to persuade other nations to do the same. This is a small step but an encouraging precedent. As nations work together on such projects, getting to know each other better, perhaps ancient hostilities will diminish and political differences will become more manageable.

Needed: constructive goals and inspiring leadership

References

[1] Omar Bradley, *A General's Life*, page 528

[2] L. Fletcher Prouty, *The Secret Team*

[3] Edwin E. Moise, *Tonkin Gulf and the Escalation of the Vietnam War*, pages 102-103

[4] Arthur M. Schlesinger, Jr., *A Thousand Days*, page 219-243

[5] Arthur M. Schlesinger, Jr., *A Thousand Days*, page 233

BIBLIOGRAPHY

Adams, Charles, *When in the Course of Human Events* (Lanham: Rowman and Littlefield, 2000)

Adams, Henry, *The Education of Henry Adams* (New York: Washington Square Press, 1963)

Albertini, Luigi, *The Origins of the War of 1914* (London: Oxford University Press, volume 2, 1957)

Auchincloss, Louis, *Woodrow Wilson* (New York: Viking, 2000)

Austin, Anthony, *The President's War* (Philadelphia: J. B. Lippincott, 1971)

Balfour, Michael, *The Kaiser and His Times* (Boston: Houghton Mifflin, 1964)

Bancroft, Hubert H., *History of California* (San Francisco: A. L. Bancroft, volume 2, 1885)

Bancroft, Hubert H., *History of California*, (San Francisco: A. L. Bancroft, volume 4, 1886)

Bane, Suda Lorena, *The Blockade of Germany After the Armistice* (New York: H. Fertig, 1972)

Barnes, Harry E., *The Genesis of the World War* (New York: Alfred A. Knopf, 1929)

Barnhart, John D., *Indiana to 1816* (Indianapolis: Indiana Historical Bureau, 1971)

Beesly, Patrick, *Room 40* (London: Hamilton, 1982)

Bemis, Samuel F., *A Diplomatic History of the United States* (New York: H. Holt and Company, 1936)

Benn, Carl, *The War of 1812* (New York: Routledge, 2003)

Bernstorff, Johann H., *My Three Years in America* (London: Skeffington, 1920)

Bonner-Smith, D., editor, *The Second China War* (Westport: Hyperion Press, 1980)

Booth, Martin, *Opium: A History* (New York: St. Martin's Press, 1998)

Borneman, Walter R., *1812* (New York: Harper Collins, 2004)

Bowler, R. Arthur, "Propaganda in Upper Canada in the War of 1812" (*American Review of Canadian Studies*, 18 (1): 11-32)

Bradley, Omar, *A General's Life* (New York: Simon and Schuster, 1983)

Braisted, William R., *U.S. Navy in the Pacific* (Austin: University of Texas Press, 1958)

Brockman, R. John, *Commodore Robert F. Stockton* (Amherst: Cambria Press, 2009)

Bryan, Williams Jenning, *The Memoirs of William Jennings Bryan* (Port Washington: Kennikat Press, volume 2, 1971)

Bui Tin, *From Enemy to Friend* (Annapolis: Naval Institute Press, 2002)

Bunsen, Frances Baroness, *Memoir of Baron Bunsen* (London: Longmans, Green, and Company, volume 2, 1868)

Carter, Miranda, *George, Nicholas and Wilhelm* (New York: Alfred Knopf, 2010)

Chesnut, Mary Boykin, *A Diary from Dixie* (New York: D. Appleton, 1905)

Churchill, Winston S., *The World Crisis* (London: T. Butterworth, second edition, volumes 1 and 2, 1923)

Churchill, Winston S., *The World Crisis* (New York: Scribner's Sons, 1931 edition) This printing is one volume.

Clark, Christopher, *The Sleepwalkers* (New York: HarperCollins, 2012)

Congressional Record, October 21, 1939

Crowell, Benedict, *America's Munitions* (Washington: War Department, 1919)

Davis, Jefferson, *The Rise and Fall of the Confederate Government* (Richmond: Garrett and Massie, 1938)

Davis, Robert C., *Christian Slaves, Muslim Masters* (New York: Palgrave Macmillan, 2003)

Dawson, Sarah Morgan, *The Correspondence of Sarah Morgan* (Athens: University of Georgia Press, 2004)

DeConde, Alexander, *A History of American Foreign Policy* (New York: Charles Scriber's Sons, first edition, 1963)

DeConde, Alexander, *The Quasi-War* (New York: Charles Scribner's Sons, 1966)

Detzer, David, *Allegiance* (New York: Harcourt, 2001)

Dewey, George, *The Autobiography of George Dewey* (St. Clair Shores: Scholarly Press, 1971)

Dillon, Richard, *Fool's Gold* (New York: Coward-McCann, 1967)

Donald, David H., *Lincoln* (New York: Simon and Schuster, 1995)

Doubleday, Abner, *My Life in the Old Army* (Fort Worth: Texas Christian University Press, 1998)

Doubleday, Abner, *Reminiscences of Forts Sumter and Moultrie* (New York: Harper & Brothers, 1876)

Dufour, Charles L. *The Mexican War* (New York: Hawthorn Books, 1968)

Eisenhower, Dwight D., *The White House Years,* (Garden City: Doubleday, volume 1, 1963)

Elliott, Charles W., *Winfield Scott* (New York: Macmillan, 1937)

Elliott, David, *The Vietnamese War* (Armonk: East Gate, 2007)

Fall, Bernard, *The Two Viet-Nams* (New York: Praeger, 1963)

Fall, Dorothy, *Bernard Fall, Memories of a Soldier-Scholar* (Washington, D.C.: Potomac Books, 2006)

Farwell, Byron, *Over There* (New York: W.W. Norton, 1999)

Fay, Sydney Bradshaw, *The Origins of the World War* (New York: Free Press, 2 volumes, 1966)

Ferguson, Niall, *The Pity of War* (New York: Basic Books, 1999)

Fisher, John, *Memories and Records*, (New York: George H. Doran, volume one, 1920)

Fleming, Thomas, *The Illusion of Victory* (New York: Basic Books, 2004)

Fox, John, *Macnamara's Irish Colony and the United States Taking of California in 1846* (Jefferson, North Carolina: McFarland & Company, 2000)

Gilbert, Martin, *The First World War* (New York: Henry Holt, 1994)

Goldberg, Harvey, *The Life of Jean Jaures* (Madison: University of Wisconsin Press, 1962)

Graham, Gerald S., *The China Station* (New York: Clarendon Press, 1978)

Grant, Ulysses S., *Personal Memoirs* (London: Sampson, Low, 1886, 2 volumes)

Grey, Edward, *Twenty-Five Years* (New York: Frederick A. Stokes Company, volumes 1 and 2, 1937) The 1937 printing combines two volumes in one; each volume numbers pages in its own sequence.

Hague, Harlan, *Thomas O. Larkin* (Norman: University of Oklahoma Press, 1990)

Halpern, Paul G., *A Naval History of World War I* (Annapolis: Naval Institute Press, 1995)

Harris, Susan K., *God's Arbiters* (New York: Oxford University Press, 2011)

Hazlehurst, Cameron, *Politicians at War* (London: Jonathan Cape, 1971)

Hendrick, Burton J., *The Life and Letters of Walter H. Page* (Garden City: Doubleday, 1970, volumes 1-3)

Higham, Charles, *Trading with the Enemy* (New York: Delacorte Press, 1983)

Hitchcock, Ethan Allen, *Fifty Years in Camp and Field* (Hallandale: New World Book Manufacturing, 1971

Hoffman, David E., "Valery Yarynich, the man who told of the Soviets' doomsday machine" (*Washington Post*, December 21, 2012, page A27)

Hofstadter, Richard, *The American Political Tradition* (New York: Alfred A. Knopf, 1948)

Hoogenboom, Ari, "Gustavus Fox and the Relief of Fort Sumter" (*Civil War History*, volume 9, pages 383-398, 1963)

Horsman, Reginald, *The War of 1812* (New York: Alfred A. Knopf, 1969)

House, Edward M., *The Intimate Papers of Colonel House* (Cambridge: The Riverside Press, volumes 1 and 2, 1926)

Howarth, Stephen, *To Shining Sea* (Norman: University of Oklahoma Press, 1991)

Hurd, Douglas, *The Arrow War* (New York: MacMillan, 1967)

Jefferson, Thomas, *The Works of Thomas Jefferson* (New York, G. Putnam's Sons, 1905),

Karnow, Stanley, *In Our Image* (New York: Random House, 1989)

Knox, Dudley W., *A History of the United States Navy* (New York: G. P. Putnam's Sons, 1936)

Kohlsaat, H. H., *From McKinley to Harding* (New York: Charles Scribner's Sons, 1923)

Lansing, Robert, *War Memoirs of Robert Lansing* (New York: Bobbs Merrill, 1935)

Lawrence, Mark A., *The Vietnam War* (Oxford: Oxford University Press, 2008)

Lichnowsky, Prince Karl Max, *My Mission to London* (New York: George H. Doran Company, 1918)

Lincoln, Abraham, *Abraham Lincoln Papers at the Library of Congress*, "Orville H. Browning to Abraham Lincoln, Sunday, February 17, 1861"

Linn, Brian M., *The Philippine War* (Lawrence: University Press of Kansas, 2000)

Love, Robert W., *History of the U.S. Navy 1775-1941* (Harrisburg: Stackpole Books, volume 1, 1992)

MacDonogh, Giles, *The Last Kaiser* (London: Weidenfeld & Nicolson, 2000)

Madison, James, *Journal of the Federal Convention*, edited by E.H. Scott (Freeport: Books for Libraries Press, 1970)

Mahan, Alfred Thayer, *The Influence of Sea Power Upon History* (New York: Barnes and Noble Books, 2004)

Marshall, S. L. A., *World War I* (Boston: Houghton Mifflin, 1964)

Massie, Robert K., *Dreadnought* (New York: Random House, 1991)

McCoy, Alfred, editor, *The Colonial Crucible* (Madison: University of Wisconsin Press, 2009)

McMeekin, Sean, *1914: Countdown to War* (New York: Basic Books, 2013)

McMeekin, Sean, *The Russian Origins of the First World War* (Cambridge: Harvard University Press, 2011)

McNamara, Robert, *In Retrospect* (New York: Times Books, 1995)

McPherson, James M., *Battle Cry of Freedom* (New York: Oxford University Press, 1988)

McPherson, James M., *War on the Waters* (Chapel Hill: University of North Carolina Press, 2012)

Mee, Charles L., *The End of Order* (New York: Dutton, 1980)

Meyer, G. J., *A World Undone* (New York: Delacorte Press, 2006)

Moise, Edwin E., *Tonkin Gulf and the Escalation of the Vietnam War* (Chapel Hill: University of North Carolina Press, 1996)

Morison, Samuel Eliot, *Three Centuries of Harvard* (Cambridge: Harvard University Press, 1936)

Morison, Samuel Eliot, *The Oxford History of the American People* (New York: Oxford University Press, 1965)

Morley, Viscount John, *Memorandum on Resignation* (New York: MacMillan Company, 1928)

Mosely, Leonard, *Dulles* (London: Hodder and Stoughton, London, 1978)

Musicant, Ivan, *Empire by Default* (New York: Henry Holt, 1998)

Muzzey, David S., *A History of Our Country* (New York: Ginn and Company, 1941)

Nicolay, John, *An Oral History of Abraham Lincoln* (Carbondale: Southern Illinois University Press, 1996

Nicolay, John G.; Hay, John M., *Abraham Lincoln a History* (New York: The Century Company, 1917)

Olcott, Charles S., *Life of William McKinley* (Boston: Houghton Mifflin, volume 2, 1972)

O'Sullivan, Patrick. *The Lusitania* (Dobbs Ferry: Sheridan House, Inc., 2000)

O'Toole, George J. A. *The Spanish War* (New York: Norton, 1984)

Paleologue, Maurice, *An Ambassador's Memoirs* (London: Hutchinson, volume 1, 1923-1925)

Palmer, Michael A., *Stoddert's War* (Annapolis: Naval Institute Press, 1987)

Parton, James, "Jefferson American Minister in France" (*Atlantic*, volume 30, October 1872)

Peeke, Mitch, et alia, *The Lusitania Story* (Annapolis: Naval Institute Press, 2002)

Peterson, H. C., *Propaganda for War* (Norman: University of Oklahoma press, 1939)

Ponsonby, Arthur, *Falsehood in War-Time* (Torrance: Institute for Historical Review, 1980)

Porter, David D., *The Naval History of the Civil War* (Mineola: Dover Publications, 1998)

Powell, Colin, *My American Journey* (New York: Ballantine Books, 2003)

Powell, Jim, *Wilson's War* (New York: Crown Forum, 2005)

Price, Glenn W., *Origins of the War with Mexico* (Austin: University of Texas Press, 1967)

Pringle, Henry F., *Theodore Roosevelt* (New York: Harcourt, Brace, 1931)

Prouty, L. Fletcher, *The Secret Team* (Englewood Cliffs: Prentice Hall, 1973)

Rappaport, Armin, *The British Press and Wilsonian Neutrality* (Stanford: Stanford University Press, 1951)

Revere, Joseph Warren, *A Tour of Duty in California* (New York: C. S. Francis and Company, 1849)

Rhodes, James Ford, *A History of the Civil War* (New York: Macmillan, 1917)

Riha, Thomas, editor, *Readings in Russian Civilization,* "The Durnovo Memorandum" (Chicago: University of Chicago Press, volume 2, 1969.)

Rogers, James Grafton, *World Policing and the Constitution* (Boston: World Peace Foundation, 1945)

Roosevelt, Theodore, *The Naval War of 1812* (New York: G.P. Putnam's Sons, 1889)

Rosenus, Alan, *General Vallejo* (Berkeley: Heyday Books, 1999)

Russell, William, *My Diary North and South* (New York: Harper and Brothers, 1863)

Sada, Georges, *Saddam's Secrets* (Brentwood: Integrity Publishers, 2006

Sansom, Robert L., *The Economics of Insurgency* (Cambridge: M.I.T. Press, 1970)

Savage, Carlton, *Policy of the United States Toward Maritime Commerce in War* (Washington: GPO, Division of Research and Publication, 1934)

Schlesinger, Arthur M., *A Thousand Days* (New York: Fawcett Premier, 1965)

Schlesinger, Arthur M., *The Imperial Presidency* (Norwalk: Easton Press, 1988)

Schroeder, John H., *Mr. Polk's War* (Madison: University of Wisconsin Press, 1973)

Scott, David, *China and the International System*, (Albany: State University of New York Press, 2008)

Scott, Winfield L., *Memoirs of Lieut.-General Scott, LL.D*, (New York: Sheldon & Company, 1864)

Shaw, Bernard, *Agitations* (New York: Frederick Ungar Publishing, 1985)

Shultz, Richard H. Jr., *The Secret War Against Hanoi* (New York: HarperCollins, 1999)

Simms, Brendan, *Europe: The Struggle for Supremacy* (New York: Basic Books, 2013)

Simpson, Colin, *The Lusitania* (Boston: Little, Brown, and Company, 1985)

Smith, Elbert, *The Presidency of James Buchanan* (Lawrence: University of Kansas Press, 1975)

Smith, Justin H., *The War with Mexico* (Gloucester: P. Smith, 1963)

Smith, Richard Norton, *An Uncommon Man* (Worland: High Plains Publishing Company, 1984)

Smythe, William E., *The Conquest of Arid America* (Seattle: University of Washington Press, 1969)

Social Justice, July 3, 1939

Stieve, Friedrich, *Isvolsky and the World War* (Freeport: Books for Libraries Press, 1971)

Stinchcombe, William, "The Diplomacy of the XYZ Affair," *William and Mary Quarterly*, volume 34, pages 590-617

Stone, Norman, *World War One* (New York: Basic Books, 2009)

Strabolgi, Joseph M. Kenworthy, *Freedom of the Seas* (London: Hutchinson & Co., 1928)

Sulzberger, C. L., *The Fall of Eagles* (New York: Crown Publishers, 1977)

Swanberg, W. A., *First Blood* (New York: Scribner, 1957)

Swing, Raymond, *"Good Evening!"* (New York: Harcourt, 1964)

Tansill, Charles C., *America Goes to War* (New York: Little, Brown, 1942)

Tansill, Charles C., *Back Door to War* (Chicago: Henry Regnery Company, 1952)

Taylor, A. J. P., *The Struggle for Mastery in Europe* (Oxford: Clarendon Press, 1954)

Taylor, Edmond, *The Fall of the Dynasties* (Garden City: Doubleday, 1963)

Toll, Ian W., *Six Frigates* (New York: W.W. Norton, 2006)

Tumulty, Joseph, *Woodrow Wilson as I Know Him* (Garden City: Doubleday, 1921)

Turner, John Kenneth, *Shall It Be Again?* (New York: B.W. Huebsch, Inc., 1922)

U.S. Congress, Senate, Committee on Foreign Relations; *The Gulf of Tonkin, The 1964 Incidents*; Hearing, 90th Congress, 2nd Session; February 20, 1968 (Washington: Government Printing Office, 1968)

U.S. Department of State, *Papers Relating to the Foreign Relations of the United States, 1914 Supplement, The World War* (Washington: Government Printing Office, 1928, page 44)

U. S. Department of State, *Right to Protect Citizens in Foreign Countries by Landing Forces* (Washington: Government Printing Office, 1912)

U. S. War Department, *The War of the Rebellion: A Compilation of the Official Records of the Union and Confederate Armies* (Washington: 1880.) This material is available online.

Van Alstyne, R. W., *The Rising American Empire* (New York: Oxford University Press, 1960)

Viereck, George S., *The Strangest Friendship in History* (New York: Liveright, 1932).

White, John A., *Transition to Global Rivalry* (Cambridge: Cambridge University Press, 1995)

Will, George, "Approaching Carter Territory," *Washington Post*, March 4, 2014.

Wildman, Edwin, *Aguinaldo* (Boston: Lothrop, 1901)

William II, *The Kaiser's Memoirs* (New York: Harper and Brothers, 1922)

Williams, Kenneth P., *Lincoln Finds a General* (Bloomington: Indiana University Press, 1985)

Wills, Garry, *James Madison* (New York: Henry Holt, 2002)

Windchy, Eugene G., "The Right to Make War" (*New Republic*, January 29, 1972)

Windchy, Eugene G., *Tonkin Gulf* (Garden City: Doubleday, 1971)

Windchy, Eugene G., "War Powers Act Inapplicable to Syria" (*Washington Times*, September 9, 2013)

Wise, Jennings C., *Woodrow Wilson* (Cornwall: The Paisley Press, 1938)

Wong, J., *Deadly Dreams* (Cambridge: Cambridge University Press, 1998)

Yardley, Herbert O., *The American Black Chamber* (Laguna Hills: Aegean Park Press, 1990)

Yen, Ch'ing-huang, *Coolies and Mandarins* (Singapore: Singapore University Press, 1985)

Young, Stephen, "How North Vietnam Won the War," *Wall Street Journal;* August 3, 1995